Terrorism and Modern Literature

Terrorism and Modern Literature, from Joseph Conrad to Ciaran Carson

ALEX HOUEN

OXFORD

UNIVERSITY PRESS

OXFORD

UNIVERSITY PRESS

Great Clarendon Street, Oxford OX2 6DP

Oxford University Press is a department of the University of Oxford.
It furthers the University's objective of excellence in research, scholarship,
and education by publishing worldwide in

Oxford New York

Auckland Bangkok Buenos Aires Cape Town Chennai
Dar es Salaam Delhi Hong Kong Istanbul Karachi Kolkata
Kuala Lumpur Madrid Melbourne Mexico City Mumbai Nairobi
São Paulo Shanghai Singapore Taipei Tokyo Toronto

Oxford is a registered trade mark of Oxford University Press
in the UK and in certain other countries

Published in the United States
by Oxford University Press Inc., New York

British Library Cataloguing in Publication Data

Data available

Library of Congress Cataloging in Publication Data

Data available

ISBN 0-19-818770-X
ISBN 0-19-818771-8 (Pbk.)

1 3 5 7 9 10 8 6 4 2

Typeset by Hope Services (Abingdon) Ltd
Printed in Great Britain
on acid-free paper by
T. J. International Ltd,
Padstow, Cornwall

For my father, MARIO,
and my sister, MARIA-CRISTINA

Acknowledgements

THIS BOOK BEGAN as a Ph.D., and I am particularly grateful to Gillian Beer for her support and careful supervision of the thesis. I am also indebted to a number of other individuals: Bruce Gardiner, for inspiring me to begin the project in the first place; Keith Carabine, for discussions on Conrad; Rod Mengham, Trudi Tate, and Patricia Waugh, for keeping me on track with meticulous criticism of the various drafts; Julian Murphet, for good arguments about theory; Geoff Gilbert (my Paul Weller of modernism), for the talks and talks; Margaret Scanlan, for opening up new literary lines of inquiry into terrorism; and Matt Campbell, for edifying insights into Northern Irish poetry and politics. Special thanks are due to the students of my 'Terrorism and Modern Literature' course who have consistently opened my eyes to new possibilities of interpretation. I have also benefited greatly from the editorial care offered by Sophie Goldsworthy, Sarah Hyland, and Frances Whistler in seeing the book through its final stages of preparation. Last and least, I should like to pay tribute to Boots™ earplugs for providing me with a silence I could always trust.

Part of Chapter 1 first appeared as '*The Secret Agent*: Anarchism and the Thermodynamics of Law' in *ELH* 65: 4 (1998). A shorter version of Chapter 4 first appeared as 'Walter Abish: Plotting a Terrorism of Postmodernist Fiction', in the MHRA's *Modern Language Review, Yearbook of English Studies* 30 (2000). Grateful acknowledgement is made to the editors for permission to reprint the material here.

I am also grateful to the following for granting permission to reprint material:

Excerpts from 'Enemy of the Stars' and 'To Suffragettes' Copyright © 1981 by the Estate of Mrs G. A. Wyndham Lewis by permission of the Wyndham Lewis Memorial Trust. Reprinted from *Blast 1* with the permission of Black Sparrow Press.

Excerpts from 'The Crowd Master' Copyright © 1981 by the Estate of Mrs G. A. Wyndham Lewis by permission of the Wyndham Lewis Memorial Trust. Reprinted from *Blast 2* with the permission of Black Sparrow Press.

Lines from Ezra Pound, *The Cantos of Ezra Pound* Copyright © 1934, 1937, 1940, 1948, 1956, 1959, 1962, 1963, 1966, and 1968 by Ezra Pound. Reprinted by permission of Faber & Faber and New Directions Publishing Corp.

Letters of John Kasper to Ezra Pound reprinted by permission from the Lilly Library at Indiana University, Bloomington, and the Yale Collection of American Literature, Beinecke Rare Book and Manuscript Library, Yale University.

Excerpts from *How German Is It* Copyright © 1979, 1980 by Walter Abish, reprinted by permission of New Directions Publishing Corp. and Pollinger Ltd.

Lines from 'Once Alien Here' © 1948 by John Hewitt, reprinted by kind permission of The Blackstaff Press.

Lines from Tom Paulin, 'Desertmartin' from *The Liberty Tree* © 1983, reprinted by kind permission of the author and Faber & Faber.

Lines from Ciaran Carson, *Belfast Confetti* © 1989, reprinted by kind permission of the author, The Gallery Press, and Wakeforest University Press.

Every effort has been made to clear the necessary permissions. Any ommissions will be rectified in future reprints.

Contents

Introduction

In the beginning was the *word* . . . terrorism. The various types
of fictionalization—representation by the media, political ma-
nipulation, academic definitions, the imaginary archetype informing the thriller—find their genesis and nourishment in the
play with meaning and confusion of contexts inherent in the
word 'terrorism'.

Joseba Zulaika and William Douglass, *Terror and Taboo*[1]

Figuring 11 September 2001

Words, fictionalization, plays with meaning—these are the last things
that most people associated with the impact of the terrorist attacks in
America on 11 September 2001. It was a day in which terrorism
exploded into a sheer viscerality of fact: four planes hijacked by Is-
lamic extremists had crashed into the World Trade Center, the Pentagon, and a field in Pennsylvania within a few hours of each other.
Shortly after, both towers of the World Trade Center collapsed. The
total casualties were immediately in the thousands; the world was
suddenly being confronted with the most devastating act of terrorism
in history. Television footage of the aftermath made the devastation
all too apparent; images of the Trade Center towers collapsing, and
of shocked and bloodied casualties, said it all. It was as if the media
itself had gone into shock. Struggling to comprehend what had happened, news programmes around the world reverted to replaying
endlessly the images of the planes smashing into the towers. It was
more real than real; too real to be real. As one television critic commented a few days after the events: 'at the early stages, the vividly
cinematic image of a plane flying into a skyscraper was still entirely
comprehensible—if only in the context of a big picture, blow-the-
budget, widescreen special effect made somehow, obscenely real'.[2]

---

[1] Joseba Zulaika and William Douglass, *Terror and Taboo: The Follies, Fables, and Faces of
Terrorism* (London: Routledge, 1996), 16, Zulaika's and Douglass's emphasis. Hereafter
cited as *TT*.

[2] Kathryn Flett, 'Images that Mocked all Powers of Description', *The Observer* (16 September 2001): 19.

Other commentators reacted similarly, finding it impossible to respond to the impact of 11 September without making analogies to other events, other images. '[W]hat strikes me first', wrote another television critic, 'is that the most vividly appalling images are all, in a strange way, palimpsests reflecting other images from the nation's visual memory, whether factual or fantastic.'[3] Along these lines, many commentators—including eye-witnesses—cited Pearl Harbour as a historical precedent, or invoked Hollywood films such as *Independence Day*, in which Manhattan is flattened by extra-terrestrials. For others, the cloud of smoke and dust that hung over New York city in the aftermath evoked the nuclear mushroom-clouds of Hiroshima and Nagasaki. It appeared to be unanimous: unless you were one of the victims, the terrifying reality of the events could only be experienced and expressed *as hyperbole*—as surpassing the normal limits of experience and expression. All of a sudden, then, the figurative, if not the fictional, was at the very heart of the disaster.

Faced with the task of expressing the inexpressible, many newspapers and magazines printed responses from literary authors. But for many of these authors it no longer seemed as if writing was up to the job. Iain McEwan, Jay McInerney, and Zadie Smith, for example, all wrote about feeling that the events of 11 September had rendered literary endeavours futile.[4] Other writers, though, felt compelled to respond precisely because of the events' perceived symbolic nature. 'The Pentagon is a symbol, and the World Trade Center is, or was, a symbol, and an American passenger jet is also a symbol—of indigenous mobility and zest, and of the galaxy of glittering destinations',[5] wrote Martin Amis. The terrorists, like skilful authors, had plotted with cunning, he argued: 'It was well understood that an edifice [The World Trade Center] so demonstrably comprised of [*sic*]

---

[3] Mark Lawson, 'The Power of a Picture', *The Guardian*, G2 (13 September 2001): 10.

[4] See Iain McEwan, 'Only Love and Then Oblivion. Love Was All They Had to Set Against Their Murderers', *The Guardian* (15 September 2001): 1; Jay McInerney, 'Brightness Falls', *The Guardian*, Saturday Review (15 September 2001): 1; and Zadie Smith, 'How it Feels to Me', *The Guardian*, Saturday Review (13 October 2001): 8.

[5] Martin Amis, 'Fear and Loathing', *The Guardian*, G2 (18 September 2001): 4. *The Guardian*, in particular, offered a range of responses from literary writers; see, for example: Umberto Eco, 'The Roots of Conflict', *The Guardian*, Saturday Review (13 October 2001): 2; Arundhati Roy, 'The Algebra of Infinite Justice', *The Guardian*, Saturday Review (29 September 2001): 1–2; Salman Rushdie, 'Let's Get Back to Life', *The Guardian*, Saturday Review (6 October 2001): 1; and Salman Rushdie, 'A War that Presents Us All With a Crisis of Faith', *The Guardian*, Saturday Review (12 November 2001): 12.

concrete and steel would also become an unforgettable metaphor.'[6] But it might be contested that the tangible physicality of the buildings and bodies involved means that the event was anything but metaphorical. Amis was certainly not alone in reading 11 September figuratively, though. Osama bin Laden, the figure accused of orchestrating the 11 September attacks, offered similar interpretations:

The 11 September attacks were not targeted at women and children. The real targets were America's *icons* of military and economic power.[7]

America [was] struck by God Almighty in one of its vital organs, so that its greatest buildings are destroyed. Grace and gratitude to God. America has been filled with horror from north to south and east to west, and thanks be to God that what America is tasting now is only a *copy* of what we have tasted.[8]

On the one hand, then, the attacks are a mere 'copy' for bin Laden, an imitation, as he goes on to argue, of the effects US foreign policy has had on Muslims in Palestine and Iraq. But, on the other hand, targeting the 'icons' of America's 'military and economic power' has led to a strike on America's entire body-politic. The attacks are thus simultaneously hyperbolized *and* diminished through being explained *as figurative events*. As imitations, the effects, *in reality*, are nothing compared to American precedents; as iconic attacks their material impact extends to more than the destruction of the buildings and people involved.

For many critics, the mass of rhetorical polemicizing surrounding terrorism makes sifting the factual from the figurative all the more exigent. Responding to 11 September, Edward Said, for example, wrote that 'what is bad about all terror is when it is attached to religious and political abstractions and reductive myths that keep veering away from history and sense'.[9] For Said, these abstractions and myths are evident not only in bellicose exhortations such as bin Laden's, but also in the pronouncements on bin Laden from the US government and media:

---

[6] Amis, 'Fear and Loathing', 4.

[7] Quoted in Hamid Mir, interview with Osama bin Laden, 'Muslims Have the Right to Attack America', *The Observer* (11 November 2001): 2, my emphasis.

[8] Quoted in Audrey Gillan, 'Bin Laden Appears on Video to Threaten US', *The Guardian* (8 October 2001): 1, my emphasis.

[9] Edward Said, 'Islam and the West are Inadequate Banners', *The Observer* (16 September 2001): 27. See also Said's 'Identity, Negation, Violence', *New Left Review* 171 (September/October 1988): 49–60.

Osama bin Laden's name and face have become so numbingly familiar to Americans as in effect to obliterate any history he and his shadowy followers might have had before they became stock symbols of everything loathsome and hateful to the collective imagination.[10]

Considering this in relation to the other statements I have quoted concerning 11 September, it would appear that the entire event amounted essentially to a monumental collision of symbols, metaphors, and other shadowy 'figures'. For Zulaika and Douglass, such a view is applicable to terrorism more generally: 'terrorism' as a term is primarily a 'rhetorical product' (*TT*, 23); as they argue in the above epigraph, the effects of this rhetoric are evidenced in all of the various mediations of terrorism. Chris Hables Gray makes similar claims about contemporary war in general. With the predominance of information technology and global networks of power, war has become both 'postmodern' and 'discursive', he argues: '*its unity is rhetorical*'.[11] What characterizes it are 'the metaphors and symbols that structure it, not . . . any direct continuity of weapons, tactics, or strategy between its various manifestations . . .'.[12] Taking up Said's point, though, to what extent does this perceived prevalence of rhetoric, discourse, and fictionalization surrounding terrorism amount to an obliteration of its 'history'? Is terrorism primarily a matter of discursive and figurative practices?

Any survey of statements made by politicians in the aftermath of 11 September would certainly suggest that rhetoric and the figurative did play a major part in the event and the responses to it. Just as media commentators struggled for words, politicians—understandably—also turned to hyperbole in order to convey the enormity of the situation. The attacks on the buildings were declared to be not just an attack on the US as a whole, as bin Laden suggested; for US Secretary of State Colin Powell, 'It wasn't an assault on America. It was an assault on civilization, it was an assault on democracy',[13] and on 'the twenty first century'[14] itself. Similarly, United Nations (UN) Secretary

---

[10] Edward Said, 'Islam and the West are Inadequate Banners', *The Observer* (16 September 2001): 27.

[11] Chris Hables Gray, *Postmodern War: The New Politics of Conflict* (New York: Guilford Press, 1997), 243.

[12] Ibid.

[13] Colin Powell, 'Interview on BBC News' (US State Department Web-Site, 21 September 2001), <http:www.state.gov/secretary/rm/2001/index.cfm?docid=5004>.

[14] Colin Powell, 'Remarks to the Overseas Security Advisory Committee' (US State Department Web-Site, 7 November 2001), <http://www.state.gov/secretary/rm/2001/index.cfm?docid=5974>.

General Kofi Annan announced the events of 11 September to be 'an attack on humanity, and humanity must respond as one'.[15] To return to Said, these are clearly instances of attaching 'political abstractions' to the events; but do the statements mark a wholesale divergence from 'history and sense'? For in some senses, the tenor of hyperbole does reflect the overreaching impact of the terrorism. It might not have been an assault on the whole of 'humanity' or on 'humanity' as an ideal, but there were citizens from eighty different countries who died in the attacks. Similarly, one might take issue with the event being an attack on 'civilization', but the effects of the terrorism were indeed global, with industries, financial markets, jobs, and political alliances being immediately affected worldwide.

What does it mean to suggest that the terrorism of 11 September was not simply experienced as hyperbole, but in some ways took place as such? The etymology of 'hyperbole' splits the word into a number of different directions: in Greek the verb *huperballein* has several meanings: 'to overshoot', 'to exceed all bounds', 'to go on further and further', and 'to pass over, cross, or traverse (mountains, rivers, etc.)' (LSJ). The history of 11 September along with the subsequent 'war against terrorism' waged in Afghanistan by US and British forces is a history of the hyperbolic in all these senses. That is not to say that the historical is usurped by an abstract figure, or that the terrorism amounted only to discourse and rhetoric. As the etymology of hyperbole shows, it oversteps itself as a term. Denoting both discursive and material excesses, it cannot contain itself. And in the instance of 11 September, such excesses produced transferences *between* discourse and material events. In this sense, the hyperbolic was implicated in the events in a number of ways: in the massive devastation (physical *and* symbolic) and loss of life caused by the plane attacks; in the physical shock of the attacks transmitted through televisual images; in the figurative language used in responses by commentators in the media; in the contagious impact of the terrorism spreading into areas of economics, politics, and culture worldwide; and in the political rhetoric that helped to legitimize and precipitate the subsequent war against terrorism waged amidst Afghanistan's mountain ranges.

---

[15] Quoted in US Bureau of Public Affairs, 'United Against Terrorism' (US State Department Web-Site, 7 November 2001), <http://www.state.gov/r/pa/rls/index.cfm?docid=5968>.

The hyperbolic as I have described it is not limited to 11 September, though; rather, it is an index of the way that performative aspects of discourse generally, and figurative language in particular, can affect the nature of material events, just as material events can modulate discursive practices.[16] It is not simply a question, then, of material history being obscured by the subsequent force of rhetorical responses, for political rhetoric effected its own intervention in the events of 11 September right from the start—not least in shifting the status of the attacks from 'terrorism' to 'war'. As Secretary of State Powell explained in an interview: 'the American people had a clear understanding that this is war. That's the way you see it. You can't see it any other way, whether legally that is correct or not.'[17] The attacks were thus felt to be so excessive that combating them was taken to be a matter that exceeded the bounds of law. This recourse to hyperbole was subsequently enforced legally by the US, UK, and other NATO allies who invoked Article 5 of the North Atlantic Treaty, which states that an attack directed from abroad on any one of NATO's member states will be considered an attack against them all.[18] The part was made to stand for the whole; power and synecdoche were thus entwined, and the war against bin Laden and the Taliban regime in Afghanistan was set in motion. Again, though, to say that this amounts to the whole affair being essentially discursive is to lose sight of the fact that the *force* of such political rhetoric is already inextricably linked to, and facilitated by, legal, political, military, economic, and financial networks of power—not to mention the physical impact of terrorist attacks themselves.

11 September and its aftermath is just one instance of how the figurative has been imbricated in terrorism's events and history in complex, material ways. Once we realize that the terrifying effects of terrorism are produced and exacerbated by such interactions, then we are faced with further questions. For example: is the figurative as

---

[16] My ideas on performativity in general are indebted to Gilles Deleuze's and Félix Guattari's work on relations between linguistic performativity and materiality—exemplified in *A Thousand Plateaus: Capitalism and Schizophrenia*, trans. by Brian Massumi (Minneapolis: University of Minnesota Press, 1987), ch. 4; also, Judith Butler's *Excitable Speech: A Politics of the Performative* (Routledge: London, 1997).

[17] Colin Powell, 'Interview on ABC News' (US State Department Web-Site, 12 September 2001), <http:www.state.gov/secretary/rm/2001/index.cfm?docid=4188>.

[18] See US Bureau of Public Affairs, 'The United States and the Global Coalition Against Terrorism, September–November 2001' (US State Department Web-Site, November 2001), <http://www.state.gov/r/pa/pubs/fs/index.cfm?docid=5889>.

volatile in what it can signify and do as the violence itself? If so, does the history of terrorism show that violence and the figurative have interacted differently according to historical context? These are the sorts of questions that I shall be pursuing throughout this study, and I shall be addressing them by examining the ways in which several literary writers have been interested in similar questions. From Robert Louis Stephenson and Joseph Conrad to Seamus Heaney and Ciaran Carson, it is not surprising that writers such as these have been compelled and concerned by terrorism considering that there has always been so much discussion of its symbolic nature and its mediation. Before turning to the issue of the literary responses in more detail, though, we first need to address questions about the definitions and discourses of terrorism more generally.

Definitions and Discourses of Terrorism

There is still no internationally accepted definition of terrorism.[19] The much-quoted adage 'one person's terrorist is another person's freedom fighter' has been borne out in numerous international conventions on terrorism. Nowhere is the ambiguity of the term more evident than in the inconsistency of its application: for example, organizations such as the African National Congress (ANC) in South Africa, and the Palestine Liberation Organization (PLO) that were once widely declared to be 'terrorist' have over recent years been accepted internationally as legitimate political parties, the ANC going on to form the government in South Africa after the dismantling of apartheid. This ambiguity surrounding terrorism has meant that, to a great extent, combating it has entailed trying to clarify the general, definitional haze. Individual governments have been swift to ratify

---

[19] The academic literature on defining terrorism is vast. For an overview of different definitions, see Alex Schmid and Albert Jongman, *Political Terrorism: A New Guide to Actors, Authors, Concepts, Data Bases, Theories and Literature* (New Brunswick, NJ: Transaction Books, 1988). Notable contributions to the debate on definition include: Walter Laqueur, *The Age of Terrorism* (London: Weidenfeld & Nicolson); Conor Gearty (ed.), *Terrorism* (Aldershot: Dartmouth, 1996); Grant Wardlaw, *Political Terrorism: Theory, Tactics, and Counter-measures* (Cambridge: Cambridge University Press, 1989), ch. 1; Bruce Hoffman, *Inside Terrorism* (London: Victor Gollancz, 1998), ch. 1; Michel Wieviorka, *The Making of Terrorism*, trans. by David Gordon White (1988; Chicago: University of Chicago Press, 1993), ch. 1; William Perdue, *Terrorism and the State: A Critique of Domination Through Fear* (Westport: Praeger, 1989), ch. 1; Yonah Alexander and Seymour Maxwell Finger (eds.), *Terrorism: Interdisciplinary Perspectives* (New York: John Jay, 1977); and Conor Gearty, *The Future of Terrorism* (London: Phoenix, 1997).

their own definitions, but when terrorism takes on international dimensions, as 11 September clearly did, the problem remains. Faced with this quandary, international law generally, and the UN in particular, has been forced to approach terrorism indirectly by agreeing to outlaw specific types of action, including hostage-taking, hijacking, and attacks on diplomats.[20] At the same time, individual nation-states have not been required to agree that these actions are instances of 'terrorism'. As Adrian Guelke has commented: 'This was an important consideration for states fearful that the labelling of particular actions as terrorist would be used to legitimize interventions in the name of counter-terrorism.'[21] Yet one of the results of this is further equivocation about militancy and legitimation in general. The 11 September attacks, for example, have widely been described as acts of 'terrorism', involving hijacking, hostage-taking of civilians, and indiscriminate loss of life. Yet because such actions are not defined as terrorism in international law, they were able to be characterized as acts of 'war'. The distinction between the two was thus rendered ambiguous, with both the US and UK governments producing new anti-terrorism legislation at the same time as waging war in Afghanistan.

The definitions of terrorism put forward in the legislation of individual nation-states also involve ambiguity. In part, the definitions are deliberately general so as to allow for maximum flexibility in applying the law. After the 1995 Oklahoma City bombing by Timothy McVeigh, for example, the US government introduced an 'Anti-Terrorist Act' (1995) extending both counter-terrorist measures and the definition of domestic terrorism. In particular, the Act also widened the performativity of terrorism to include the 'threat, or attempt, or conspiracy' to commit any of the proscribed actions it listed as 'terrorist'.[22] The UK government's 'Terrorism Act' (2000)—which I shall be discussing at more length in my Conclusion—similarly extended the definitions from previous Acts to incorporate a host of performative potentials. 'Terrorism' is defined as the 'use or threat of action' to 'influence the government or to intimidate the public' in

[20] On terrorism and international law, see Rosalyn Higgins and Maurice Flory (eds.), *Terrorism and International Law* (London: Routledge and London School of Economics, 1997), and Adrian Guelke, *The Age of Terrorism and the International Political System* (London: Tauris Academic Publishers, 1995).

[21] Guelke, *The Age of Terrorism and the International Political System*, 166.

[22] Quoted in American Civil Liberties Union, 'Civil Liberties Implications of the Anti-Terrorism Act of 1995' (American Civil Liberties Union: Freedom Network Web-Site, 1996), <http://www.aclu.org/congress/terract.html>.

order to advance 'a political, religious, or ideological cause'.[23] In this context, 'action' was also widened to include 'serious damage to property' and 'serious disruption' of 'an electronic system'.[24] As Ian Dennis has commented, one of the results of this is that computer hacking, and animal rights activism can be covered in the same way as sectarian paramilitary groups.[25] Moreover, while specifying 'use *or* threat' of such actions understandably facilitates punishing things such as bomb threats, it clearly makes the differences between action and speech, event and potential, tenuous.

Considering the growing debates and expanding legislative definitions of terrorism, it is little wonder that 'terrorism studies' has burgeoned so dramatically over the last three decades. In addition to the increasing number of government-funded institutes, 'terrorology' has taken root in a range of academic fields, including political science, history, sociology, social anthropology, and international relations. The explosion of interest has not resulted in greater consensus, though. As Guelke has argued, 'By the 1990s, the concept of terrorism had become so elastic that there seemed to be virtually no limit to what could be described as terrorism.'[26] This general vagueness of the term is precisely what has led commentators such as the social-anthropologists Zulaika and Douglass to assert that terrorism is 'first and foremost discourse' (*TT*, 14), and that this discourse is largely a matter of 'fictionalization'. As I have argued, though, such a view becomes problematic if the focus on the fictional and the figurative obscures the physical effects of terrorist violence. David E. Apter's 'mytho-logical' approach to political violence in general is exemplary of this. Like Zulaika and Douglass, Apter advocates a discursive approach to terrorism, and stresses the importance for separatist groups of first engendering separatist narratives: 'Each inversionary movement generates its own discourse by means of which it defines its principles, goals, and establishes boundaries which give rise to outrage when violated or penetrated.'[27] Naming a disparate set of

[23] The Home Office, London, 'Terrorism Act 2000' (Her Majesty's Stationery Office Web-Site, 2000), 1.1, <http://www.hmso.gov.uk/acts/acts2000/20000011.htm>.

[24] Ibid.

[25] Ian Dennis, editorial, 'The Terrorism Act 2000', *The Criminal Law Review* (December 2000): 931–2.

[26] Guelke, *The Age of Terrorism and the International System*, 1.

[27] David Apter, 'Political Violence in Analytical Perspective', in *The Legitimization of Violence*, ed. by David Apter (London: Macmillan, 1997), 6. Apter discusses his notion of 'mytho-logics' further in *Rethinking Development: Modernization, Dependency and Postmodern Politics* (Newbury Park: Sage, 1987), ch. 10.

philosophers and literary theorists as inspiration—including Plato, Lévi-Strauss, Roland Barthes, Pierre Bourdieu, Guy Debord, Fredric Jameson, Jean Baudrillard, Michel Foucault, Peter Brooks, Terry Eagleton, and Georges Bataille—Apter generates his own discourse for containing the diversity of political violence, but neglects to attend to the stark theoretical divergences between these figures he cites. Just as questionable is his assertion that terrorists' actions are representative figures of the narratives they have created: 'There is a troping of facts. Events become metaphors, as part of a narrative process and metonyms for a theory.'[28] It is one thing to state this transformation as a strategy of terrorists; it is another to accept the transformation as reality. Clearly, turning terrorism into a matter of narrative, theory, and 'symbolic capital' makes it easier to theorize. But what about the violence itself? What of its own impact on the production of legislation or force of discourse? What of its influence in precipitating or terminating political negotiations? Is it always textualized in advance, or can it manifest its own volatile performativity?

Zulaika and Douglass are among the very few commentators who do address issues of performativity and 'ritualization' in order to examine how violence and discourse can become compounded in terrorism and its mediation. Terrorist actions complicate the notion of it as mere 'rhetorical product', they argue: 'If anything, "terrorism" is a succesion of actions; its real efficacy lies in its power to provoke, through sudden actions, disruptions of the existing order' (*TT*, 76). The physical, non-linguistic aspects of terrrorism are thus recognized as having a distinct role. And the way this role becomes significant, they state, is through ritualization: 'the appropriate way of getting at the nonverbal components of violence is to study its ritual practice . . .' (*TT*, 84). In so far as terrorist events frequently appear to be choreographed by the perpetrators as media spectacles, and often involve attacks on 'symbolic' buildings, such ritualization is clearly evidenced. As Zulaika and Douglass argue, though, rituals are also 'repetitive and stereotyped forms' (*TT*, 84). The material impact of terrorism is thus theoretically absorbed by them and becomes overdetermined. But how useful is this concept of ritualization if the terrifying nature of terrorism is partly attributable to its capacity to disrupt the security of everydayness? What of the sudden attack that terrifies through anonymity and the lack of any warning signs? What of the

---

[28] Apter, 'Political Violence in Analytical Perspective', 1.

bombing or assassination that is designed simply to take the enemy by surprise and cause as much harm as possible?

Producing a narrative or theory that outlines an aetiology of terrorism and accounts for its effects is obviously a form of counter-terror in itself. Indeed, much of terrorology is concerned primarily with compiling statistics, psychological reports, and other data in order to advise and report on effective anti-terrorist policies. Yet in the studies that are more concerned with analysing terrorism's impact on culture more generally, rigid theoretical constructions of the phenomenon also predominate, particularly regarding terrorism's relation to the media. The view that terrorism and the media form a 'symbiotic relationship' is certainly commonplace, although there is significant disagreement about what form the symbiosis takes. For commentators such as Russell F. Farnen, the media is the dominant partner: 'what we know as terrorism is actually a media creation: mass media define, delimit, delegitimize, and discredit events that we have not actually seen . . .'.[29] Those like H. H. A. Cooper are more cautious: 'The media certainly does not create the terrorist, but like a skilful make-up artist, can assuredly make of him either a Saint or a Frankenstein's monster.'[30] In contrast to these views, other commentators assert that it is the terrorists who direct the show. J. Bowyer Bell, for example, argues that 'To be free means that the media are open to capture by spectacular events. And the media have been captured, have proven totally defenseless, absolutely vulnerable.'[31] This has certainly been a view held by governments in the past, the UK Prime Minister Margaret Thatcher, for example, famously declaring that the media provides 'the oxygen of publicity on which [terrorists] depend'.[32] Accordingly, the UK government at one time placed a Broadcast Ban preventing members of proscribed organizations in Northern Ireland from talking on UK television or radio. The US government was similarly critical of media reportage when Shi'ite

---

[29] Russell F. Farnen, 'Terrorism and the Mass Media: A Systemic Analysis of a Symbiotic Process', *Terrorism* 13: 2 (1990): 140. See also: Steven Livingston, *The Terrorism Spectacle* (Boulder and Oxford: Westview Press, 1984); and Philip Schlesinger, Graham Murdock, and Philip Elliott (eds.), *Televising Terrorism: Political Violence in Popular Culture* (New York: Commedia, 1983).

[30] H. H. A. Cooper, 'Terrorism and the Media', in Alexander and Finger (eds.), *Terrorism: Interdisciplinary Perspectives*, 154.

[31] J. Bowyer Bell, 'Terrorist Scripts and Live-Action Spectaculars', *Columbia Journalism Review* 17: 1 (1978): 50.

[32] Quoted in Hoffman, *Inside Terrorism*, 145.

Muslims hijacked TWA flight 847 in June 1985. With television stations such as ABC and CNN having fought over the chance to conduct live interviews with both the hostages and their captors, Thomas Luken, a member of the Telecommunications, Consumer Protection, and Finance Subcommittee of the US House of Representatives, reported that 'Many of the members of the subcommittee are deeply concerned with the astonishing spectacle of T.V. news shows from the Middle East apparently "co-produced by television and the terrorists".'[33] The coverage certainly had not aided the government in resisting the terrorists' demands. The exposure of the hostages' ordeal intensified the domestic pressure on the government to accede, which it did, convincing Israel to release 766 imprisoned Shi'ites in return for the hostages' release.

Clearly, the hijacking of the TWA flight does demonstrate that terrorism and media coverage have been compounded all too effectively, but it also shows that public opinion and government policy can play a part in the dynamic, too, making the symbiosis all the more unstable. To delimit terrorism within a generalized relation to the media is thus to fail to account for the various factors that can contribute to its effects and mediation. The media has itself been affected by government policy, and not only through measures such as broadcast bans. After US Secretary of State Alexander Haig declared in 1981 that international terrorism had 'take[n] the place of human rights'[34] on the US government's agenda, the *New York Times*'s coverage of the phenomenon increased by 60 per cent. That terrorists themselves have adopted a variety of stances towards the media is another reason why the notion of a binary symbiosis is problematic. As Michel Wieviorka has commented, 'From the point of view of the terrorists . . . there exists no single relationship between terrorists and the media'.[35] For while some groups have actively sought media publicity, others, like the Peruvian *Sendero Luminoso* (Shining Path), have shunned the popular media and created their own underground presses. In some instances, terrorists' antipathy towards the media has even extended to making attacks on it—as, for example, with the bombing of *The Times*'s offices in London by Irish-American 'Fenians' in 1881, and the arson attack on *Bild-Zeitung*'s buildings by West German militants in 1968. For Wieviorka, the evident diversity of

---

[33] Quoted in Perdue, *Terrorism and the State*, 47.
[34] Quoted in Reuben Miller, 'The Literature of Terrorism', *Terrorism* 11: 1 (1988): 78.
[35] Wieviorka, *The Making of Terrorism*, 43.

relations means that the symbiosis must be approached both 'synchronically' in terms of the particular context, and 'diachronically' in terms of historical continuities and shifts.[36] My position is that this combination of synchronic and diachronic analyses also needs to be applied to the figurative aspects of terrorism more generally.

That so much terrorism has been about contesting history is another reason for taking a historical approach. Consider, for example, McVeigh's bombing on 19 April 1995 of the Alfred P. Murrah building in Oklahoma City in which 168 people died.[37] The date of the attack was carefully chosen as a response to the disaster in Waco, Texas, on 19 April 1993, in which US Federal forces attacked the camp of a separatist, religious group, the Branch Dravidians. The destruction of the Murrah building—caused by a primitive fertilizer bomb—was thus aimed at protesting against the Federal government's perceived interference in the local affairs of the nation's states. That the bombing was largely about contesting history is borne out by various social critics. For Ardyce and James Masters, if McVeigh had reportedly been awaiting an 'imminent Civil War' prior to the explosion, this was what the attack fomented: 'the rhetoric we have been hearing reminds us of the nullification rhetoric before the Civil War . . . We have that sinking feeling that a civil war has already begun.'[38] In one sense this analysis of the situation is figurative; it draws on analogy. In another sense, the militancy was an attempt to make such an analogy real and to galvanize the incendiary rhetoric and utopian separatism that had already taken root. As Michael Barkun has pointed out, McVeigh's bombing was partly inspired by right-wing conspiracy theory.[39] Among the groups in which McVeigh circulated, states Barkun, the idea that the US Federal government is operated by a host of secret organizations masquerading as the 'New World Order'—of which the UN is the public face—was common currency. Such paranoia also literally involved fiction in the form of novels like William Pierce's *The Turner Diaries*, which portrays

[36] Ibid., 43–51.

[37] For a history of terrorism in America prior to the Oklahoma City bombing, see Jeffrey D. Simon, who discusses the incident in *The Terrorist Trap: America's Experience with Terrorism* (Bloomington: Indiana University Press, 1994).

[38] Ardyce and James Masters, 'Reflections on the Oklahoma City Bombing', *The Journal of Psychohistory* 23: 1 (Summer 1995): 29. See also Lloyd deMause, 'The Apocalypse in Our Heads', ibid., 24.

[39] Michael Barkun, 'Religion, Militias and Oklahoma City: The Mind of Conspiratorialists', *Terrorism and Political Violence* 8: 1 (Spring 1996): 50–79.

a bombing similar to that in Oklahoma City—McVeigh owned a copy of it. In an interview with James Coates, Pierce revealed that he had in turn been inspired by another novel, *The John Franklin Letters*, in which an America controlled by a global Communist regime is rescued by right-wing, rural revolutionaries.[40] According to Zulaika and Douglass (*TT*, 10), Coates's factual report on 'The Order', an anti-Semitic group that carried out armed robberies and killed a Jewish talk show host, was also taken by McVeigh as encouragement.

Part of what is terrifying about events like 11 September or the Oklahoma City bombing is that they turn the anomalous into physical reality. Blowing a hole in the very fabric of everydayness, they become an event that seems to exceed both the past and present. This was precisely one of McVeigh's intentions: to refigure relations between the two. Such terrorism is not just a rupture *in* history, then, but a rupture *of* history, in which the anachronistic and the utopian are made inexplicably incarnate.

'You couldn't figure me out then, and you can't figure me out now',[41] claimed Theodor Kaczynski, also known as the 'Unabomber'. In Kaczynski's case, historical revanchism and the figurative also collide.[42] Sending letter bombs to academic scientists, airline employees, and others over a period of eighteen years, Kaczynski waged his campaign against what he perceived to be the technological evils of contemporary mass-culture. Much taken with Joseph Conrad's novel about nineteenth-century terrorism, *The Secret Agent*—which I shall be discussing in the following chapter—Kaczynski variously signed himself as 'Konrad', 'Conrad', and 'Korzeniowski' (Conrad's original Polish surname) in several Sacramento hotels, and kept a copy of the novel in his Montana hut where he lived as a recluse. His 35,000 word manifesto, 'Industrial Society and Its Future' was eventually published by the *Washington Post* and the *New York Times* in return for his discontinuing the violence, and was distinctly nineteenth century in its arguments and tone. The letter-bombs that persuaded the papers to publish the manifesto—and the Federal Bureau of Investigation (FBI) to spend a reported $50 million in

[40] John Kifner, 'Oklahoma Blast: A Tale in Two Books', *New York Times* (21 August 1995): A12.
[41] Quoted in Zulaika and Douglass, *TT*, 91.
[42] See Joan Didion's review of books about Kaczynski, 'Varieties of Madness', *The New York Review of Books* 45: 7 (23 April 1998): 17–21; and Anne Eisenberg, 'The Unabomber and the Bland Decade', *Scientific American* 278: 4 (30 April 1998): 27.

tracking him down—were similarly atavistic, being composed initially of match-heads. This is not to say that Kaczynski's militancy was a laughing matter: three people died and twenty-three were injured by his bombs over the course of his campaign. What is contentious is his historical status.

For Mark Seltzer, Kaczynski was a 'serial killer', which he sees as being an extreme, though in many ways exemplary, figure of contemporary, American culture.[43] Information technology and widespread mechanization have led to a blurring of lines between the private and the public, the physical and the psychological, perception and representation, Seltzer argues. The result is a traumatic space of socialization. Serial killing is a symptom of, and response to, this repetitive 'wound culture' (in Greek, '*trauma*' means 'wound') and its 'pathological public sphere', which is 'everywhere crossed by the vague and shifting lines between the singularity of the subject, on the one side, and collective forms of representation, exhibition, and witnessing, on the other'.[44] In the act of murder, states Seltzer, the serial killer attempts to redefine boundaries between psychological and corporeal wounding, life and death, self and others. But because the killing is already influenced by the public sphere's pathology, the serial killer's separatist labour is never complete. Is this public sphere so homogeneously pervasive, though? What about forms of pathology that develop through withdrawal from social spaces? Certainly Kaczynski's violence provoked terror in the media and government largely because he appeared to be a social and historical outsider. The US government's sophisticated surveillance, and its development of character profiles using computer technology developed for market research, can themselves be viewed as attempts to reduce the threat of anomalous archaism to the statistical. Furthermore, the 'serial killer' appellation was used strategically by the government as a means of countering Kaczynski's claims that he was fighting an ideological campaign. Prior to the publication of his manifesto, an FBI agent told *Newsweek* that 'he does not appear to be a serial killer in the mold of Ted Bundy, John Wayne Gacy, or Jeffrey Dahmer. He is not, from the available evidence, a sexually driven psychopath.'[45] But as Zulaika and Douglass point out, when law-enforcement officials became concerned at the media publicity surrounding Kaczynski, they

---

[43] Mark Seltzer, *Serial Killers: Death and Life in America's Wound Culture* (New York: Routledge, 1998), 17–18.

[44] Ibid., 254.   [45] Quoted in Zulaika and Douglass, *TT*, 93.

swiftly cast him as a copy-book psychopath. After the publication of his manifesto, they declared that whereas they had 'previously thought the suspect might be a terrorist with a political agenda', they now considered him to be 'a serial murderer who kills to satisfy an inner psychological need'.[46]

With so much equivocation over the definitions, discourses, and figurative aspects of terrrorism, contribution to the debates from literary critics and theorists is timely. To date, though, the few significant responses have been limited to analysing terrorism as a form of social theatre. John Orr, editor of *Terrorism and Modern Drama* (1990), emphasizes terrorists' dramaturgical tendencies in his introduction:

Acts of violence against property or people are staged for different audiences simultaneously, sometimes to frighten, often to intimidate, usually to provoke the state enemy into excessive and unpopular counter-terror, but always to ensure that the act itself cannot be ignored. Such outrages would be nothing without their dramatic impact. They are the unlikely fusion of two contradictory things: spectacle and secrecy.[47]

The 'act' of violence is also an act of communication, then. But can it be said that terrorists are in control of its management and staging? Does the terrorists' 'secrecy' mean that they can direct everything from behind the scenes, or does it mean that they cannot control the representation of themselves or their actions? As far as David Miller is concerned, for example, 'violence is an ineffective means of communicating politically with a mass public because the medium of communication distorts the message'.[48] What Orr fails to address adequately is the question of whether the 'spectacle' of terrorism might mediate the 'acts'. Furthermore, if the script is written *after* the act, then are we still dealing with something that can be termed 'theatre'? And is there only one script? That the production of terrorism involves both actions and complicated power relations is subsequently acknowledged by Orr:

Terrorism . . . is two things, both *event*, the things that happen, and *process*, that is to say, it consists of the relationships developing between protagonists, the dyadic relationship of terrorists and authorities, and the triadic relationship of state, terrorists and public.[49]

[46] Quoted in Zulaika and Douglass, *TT*, 93.
[47] John Orr, 'Introduction', in *Terrorism and Modern Drama*, ed. by John Orr and Dragan Klaic (Edinburgh: Edinburgh University Press, 1990), 2.
[48] David Miller, 'The Use and Abuse of Political Violence', *Political Studies* 32: 3 (1984): 416.
[49] Orr, 'Introduction', 3, Orr's emphases.

But while Orr charts the basis of an overall interaction here, he does not consider the nature of the dynamics—how the interactions operate, or whether they are structurally constant. The juxtaposition of 'event' and 'process' begs the question of *how* violence and representation, for example, become compounded in the first place.

In contrast, Anthony Kubiak, in *Stages of Terror* (1991), does endeavour to offer a theory of how terrorism's violence and mediation become entangled. Like Zulaika and Douglass, he prefaces his investigation by foregrounding the role played by the media: 'Terrorism first appears *in culture* as a media event. The terrorist, consequently, does not exist before the media image, and only exists subsequently *as* a media image in culture.'[50] In light of this, Kubiak argues that we need to 'reverse' the usual emphasis on the 'symbiosis' of the two: 'the media do not merely need and support terrorism, they construct it mimetically as a phenomenon'.[51] As I have already shown, such a view is not uncommon in terrorism studies more generally, and not without its critics. Not unaware of the problem, Kubiak goes on to discuss the issue of forgetting that terrorism involves a violence that is all too real:

For us, the *terror* of mediated terrorism does not exist, because it has been obliterated by the repetitions of its own abstracted image. This repetition deadens the initial impact, and finally blurs the distinction between immediate violence, and the mediated images of violence, between the terror that exists within the mind and within the theatre, and the 'theatre of terrorism', which exists only in the media.[52]

But how can a process that 'blurs the distinction' between the mediation and the immediacy of violence amount only to mediation? How can representation become confused with the event it represents and yet still remain resolutely 'abstracted'? Cannot the contiguity of event and reportage facilitate an unstable contagiousness or *immediation* of terror? Such questions remain unadressed in Kubiak's study.

Literary Approaches to Terrorism

The issue of how figurative aspects of terrorism and its mediation are *variously* bound to contagions and transferences between discourses,

[50] Anthony Kubiak, *Stages of Terror: Terrorism, Ideology, and Coercion as Theatre History* (Bloomington: Indiana University Press, 1991), 1, Kubiak's emphasis.
[51] Ibid., 2.   [52] Ibid., 157, Kubiak's emphases.

events, and cultural processes more generally thus remains largely unexamined in terrorism studies. Yet is not as if such questions have been without importance for literary writers. Indeed, in attempting to trace the complex dynamics of terrorism, there is much to be learned from the examinations of it from within literature itself. By analysing how different literary writers have responded to specific instances of terrorism in the twentieth century, I shall thus be aiming to offer a more adequate account of terrorism's figurative aspects, at the same time as asking to what degree these literary responses have meant trying to refashion the force of literature itself. With readings of Joseph Conrad's writings on Anarchism and Russian Nihilism, Wyndham Lewis's responses to Syndicalism and militant Suffragism, Ezra Pound's involvement in anti-Semitic and anti-Integrationist activism, Walter Abish's depiction of 1970s West German left-wing militancy, and Ciaran Carson's poems on paramilitary violence in Belfast, the modes of literature discussed will be as various as the terrorism the authors deal with. At no stage shall I be offering a generalized definition or aetiology of terrorism, though. Instead, I shall examine actions and pronouncements of specific movements and individuals that have been declared 'terrorist' by governments and social commentators, and then look at how the literary authors have sought to engage with the issues of mediation and cultural contagion that each instance has involved.

In part, then, my approach will be to look at the way terrorism has been caught up in wider cultural fields that are not reducible to a triangle of terrorists, government, and the media. I shall also be using the works of the literary authors as focal points, and as guides for proposing new figurations of terrorism's historical volatility. The 'figures' of terror and violence that I shall be examining throughout the book thus include the figures of the writer and the terrorist in various ways. More specifically, though, I shall be focusing on the tropes and stylistic strategies that writers have used to represent, mediate, and sometimes even practise, terrorism. The fact that terrorism's figurative dimensions have entailed differing types of cultural transference is precisely why literary writers have sought to develop new tropological and stylistic strategies in response. In that sense, the figurations are not mere abstractions. Bound up with the very relations of force and discourse that they engage with, they also present their own power of performativity and critique. Taken as manifestations of the way literature has itself resisted and been subject to cultural contamination, it will thus be important to discuss the tropes' performativity both in terms of history, literary periodicity, and genre.

Bearing that in mind, I am in no way offering this book as an historical overview of modern terrorism or the literature on it. While it covers writings on a range of terrorism, from the late-Victorian period to the contemporary, it is very much limited. My focus on literature written in English has been one reason why I am not discussing groups such as the Basque *Euszkadi ta Askatasuna* (ETA), the Algerian *Front de Libération Nationale* (FLN), the Palestinian HAMAS, or the Japanese Red Army (JRA), to name but a few. The literature is simply not there. The majority of the terrorism and literature that I consider is thus centred in the UK and the US, although given the international dimensions of both literary and terrorist practices in the twentieth century, I have invariably discussed them in relation to a wider—mostly European—context. Limiting my analyses to Western literature and terrorism is also intended to give the study a focus both in terms of history and literary periodicity. So although I have not sought to offer a unified critical narrative about terrorism and modern literature—there are too many discontinuities—I have drawn a series of connections between the chapters that relate to notable shifts in the UK, US, and Europe more generally; for example, in areas of modernist literary practice, terrorism legislation, literary criticism, and postmodern theory. But while it is true that the Western discourses about terrorism, particularly from the US, have become increasingly hegemonic, I am not suggesting that they are the only ones that deserve to be heard. As I hope will become clear, other voices are already implicated in much of the legislation and discourses, concerned as they are with addressing the impact of 'alien' forces. And while the sample of terrorism and texts included here is relatively small, my aim is to show in detail some of the different ways that terrorism and its figuration have interacted so that the complex nature of the dynamic will become clear.

Finally, I should also explain the choice of period that the book covers. Several terrorologists have pointed out that the practice of terrorism is an ancient one—assassination, for example, being a favourite tactic of the *Sicarii* in Palestine during the first century AD, and of the *Hashishin* ('eaters of hashish'), commonly known as the 'Assassins', in Persia between the eleventh and thirteenth centuries AD. The first recorded usage of the term 'terrorism' given by the *OED* is not until 1795, though, when Edmund Burke associated it with the regime of terror that arose in France during 1793–4 in the aftermath of the Revolution. Initially, then, the word denotes a repressive regime. In terms of the covert terrorism of modern times, most commentators have placed its beginnings in the mid- to late nineteenth century, associating it with the subversive militant tactics of the Russian Nihilists and Irish 'Fenians' in the 1860s and 1870s, along with developments in explosives and the advent of a mass media.[53] By looking at literary responses to terrorism in discrete periods between the 1880s and 1980s, I have thus attempted to question the 'modern' both in terms of the literature and the militancy. My interest has partly been to show how the writers' approaches to terrorism are also attempts at refiguring relations between literature and other areas of cultural life. The literary writings on terrorism are no less experiments in the force of literature itself, I argue; accordingly, I have sought to present these experiments as refigurings of modernist and postmodernist literary practices respectively.

My analysis of terrorism through literature is also intended as a contribution to debates about terrorism's figurative aspects more generally. For while many literary and critical theorists contend that we have moved from modernity to postmodernity, from capitalism to 'late-capitalism', from structuralism to poststructuralism—and, moreover, that these shifts have had profound influences on sociopolitical practices generally—it is rare to see these terms or debates being filtered into terrorism studies, despite its frequent references to fictionalization and theories of discourse.[54] The historical jumps between the chapters are thus intended to contrast the ways that modernism and postmodernism, for example, can be used to examine terrorism and its mediation. These jumps in history also correspond to wider shifts in power. As William Perdue has argued, developments in international terrorism must be viewed in relation to the

---

[53] See, for example, Franklin L. Ford, 'Reflections on Political Murder: Europe in the Nineteenth and Twentieth Centuries', in *Social Protest, Violence and Terror in Nineteenth- and Twentieth-century Europe*, ed. by Wolfgang J. Mommsen and Gerhard Hirschfield (London: Macmillan, 1982), 4; Laqueur, *The Age of Terrorism*, 33; Robert A. Friedlander, 'The Origins of International Terrorism', in Alexander and Finger (eds.), *Terrorism: Interdisciplinary Perspectives*, 34–5; and Wardlaw, *Political Terrorism*, 18–19.

[54] James Der Derian's study, *Antidiplomacy: Spies, Terror, Speed and War* (Oxford: Blackwell, 1992) is an exception to this. Writing from within the field of International Relations theory, Der Derian argues that with terrorism, espionage, and war being increasingly affected by developments in information technology, a 'poststructuralist' approach is necessary for addressing the changing horizons of global power relations.

increasing 'supersedure of Great Britain by the United States'[55] as
the dominant economic and military power. Similarly, many theorists of postmodernism have claimed that the increasingly global networks of economics, finance, and information are largely driven by
American mass-culture. The opening chapters on Conrad and Lewis
thus concentrate on how radical militancy was tied to questions of national community in Britain and Europe during the first three
decades of the twentieth century. The chapter on Pound focuses on
his activism against international capital in the 1940s and 1950s, and
moves from a European context to an American one. The chapter on
Abish examines the way 1970s left-wing terrorists in West Germany
were largely attacking what they perceived to be an invidious mixture
of local neo-Nazism and American 'Imperialism'. And the concluding chapter on Northern Irish poetry about the 'Troubles' addresses
the extent to which the concept of postmodern, globalized power
might itself be something that has been contested in the region.

Before turning to Conrad, though, we need to return briefly to the
late-Victorian period and the first terrorist bomb attacks on London
carried out by Irish and American-Irish Republicans. Coupled with
concerns about the Anarchism that was beginning to spread internationally, this militant Republicanism and the responses it provoked
laid down the legacy of terrorism that Britain inherited at the beginning of the twentieth century.

Fenians and Anarchists

The group that encouraged much of the early Republican militancy
was the Irish Revolutionary Brotherhood (IRB), which later became
the Irish Republican Brotherhood. Set up in 1858 by James Stephenson, it built centres of activity in Dublin and New York—the term
'Fenian', derived from the ancient Irish army called the 'Fianna',
came to be applied to both branches.[56] Essentially, the movement
was opposed to Britain's 1801 Act of Union which had divested Ireland of self-determination. Still suffering from the effects of the Great
Famine of 1845–9, and unable to change legislation controlling land

[55] Perdue, *Terrorism and the State*, 21.

[56] On the Fenians generally, see Thomas E. Hachey, *Britain and Irish Separatism: From the
Fenians to the Free State, 1867–1922* (Washington, DC: Catholic University of America Press,
1984); León Ó Broin, *Revolutionary Underground: The Story of the Irish Republican Brotherhood,
1858–1924* (Dublin: Gill and Macmillan, 1976); and R. V. Cornerford, *The Fenians in Context:
Irish Politics and Society, 1848–82* (Dublin: Mercier, 1978).

rights and production, Republicans perceived the the Act to be 'the source of Ireland's political, social, and economic evils',[57] and so decided to act for themselves. The first Fenian sorties on British soil were in 1867 with an attack on a police-van carrying Fenian prisoners in Manchester, and the bombing of Clerkenwell Prison in which twelve people died and 100 were injured. At this stage, the intention was not to initiate a protracted offensive but to rescue captured group-members. After three men were executed for the Manchester affair and another man hanged for the Clerkenwell attack, however, the call for an intensive bombing campaign became more fervent. This was especially so in America, where Fenians were able to publish incitements and organize funding with impunity.[58] Consequently, on being released from prison in England, Jeremiah O'Donovan Rossa, John Devoy, and other prominent Fenians travelled to New York city where, on 20 June 1872, they formed *Clan na Gael*, otherwise known as the 'United Brotherhood'. Using Patrick Ford's newspaper, *Irish World*, as a mouthpiece, the group issued a series of requests for men and money:

The Irish cause requires skirmishers. It requires a little band of heroes who will initiate and keep up without intermission a guerrilla warfare—men who will fly over land and sea like invisible beings—now striking the enemy in Ireland, now in India, now in England itself, as occasion may present.[59]

John Holland, an ex-schoolmaster from County Clare and a friend of Devoy's, took this aim of subversion literally and offered to build the first torpedo-submarine. Explaining his objective in 1873, he described the nature of such a craft: 'It is not like other small vessels, compelled to select for its antagonist a vessel of about its own or inferior power; the larger and more powerful its mark, the better its opportunity.'[60] Holland's designs had already been turned down by the US Navy, but Ford was more optimistic, maintaining that a fleet of ten Irish privateer vessels could clear the seas of English commerce within six months. Many others agreed: *Fraser's Magazine* carried an

---

[57] Peter Alter, 'Traditions of Violence in the Irish National Movement', in Mommsen and Hirschfield, *Social Protest*, 137.

[58] For a discussion of American Fenianism from this time, see 'Fenianism—its Force and its Feebleness: By an Ex-Member of the Fenian Directory', *Blackwood's Edinburgh Magazine* 131: 798 (April 1882): 454–67.

[59] Quoted in Ó Broin, *Revolutionary Underground*, 35.

[60] Quoted in Dan van der Vat, *Stealth at Sea: The History of the Submarine* (London: Weidenfeld & Nicolson, 1994), 30.

article stating that 'sub-aqueous tactics' would 'neutralise the vast improvements in naval art due to steam-power',[61] while the British Admiralty declared submarines to be 'underhand, unfair, and damned un-English',[62] and refused to consider building them until 1901. Such acerbity was no doubt attributable to the fact that Americans had a history of trying to develop submarines for attacking the British navy. The first attempt to sink a surface ship with a submersible craft was in 1776 by an American, David Bushnell, on a British vessel. The submarine had a drill with which it was supposed to bore a hole in the ship for an explosive to be attached—none of the attempts was successful. The next serious effort was by an Irish-American, Robert Fulton, in 1801. Like Bushnell's craft, his submarine could not dive but propelled itself just below the surface; it did, however, manage to sink a ship in a demonstration. The first successful attack by a truly submersible craft was not until the American Civil War, though, with the sinking of the USS *Housatonic* by James McClintock's *H. L. Hunley* on 17 February 1864. Along with the invention of the self-propelled torpedo by Robert Whitehead in 1868, this would have been the inspiration for Holland's design. But after having built a small experimental prototype, and having received more than $20,000 from *Clan na Gael* funds, Holland's subsequent creations were fraught with failure. As a result, the Fenian movement withdrew its support, and Holland did not succeed in his project until the 1890s when the US Navy finally approved his designs.

As León Ó Broin argues, the Fenian's financing of the submarine probably prevented the movement from initiating more effective modes of militancy.[63] Nevertheless, even if it did not become an actuality, the possibility of submarine and torpedo warfare made a definite social impact, as is evident from popular fiction of the time. Mary Richardson Lesesne's *Torpedoes; or, Dynamite in Society* (1883), for example, is not at all about torpedoes or submarines, yet it uses both as a general metaphor for the arson attack and social connivances featured in its plot:

Under-water hostilities are carried on in society to a fearful extent, and many schools engaged in drilling in deadly work are without signs of their true

[61] Cyprian Bridge, 'Sub-Aqueous Warfare', *Fraser's Magazine* 98 (October 1878): 463.
[62] Quoted in van der Vat, *Stealth at Sea*, 33. See also Waldon Fawcett, 'The Submarine Boat and its Future', *Scientific American* 81: 24 (9 December 1899): 376–7.
[63] Ó Broin, *Revolutionary Underground*, 238.

character. If the little work now offered to the public can serve as a 'don't anchor' to some young unwary voyagers, it will not be in vain.[64]

When the terror associated with such subversive combat derives from its secrecy, the fact that it is nowhere evident does not bury fears so much as sow them. Thus, for Lesesne, the submarine warfare that has not taken place is nevertheless endemic to society in other forms. Similarly, Donald MacKay's *The Dynamite Ship* (1888), a utopian narrative of Fenian revolution, creates its own 'signs' with which to represent the 'true character' of the group's marine militancy. The novel figures three Republicans: Lubin, an Irishman; Heyward, an American; and Alexander; an Englishman, who transform a steam-yacht into a military vessel with unheard of capacities for shooting dynamite projectiles. After sailing silently into the Thames and reducing London to rubble, the group negotiate new terms for Irish Home Rule. The terror of the ship's destructive force is prefigured by its invisibility: 'like a spectre from the shades of darkness' evidencing 'no sails, no flags, no steam, no smoke',[65] its new, terrifying power is largely its ethereality.

If submarine terror was largely distilled and disseminated through mythifying, the assault on English cities by Fenian bombers between 1881 and 1887 produced considerably more damage, fear, and fictions. The 1867 attack on Clerkenwell Prison had involved barrels of gunpowder which, because of the amount needed to produce the desired effect, was an unwieldy substance for subversion. But with Alfred Nobel's inventions of dynamite in 1863, and the fulminate mercury detonating process in 1867, the possibility of carrying out successful, clandestine operations was greatly increased. The first Fenian dynamite attack was near Manchester at the Salford Barracks on 14 January 1881; by 1883, with a bomb having gone off near the House of Commons on 15 March, the media was saturated with articles on the situation. Some commentators were dismissive of the events, arguing, for example, that the battle against dynamite 'is made very much easier by the fact that it is only . . . a specially base and evil form of ordinary crime'.[66] Others asserted that the explosive presented a new international crisis: 'The bad and the mad have obtained from science command of a strong weapon of destruction,

[64] Mary Richardson Lesesne, *Torpedoes; or, Dynamite in Society* (Galveston, Tex.: Shaw & Baylock, 1883), 6.
[65] Donald Mackay, *The Dynamite Ship* (New York: Manhattan, 1888), 5, 155.
[66] 'The Dynamite Plot', *Saturday Review* 55: 1433 (14 April 1883): 516.

which they can carry about, can conceal, and can use without committing suicide, and the whole world is the worse for a "triumph of intellect". '⁶⁷ Responding to this heated diversity of opinion, an article in *The Spectator* offered a general, psychological synopsis of the threat, stating that dynamite produced effects on the 'imagination' more than anything else. The terror was attributable to three main factors, it argued: first, 'by the belief that numbers must die', which is the 'secret of the panic in individuals caused by cholera'; second, by the 'horror' of 'unaccustomed modes of death' whereby 'improbable possibilities' are countenanced by individuals; third, 'by the absence of personality in dynamite. We expect it to explode . . . without any man there and then manipulating it.'⁶⁸ From this perspective, what was terrifying about dynamite-terrorism was not simply its propensity to kill. It was also its impersonal randomness, which revealed to people that they were *already living as potential statistics*, already living as anonymous figures in a crowd. Dynamite's explosivity underscored the fact that instead of death and its significance being managed and contained within specific private and public spaces—such as the family home, the battleground, hospital, church, and cemetery—death could break into any space at any time. 'Dynamite is like Banquo's ghost', announced the Anarchist Lizius, 'it keeps on fooling around somewhere or other in spite of his satanic majesty.'⁶⁹

That the Fenian movement was more interested in promulgating terror than causing casualties is evident from its concerted targeting of national landmarks. That is not to say that tactics such as assassination were not also employed: Queen Victoria was shot at on 29 February 1872, and the Chief Secretary for Ireland, Lord Frederick Cavendish, and his deputy were killed with knives by the 'Irish Invincibles' in Dublin's Phoenix Park on 6 May 1882.⁷⁰ Generally, though, the attacks were on buildings, the most notable being on London's Victoria Station on 25 February 1884; Nelson's Column on 30 May 1884 (unsuccessful); and Westminster Hall, the Houses of Parliament, and the Tower of London almost simultaneously on 24 January 1885. The panic resulting from such events was intensified

⁶⁷ 'The Dynamite Danger', *The Spectator* 2856 (24 March 1883): 383. See also 'Dynamite', *Cornhill Magazine* 3: 15 (September 1884): 273–91, which attempts to alleviate fears by giving a scientific account of dynamite's composition and explosivity.
⁶⁸ 'The Fear of Dynamite', *The Spectator* 2859 (14 April 1883): 478.
⁶⁹ 'Lizius', contribution to *Alarm*, quoted in Laqueur, *The Terrorism Reader*, 111.
⁷⁰ See K. R. M. Short, *The Dynamite War: Irish-American Bombers in Victorian Britain* (Dublin: Gill and Macmillan, 1979), 75–6.

by the press's reportage. Commenting on the bombing of the Local Government Board and *The Times* offices on 15 March 1884, the *Annual Register* for that year stated that 'Alarming stories of the discovery of arms and explosives were greedily swallowed, and the fears of the public were fostered by sensational reports of the most trivial circumstances.'[71] The reference to the public's 'swallowing' of the news aptly highlights the way in which the distinctions between the tangible impact of the attacks was spread by the reports themselves.

Some of the newspapers had their own views on counter-terrorist ploys, though. After the 1884 bombing of Victoria Station, for example, *The Times* argued that gathering data would help defuse the situation:

Mysterious explosions now-a-days occur in London with the regular irregularity which tempts the statistical mind to strike an average, and thus bring them under the reign of law. The chance of an explosion in any given month will shortly be calculable, and after time the date may even accumulate to such an extent as to fix the probable locality of the next catastrophe.[72]

In this sense, newspaper reports are imagined as having a general apotropaic function. The desire to counter terror is also particularly evident in attempts to reduce the effects to a series of minute, factual details: 'The property destroyed included a waiting room, a booking office, and a luggage depository office (called a cloak room), covering in all a space of about 45 feet square'; 'The wrecked premises were then carefully photographed from different points of view to show how the wreckage had fallen, and no detail, however trifling it might seem, was neglected.'[73] Yet clearly this also had the adverse effect of associating the 'trifling' and the trivial with catastrophe, as the *Annual Register* stated. The impact of the Fenians' terrorism was thus not reducible either to its violence or the reports on it; rather, it elicited an admixture of the two to rival nitro-glycerine in volatility. The exiled Russian Nihilist 'Stepniak' (Sergei Kravchinsky) later denounced the papers' reports accordingly: 'it is the sensational journalism which deserves the palm for its efforts in spreading and protracting the dynamite epidemics'.[74]

[71] *Annual Register, 1884: A Review of Public Events at Home and Abroad* (London: Ridingtons, 1885), 8.

[72] 'The Outrage at Victoria Station', *The Times* (27 February 1884): 10, author's emphasis.

[73] Ibid.

[74] 'Stepniak', 'The Dynamite Scare and Anarchy', *The New Review* 6 (May 1892): 541.

With the Fenians putting faith in symbolism and synecdoche by attacking the nation through buildings like Nelson's Column and the Houses of Parliament, and with the media variously assuaging and augmenting public fears with its reportage, many novelists felt driven to respond. Tom Greer's *A Modern Daedalus* (1885), for example, is a utopian narrative in which the Irish narrator, John O'Halloran, invents a pair of wings that enables him to fly. Having resisted entreaties from both Irish Republicans and the British government to use the machine in battle, O'Halloran eventually builds up his own squadron of flying subversives, destroys the British forces in Ireland by dropping bombs on them, and so secures a new Irish Republic. In his preface, Greer defends himself against possible accusations of harbouring Fenian sympathies: 'Let no reader suppose that this is the work of an enemy of England. . . . I am a lover of England and believe in the necessity of a firm and lasting union between the two countries.'[75] But this claim is offset by his subsequent assertion that while the text is 'purely imaginary', the 'ideas and forces with which it deals are real and may at any moment be brought into active play by the development of the "resources of civilisation" '.[76] If the ideas are none the less real, then exercising the imagination on them becomes a potentially incendiary act.

Whereas Greer is fascinated in portraying acts of terrorism, Edward Jenkins is more interested in counter-terror. In his *A Week of Passion; or, The Dilemma of Mr George Barton the Younger* (1884), the story opens on '26 June 188—' with an explosion at Regent Circus that immediately provokes cries of 'Fenians', 'Dynamite', and 'Nitro-Glycerin' [*sic*].[77] But it is not the actual 'effects of the explosion' that clears a space in the crowd, we are told; it is instead the ensuing 'terror' which 'decentralises a mob in the midst of which some catastrophe has happened'.[78] Moreover, this terror is not so much caused by the spectacle of death as by the destruction of spectacle, the general anonymity of the violence:

There were no palpable signs except that rain of flesh and blood, which had sent a ghastly thrill of horror through the crowd, and a dent in the roadway about the size of a French wash-basin. . . . A horrible crime had been

---

[75] Tom Greer, *A Modern Daedalus* (London: Griffith, Farran, Okeden & Welsh, 1885), v.
[76] Ibid., vi.
[77] Edward Jenkins, *A Week of Passion; or, The Dilemma of Mr. George Barton the Younger* (1884; London: Bliss Sands, 1897), 9.
[78] Ibid.

committed in the presence of a thousand people, and there appeared to be no traces left, either of the victim or the perpetrator.[79]

So, on the one hand, the *act* of violence never really occurs in Jenkins's text—the subsequent comparison of the 'dent' left by the explosion to a 'French wash-basin' further domesticates and diminishes its impact. On the other hand, because the violence destroys the signs of itself and the agency behind it, the event demonstrates publicly that everyone's individuality is all the more susceptible to being erased through arbitrary acts. This is mitigated by Detective Sontag, however, who finds a hand of the victim and eventually deduces that it belonged to an estate agent, George Barton, and that he was killed not by Fenians but by a firm of maleficent solicitors angry at his investigations into their improper business practices. By tracing the motivations and events leading up to the explosion, the case is solved and the terror allayed—even if Barton remains dead. In this way, the *significance* of the murder is largely detached from the event itself and instead made into a matter of plotting causes. A complicity between novelists' and detectives' work can thus be made explicit: 'the real artist', declares Sontag, 'has . . . an intuitive sense of the *character* of the object he looks at. Every good detective is an artist with the poetry suppressed.'[80] In this respect, Greer and Jenkins offer contrasting portrayals of terrorism's mediation. For while Jenkins figures a distinction between violence and terror, thereby affirming a greater capacity for narrative to mediate the effects of violence, Greer suggests that narrative and mythification can themselves embody latent forces that may be brought into 'active play'.

These novels by Greer and Jenkins are just two instances of how relations of representation and violence could be figured differently regarding the terrorism of the time. Such inconsistency in dealing with the issue could also be used strategically, as in the novel *The Dynamiter* (1885) by Robert Louis Stevenson and his wife, Fanny Van de Grift Stevenson. The story concerns three impecunious young Londoners, Paul Somerset, Harry Desborough, and Edward Challoner, who decide to become detectives when they read an advertisement offering a £200 reward for information about the identity or whereabouts of a tall, broad, moustached man last seen the day before in Green Park. The three protagonists go their separate ways, and the narrative divides into three 'adventures' accordingly. By

---

[79] Jenkins, *A Week of Passion*, 10.   [80] Ibid., 33, Jenkins's emphasis.

chance, though, they all encounter the mendacious Fenian Clara Luxmore, who offers each a different account of her life-story and identity, and turns out to be an accomplice of the terrorist, M'Guire—the man wanted in the advertisement. Thus, the disruptive schemes of the Fenians are themselves foiled by accident, as the chain of chance meetings leads the protagonists to M'Guire despite Clara's dissimulation. The novel's plot of counter-terror is further bolstered by its depiction of the terrorists' attacks, for these only ever amount to their own 'report': 'suddenly, without one premonitory rustle, there burst forth a report of such a bigness that it shook the earth and set the echoes of the mountains thundering from cliff to cliff . . . at the same time the lights in the windows turned for one instant red and then expired.'[81] As in Jenkins's text, violence itself never really takes place, for the explosions invariably destroy their own force; the bomb M'Guire throws into the Thames after a series of misadventures is exemplary: 'a momentary fountain rose and disappeared' (*Dynamiter*, 117). Consequently, terrorist events are always absorbed safely into the quotidian, as the collocation of the bombings with 'the report of a champagne cork' (*Dynamiter*, 76) implies. The obvious punning play on 'report' suggests that violence is ultimately supervened by the textual—which we find another terrorist, Zero, decrying to Somerset: 'Conceive me now, accused before one of your unjust tribunals; conceive the various witnesses and the singularity of their reports' (*Dynamiter*, 105). This is further emphasized in the two main accounts of explosions, newspapers featuring among the main casualties on both occasions. Zero's only claim to fame is 'the outrage of Red Lion Court', in which, Somerset derisively states, 'a scavenger's barrow and some copies of the *Weekly Budget*' (*Dynamiter*, 108) were destroyed. As Zero rejoins, though, 'a child was injured also'. Vengeance for this is ultimately exacted; after Zero accidentally blows himself up the only visible victim is a news-stand:

instantly, with a formidable report, the dynamite exploded. When the smoke cleared away the stall was seen much shattered, and the stall keeper running forth in terror among the ruins; but of the Irish patriot or the Gladstone bag no adequate remains were to be found. (*Dynamiter*, 182)

A catastrophe of disappearance or a disappearance of catastrophe? The 'reports' of the novel are potentially both, the ambiguity being

---

[81] Robert Louis Stevenson and Fanny Van de Grift Stevenson, *The Dynamiter* (Stroud: Sutton, 1991), 23, hereafter cited as *Dynamiter*.

used strategically in such a way that violence and accidents can always happen, but only to terrorists, while simultaneously never happening, for these events take place *as signs*. Fighting terrorism thus becomes a matter of fighting phenomenality. Yet the Stevensons also sabotage their own plot in so far as presenting an intrinsic absurdity of violence makes it all the more tragic when death occurs—as in the instance of the child. Moreover, depicting the significance of violence as fundamentally textual only lends credibility to Stepniak's claim that 'sensational journalism' actually spreads and protracts terrorism's effects.

The Fenian dynamite scare ended in a whimper rather than a bang in Britain, not because it was successfully muted by mediation but because by 1887 *Clan na Gael* and O'Donovan Rossa's 'skirmishers' had decided to cease their 'guerrilla' activities. This was due to a number of factors: the creation by the metropolitan police of a 'Special Irish Branch' and a general increase in surveillance; a split within *Clan na Gael*; proposals by the British Prime Minister, Gladstone, for Home Rule in 1886 (defeated by dissident Liberals); and increasing opposition by the IRB to covert militancy in favour of political negotiation.[82] Yet the trauma of the bombings had certainly left its mark, and by the 1890s the British media was full of reports on the Anarchist bombings that were becoming increasingly common on the continent and in Russia. If the Stevensons' novel was intended to show how terrorism's volatility could be defused textually and ideologically, this is precisely what many Anarchists were contesting.

Anarchism was officially founded by Mikhail Bakunin after he was expelled in September 1872 from the International Working Men's Association on account of his opposition to the running of the organization, and to Marx's belief that a proletarian revolution would eventuate without the aid of incendiary acts.[83] For Bakunin, advocating radical vitalism and violent subversion went hand in hand. Abstract ideas are 'always produced by life', he argued; the Anarchist revolutionary method would thus arise 'spontaneously within the people and destroy everything that opposes the broad flow of popu-

[82] See Short, *The Dynamite War*, 229–42.

[83] On Anarchism's inception and development, see Peter Marshall, *Demanding the Impossible: A History of Anarchism* (London: HarperCollins, 1992); David Miller, *Anarchism* (London: Dent, 1984); and George Crowder, *Classical Anarchism: The Political Thought of Godwin, Proudhon, Bakunin, and Kropotkin* (Oxford: Clarendon, 1991).

lar life so as to create new forms of free social organization'.[84] Similarly, Peter Kropotkin, a Russian Prince who settled and wrote in England from 1878 onwards, proposed a form of Anarchist Communism whereby state governance would be replaced with collective 'free agreements'. The result, he claimed, would be freedom from 'obedience towards individuals or metaphysical entities'.[85] The Anarchists' bombings were thus seen to be fighting for a radical physicality, just as the Fenians' subversions had been blamed on renegade developments of 'Science'. This was especially the view in popular fiction, which invariably yoked Anarchist militants and dangerous scientists together. Grant Allen, author of an amateur book on physics, *Force and Energy: A Theory of Dynamics* (1888), also wrote a novel, *For Maimie's Sake: A Tale of Love and Dynamite* (1886), in which a scientist, Sydney Chevenix, develops a form of silent dynamite that leaves no trace of itself. Despite his professed philanthropic intentions, Chevenix still muses over its potentially revolutionizing effects on warfare—'the unsuspecting savages don't even know they're being shot'[86]—as does his Polish assistant, Stanislas Benyowski, who is actually a member of the Nihilist group 'The People's Will'. Amounting to a form of anti-matter, what is terrifying about the dynamite is its effect of rendering violence an immaculate deception.

In E. Douglas Fawcett's *Hartmann the Anarchist; or, The Doom of the Great City* (1893), it is the invention of a new, lightweight, 'Utopian', high-tensile metal that aids some German Anarchists, allowing them to build the first successful airship, or 'aëronef'. Set in the future around 1920, the novel presents the Anarchists destroying London by aerial bombardment in order to overturn 'the Sin of this industrial age'.[87] The text thus presents a cross-fertilization of genres, mixing the dynamite-terrorism novel with the futurist-dystopian war novel which had become increasingly popular in Britain ever since developments in weaponry and travel made a battle with either Germany or France seem increasingly likely. Sir George Chesney's *The Battle of Dorking* (1871) was the precursor of these war novels, and portrayed a

    [84] Mikhail Bakunin, *Statism and Anarchy*, trans. by Marshall S. Shatz (Cambridge: Cambridge University Press, 1990), 133.
    [85] Peter Kropotkin, 'Anarchism', in *Anarchism and Anarchist Communism* (London: Freedom, 1987), 7.
    [86] Grant Allen, *For Maimie's Sake: A Tale of Love and Dynamite* (London: Chatto & Windus, 1886), 27.
    [87] E. Douglas Fawcett, *Hartmann the Anarchist; or, The Doom of the Great City* (London: Arnold, 1893), 82.

German invasion of Britain. Others forecast attacks by sea, air, or channel tunnel—the construction of which had been seriously considered in the early 1880s.[88] While Fawcett's novel is wholly imaginary, it captures well the fear in Britain of becoming increasingly prone to inimical forces of internationalism and technology. Such responses obviously had a double-edge, though, for if portraying a potential threat is in some sense cathartic, it also gives the potential and the 'alien' certain, concrete forms.

Aristotle's definition of man as '*zoón politikon*', a political animal, certainly did not extend to 'terrorists' as far as the popular media was concerned. Viewed as being devoid of politics, they were cast simply as animals, or rather *anti-human* life-forms, as we shall see in the following chapter. This is presented literally in H. G. Wells's *The War of the Worlds* (1898), in which London is terrorized by 'Martians' with sophisticated technology and weaponry. Terrorism in the novel is not just associated with the flouting of war conventions, but also with attempts to institute an *Other world of possibility* on earth: 'No one gave a thought to the older worlds of space as sources of human danger, or thought of them only to dismiss the idea of life upon them as impossible or improbable.'[89] Yet the positing of new, 'alien' states of existence was already being nurtured on earth itself. Revisionings of geographical space and evolutionary theory by Anarchists such as Kropotkin, Elisée Reclus, and Leon Metchnikoff, along with various refigurations of materialism and thermodynamics by Anarchists, Marxists, and physicists were already being developed internationally. Many of these issues are mixed with typical images of terrorism in Wells's novel to portray the terrorizing: the aliens are octopus-like in appearance (i.e. submarine life-forms); the weapons they use shoot a 'heat-ray' that is as 'invisible' as their 'terrors'; like the terror spread by the presses they also fire canisters of poisonous vapour likened to 'ink'; they have superior technology but eventually succumb to bacteria because they have not evolved terrestrial immune systems. So although the text does not feature any specific terrorist organizations, it is in some senses more realistic than many of the other novels that do on account of its showing the sheer concatenation of factors at

---

[88] For a selection of these texts, see *The Tale of the Next Great War: Fictions of Future Warfare and Battles Still-to-come*, ed. by I. F. Clarke (Liverpool: Liverpool University Press, 1995), and *The Great War with Germany, 1890–1914: Fictions and Fantasies of the War-to-come*, ed. by I. F. Clarke (Liverpool: Liverpool University Press, 1997).

[89] H. G. Wells, *The War of the Worlds* (Bloomington: Indiana University Press, 1993), 51.

play in terrorism's impact at the time. It is this concatenation that prompted Joseph Conrad's fascination with terrorism. In the following chapter, I shall look at how he traces the extent of terrorism's cultural effects in his novels *The Secret Agent* (1907)—dedicated to H. G. Wells—and *Under Western Eyes* (1911) while drawing literature into the fray.

1. Joseph Conrad: Entropolitics and the Sense of Terror

The Secret Agent: *Anarchism and the Thermodynamics of Law*

An act of terrorism in the name of government; a work of destruction so expressive it is incomprehensible; an event so strategic that it appears to be insane. It is a matter of a phantom event. This paradoxical state of affairs is precisely what Privy Councillor Wurmt, the *Chancelier d'Ambassade* at the London embassy of a 'great power', invokes as a means of sorting out the affairs of state within England in his meeting with Adolf Verloc, *agent provocateur*: 'What is required at present is not writing, but the bringing to light of a distinct, a significant fact', in order to exacerbate national 'unrest'.[1] The central terrorist action of *The Secret Agent* (1907), based on the actual self-detonation of the Anarchist Martial Bourdin in Greenwich in 1894, is thus prefigured as state '*propagande par le fait*'—'propaganda by deed', as it is translated in English, though it could equally be rendered 'propaganda by fact'.[2] The term was officially introduced in 1876 at the Anarchist International to inaugurate a policy of political violence that would assert a radical materiality for overturning *meta*physics and the state in one blow.[3] Yet in *The Secret Agent* (1907) it is to be put to wholly different ends. Provocation is necessary, Verloc is told by Wurmt, because of the 'general leniency of the judicial procedure' (*SA*, 55) in Britain, a point Mr Vladimir, the First Secretary of the embassy, reiterates: 'This country is absurd with its regard for individual liberty' (*SA*, 64). What is referred to here is the granting of asylum to

---

[1] Joseph Conrad, *The Secret Agent* (Harmondsworth: Penguin, 1990), 56, hereafter cited as *SA*.

[2] Norman Sherry in *Conrad's Western World* (Cambridge: Cambridge University Press, 1971), offers a detailed analysis of the Martial Bourdin affair and other political matters relating to *The Secret Agent* (219–59).

[3] See Caroline Cahm, *Kropotkin and the Rise of Revolutionary Anarchism, 1872–1886* (Cambridge: Cambridge University Press, 1989), chs. 4 and 5.

political fugitives that Britain extended under the 'Extradition Act' (1870) and then the 'Aliens Act' (1905), both of which helped to support the relatively nascent legal category of political crime.[4] As far as many European nations were concerned, Britain's asylum policy simply helped terrorists, and undermined the stricter European legislative measures—it was not until 1914 that Britain followed most of Europe in registering, and retaining records on, resident 'aliens'.[5] Moreover, the British government seemed actively uninterested in colluding with Europe over anti-terrorism; for example, it did not send representatives to the 1898 Rome Conference which was aimed at producing common European anti-terrorist policies. This reticence is clearly what Mr Vladimir is aiming at when he tells Verloc that there must be a 'dynamite outrage' in Britain before the 'Milan Conference' (*SA*, 70) reconvenes.

By the 1890s, Anarchist activity had certainly taken on international proportions. As well as numerous dynamite attacks in Europe and the USA, there was a series of assassinations of heads of state: President Carnot of France was killed in 1894; the Spanish Prime Minister del Castillo in 1897; King Umberto of Italy in 1900; and President McKinley of the USA in 1901.[6] Faced with this growing epidemic of violence, many British newspapers and periodicals declared their government's legislation on political crime and asylum to be short-sighted. 'For the Anarchists' benefit a monstrous contradictory contrivance is tolerated called "political crime" ',[7] declared *Blackwood's Magazine* (a periodical that Conrad once said '[is] the only one for which I really care to work').[8] *The Times* was similarly antipathetic: ' "political" is a question-begging epithet . . . the real grounds upon which an action must be judged have nothing to do with artificial classification'.[9] Attempting to define the phenomenon was no less

[4] For a detailed discussion of the genesis of the concept of the political offender in Britain in the nineteenth century, see Leon Radzinowicz and Roger Hood, *A History of English Criminal Law, Volume 5: The Emergence of Penal Policy in Victorian and Edwardian England* (Oxford: Clarendon, 1990); and Barton L. Ingraham, *Political Crime in Europe: A Comparative Study of France, Germany, and England* (Berkeley: University of California University Press, 1979).

[5] David Glover discusses immigration and the Aliens Act in relation to *The Secret Agent* in 'Aliens, Anarchists and Detectives: Legislating the Immigrant Body', *New Formations* 32 (Autumn/Winter 1997): 22–33.

[6] See David Miller, *Anarchism* (London: Dent, 1984), 97–146.

[7] 'Charles Whibley' (William Blackwood), 'Musing without Method', *Blackwood's Magazine* 170: 1032 (October 1901): 561.

[8] Quoted in Sherry, *Conrad's Western World*, 250.

[9] 'Political Crime', *The Times* (12 March 1896): 11.

difficult for the law. Introduced as a category first in 1820, Cesare Lombroso went on to characterize political crime as '*crime passionel*'— a definition that was later supported by Lord Carnarvon at the 'International Penitentiary Commission' in 1872: 'crimes of passion', 'mere political crimes', he asserted, 'should not be punished by ordinary imprisonment, but by simple detention in a fortress'.[10]

However, while political crime was presented as a privileged species of offence, the issue of what constituted a politically criminal act remained unclear. When Angelo Castioni was arrested in Britain in 1891 at the request of the Swiss government for having murdered Luigi Rossi, the judges defined political crime as an act 'committed as incidental, and in furtherance of, political insurrection'.[11] But they still admitted the impossibility of giving specific examples. Subsequently declared justifiable only in a civil war, political crime therefore had to bear some resemblance to state rebellion.[12] As a result, Anarchist violence was frequently denied the status of political crime, particularly by the press: 'the anarchist is not a political assassin; he is merely a noxious beast',[13] asserted the *Saturday Review*: 'anarchism has no politics'.[14] This general ambivalence surrounding political criminality is symptomatic of the problems that terrorist violence and anti-terrorist legislation presented for British liberalism at the time. For when it came to the possibility of political crime taking place in Britain itself, the government's stance was contradictory. The granting of asylum to foreign fugitives was largely indicative of the suspicion with which other governments were viewed; the Extradition Act and the Aliens Act only recognized political crime as something which took place *elsewhere*. Thus, when the Suffragettes in 1908 attempted to justify their militancy on the grounds of political insurrection, the government declared that the Extradition Act was not applicable to offences committed within the country.[15]

In an extreme way, Britain's paradoxical stance on political violence is what Mr Vladimir is attempting to match with his plan of creating a terrorist 'outrage' in order to elicit more stringent policing. His idea takes on an absurdist tone, though, when he explains to

[10] Quoted in Radzinowicz and Hood, *A History of English Criminal Law*, 402.
[11] Quoted in Ingraham, *Political Crime in Europe*, 206.
[12] See James Fitzjames Stephens, *A History of the Criminal Law in England* (London: Macmillan, 1883), 69–80.
[13] 'Anarchists as Pests', *Saturday Review* 101 (9 June 1906): 712.
[14] 'Anarchism, Socialism and Rubino', *Saturday Review* 94 (22 November 1902): 634.
[15] See Radzinowicz and Hood, *A History of English Criminal Law*, 442–4.

Verloc his 'philosophy of the bomb': 'A bomb outrage to have any influence on public opinion must go beyond the intention of vengeance
or terrorism', he argues: 'it must be purely destructive. It must be
that, and only that . . .' (*SA*, 66). Attacks on property, religion, and
churches fail to disturb the quiescence of the everyday, he states, for
insurrection has become a mere media phenomenon: 'Every newspaper has ready-made phrases to explain such manifestations away'
(*SA*, 66). An act without authorship is thus required, he argues, an
epiphanous devastation irreducible to the familiar: 'what is one to say
to an act of destructive ferocity so absurd as to be incomprehensible,
inexplicable, almost unthinkable; *in fact*, mad?' (*SA*, 67, emphasis
mine). Such an attack would be an assault on 'the whole social creation', Mr Vladimir continues, which is why he wants it to involve an
attack on 'science', the last 'sacrosanct fetish' of the 'bourgeoisie':
'They believe that in some mysterious way science is at the source of
their material prosperity' (*SA*, 67). The law's reinforcement is thus
imagined as eventuating from an attack on the laws of nature. Moreover, the synecdochical assault on 'Astronomy' that is decided
upon—an attempt on the Greenwich Observatory—carries the
added effect of being viewed as a global event: 'the whole civilised
world has heard of Greenwich' (*SA*, 68).

In all of this, the connection made between the politicizing of law
and the grounding of the social in science reflects a wider debate that
was taking place in the late-Victorian period. In an age of positivism,
when biology and physics were in their ascendancy and questioning
preconceived notions of nature in general, the application of science
to the social body was widespread. As Robert Young has commented:
'it was the nineteenth-century debate which led to the conclusion that
morality and social theory could be natural science'.[16] Walter Pater,
for example, proclaimed the 'empirical study of facts' to be the rem-
edy for the 'disabused soul of the century'.[17] Asserting a facticity of

---

[16] Robert Young, 'The Historiographical and Ideological Contexts of the Nineteenth-
Century Debate on Man's Place in Nature', in *Changing Perspectives in the History of Science*, ed.
by Mikulas Teich and Robert Young (London: Heinemann, 1973), 403.

[17] Walter Pater, 'Prosper Mérimée' (1890), in *Miscellaneous Studies* (London: Macmillan,
1910), 16. See also Donald Benson, 'Facts and Constructs: Victorian Humanists and Scientific Theorists on Scientific Knowledge', in *Victorian Science and Victorian Values: Literary
Perspectives*, ed. by James Paradis and Thomas Postlewait (New York: The New York Academy of Sciences, 1981), 299–318; and Brian Wynne, 'Physics and Psychics: Science, Symbolic Action, and Social Control in Late Victorian England', in *Natural Order: Historical
Studies of Scientific Order*, ed. by Barry Barnes and Steven Shapin (Beverley Hills: Sage, 1979),
169–86.

law was certainly prevalent in politics and the sciences alike, and frequently led to cross-referencing. The scientist Thomas Huxley predicted that physiology would 'extend the realm of matter and law until it is coextensive with knowledge, with feeling, with action'.[18] The very possibility of rational political life depends on it, he argued. Only by treating political matters as a scientific problem would 'the perpetual oscillation of nations between anarchy and despotism . . . be replaced by the steady march of self-restraining freedom'.[19] Herbert Spencer was attempting precisely this marriage of politics and science by developing a theory of sociology along the lines of evolution. Society evolves as a movement from a state of 'incoherent homogeneity to a coherent heterogeneity', he writes, 'accompanying the dissipation of motion and integration of matter'.[20] In contrast, for Anarchist writers such as Leon Metchnikoff, Elisée Reclus, and the Russian Prince Kropotkin, evolution theory was useful for outlining an alternative form of social co-operation that would not need a state to preside over it.[21] In the most extreme cases, evolution was also viewed by some Anarchists as legitimating the use of violence; in 1894 George Etievant, after being sentenced to five years for stealing dynamite, told the court:

Everything from the jellyfish to the elephant, from the blade of grass to the oak, from the atom to the star proclaim it. . . . The movements of the infinitely small as those of the infinitely great, act and react continuously on each other. And since they all react on us, we have a right to react on them; for we have a right to live . . .[22]

But while science was viewed as correlating natural law and political legitimacy in a number of ways, advances in physics were perceived as threatening the stability of natural life. Expounded first by

---

[18] Thomas Huxley, *Selections from the Essays of T. H. Huxley*, ed. by Alburey Castell (New York: Appleton-Century-Crofts, 1948), 21. For a criticism of Huxley from one of his contemporaries, see W. H. Mallock, 'Physics and Sociology', *Contemporary Review* 68 (December 1895): 883–908.

[19] Thomas Huxley, 'Science and Culture', in *Science and Culture, and Other Essays* (London: Macmillan, 1881), 23.

[20] Herbert Spencer, 'First Principles' (1867), in *On Social Evolution: Selected Writings of Herbert Spencer*, ed. by J. D. Y. Peel (Chicago: University of Chicage Press, 1972), 71.

[21] See e.g. Kropotkin, 'The Scientific Bases of Anarchy', *Nineteenth Century* 21 (February 1887): 238–52; Metchnikoff, 'Revolution and Evolution', *Contemporary Review* 50 (September 1886): 412–37; and Reclus, 'The Evolution of Cities', *Contemporary Review* 67 (February 1895): 246–64. Con Coroneos relates Conrad's urban depictions to the work of such writers in 'Conrad, Kropotkin and Anarchist Geography', *The Conradian* 18 (Autumn 1994): 17–30.

[22] Quoted in 'Anarchy at the Bar', *Commonweal* (12 May 1894): 67.

Sadi Carnot in 1824, thermodynamics was subsequently taken up in Britain by scientists such as James Clerk Maxwell, James Thomson, William Thomson (later Lord Kelvin), John Tyndall, Balfour Stewart, and Peter Guthrie Tait. The second law of thermodynamics states that the universe is moving towards a maximum state of 'entropy' in terms of energy flow; the neologism—a coupling of the Greek '*energeia*' (energy) and '*tropé*' (transformation or turn; cognate of 'trope')—was coined by Rudolph Clausius in 1865.[23] Work and motion (kinetic energy) convert into heat, but while all work can be converted as such, not all heat can be transformed back into work. This is the 'Principle of Dissipation of Energy', which asserts that although the total quantity of energy in the universe remains constant (the 'Law of Conservation'), its quality or 'usefulness' is continually being degraded. Moreover, as heat manifests and requires a *differential* of temperatures (Carnot), the more that heat is expended, the more everything tends towards a homogeneous and thus enervated state.

The social implications of thermodynamics were met with widespread dismay, not least because many of the scientists wrote in popular journals of the time. That many physicists were themselves uncomfortable with the social ramifications did not help to allay fears. Josef Loschmidt, for example, declared his intention to 'destroy the terroristic nimbus of the second law, which has made it appear to be an annihilating principle for all living beings'.[24] Intense debates ensued as to the interconvertibility of work and heat, as scientists attempted to counteract the possibility of global melt-down. Balfour Stewart in the very popular *The Conservation of Energy* (1873), and *The Unseen Universe* (1875) which he wrote with Peter Guthrie Tait, set about reconciling thermodynamics with a Christian ethos, interpolating in the latter work a plethora of literary quotations as authoritative evidence. The universe in general is figured by them as a volatile system, a substance like 'gun cotton' or 'nitro-glycerine',[25] in which heat is literally the leveller of all: 'the tendency of heat is

---

[23] For an introduction to the historical development of thermodynamics in the nineteenth century, see Stephen G. Brush, *The Temperature of History: Phases of Science and Culture in the Nineteenth Century* (New York: Franklin, 1978), also his *The Kind of Motion We Call Heat: A History of the Kinetic Theory of Gases in the Nineteenth Century*, 2 vols. (Amsterdam: North Holland, 1986); and Crosbie Smith and M. Norton Wise, *Energy and Empire: A Biographical Study of Lord Kelvin* (Cambridge: Cambridge University Press, 1989).

[24] Brush, *The Temperature of History*, 66.

[25] Balfour Stewart, *The Conservation of Energy: An Elementary Treatise on Energy and its Laws* (London: Henry S. King, 1873), 137, hereafter cited as *CE*.

towards equalization: heat is par excellence the communist of our universe and will undoubtedly bring the system to an end'.[26] This nihilistic view is reversed, though, when the dissipation of kinetic energy is said to be conserved as 'ether', which they view as an eternal, directing force. 'Life', they assert, is controlled by an ethereal government: 'We . . . look upon the laws of the universe as those laws according to which the beings of the universe are conditioned by the Governor thereof, as regards time, place, and sensation'(*UU*, 47).[27] Total government authority is thus accorded the status of natural law. In this sense, the transformation from the seen to the unseen, from the physical to the ethereal, is indissociably a matter of en-*troping* states of affairs. Such metaphorizing is merely one example of the more general transferences taking place as a result of dialogues between politics, law, and science at the time.[28] As Gillian Beer has argued, the widespread implications of thermodynamic theory meant that it was seen to have unlimited applicability: 'It could be made into a description of mind; it could become grounds for spiritualism; it could provide a vocabulary for degenerationism; it could dislimn all boundaries and disturb all organizations.'[29] Bearing the volatility of these cultural exchanges in mind, we can form a different conception of the connection between narrative and politics within *The Secret Agent*—'this simple tale of the nineteenth century' (*SA*, 5)—by analysing the images of thermodynamics that abound throughout the text, recognizing that they are intrinsic to issues of fact and fabrica-

---

[26] Balfour Stewart and Peter Guthrie Tait, *The Unseen Universe; or, Physical Speculations on a Future State* (London: Macmillan, 1875), 91, hereafter cited as *UU*.

[27] The 'Governor' is indebted to Maxwell's hypothetical 'demon'—which Maxwell had written of to Tait on 11 December 1867. Imagine two vessels, A and B, separated by a diaphragm 'without mass', he explained, and 'a being' who knows the relative velocities of molecules in both. By simply operating the diaphragm and directing molecules with a higher velocity into A, the demon elicits a difference in temperatures between the two vessels. The energy in A is thus increased while that in B decreases, even though 'no work has been done: only the intelligence of a very neat fingered being has been employed' (quoted in C. G. Knott, *The Life and Scientific Work of Peter Guthrie Tait* [Cambridge: Cambridge University Press, 1911], 213). The physical law of dissipation is thus not denied, it is supervened by an agency that operates independently, supposedly like a mind controlling its body.

[28] On the impact of thermodynamics on literature, and on literary and rhetorical figures as being intrinsic to Victorian scientific theorizing, see Gillian Beer, *Open Fields: Science in Cultural Encounter* (Oxford: Clarendon, 1996), chs. 10–13; and Greg Myers, 'Nineteenth-Century Popularizations of Thermodynamics and the Rhetoric of Social Prophecy', in *Energy and Entropy: Science and Culture in Victorian Britain*, ed. by Patrick Brantliger (Bloomington: Indiana University Press, 1990), 307–38.

[29] Beer, *Open Fields*, 301.

tion, stability and transformation, and engage with an entire landscape of debate at that time.

Stewart and Tait's notion of violent transformations being caused by the 'slightest impulse' is applicable to the genesis of *The Secret Agent* as recounted by Conrad in the 'Author's Note' he added twelve years after the novel's publication.[30] A recalled statement of Sir William Harcourt, the Home Secretary, to Assistant Commissioner Anderson regarding an Anarchist 'outrage'—'All that's very well. But your idea of secrecy over there seems to consist of keeping the Home Secretary in the dark' (*SA*, 40)—exploded instantly, for Conrad, into vistas of narrative imagery: 'of South America, a continent of crude sunshine and brutal revolutions . . . the reflector of the world's light. Then the vision of an enormous town . . . more populous than some continents . . . a cruel devourer of the world's light' (*SA*, 40–1). The Latin American insurgency that he had already portrayed in *Nostromo* is juxtaposed with an entropic cityscape that is figured in the novel as London. The catalyst for the story is thus explicitly imagined in terms of thermodynamics, for it was the sun, seemingly the central energy source of the world, that was placed at the centre of much of the scientific debate.[31] Within the narrative, the first survey of London also involves an image of 'diffused' light cast by a 'bloodshot' sun:

Mr Verloc was going westward through a town without shadows in an atmosphere of powdered old gold. There were red, coppery gleams on the roofs of houses, on the corners of walls, on the panels of carriages, on the very coats of horses, and on the broad back of Mr Verloc's overcoat, where they produced a dull effect of rustiness. (*SA*, 51)

Blazing with metaphor as much as light, the diffusion is presented as a slide in wealth as we move from the sheen of 'old gold' to 'coppery gleams' and finally to 'rustiness'—all of which flows into Verloc's

---

[30] Michael Whitworth's 'Inspector Heat Inspected: *The Secret Agent* and the Meanings of Entropy', *The Review of English Studies* 49: 193 (1998): 40–59, is the only other study of the novel to date in terms of thermodynamic theory. For examinations of Conrad's work in terms of biology and evolution, see Redmond O'Hanlon, *Joseph Conrad and Charles Darwin: The Influence of Scientific Thought on Conrad's Fiction* (Edinburgh: Salamander, 1984); Allan Hunter, *Joseph Conrad and the Ethics of Darwinism: The Challenges of Science* (London: Croom Helm, 1983); and George Levine, 'The Novel as Scientific Discourse', in *Why the Novel Matters: A Postmodern Perplex*, ed. by Mark Spilka and Caroline McCracken-Fleischer (Bloomington: Indiana University Press, 1990), 238–45.

[31] See, for example, William Thomson, 'On the Age of the Sun's Heat', *Macmillan's Magazine* 5 (March 1862): 388–93; Balfour Stewart and J. Norman Lockyer, 'The Sun as a Type of the Material Universe', *Macmillan's Magazine* 18 (July 1868): 246–52.

summation that 'these people had to be protected. Protection is the first necessity of opulence and luxury' (*SA*, 51).

But what if the stability of social fabric, its very energy, depends on a sun which, according to the scientists, is living on borrowed capital? Stewart raises the problem in precisely these terms. Potential energy is like 'capital', kinetic energy is like 'the act of spending', and the sun is the 'primordial capitalist'—'in the position of a man whose expenditure exceeds his income' (*CE*, 26, 152).[32] Thermodynamic laws are thus made to operate pessimistically as laws of capitalism. But any potential danger of energetic bankruptcy is overcome when Stewart once again posits capital as an 'ethereal' force. The consequence of this, he claims, is that there can be no degradation or production of energy or wealth, only exchange: 'the world of mechanism is not a manufactory in which energy is created, but rather a mart' (*CE*, 341). Thomas Huxley develops the capitalist metaphor further. Discussing the first breath of an infant in terms of labour, capital is the energy or 'work-stuff' drawn on, which he compares to the 'powder' of a 'loaded gun'.[33] The force of work is subsequently debilitated, though, when he asserts that all labour is dependent on the existence of a prior stock of 'work-stuff'. Consequently, labour is made incidental to capital, in effect contributing nothing, while capital itself remains theoretically self-creating and inexhaustible.

If capitalist law depends on remaining independent of volatile bodies, however, the material side of life becomes dangerous, as we see Conrad's Anarchist, Michaelis, claiming: 'History is dominated and determined by the tool and production—by the force of economic conditions. Capitalism has made socialism, and the laws made by the capitalist for the socialist are responsible for anarchism' (*SA*, 73). On Huxley's terms, Michaelis is certainly his own body of potentially explosive 'work-stuff': 'He had come out of a highly hygienic prison round like a tub, with an enormous stomach and distended cheeks' (*SA*, 74). Several critics have noted the fascination with obese and emaciated bodies in the novel, but it is in the context of writings such as those of Huxley, Stewart, and Tait that we can fully appreci-

---

[32] In a letter of 7 October 1907 to Robert Cunninghame Graham responding to the latter's praise of the novel, Conrad wrote: 'By Jove! If I had the necessary talent I would like to go for the true anarchist—which is the millionaire. Then you would see the venom flow. But it is too big a job' (Cedric Watts, *Joseph Conrad's Letters to R. B. Cunninghame Graham* [Cambridge: Cambridge University Press, 1969], 170).

[33] Thomas H. Huxley, 'Capital—The Mother of Labour', *Nineteenth Century* 27 (March 1890): 514.

ate their import.[34] As a result of theorizing about materialism more than practising it, Michaelis appears to embody the very image of the bourgeoisie, for which we also find Verloc being berated by Mr Vladimir earlier: 'You—a starving proletariat—never!' (*SA*, 58). Bodily inertia, the indulgence in consumption over production, is a form of entropy in itself. So, for Mr Vladimir, Verloc's obesity is cast as evolutionary degeneracy: 'He's fat—the animal' (*SA*, 57), which is all the more reason to force him to plant the bomb: 'no pay without work' (*SA*, 62). In contrast to Michaelis and Verloc, the terrorist, Yundt, looms spectrally thin, dreaming of a group of fellow 'destroyers' who would employ death 'for the good and all in the service of humanity' (*SA*, 74). Figure of his own dream of destruction, Yundt is presented in a more terrifying light than either Michaelis or Verloc, yet his nihilistic ideas are depicted as corroding his power: 'The shadow of his evil gift clung to him . . . useless, ready to be thrown away on the rubbish heap of things' (*SA*, 78). Laws of bodies and the embodiment of law are thus entangled, just as they were in the writings of the criminologist Lombroso, who believed that physiognomy could provide the 'juridical basis of political crime . . .'.[35] It is Lombroso whom Yundt declares 'an ass' after another revolutionary, Ossipon, cites the criminologist when suggesting that Verloc's 'simple' brother-in-law, Stevie, shows signs of being 'degenerate' (*SA*, 77). 'Teeth and ears mark the criminal? Do they?', responds Yundt: 'And what about the law that marks him still better—the pretty branding instrument invented by the overfed to protect themselves against the hungry?' (*SA*, 78).[36]

This conundrum of physical force is posed as a problem of temporality in Ossipon's subsequent meeting with a terrorist known as 'the Professor' when they discuss the detonator and flask of explosives that the latter wears at all times. Guaranteeing freedom in the event of any police apprehension, the device works on 'the principle of the pneumatic instantaneous shutter for a camera lens' (*SA*, 91), and the effects

---

[34] See James F. English, 'Anarchy in the Flesh: Conrad's "Counterrevolutionary" Modernism and the *Witz* of the Political Unconscious', *Modern Fiction Studies* 38 (Autumn 1992): 616–30; and J. Hillis Miller, *Poets of Reality* (Cambridge: Harvard University Press, 1966), 49–53.

[35] Cesare Lombroso, 'Illustrative Studies in Criminal Anthropology: The Physiognomy of the Anarchists', *The Monist* 1: 3 (April 1891): 336.

[36] The discussion between Conrad's Anarchists can be compared to that of the public-house revolutionaries in Henry James's (generally oblique) book on Anarchism, *The Princess Casamassima* (1886; Harmondsworth: Penguin, 1987), ch. 21.

of its irreversibility are immediate. Its only imperfection, says the Professor, is that the actual detonation is not immediate: 'A full twenty seconds must elapse from the moment I press the ball till the explosion takes place' (*SA*, 92). For Ossipon, this lapse is more terrifying than the instant of death itself, but for the Professor the resolve required to face the horror is the source of his 'force of personality': 'What is effective is the belief those people have in my will to use the means. That's their impression. It is absolute. Therefore I am deadly' (*SA*, 92–3). A whole ethics of the individual versus the masses is outlined by him in terms of this division between life and death:

> They depend on life, which in this connection is a historical *fact* surrounded by all sorts of restraints and considerations, a complex, organized *fact* open to attack at every point; whereas I depend on death which knows no restraint and cannot be attacked.   (*SA*, 93, emphases mine)

Just how much the Professor can claim to have freed himself from the constraint of factual life appears questionable in so far as death is the one experience he cannot possess, the one event that would prevent him from 'having' an experience. Incapable of *being* death, he can only adopt a relation of simile and become *deadly*. His death would remain the one thing that would exist only for others, then, a mediated after-image robbed of its social transcendence—as Mr Vladimir has told Verloc, the newspapers have 'ready-made phrases to explain such manifestations away' (*SA*, 66). For this reason, the Professor's power is dependent on the social body he wishes to attack. His terror is predicated on the promise of death *and* its deferral.[37] The passage of time itself thus threatens to absorb the impact of his terror—'I *am* the force. . . . But the time! . . . Give me the time!' (*SA*, 264, Conrad's emphasis)—and exacerbate his worst doubt; that the masses are 'impervious to fear' and even have 'death' on their side. In this sense, Conrad's image of the detonator implicates the dynamics of social life more generally, just as 'nitro-glycerine' did for Stewart and Tait. The instant threatens everyone with death and irreversibility, yet it also ensures that the effects of an event are carried through time. An instance of this is given when Inspector Heat inspects the bloody

---

[37] Maurice Blanchot, in *The Writing of the Disaster*, trans. by Ann Smock (1980; Lincoln: University of Nebraska Press, 1992), discusses this impossibility of arrogating one's own death: 'he who opens, as Heidegger said, *the possibility of impossibility*—or again, he who believes himself to be master of un-mastery—lets himself get caught in a sort of trap and halts eternally (halts, obviously, just an instant) at the point where, ceasing to be a subject . . . he comes up against death as that which doesn't happen . . .' (70, Blanchot's emphasis).

remains of Stevie after the latter has tripped over the bomb that he was unwittingly carrying to Greenwich for Verloc: '[Inspector Heat] evolved a horrible notion that ages of atrocious pain and mental torture could be contained between two successive winks of an eye' (*SA*, 107). Conrad's indirect connection of the camera shutter with the detonator thus links the image of disaster to a disaster of images. The chiasmus is evident in the instance of Stevie's exploded flesh embodying, for Heat, 'all he had ever read in popular publications of long and terrifying dreams . . .' (*SA*, 107).[38] By this point in the novel, then, violence and entropy are also being linked to the force of literature itself.

If Conrad's image of energy confounds apocalypse by imbricating life and death, the individual and the social, within one circulation, the physical substance of life is also figured as facilitating subversion, as we are told after Inspector Heat has confronted the Professor:

[Heat's] wisdom was of an official kind, or else he might have reflected upon a matter not of theory but of experience that in the close-woven stuff of relations between the conspirator and the police there occur sudden solutions of continuity, sudden holes in space and time.   (*SA*, 105)

A novel image of a political unconscious begins to take shape along these lines, incorporating transferences of energy that are strikingly similar to those theorized by Henri Bergson. For Bergson, 'the flux of time is reality itself'.[39] The passage of time is essentially one of 'becoming', of 'dissociation and division', in which past and present, virtual and actual, matter and memory coexist in every moment, 'always interpenetrat[ing] each other'.[40] And because *every* moment that passes is also passed on within this temporal flow, 'a single duration will pick up along its route the events of the totality of the material world'.[41]

---

[38] Stewart and Tait present a similar combination of force and image in their notion of energy-pictures: 'A picture of the sun may be said to be travelling through space with an inconceivable velocity, and, in fact, continual photographs are thus produced and retained. A large portion of the universe may thus be said to be invested in such pictures' (*UU*, 158).

[39] Henri Bergson, *Creative Evolution*, trans. by Arthur Mitchell (1907; London: Macmillan, 1920), 374. See also James T. English, 'Scientist, Moralist, Humanist: A Bergsonian Reading of *The Secret Agent*', *Conradiana* 19 (1987): 139–56; and M. A. Gillies, 'Conrad's *The Secret Agent* and *Under Western Eyes* as Bergsonian Comedies', *Conradiana* 20 (1988): 195–213.

[40] Henri Bergson, *Matter and Memory*, trans. by Nancy Margaret Paul and W. Scott Palmer (1896; New York: Zone, 1991), 67.

[41] Henri Bergson, *Duration and Simultaneity*, trans. by Leon Jacobson, (1922; Indianapolis: Bobbs-Merrill, 1965), 47.

In this way, the past is conserved in matter as a form of energy, the formulation owing a considerable debt to thermodynamic theory:

It works in two complementary ways—in one, by an explosive action, it liberates instantly, in the chosen direction, energy which matter has been accumulating a long time, in the other, by a work of contraction, it gathers into a single instant the incalculable number of small events which matter holds distinct, as when we sum up in a word the immensity of history.[42]

Bergson outlines an ethics of agency here. Despite the simultaneity of past and present in duration, the subject effects a hiatus, explodes the connection, thereby being accorded a space of time to choose a word or course of action. In *The Secret Agent*, however, such freedom is problematic in so far as the word 'phantom' which begins to 'sum up' the 'immensity of history' for Verloc also threatens his autonomy. Contemplating the fragility of his situation in general, he is visited by a vision of the main cause of his worries:

The prospect was as black as the window-pane against which he was leaning his forehead. And suddenly the face of Mr Vladimir, clean-shaved and witty, appeared enhaloed in the glow of its rosy complexion like a sort of pink seal impressed on the fatal darkness.

This luminous and mutilated vision was so ghastly physically that Mr Verloc started away from the window, letting down the venetian blind with a great rattle. (*SA*, 84)

Much as Verloc would like to exorcize Mr Vladimir from his memory, the thought of him remains as insurmountable as the prospect of fatal darkness itself. All the more persistent for being repressed, Vladimir's spectre has already transgressed the distinctions between past and present, matter and memory, inside and outside, that Verloc tries to draw in his action of letting down the blind.

Freud and Breuer theorized hysterical phenomena as operating in a similar way. Using thermodynamics to theorize the dynamics of the unconscious, as Michel Serres has pointed out,[43] the force of a traumatic event is conserved all the more when denied its effects, and keeps on acting long after its occurrence: 'We must presume that the physical trauma—or more precisely, the memory of the trauma—

---

[42] Henri Bergson, 'Life and Consciousness' (1911), in *Mind Energy*, ed. and trans. by H. Wildon Carr (London: Macmillan, 1920), 17, see also 14–15.

[43] See Michel Serres, 'The Origin of Language: Biology, Information Theory, and Thermodynamics', in *Hermes: Literature, Science, Philosophy*, ed. by Josué V. Harari and David F. Bell (Baltimore: Johns Hopkins University Press, 1992), 71–83.

acts like a foreign body, which long after its entry must continue to be regarded as an agent that is still at work.'[44] The trauma's force is indissociable from the vacillation between memory and body that is described in this passage. The unconscious itself is a secret agent, for the traumatic event already exists as a memory but never ceases to happen again, forming links with other times: 'traumatic scenes do not form a simple view, like a string of pearls, but ramify and are interconnected like genealogical trees'.[45] In this sense, Freud's and Breuer's early psychoanalytic writings on hysteria and trauma are particularly pertinent to the issue of terrorism at the time—particularly in so far as they posit transferences between the body and mind, violence and terror. But while these transferences involve exchanges of energy that threaten the subject's agency, they are nevertheless limited for Freud and Breuer to exchanges *in* the subject between consciousness and the unconscious. In Conrad's novel, though, the image of a political unconscious begins to develop around transferences *between* subjects, such that interconnections of terror and violence are more actively involved in a wider social field.[46]

Grant Allen had already seen the potential for linking terrorism to the unconscious in his popular novel *For Maimie's Sake: A Tale of Love and Dynamite* (1886). The main terrorist group in the text is ruled over by a power called 'the Unconscious', which the Polish revolutionary Benyowski describes after having been chosen to carry out an assassination: 'The old fashioned mind would have seen in this the finger of providence. We see in it rather the working of the Unconscious.

---

[44]   Sigmund Freud and Josef Breuer, *Studies on Hysteria* (1893–5), in *The Standard Edition of the Complete Psychological Works of Sigmund Freud*, ed. and trans. by James Strachey, 24 vols. (London: Hogarth and the Institute of Psycho-analysis, 1955), ii: 13. The connection between thermodynamics and the unconscious is made in Breuer's 'Theoretical' section, ii: 193–4, 203, 207 n.1, where he uses analogies of steam engines, electrical currents, and telegraphic wires.

[45]   Freud and Breuer, *Studies on Hysteria*, 211.

[46]   Regarding Conrad and the political unconscious, see Fredric Jameson, *The Political Unconscious: Narrative as a Socially Symbolic Act* (London: Methuen, 1981), ch. 5. Interestingly, the main passage—from *Typhoon*—which Jameson presents as an example of Conradian style countering dominant ideology with a 'utopic' narrative space is also one concerned with thermodynamics. Jameson sees the incorporation of a 'late nineteenth-century positivist Wellsian metaphysic of entropy' as 'nonideological': 'In such "purer" descriptive passages, the function of the literary representation is not to underscore or to perpetuate an ideological system; rather the latter is cited to authorize and reinforce a new representational space' (231). While I concur with this view of Conrad's style and imagery as exercising its own potentials, I would argue that rather than carving out a 'utopic' space, it is because thermodynamics *was* ideologically an issue of sensation, perception, and bodies that Conrad's entropic images present a direct and immanent engagement with ideology.

Both are immutable, divine, mysterious.'[47] In *The Secret Agent* the machinations of a social unconscious are evident in the confrontation Winnie has with Verloc after she has learned of his involvement in her brother Stevie's death. The effect of the news on Winnie, coupled with Verloc's insensitive attempts at consoling her, is portrayed as a thermodynamics of grief: 'It was the effect of a white-hot iron drawn across her eyes; at the same time her heart, hardened and chilled into a lump of ice, kept her body in an inward shudder . . .' (*SA*, 219). Faced with her unresponsive despair, Verloc grapples with the problem of explaining that: 'a notion grows in a mind till it acquires an outward existence, an independent power of its own, and even a suggestive voice . . . a man may be haunted by a fat, witty, clean-shaved face till the wildest expedient to get rid of it appears a child of wisdom' (*SA*, 216). He does not need to explain, though, for Winnie, after being confronted suddenly with the 'crushing memory' and 'exhausting vision' of her life of labour when she had lived with Stevie in Belgravia, is subsequently possessed by the thought that 'This man took the boy away to murder him': 'It was in her veins, in her bones, in the roots of her hair' (*SA*, 223). So unbearable is this conception for her that it takes on its own bastard reality: 'across that thought (not across the kitchen) the form of Mr Verloc went to and fro . . . stamping with his boots upon her brain' (*SA*, 225). Thought, memory, and the past join forces, turning both Winnie and Verloc into virtual automata. For Winnie, the impact the disaster has on her sense of outrage outweighs any other catastrophe: 'the most violent earthquake of history could only have been a faint and languid rendering' of her 'moral shock' (*SA*, 229). Matters worsen, though, when Verloc suggests that she is as responsible for Stevie's death as he is. Advancing, knife in hand, 'the resemblance of her face with that of her brother grew with every step' (*SA*, 234). Winnie literally becomes a double-agent, possessed by the past at the same time as embodying it, the very transference of energy becoming a living metaphor (in Greek, '*metapherein*' means 'to transport').[48] This uncanny movement is also

---

[47] Grant Allen, *For Maimie's Sake: A Tale of Love and Dynamite* (London: Chatto & Windus, 1886), 46.

[48] For the *Star*'s anonymous reviewer of the novel, this double-agency also extends to the scene of reading: 'The murder of Verloc is one of the most intensely dramatic murders in fiction. Its imaginative realism is diabolical. . . . You see Verloc seeing the shadow of the arm with the clenched hand holding the carving-knife. You think out the plan of defence which he thinks out' (*Star* [5 October 1907]: 1, quoted in Norman Sherry (ed.), *Conrad: The Critical Heritage* [London: Routledge, 1973], 198).

intrinsic to her stabbing of Verloc, whereby the agency at work extends between two ages: 'Into that plunging blow, delivered from the side of the couch, Mrs Verloc put all the inheritance of her immemorial and obscure descent, the simple ferocity of the age of caverns, and the unbalanced nervous fury of the age of bar-rooms' (*SA*, 234). The whole scene thus presents a revision of thermodynamics itself.[49] Energy is conserved as potentiality, but does not remain ethereal, inconvertible, or unaffected by the living, for Winnie's action is figured as drawing upon what Bergson refers to as an 'immensity of history'.

If potentiality is no longer simply abstracted energy, but rather an immanent possibility of force, the security of the body-politic is rendered fragile. The 'secret agent' in the novel is this thermodynamic force, the movement of physical mass suggesting new potentials of social movement. Conrad's belief in a connection of physics to mass consciousness is manifest in a letter to Edward Garnett (29 September 1898), which he wrote after staying with his radiologist friend, Dr John McIntyre. Having discussed radiation with McIntyre and witnessed the novelist and scientist, Neil Munro, behind an X-ray machine,[50] Conrad reports asking if it were not the case that:

The secret of the universe is in the existence of horizontal waves whose varied vibrations are at the bottom of all states of consciousness. . . . Therefore it follows that two universes may exist in the same place and in the same time— and not only two universes but an infinity of different universes—if by universe we mean a state of consciousness. And, note, *all* (the universes) composed of the same matter, *all matter* being only that thing of inconceivable tenuity through which the various waves (electricity, heat, sound, light, etc.) are propagated, thus giving birth to our sensations—then emotions—then thought.[51]

To which McIntyre reportedly replied 'it was so', and that, moreover, 'there is no space, time, matter, mind as vulgarly understood, there is only the eternal something that causes the waves'.[52]

---

[49] A revision of the second law of thermodynamics appeared with Henri Poincaré's 'recurrence theorem', of which he gave mathematical proof in 1890. It stated that any mechanical system with fixed total energy must eventually return arbitrarily close to its initial state. See Poincaré's 'Sur le probleme des trois corps et les équations de dynamique', *Acta Mathematica* (February 1890): 1–270.

[50] X-rays were discovered in 1895 by Conrad Röntgen, who suggested they might be related to ether—see Smith and Wise, *Energy and Empire*, 491–3.

[51] Joseph Conrad, *The Collected Letters of Joseph Conrad, 1898–1902*, ed. by Frederick R. Karl and Laurence Davies, 5 vols. (Cambridge: Cambridge University Press, 1986), ii: 94–5, Conrad's emphases. Hereafter cited as *Letters*.

[52] Ibid., 95.

Despite Conrad's obvious engagement with scientific theory, I do not want to suggest that he views it without scepticism. In a 1913 letter to Warrington Davis, for example, he states that whereas science 'at best can only tell us—it seems so', Art can 'call on us with authority to behold! to feel!'[53] So, in *The Secret Agent*, his interest is partly in showing how the 'turnings' of energy involve lived experience. Another of the novel's innovations is to show how these turnings might have political consequences—individual events are posed as being inseparable from wider plots. Endeavouring to assure the Secretary of State, Sir Ethelred, that a solution to the bombing is inevitable, the Assistant Commissioner declares: 'this affair, I make so bold to say, is episodic; it is no part of any general scheme, however wild' (*SA*, 145). And on his second visit, after having discovered Verloc's culpability, he informs Sir Ethelred that what he had discovered was merely a 'psychological state' (*SA*, 201), a 'domestic drama' (*SA*, 204). But the possibility that an episode might *not* be connected to a general scheme is precisely what threatens the efficacy of surveillance and control. Inspector Heat is thus forced to admit his rashness in trying to mollify the Assistant Commissioner over the bombing with the comment: 'I can tell you at once, none of our [Anarchists] had anything to do with it' (*SA*, 106)—referring to the revolutionaries known to, or in the service of, the police. If, for Stewart and Tait, 'heat' threatens to 'bring the system to an end' because of its levelling tendencies, the tendency of Inspector Heat in *The Secret Agent* is also towards equalization as he draws the Anarchist and the law into collusion. This is what sustains the efficiency of the social system. His 'private friendship' with Verloc means that in exchange for protection, 'when I want an address in a hurry, I can always get it . . .'(*SA*, 139).

But if effective government is shown to depend on blurring the distinctions between crime and law, bureaucracy and the individual, public and domestic, this also threatens governmental and legislative stability. On the one hand, that everything is connected leads to the discovery of Verloc's involvement. The event of Heat finding Verloc's address on Stevie's lapel sets a whole chain of events into motion, as Verloc bemoans: 'A small tiny fact had done it. It was like slipping on a bit of orange peel in the dark and breaking your leg' (*SA*, 215). On the other hand, this complexity means that supposedly extraneous elements affect politics and the law. Verloc's orchestration

---

[53] Letter to Warrington Davies (20 June 1913), in Karl and Davies, *Letters*, v: 238.

of the bombing is partly determined by the sheer financial exigency of having to support Winnie, Stevie, and their mother; the Assistant Commissioner endeavours to protect Michaelis on account of the latter's intimacy with one of his wife's society friends. Thus, the body-politic can no longer maintain its distance from the movement of its component parts, let alone control them. Yet for Inspector Heat this is essential for the functioning of state bureaucracy. The 'complex organism' that is a department 'does not know so much as some of its servants. Being a dispassionate organism, it can never be perfectly informed. It would not be good for its efficiency to know too much' (*SA*, 109). Such a propagation of ignorance is, however, what the Assistant Commissioner complains of to Heat: 'Your idea of secrecy seems to consist of keeping the chief of department in the dark' (*SA*, 140)—echoing the original recounted statement that was for Conrad a catalyst for the whole novel.

It all amounts to a depiction of bureaucratic Being that is uncannily like an *inverse* image of Stewart and Tait's ethereal 'Governor', and their earlier image of the 'Commander' of 'Life' who

knows too well to expose his person; in truth he is never seen by any of his subordinates. He remains at work in a well guarded room, from which telegraphic wires lead to the headquarters of the various divisions. He can thus, by means of these wires, transmit his orders to the generals of these divisions, and by the same means receive back information.[54]   (*CE*, 150)

In place of this image of 'Life' under martial law, *The Secret Agent* offers the figure of the Assistant Commissioner under siege:

'Here I am stuck in a litter of paper', he reflected, with unreasonable resentment, 'supposed to hold all the threads in my hand and yet I can but hold what is put in my hand, and nothing else. And they can fasten the other ends of the threads where they please.' (*SA*, 127)

This image of politics is as tied to the conception of an organized substance of life as much as thermodynamics for Stewart and Tait was linked to political and legal stability. Everything is drawn into the one image, as in the instance of Stevie's obsessive sketching of circles, because the physical mass depicted by Conrad entails that an event can

[54] By the 1870s, the British Empire was connected by a vast network of submarine telegraphic cables, extending across the Atlantic, as well as to Gibraltar, India, Singapore, Hong Kong, Australia, and New Zealand. See Bruce J. Hunt, 'Doing Science in a Global Empire: Cable Telegraphy and Electrical Physics in Victorian Britain', in *Victorian Science in Context*, ed. by Bernard Lightman (Chicago: The University of Chicago Press, 1997), 312–33.

ramify and form a genealogy of connections like Freud's hysterical phenomena. Discussing 'intracerebral' excitations, Breuer argues that the analogy of a telephone wire which is 'only excited at the moment at which it has to function' is not adequate: 'We ought to liken [the excitations] to a telephone line through which there is a constant flow of galvanic current and which can no longer be excited if that current ceases.'[55] With Conrad's image of excitability, energy waves are 'intercerebral' and are not limited to subjective duration—they combine the individual with the social. This is why rather than simply becoming ethereal, past actions can become latent—lurking possibilities. And just as the relating of governmentality and science was important for physicists and politicians alike, so the fragility of the bureaucratic organism that arises from the loss of distinction between the political and the criminal is linked in *The Secret Agent* to both a fabrication of facts and an instability of law:

That the spy will fabricate his information is a mere commonplace. But in the sphere of political and revolutionary action, relying partly on violence, the professional spy has every facility to fabricate the very facts themselves, and will spread the double evil of emulation in one direction, and of panic, hasty legislation, unreflecting hate in the other.   (*SA*, 144)

Conrad thus sketches a landscape of critique in showing that the creation of zones of ambiguity and double-agency bolsters the functioning of the system. The possibility of 'political crime' is essential for the state's law. The result of the dissipation of the body-politic, however, is that it comes to incorporate everything, permeating every aspect of life. Yet the movement of force portrayed in Conrad's phantasm-images also denies the possibility of a political space existing that is not haunted by an infinitude of events and ideas—all of which can potentially influence political legislation and action.

So how do we deal with the fact of Conrad's literary politics in the novel? Rather than raising the issue in terms of left or right proclivities, we should do better, I should argue, to make the distinction that Deleuze and Guattari make, in *A Thousand Plateaus*, between the 'molecular' or 'micropolitical', and the 'molar' or 'macropolitical', the terms being derived from physics itself:[56]

---

55 Freud and Breuer, *Studies on Hysteria*, 193.
56 Grant Allen, for example, differentiates between molecular and molar forces: 'energies which separate Masses and resist the aggregation of Masses may be summed up under the title Molar Forces' (*Force and Energy: a Theory of Dynamics*, [London: Longman, 1888], 19).

everything is political, but every politics is simultaneously a *macropolitics* and a *micropolitics*. Take aggregates of the perception or feeling type: their molar organization, their rigid segmentarity, does not preclude the existence of an entire world of micropercepts, unconscious affects, fine segmentations that grasp or experience different things, are distributed and operate differently.[57]

The imbrication of 'state' molarity with 'collective' or 'mass' molecularity made by Deleuze and Guattari is evident throughout the *The Secret Agent*, producing a vision of what we might term *entropolitics* that disrupts the opposition between a revolutionary and a conservative ethos.[58] For example, the phantasmic transformation of energy problematizes Michaelis's idea of pure materiality, but turns texts and images themselves into quasi-corporeal events, and so facilitates precisely the type of contagion frequently associated with the Anarchist threat: 'it has become a disease which is transmitted from one mad dog to another as hydrophobia is transmitted from one mad dog to another', declared the *Saturday Review*.[59] Similarly, in portraying state bureaucracy as bound to series of connections that spread beyond its control, Conrad asserts an atomism of the social corpus that was also associated with Anarchism. There is no Anarchist body-politic, argued the *Arena*, it is a 'mass of individual cells, nucleating together in temporary forms, free to break up at any moment . . . its type is the jelly fish or sponge'.[60] Yet such a scattered, dissipated organism is countered in the novel by the images of temporal and material continuity manifest in Winnie's metamorphosis, Verloc's hallucinations, and Ossipon's detonator. Entropolitics thus combines states of disaggregation and continuity so that the body-politic is inherently tropological in its dynamics, at the same time that images and texts are

---

[57] Gilles Deleuze and Félix Guattari, *A Thousand Plateaus: Capitalism and Schizophrenia*, trans. by Brian Massumi (Minneapolis: University of Minnesota Press, 1987) 213, authors' emphases. They offer Kafka's portrayals of bureaucracy as exemplary of the 'micropolitical': 'If Kafka is the greatest theorist of bureaucracy, it is because he shows how, at a certain level (but which one? it is not localizable), the barriers between offices cease to be "a definite dividing line" and are immersed in a molecular medium (*milieu*) that dissolves them . . .' (214). Regarding Deleuze and Guattari's relation to Anarchist thinking, see Todd May, *The Political Philosophy of Poststructuralist Anarchism* (Philadelphia: University of Pennsylvania Press, 1994), chs. 3 and 4.

[58] On relating the text's politics to a wider social organicism, see also Avrom Fleishman, *Conrad's Politics: Community and Anarchy in the Fiction of Joseph Conrad* (Baltimore: Johns Hopkins University Press, 1967), 187–214.

[59] 'Anarchy and Assassination', *Saturday Review* 92 (14 September 1901): 324.

[60] R. Heber Newton, 'Anarchism', *Arena* 27: 1 (January 1902): 2.

incorporated into physical transferences. And it is here that the radical nature of Conrad's vision lies; in branding the work of literature into the very substance of political life.

Sublime Subversions: Female Terrorism and Popular Victorian Fiction

In the 'Author's Note' that Conrad later added to *The Secret Agent*, he gestures towards the text's powers of contagion: 'I have no doubt', he writes, 'that there had been moments writing the book when I was an extreme revolutionist . . .' (*SA*, 42). Nevertheless, he continues, 'I have not intended to commit a gratuitous outrage on the feelings of mankind' (*SA*, 43). Both of these statements suggest that Conrad believed his writing on terrorism involved exploring the force of literature itself. But while he asserts general tendencies of entropolitics in *The Secret Agent*, it is manifestly not the case that all the characters interact with these tendencies in the same way. Indeed, in the 'Author's Note' Conrad essentially sees the 'anarchistic' story as residing essentially with Winnie. She is, after all, the only character who performs a serious act of violence against another in the text. Yet, as we have seen, her murdering of Verloc is also a form of double-agency to the extent that she becomes possessed by a force of the past. To what extent can such possession be mediated or resisted, then? Are exchanges of force inherently arbitrary, accidental? If not, what role is played by the state of mind or the sex of an individual in determining or performing violence and terror? These questions were pertinent to a wide range of Conrad's contemporaries who were variously attempting to address the ways that science, sex, politics, and Being might relate to individual agency. Perhaps no one was quite so assiduous in thinking about how *all* of these fields might impact on subjectivity, though, as Friedrich Nietzsche.

That events might occur without there being an overarching agency is seen to be the most terrifying form of Nihilism by Nietzsche in *The Will to Power* (written between 1883 and 1888): 'existence as it is without meaning or aim, yet recurring inevitably without any finale of nothingness: the "eternal recurrence." This is the most extreme form of nihilism.'[61] As Maurice Blanchot points out, Nihilism is not tied to nothingness for Nietzsche, but to 'being' itself: it is 'the impossibility of there being a final outcome. . . . Nothing ends; it all

    [61] Friedrich Nietzsche, *The Will to Power*, trans. by Walter Kaufmann and R. J. Hollingdale (London: Vintage, 1968), 35.

begins again.'[62] If Being is mutable through repetition, everything is of necessity at the mercy of a continual revaluation, open to an infinite variety of forces. 'What does Nihilism mean? *That the highest values devalue themselves.* The aim is lacking; "why?" finds no answer.'[63] Yet it is through the experience of the 'eternal return' that Nietzsche's Zarathustra, like Conrad in front of the X-ray machine, realizes he is implicated in a general 'Will to Power' whereby 'all things are bound fast together':[64]

a play of forces and waves of forces, at the same time one and many, increasing here and at the same time decreasing there: a sea of forces flowing and rushing together, eternally changing, eternally flooding back, with tremendous years of recurrence . . . *This world is the will to power—and nothing besides!* And you yourselves are this will to power—and nothing besides![65]

Confronted by this network of forces, the 'Overman' (*Übermensch*) is the name Nietzsche gives to the individual who can affirm that subjectivity is not the ultimate limit. Only by so affirming can the Overman announce, as Nietzsche does in *Ecce Homo* (1908), that 'all of history is I'. To do so is to bring the numinous down to earth: 'To burden one's soul with all of this—the oldest, the newest, losses, hopes, conquests, and all the victories of humanity; if one could finally crowd all of this into a single feeling . . . this godlike feeling would be called—"humaneness".'[66] But while Nietzsche proffers the Will to Power as nullifying absolute subjectivity, he later presents the Overman as *dominating* historical forces. This is most explicit in *Ecce Homo* with its acclamations of hyper-subjectivity such as: 'I am no man, I am dynamite.'[67] Nietzsche goes on to declare that a new epoch of 'great politics' will be conceived through his philosophizing: 'The concept of politics will . . . be raised entirely to that of the war of spirits; all power structures of the old society will have been

[62] Maurice Blanchot, 'The Limits of Experience: Nihilism', in *The New Nietzsche*, ed. by David B. Allison (Cambridge, Mass.: MIT Press, 1990), 126.

[63] Nietzsche, *The Will to Power*, 9, Nietzsche's emphasis.

[64] Friedrich Nietzsche, *Thus Spake Zarathustra*, trans. by R. J. Hollingdale (1892; Harmondsworth: Penguin, 1969), 179.

[65] Nietzsche, *The Will to Power*, 550, Nietszche's emphasis. Regarding thermodynamic bases of Nietzsche's 'eternal return' in terms of infinite (as opposed to finite) energy systems, see Brush, *The Temperature of History*, 70–6.

[66] Friedrich Nietzsche, *The Gay Science*, trans. by Walter Kaufmann (1882; New York: Random House, 1974), 387.

[67] Friedrich Nietzsche, *Ecce Homo*, trans. by R. J. Hollingdale and Walter Kaufmann (New York: Random House, 1967), 326.

exploded—all of them rest on lies: there will be wars like none on earth have ever been. Only beginning with me does the earth see *great politics*.'[68] Here the Will to Power reaches its most potent form in making ghosts of social power-structures. But such revolutionary character is exorcized in earlier writings and transformed into a new kind of totalitarianism. In *Beyond Good and Evil* (1886), for example, 'great politics' does not consist of an infinite set of forces, but of affirming the formation of superpowers:

I mean such an increase in the menace of Russia that Europe would have to decide to become menacing to the same degree, namely, to acquire *one will* by means of a new caste that would rule Europe, a long terrible will of its own that would cast its goals millennia hence. . . . The time for petty politics is over: the next century will bring the fight for a world dominion—the *compulsion* to great politics.[69]

Within Russia at the time, Nietzsche's writings gained currency among intellectuals from around 1890. Moreover, revolutionary writers such as Stepniak began to offer the figure of the 'Terrorist' along Overman lines. Defining Nihilism in *Underground Russia* (1883), Stepniak writes: 'It was a struggle for the emancipation of the intelligence from every kind of dependence. . . . It was the negation in the name of individual liberty, of all the obligations imposed upon the individual by society, by family life and religion.'[70] Moral despotism was as much to be destroyed as political hegemony, he argues, for the Nihilist was opposed to everything that did not stem from 'positive reason'. The fulfilment of Nihilism, however, is attained only with the advent of the 'Terrorist': 'Upon the horizon there appeared a gloomy form, who, with lofty bearing, and a look breathing forth hatred and defiance, made his way through the terrified crowd to enter with firm step upon the scene of history' (*Underground*, 31). In contrast to the 'Propagandist', who had been committed to a 'sublime test of the

---

[68] Nietzsche, *Ecce Homo*, 327, Nietzsche's emphasis.

[69] Friedrich Nietzsche, *Beyond Good and Evil*, trans. by Walter Kaufmann (New York: Random House, 1966), 131, Nietzsche's emphasis. Keith Ansell-Pearson, in *An Introduction to Nietzsche as Political Thinker* (Cambridge: Cambridge University Press, 1994), criticizes the notion of 'great politics' in terms of its lack of legitimacy, arguing that it could not be maintained 'except through ruthless forms of control' (155). See also Bernard Yack, *The Longing for Total Revolution: Philosophic Sources of Social Discontent from Rousseau to Marx and Nietzsche* (Princeton: Princeton University Press, 1986), 349–52.

[70] Sergei Kravchinsky ('Stepniak'), *Underground Russia* (London: Smith & Elder, 1883), 4, hereafter cited as *Underground*.

power of words', the Terrorist, declares Stepniak, is committed to 'Acts' (*Underground*, 33).

Stepniak had himself assassinated the Russian General Mesentzoff on 16 August 1878—the details of which do not need to be entered into, he writes, for they are 'written in letters of fire upon the records of history' (*Underground*, 42). This being said, though, Stepniak still sees the need to give an inventory of the attributes of the Terrorist more generally: 'He is noble, terrible, irresistibly fascinating, for he combines in himself the two sublimities of human grandeur: the martyr and the hero' (*Underground*, 44). The messianic nature of this seemingly spiritual militant is nevertheless opposed to adopting any godly qualities:

Proud as Satan rebelling against God, he opposed his own will to that of the man who alone, amid a nation of slaves, claimed the right of having a will. But how different is this terrestrial god from the old Jehovah of Moses! How he hides his trembling head under the daring blows of the Terrorist! (*Underground*, 44)

Like Nietzsche becoming dynamite, the Terrorist becomes pure force. He is 'immortal', writes Stepniak: 'His limbs may fail him, but, as if by magic, they regain their rigour, and he stands erect, ready for battle after battle until he has laid low his enemy and liberated the country' (*Underground*, 45). Considering this kind of emphasis by both Stepniak and Nietzsche on overcoming subjective limits, it would appear that the 'great politics' of either the Overman or the Terrorist might be open to anyone. But for Nietzsche the capacity to overcome one's self is very much an issue of sex. Zarathustra's command to women, for example, is: 'Let your hope be: May I bear the Overman!', for 'The man's happiness is: I will. The woman's is: he will'.[71] Seemingly, without an Underfemale the Overman must adopt a policy of 'self-rape'.[72]

The sort of virile heroism inherent to the 'sublime' politics that Stepniak sees the Terrorist as carrying out with his 'Acts' had long been championed by exponents of the sublime itself. In Edmund

---

[71] Nietzsche, *Thus Spake Zarathustra*, 92.

[72] On Nietzsche's contradictory positions on feminism and its relation to the Will to Power, see Keith Ansell-Pearson, 'Women and Political Theory', in *Nietzsche, Feminism and Political Theory*, ed. by Paul Patton (London: Routledge, 1993), 43–6; also Lynne Tyrell, 'Sexual Dualism and Women's Self-Creation: On the Advantages and Disadvantages of Reading Nietzsche for Feminists', in *Nietzsche and the Feminine*, ed. by Peter J. Burgard (Charlottesville: University Press of Virginia, 1994), 158–82.

Burke's *A Philosophical Enquiry into the Origin of our Ideas of the Sublime and Beautiful* (1757), for example, the confrontation with 'hideous objects' that evoke either death—'the king of terrors'—or the infinite, causes the subject to experience a heightened sense of security in having survived: 'the more frightful they make us, the greater is the pleasure we receive from the sense of our own safety'.[73] Terror and power become reciprocally constitutive for Burke: 'I know of nothing sublime which is not some modification of power' (*Enquiry*, 64); 'The power which arises from institution in kings and commanders, has the same connection with terror' (*Enquiry*, 67).[74] Yet the more the two become interchangeable, the less the subject is able to differentiate between 'natural' and 'instituted' power, cause and effect, object and experience. Burke himself states that 'far from being produced by them, [the sublime] anticipates our reasonings, and hurries us on by an irresistible force' (*Enquiry*, 57). Which is why he declares that its 'pain and terror' need to be 'modified as not to be actually noxious' (*Enquiry*, 138)—the experience must be *like* the sublime.

In Immanuel Kant's *Critique of Judgement* (1790), sublime experience similarly involves a 'formless object' that connotes 'boundlessness' and does 'violence to the imagination' in being unassimilable for it.[75] In contrast to Burke, however, Kant asserts that sublimity is not an attribute of a confronting object: 'all we are entitled to say is that the object is suitable for exhibiting a sublimity that can be found in the mind' (*CJ*, 99). If the experience shows that nature cannot be comprehended by the imagination *as a sensation*, he argues, this does not mean that it cannot be comprehended through the 'Ideas' of reason. For like nature itself, the Ideas are infinite—'not determined by anything else, whether sensation or concept' (*CJ*, 138). It is thus a super-sensibility of reason that the imagination ends up grappling with, rather than an illimitable objectivity, as it first appeared. Consequently, the 'violence' of the sublime is 'purposive' for the 'whole determination of the mind', Kant argues, and the subject becomes a 'general' in charge of his forces. As with Burke, militancy is not em-

---

[73] Edmund Burke, *A Philosophical Enquiry into the Origin of our Ideas of the Sublime and Beautiful*, ed. by J. T. Boulton (London: Routledge, 1958), 39, hereafter cited as *Enquiry*.

[74] Tom Furniss, in *Edmund Burke's Aesthetic Ideology: Language, Gender, and Political Economy in Revolution* (Cambridge: Cambridge University Press, 1993), argues that 'these metaphors . . . attempt to represent Britain as a body politic whose preservation depends on resisting revolutionary contagion' (28).

[75] Immanuel Kant, *Critique of Judgement*, trans. by J. H. Bernard (London: Macmillan, 1914), 102, 103, hereafter cited as *CJ*.

ployed simply as a metaphor; war itself, states Kant, 'has something of the sublime in it'—if the 'rights of citizens' are respected—whereas peace 'generally brings about a predominant commercial spirit, and along with it, low selfishness, cowardice and effeminacy . . .' (*CJ*, 127).

We can see, then, that the constitution and recognition of a number of distinctions rests upon the subject's capacity to arrogate the violence of sublimity—the difference between masculinity and femininity being no less at stake than that between reason and imagination, or sovereignty and subjection. But although the determination of subjectivity appears to be *subject to* the sublime, effected by it, both thinkers present sublimity as sexualized in advance. Women can only have a 'beautiful' understanding, contends Kant, 'whereas ours should be a *deep understanding*, an expression that signifies identity with the sublime'.[76] Similarly, for Burke, women are figured as beautiful objects rather than sublime subjects. The female synonymity with beauty is evident from his characterization of its epitome as:

that part of a beautiful woman where she is most beautiful, about the neck and breasts; the smoothness; the softness; the easy and insensible swell; the variety of the surface, which is never for the smallest space the same; the deceitful maze through which the unsteady eye slides giddily, without knowing where to fix, or whither it is carried. (*Enquiry*, 115)

Entailing a 'gradual variation' of exiguity as opposed to a delimitation of infinitude, beauty nevertheless becomes *more* sublime than the sublime here, for it moves beneath the limit (*sub limine*) of perception. And because this 'part' of *décolletage* extends 'by a deviation continually carrying on', its 'beginning or end' is difficult to ascertain (*Enquiry*, 115). As Barbara Claire Freeman has pointed out, then, the 'principal theorists are able to represent the sublime only through recourse to metaphors of sexual difference'.[77] But we also need to recognize that this metaphorizing is explicitly an issue concerning the force of terror. On the one hand, the violation of subjective limits and judgement culminates in a series of metaphorized equivalences: terror is power is rational is male is the subject. On the other hand, this contagious immediation of experience leads both Burke and Kant to

[76] Immanuel Kant, *Observations on the Sublime and the Beautiful*, trans. by John T. Goldthwait (1764; Berkeley: University of California Press, 1960), 78, Kant's emphasis.

[77] Barbara Claire Freeman, *The Feminine Sublime: Gender and Excess in Women's Fiction* (Berkeley: University of California Press, 1995), 4. Terry Eagleton in *The Ideology of the Aesthetic* (Oxford: Blackwell, 1990), makes the same claim: 'the distinction between the beautiful and the sublime, then, is that between woman and man' (47).

call for strictures on sublimity: in order to stimulate safely, terror must *simulate* so as not to be 'actually noxious'.[78] But how can these two modes of the sublime—'authentic' and figurative—be distinguished when the very possibility of determining relations between imagination and reason, objectivity and subjectivity, masculinity and femininity, appears to depend on experiencing sublimity in the first place?

In the period of Russia that Conrad depicts in his novel *Under Western Eyes* (1911), which I will be turning to shortly, 'true' sublimity was frequently linked to the capacity to carry out violent actions. Stepniak declares Nihilism to have 'rendered great service to its country' by recognizing women 'as having equal rights to man' (*Underground*, 23). With the large involvement of women in 'terrorist' groups in Russia, feminism and political subversion were closely allied. An eighth of listed terrorists in the 1870s were women,[79] and by the beginning of the twentieth century this figure had risen to one quarter.[80] Indeed, in the 1870s, writes Richard Stites, 'the vocation of revolutionary was the only one open to women which would greet her as equal, allow her talents to unfold, and permit her to rise to the top'.[81] Agitation among the growing female intelligentsia for the right to education led to the inauguration of courses for women, allowing them to train for professions such as medicine for the first time. And amongst the middle classes at least, the effects of feminist fervour were widespread. Spurred on by the revaluations of women's roles and by heroines in feminist novels like Nikolai Chernyshevski's *What is to be Done?* (1863), many women avoided marriage and left their husbands.

Repressive repercussions ensued, though, as Stites has pointed out: 'many of the remarks about women's desertion of their husbands and families were couched in language usually used to describe crimes against the state'.[82] Moreover, *any* woman who did not appear traditionally feminine was prone to being dubbed a female Nihilist. 'A *nigiltska* could be an auditor at a university, a girl with bobbed hair'

---

[78] Like Burke, Kant states that it is 'impossible to find satisfaction in a terror that is seriously felt' (*CJ*, 124).

[79] Richard Stites, *The Women's Liberation Movement in Russia: Feminism, Nihilism, and Bolshevism 1860–1930* (Princeton: Princeton University Press, 1978), 148.

[80] Anna Geifman, *Thou Shalt Kill: Revolutionary Terrorism in Russia, 1894–1917* (Princeton: Princeton University Press, 1993), 12.

[81] Stites, *The Women's Liberation Movement in Russia*, 153.

[82] Richard Stites, 'Women and the Russian Intelligentsia', in *Women in Russia*, ed. by Dorothy Atkinson, Alexander Dallin, and Gail Warshofsky Lapidus (Hassocks: Harvester, 1978), 41.

or 'a woman with "advanced" ideas.'[83] Even the police described women's courses as being 'a veritable sewer of anarchist disease',[84] and so great was the antipathy towards them that they were briefly shut down in the 1880s. For many, feminism was not just politically subversive, it was also sexually perverse. As far back as the White Terror of 1866, police would reportedly ask female revolutionaries taken into custody 'if they lived in sin with their male comrades'.[85] In subsequent years, a rumour was circulated about a 'beautiful nihilist' who sold her body in order to finance the radical activities of a tiny circle known as the 'Smorgon Academy'. And in 1905, the year the women's suffrage movement became active in Russia (as in Britain), Mariya Spiridonova was tortured by police after she assassinated General Luzhenovsky: 'Soldiers dragged her face down on the stone steps, extinguished cigarettes on her breasts . . . whipped her, tore out her flesh, and asked her how many lovers she had.'[86] In this sense, it was the sex as much as the violence of female radicals that was deemed a threat to social order more generally, and male hegemony in particular. Every time a *nigiltska* fired a pistol it was not just the autocracy but the rights to heroic subjectivity that were being challenged. 'Experience shows', said a St Petersburg prison official, 'that women, in terms of criminality, ability and possession of the urge to escape are hardly distinguishable from men.'[87] Vera Zasulich, a member of 'The People's Will' (*Narodnaya Volya*) who attempted to assassinate the Governor of St Petersburg, was exemplary in demonstrating a female readiness for violence. Ten members of the group—over a third—were women, and all except three were eventually imprisoned or hanged for their terrorist activities. Sofiya Perovskaya also followed Zasulich's example, planning the assassination of Alexander II in 1881—she became the first female terrorist to go to the scaffold. Tolya Ragozinikova was another, shooting the prison administrator of a St Petersburg prison at which corporal punishment was used to discipline the prisoners. Her motivation, she claimed, was martyrdom for the love of the people: 'Only a higher duty forced me to do this deed. No, not even duty, but love, a great love of mankind. For its sake I sacrificed all I had. How good it is to love people. How much strength one gains from such love.'[88]

[83] Stites, *The Women's Liberation Movement in Russia*, 105.
[84] Stites, 'Women and the Russian Intelligentsia', 44.   [85] Ibid., 42.
[86] Ibid., 46.   [87] Ibid., 60.
[88] Stites, *The Women's Liberation Movement in Russia*, 272.

Such actions and statements by women were ascribed a sublime politics by several commentators. 'She is not beautiful' (*Underground*, 117), declares Stepniak of Zasulich, but 'extremely reserved' (*Underground*, 118), possessed by a 'sublime craving . . . the result of an extreme idealism that is the basis of her character' (*Underground*, 120). Sophia Perovskaya, 'was beautiful' he states, 'a blonde with a pair of blue eyes' (*Underground*, 126), yet through her 'ardent temperament' she could 'elevate herself by the force of her intellect above the promptings of feeling' (*Underground*, 133), her 'great reasoning powers' triumphing over any 'romantic feeling' (*Underground*, 134). In these passages, the *nigiltska* is thus accepted as having the same capacity for violence and self-overcoming as her male counterpart. But whereas for both Stepniak and Nietzsche this could elicit a hyper-masculinity in men, the female terrorist was frequently cast as becoming something wholly other than her sex—in most cases, male. This is certainly true of the portrayals of female Nihilists in popular late-Victorian novels, in which the two modes of sublime metaphorizing evident in Burke's and Kant's writing—simulated terror versus contaminating force—are employed both to romanticize and diminish the ardour of female revolutionaries.[89]

Joseph Hatton's *By Order of the Czar: The Tragic Story of Anna Klosstock, Queen of the Ghetto* (1890), is a *Bildungsroman* in which Anna, an innocent young Polish Jew, is transformed into a recalcitrant, militant Nihilist after her village becomes another victim of the Russian autocracy's White Terror pogrom. Anna herself is sexually assaulted by the Governor of her province, General Petrovitch, and then flogged after being accused of inciting a mob. In Part II, the scene shifts to London where we find Philip Forsyth, a painter, enraptured by the face of a woman he is painting for his picture, 'Tragedy', which he intends to enter into a Royal Academy competition:

It is a beautiful face, stamped with a suffering that has no resignation in it . . . The mouth is pursed into an expression of angry revolt. If ever the time for vengeance came, you feel that this woman would not abhor the assassin's knife nor the dynamiter's shell . . .[90]

Klosstock soon arrives in London and is inevitably introduced to Forsyth, who falls immediately in love with her because of her re-

[89] For a survey of the many popular novels on terrorism written in this period, see Barbara Arnett Melchiori, *Terrorism in the Late-Victorian Novel* (London: Croom Helm, 1985).

[90] Joseph Hatton, *By Order of the Czar: The Tragic Story of Anna Klosstock, Queen of the Ghetto*, 3 vols. (London: Hutchinson, 1890), i: 199.

semblance to the figure in his painting. However, she only reveals her identity to him after revenging her assault and killing General Petrovich in Venice:

'Let him know why I am a Nihilist of the Nihilists! Let him behold my title to vengeance!'

As she spoke she tore open her dress, exhibiting a lovely white arm and part of a beautiful bust, turning at the same time with swift rapidity to exhibit her right shoulder and neck, no farther than is considered correct by ladies of fashion at balls and in the opera stalls, but sufficient to thrill iron men who had themselves been witnesses of the worst of Russian tortures. Red and blue deep ridges and welts crossed and recrossed each other, with intervals of angry red patches of red and weird daubs of grey that blurred and blotted out all remains and tokens of the beautiful form with which nature had endowed one of its loveliest creatures.[91]

More apposite for a description of an expressionist painting, the graphic references to 'angry red patches of red' and 'weird daubs of grey' amount to a blurring of the difference between her beauty and sublimity. Appearing as both an alluring and terrifying figure, it becomes unclear whether it is the exhibition of her 'beautiful bust' or her 'welts' which would be 'sufficient to thrill' the witness of the 'worst of Russian tortures'. The crossings and recrossings of her 'ridges' thus mark the point at which the spectacle of flogging and the aesthetics of portraiture become confused.

L. T. Meade's *The Siren* (1898) exhibits a similar array of interlacings. The story commences with Colonel George Nugent discovering that his long-lost daughter, Vera, born to his Russian ex-wife, has been found in Russia, where she has been fraternizing with Nihilists. On meeting her, this blight on her character is ameliorated for Nugent by her devastating beauty: 'She is ten times more beautiful than her mother ever was.'[92] But when he, along with her cousin, stepmother, stepsister, and innumerable men, fall passionately in love with her, it soon becomes clear that she is literally a *femme fatale*: 'I know I possess the gift of beauty', she declares, 'I regard it as a very strong weapon';[93] 'It can sting, crush, destroy, it can be a snake in the grass.'[94] Everyone she knows is eventually willing to die for her, as she informs her cousin, Frank: 'I could name twenty, thirty, men who would die for me, I could even mention women who would go to that length of devotion.'[95] Nihilism and subversion thus become

---

[91] Ibid., iii: 179–80.   [92] L. T. Meade, *The Siren* (London: F. V. White, 1898), 69.
[93] Ibid., 84.   [94] Ibid., 100.   [95] Ibid., 151.

increasingly caught within a web of transgressive desire, all of which is resolved when Vera chooses to kill herself rather than carry out an assassination. Such a conclusion is no doubt what provoked Alice Stopford Green, writing of women's place in literature, to pose the real task of female sublimity as one of *transforming* 'war and destruction' rather than performing it: 'With a sublime economy she [Woman] is everlastingly busy retrieving the waste of the world'; 'If she is to deliver her true message, or to be the apostle of a new era, she must throw aside the curiosity of the stranger and the license of the anarchist.'[96]

Stepniak would have disagreed. His novel *The Career of a Nihilist* (1889) features several female terrorists and repeatedly extolls their sublime martyrdom. After being told of the self-sacrifice of a fellow terrorist, the character Tania experiences a 'moment of moments' in which she resolves to commit herself fully to the cause:

It was as if she had outgrown in an instant her girlhood and her womanhood, her motherly instincts reaching their maturity within her maiden breast, and this young man, whom she had never seen, had been her own child, torn by cruel enemies from her arms . . .[97]

Anna becomes fully developed psychologically only by contemplating self-sacrifice, just as for Kant sublime 'violation' is wholly 'purposive' for organizing the mind. But because the death can only be experienced vicariously, the change remains intrinsically metaphorical for her—'It was as if . . .'—and both the event of death and the *conception* of it are 'torn' from her as soon as they are born(e). The violence of this 'moment of moments' is simultaneously transferred and deferred, for its force of contagion *is* its metaphorizing. As soon as she is overcome by the experience, Andrey Kojukhov, another Nihilist, is overcome by her: 'she was terribly beautiful at that moment';[98] 'only tonight did he know what love for a woman is like'.[99]

For Kant, the spectacle of someone else suffering is analogous to what the imagination provides for reason. Sublimity occurs, he says, only when the imagination is no longer capable of assimilating the object confronting it, and 'this might actually reveal itself only through self-sacrifice [*Aufopferungen*]' (*CJ*, 131). The threat of sublimity

---

[96] Alice Stopford Green, 'Women's Place in the World of Letters', *Nineteenth Century* 41 (June 1897): 970, 974.

[97] Sergei Kravchinsky ('Stepniak'), *The Career of a Nihilist* (London: Scott, 1889), 94, hereafter cited as *Career*.

[98] Ibid., 94.   [99] Ibid., 98.

is thus doubly distanced for reason: first, because the imagination is made to suffer it; second, because its sacrifice also amounts necessarily to an extinguishment of the experience itself. Left with only a ghostly idea of sublimity, reason would be forced to augment its conception of it with an even more powerful act of imagination so as to recast the force of the experience it is supposed to appropriate.

Kojukhov faces a similar dilemma in Stepniak's novel when the desire for martyrdom aroused by Anna is rekindled by the spectacle of his fellow terrorists about to be hanged by the police. This time, it is the 'face of the beautiful woman', Zina, on the scaffold that excites his passions—so much that he has to leave the scene. The thought of her execution is enough to inflame his desire to become a martyr once and for all:

If we have to suffer—so much the better! Our sufferings will be a new weapon for us. Let them hang us, let them shoot us, let them kill us in their underground cells. The more fiercely we are dealt with, the greater will be our following. I wish I could make them tear my body to pieces . . .[100]

If, for Kant, the violent spectacle can precipitate a mastery of subjective limits, for Kojukhov its transferential force constitutes an ideality of community. Nothing will be enough to destroy this 'us', yet it will always need to be destroyed more. Consequently, the very event that founds a sense of terroristic collectivity also suspends it. The only way in which the individual could become fully incorporated into it is through more violence—'I wish I could make them tear my body to pieces . . .'. As in Hatton's novel, then, beauty and sublimity are not divided along lines of sex; nor do they mark divisions between imagination and reason. Instead, sublimity destabilizes the very divisions it is supposed to install.

The admixture of sexuality and politics in these novels has not gone unnoticed by critics. Barbara Melchiori, commenting on the spectacle of Klosstock's back in *By Order of the Czar*, writes that the passage seems 'curiously suspect—Victorian pornographers had a penchant for scenes in much the same tone'.[101] David Trotter is similarly

---

[100] Ibid., 288–9.

[101] Melchiori, *Terrorism in the Late-Victorian Novel*, 179. As Melchiori herself points out, though, Hatton's inspiration for this passage was the following statement of abuse from Theodora Osnavitch that appeared in the *Brooklyn Times* in 1881: 'That is why I am a Nihilist . . . in half a minute [she] had bared herself to the waist. The front of her form from neck to belt might have passed as the model for the Venus di Milo. But the back! Ridges, welts, and furrows that crossed and interlaced as if cut out with a red hot iron . . .' (quoted in *Terrorism and the Late-Victorian Novel*, 172–3).

critical of the scene: 'the most potent symbol, Anna's back, is a hi-eroglyph rather than a manifesto; the injury condensed in its ruin will never enter into political process. Hatton doesn't really know what to do with it.'[102] Both *The Siren* and *By Order of the Czar* aspire to 'politi-cal commentary', Trotter argues, yet 'their fascination with women's bodies deflects them into sado-masochism'.[103] But as we have seen in the historical accounts cited, such deflections were also endemic in Russia at the time, as well as in the thought of writers such as Nietzsche and Stepniak, Burke and Kant. As I have been arguing, the extent to which violence, aesthetics, and political ideology can be sep-arated is a question posed by the sublime itself. I am not, however, suggesting that the confusions of this period can simply be accounted for by rereading Burke's or Kant's texts. Nor am I suggesting that the sublime is in some way metahistorical. As we have seen in the texts of this period that invoke it, the performativity of the sublime is itself volatile. Thus, in the following reading of Conrad's *Under Western Eyes*, at the same time as showing how he uses images of the sublime to address Russian Nihilism and Anarchism, I shall also attend to the ways in which he refigures the dynamics of sublimity itself.

Under Western Eyes: *The Sense of Terror*

By 1905, the year of the first Russian Revolution, the political climate in Russia could be defined without exaggeration as being terroristic. With the formation of the Party of Socialist Revolutionaries (SRs) in 1901, terrorism had virtually become a mass movement. Whereas the Nihilist group 'The People's Will' had totalled 500 members in 1879, by 1907 the SRs boasted some 45,000.[104] As Anna Geifman states, after 1905 'terrorist enterprises . . . became part of everday life in Russia, and, as some radicals admitted, a mass psychosis developed, a true "epidemic of combat activity".'[105] The more that political vio-lence began to shape a new historical epoch, the more the epoch en-couraged the development of a new type of political violence. Not only was the terrorist campaign of the SRs and other groups such as the 'Maximalists' more intense than those of the nineteenth century, it was also both more professional and less discriminating. Geifman thus identifies a 'new breed of terrorism' as emerging at this point—

---

[102] David Trotter, *The Novel in English History* (London: Routledge, 1993), 172.
[103] Ibid.   [104] Geifman, *Thou Shalt Kill*, 262.   [105] Ibid., 22.

the 'motiveless terror' (*bezmotivnyi terror*) of the Anarcho-Communist group Black Banner (*Chernoe Znamia*) being a prime example. In Conrad's essay 'Autocracy and War' (1905), however, the crisis faced by Europe as a whole is not related to the spectacle of Russian terrorism, but rather to the seemingly indefatigable spirit of its autocracy. The absolutism of the national will is made synonymous by Conrad with a desire for nothingness. Yet within the essay itself, the vacuum that is Russia is never quite exorcized. Conrad dreams of a 'new political organism' that would take the place of 'this dreaded and strange apparition'—then, suddenly, we learn that it has already been destroyed in the Russo-Japanese war, 'never to haunt again this world . . . it has vanished for ever at last', only to be told that the 'hallucination still lasts as inexplicable in its persistence as in its duration'.[106] What strange being are we dealing with? The diplomat's remark to Bismark, '*La Russie, c'est le néant*', which Conrad cites approvingly in the essay, and in a later letter to Edward Garnett (quoted below), is not enough for him.[107] 'Russia is not a *Néant*', declares Conrad, 'she is and has been simply the negation of everything worth living for. She is not an empty void, she is a yawning chasm that has swallowed up every hope of mercy . . .'.[108]

From a Russian perspective, autocracy was also viewed as having contributed to a national Nihilism. Indeed, terrorism was seen both as a natural response to this crisis and as an attempt to rectify it. As far as Alexander Blok, a contemporary poet, was concerned, 'some different higher principle is needed. Since there is none, rebellion and violence of all sorts takes its place.'[109] So to state that the crisis posed by Russia was merely symptomatic of an autocratic spirit, as Conrad does, is to elide the fact that autocracy was being attacked in Russia itself. In response to this pressure, the Tsar's government issued a manifesto on 17 October 1905 promising full civil liberties and the election of a legislative assembly, a state *Duma*. That the burgeoning of terrorism into a national phenomenon was, as Geifman states, 'both a catalyst for and the result of Russia's internal crisis'[110] further testifies to the fact that a single, autocratic, historical agency was no longer in evidence. Moreover, by contesting the issue of national authority, several of the revolutionary movements sought to institute a

---

[106] Joseph Conrad, 'Autocracy and War', in *Notes on Life and Letters* (London: Dent, 1924), 89, 90, herefter cited as 'Autocracy'.

[107] Karl and Davies, *Letters*, iv: 489.   [108] Conrad, 'Autocracy and War', 100.

[109] Quoted in Geifman, *Thou Shalt Kill*, 19.   [110] Ibid., 20.

solidarity that would not be limited to national boundaries. The European 'solidarity' that Conrad calls for in 'Autocracy and War' is precisely what many Russian Anarchists were aiming at. Conrad's vitriol was not engendered *ex nihilo*. He had experienced the force of the Russian regime in its suppression of the Polish revolts of 1863 while living in Berdichev, in the Ukraine, as a child. Resistance to Russia was also a legacy inherited from his father, Apollo Korzeniowski, who was the main force behind a society called 'The Trinity', which was staunchly opposed to Russian occupation. While maintaining a spiritual element, the group also developed a liaison with General Mieroslawski, in Paris, who had links with Bakunin.[111] By 1861 Conrad's father was fully committed to politics, moving to Warsaw and joining the 'Reds', a revolutionary group advocating direct action. As a result, both he and Conrad's mother were convicted of political activism in October 1861.[112] For Conrad, however, none of this amounted to revolutionary activity nor to a passion for revolt. An early letter shows his disaffection with the efficacy of socialism in general: '[it] must inevitably end in Caesarism. . . . Disestablishment, Land Reform, Universal Brotherhood are but like milestones on the road to ruin. . . . All is vanity.'[113] So, in *A Personal Record*, which he published partly to show why he wrote *Under Western Eyes*, Conrad argues that if there was any insurrection it was only from a Russian perspective: 'These risings were purely revolts against Russian domination. The Russians themselves called them "rebellions", which from their point of view was the exact truth.'[114] His father was not a revolutionary, he writes, merely a 'patriot' who believed in the 'spirituality of a national existence' and who 'could not bear to see that spirit enslaved'.[115]

---

[111] Avrom Fleishman, in *Conrad's Politics*, discusses the political milieu of Conrad's early years in Poland, and the importance of writers such as Burke and Arnold in the heritage of Victorian literature that Conrad adopted and engaged with on settling in England. See also Zdzisław Najder, *Joseph Conrad: A Chronicle* (Cambridge: Cambridge University Press, 1983) ch. 1; and Eloise Knapp Hay, *The Political Novels of Joseph Conrad* (Chicago: University of Chicago Press, 1963), ch. 2.

[112] John Batchelor, *The Life of Joseph Conrad: A Critical Biography* (Oxford: Blackwell, 1994), 3.

[113] G. Jean Aubry, *Joseph Conrad: Life and Letters*, 2 vols. (London: Heinemann, 1927), i: 84–5.

[114] Joseph Conrad, *A Personal Record*, in *The Mirror of the Sea, and A Personal Record* (Oxford: Oxford University Press, 1988), vii.

[115] Ibid., viii.

But how can we judge the spirit of Conrad's writings on this issue? For at times, advocating nationalism is viewed with abhorrence by him. The reason for there being 'no Europe', he writes, is because 'nationalism' has taken precedence over 'solidarity'.[116] In *A Personal Record*, belief in spirit is also associated with the negation of authentic cultural history: 'Inspiration comes from the earth, which has a past, a history, a future, not from the cold and immutable heaven'.[117] Similar waverings over national character are evident in the 'Author's Note' of 1920 to *Under Western Eyes*, in which Conrad describes the work as 'a sort of historical novel dealing with the past', yet one that strives to represent not so much the 'political state' as the 'psychology of Russia itself'.[118] Apparently, having to characterize a national ideal rather than a particular state of affairs is dictated by the nature of the subject. The most 'terrifying' aspect of writing the novel, states Conrad, was the recognition that all of its characters—terrorist and autocrat alike—were not products of the exceptional but of 'the general—of the normality of their place, and time, and race' (*UWE*, 51). But even this stock nationality does not appear to *reside* in Russia when Conrad claims for his terrorist character, Nikita, a 'banality' of existence that has its origin in the 'so-called "disclosures" in newspaper articles, in secret histories, in sensational novels' (*UWE*, 51). The spectrality of Russia is also a certain fictionality, a cultural imagination, then, which Conrad acknowledges to Edward Garnett when he writes that the novel is 'concerned with nothing but ideas'.[119] It has to be: writing on Russia, he argues, is 'the most chimeric of enterprises' since it is 'le néant. Anybody with eyes can see it'.[120]

Conrad was not the only person in Britain to be expressing such sentiments. Indeed, his statements take on a different aspect when we consider the political import that the British press were ascribing to political events in Russia at the time. The *Contemporary Review*, *Fortnightly Review*, and *The Spectator* in particular all kept up running commentaries, publishing articles by writers such as Kropotkin and Tolstoy, as well as a host of foreign correspondents, a number of whom wrote under pseudonyms. Many of the articles are concerned with analysing autocracy and terrorism in terms of an essential 'Slavic' psychology. According to 'R. L.', 'No one can live long in

---

[116] Conrad, 'Autocracy and War', 103.   [117] Conrad, *A Personal Record*, 95.
[118] Joseph Conrad, *Under Western Eyes* (Harmondsworth: Penguin, 1989), 49, hereafter cited as *UWE*.
[119] Letter dated 20 October 1911, in Karl and Davies, *Letters*, iv: 489.   [120] Ibid.

Russia without finding strange support of the reactionaries' contention that the Autocracy, in its habits of thought and practice, mirrors perfectly the people.'[121] A similarly sweeping view is espoused by a correspondent using the *nom de plume* of 'Specto': 'the Slav temperament is profoundly subject to illusion. . . . We see it not only in the bureacracy but in the opposition and the masses. . . . Russians have hitherto been governed not by realities but by phantasms . . .'.[122] Portraying the events as fundamentally foreign to the British psyche was a way of defending the political stability of British liberal democracy. As the Extradition Act and Aliens Act decreed, political violence could only take place elsewhere. With tensions in the Baltic and Europe in general increasing, however, the fate of Russia became seen as an increasingly important issue for Britain itself. 'Perseus' perceives as much in 1905:

Never has the communal instinct of the Slav appeared so obvious in action as in the cataclysmal events which have swept the Tsardom towards the edge of Niagara, and may draw into their vortex of disaster the fortunes of every European, and perhaps of every Asiatic nation.[123]

As Conrad himself was lumped together with Russian writers as 'Slavonic', he had all the more reason to express his opposition: 'The critics detected in me a new note and as, just when I began to write, they had discovered the existence of Russian authors, they stuck that label on me under the name of Slavonism.'[124]

With hostilities between Britain and Germany increasing, the need for Britain to foster a political alliance with Russia was accepted, although there was widespread concern about forming an affiliation with an autocratic nation. For Conrad, living in England at the time, the prospect of an accord was not an agreeable one; he had already written a letter to *The Times* in 1904 denouncing Russian attacks on English fishing boats.[125] Despite opposition, though, British diplo-

---

[121] 'R. L.', 'Peace and Internal Politics: A Letter from Russia', *Fortnightly Review* 84: 463 (1 July 1905): 136.

[122] 'Specto', 'Russia's Line of Least Resistance', *Fortnightly Review* 84: 466 (October 1905): 573.

[123] 'Perseus', 'Europe and the Russian Revolution', *Fortnightly Review* 84: 468 (1 December 1905): 959.

[124] Aubry, *Joseph Conrad*, ii: 101. See also Christopher GoGwilt, *The Invention of the West: Joseph Conrad and the Double-Mapping of Europe and Empire* (Stanford: Stanford University Press, 1995), ch. 6.

[125] Zdzisław Najder, 'Conrad, Russia and Dostoevsky', in *Conrad in Perspective: Essays on Art and Fidelity* (Cambridge: Cambridge University Press, 1997), 122.

macy continued; in June 1907, news that the British Foreign Office and the St Petersburg government were drawing up an agreement over their respective claims to India and Tibet provoked a number of dissenters to sign a 'memorial' reminding the government of autocratic atrocities—George Bernard Shaw was among the signatories. In response, *The Spectator* declaimed Shaw's participation as no less comical than his plays, and went on to defend the agreement: 'The British people will have their own opinions of the actions of either party. They will be indignant to the excesses of terrorism, or the excesses of repression. To the Foreign Office Russia is, and ought to be, a whole, known to us through the ordinary diplomatic machinery . . .'.[126]

Dealing with Russia in this holistic way meant that individual instances of ignominy were downplayed. Along with the '*entente cordiale*', the Anglo-Russian agreement that eventuated was seen to be tantamount to a radical reconfiguration of continental relations: 'The *entente cordiale* and the Anglo-Russian agreement, which are evidently calculated to strengthen each other, have brought about an astonishing transformation of the European system . . .'.[127] On the one hand, then, Russia, and its relation to Britain, remained unknown quantities, which is why there was such frequent recourse in the press to figurative generalization. So while *The Spectator* declared that anyone relying on media reports remained a 'foreigner' to Russian politics, it still maintained a rhetoric of intimacy between the nations: 'the general current of English opinion is sound. It knows a friend when it sees him.'[128] On the other hand, the bureaucratic accords effected structural changes that exacerbated European tensions and aided the Russian autocracy in upholding repressive measures. As 'Perseus' argued, changes in Russia meant changes in Europe in general: 'None of the more Western or Eastern powers can prophesy with certainty that they will continue to remain detached spectators.'[129]

The collocations of representation, spectrality, and specularity that Conrad uses throughout *Under Western Eyes* to approach the issue of Anglo-Russian relations can thus be seen, once again, to engage with

---

[126] 'Paradox in Politics', *The Spectator* 4121 (15 June 1907): 930.
[127] 'Calchas', 'The Anglo-Russian Agreement', *Fortnightly Review* 87: 490 (October 1907): 545.
[128] 'Russia and Great Britain', *The Spectator* 4259 (12 February 1910): 247.
[129] 'Perseus', 'Europe and the Russian Revolution', 959.

a wider cultural debate. 'Here is given the very essence of things Russian', Conrad wrote to James Pinker of the novel, 'Not the mere outward manners and customs but the Russian feeling and thought. . . . The subject has long haunted me.'[130] Clearly, this desire for an ideal portrayal is also symptomatic of Conrad's desire to assert that he is working free from prejudice or sentiment. In the same way that the Stevensons were at pains to justify their confrontation with terrorism, so Conrad in his 'Author's Note', claims to be offering a subjective work of imagination: '[The novel] has suggested itself more as a matter of feeling than of thinking' (*UWE*, 49). But he also states that his 'greatest anxiety was in being able to strike and sustain the note of scrupulous impartiality' (*UWE*, 49). On entering the novel, the realism of the writing is the first thing we are confronted with by the middle-aged, English narrator. Introducing himself as a language teacher, he immediately relinquishes any claim to the faculty of imagination, explaining that the narrative is based on the diary left by the protagonist of the novel, Kirylo Isidorovitch Razumov. Consequently, he argues, it must be be seen more as 'documentary' than anything else. Any imagination the narrator once had has been 'smothered out of existence a long time ago under a wilderness of words. . . . the great foes of reality': 'To a teacher of languages there comes a time when the world is but a place of many words and man appears a mere talking animal not much more wonderful than a parrot' (*UWE*, 55). This theme of usurpation and substitution is continued when he turns to the story of Razumov. As the illegitimate son of Prince K——, Razumov is 'officially and in fact' without parentage. A young philosophy student, he works sedulously towards gaining recognition in his studies, his very name connoting 'reason' (*razum* in Russian) or mind.[131] Thinking of Russia itself as his only form of family, Razumov is intent on winning a medal at the university in order to gain a position so that he might best be able to represent his nation.

All his plans are thrown into disarray, however, when Victor Haldin, a student revolutionary, assassinates the Minister of the Repressive Commission, Mr de P——, the incident being based on the

---

[130] Letter dated 1 January 1908, in Karl and Davies, *Letters*, iv: 14.

[131] Critics have pointed out that the name also echoes that of Raskolnikov, in Dostoevsky's *Crime and Punishment*, who suffers similar psychological disruptions. In contrast to Razumov's name, 'Raskolnikov' connotes rebellion. On Conrad's relation to Dostoevsky, see Najder, 'Conrad, Russia and Dostoevsky'.

assassination of Viacheslav K. Plehve by SR members, Egor Sazonov and Boris Savinkov in 1904.[132] Deciding that Razumov's taciturnity would make him an ideal comrade, Haldin turns to the student for confidence and shelter. Razumov's immediate feeling is one of absolute revulsion and dismay, 'his life being utterly ruined by this contact with such a crime . . .' (*UWE*, 65). But despite the growing intensity of rancour that rises in him as Haldin justifies his actions, he represses any show of emotion that might give himself away. Endeavouring to subdue his own rising passions as well as the 'horrible discord' of Haldin's presence, a parallel soon becomes apparent between the dynamics of political and psychological repression, and also between the *raisons d'être* of the two students. As far as Haldin is concerned, his 'deed' was committed in the cause of the Russian spirit:

'You suppose that I am a terrorist, now—a destructor of what is. But consider that the true destroyers are they who destroy the spirit of progress and truth, not the avengers who merely kill the bodies of the persecutors of human dignity. Men like me are necessary to make room for self-contained, thinking men like you.' (*UWE*, 67–8)

Razumov's struggle to overcome the threat of discord through the labour of his reason is thus matched with an equally fanatical idealism in Haldin. Just as Razumov wishes to become, above all, a representative of the nation, so Haldin talks of his soul as working on behalf of Russia itself:

'No man's soul is ever lost. It works for itself—or else where would be the sense of self-sacrifice, of martyrdom, of conviction, of faith—the labours of the soul? . . . This is not murder—it is war, war. My spirit shall go on warring in some Russian body till all falsehood is swept out of the world. The modern civilization is false, but a new revelation shall come out of Russia. Ha! you say nothing. You are a sceptic. I respect your philosophical scepticism, Razumov, but don't touch the soul. The Russian soul that lives in all of us. It has a future. It has a mission, I tell you, or else why should I have been moved to do this—reckless—like a butcher—in the middle of all these innocent people— scattering death—I! I! . . . I wouldn't hurt a fly!' (*UWE*, 69–70)

---

[132] Plehve had indeed been responsible for severe repressive measures, including the suppression of student demonstrations between 1899 and 1901. See Boris Savinkov's *Memoirs of a Terrorist*, trans. by Joseph Shaplen (New York: Boni, 1931); Peter Kropotkin, 'The Revolution in Russia', *Nineteenth Century and After* 83: 316 (December 1905): 865–83; and Edward H. Judge, *Plehve: Repression and Reform in Imperial Russia* (Syracuse: Syracuse University Press, 1983).

Haldin's conviction of the rectitude of his national mission arises from being prepared to lay down his life for his country. So whereas Winnie becomes a 'double-agent' through an *immanent* transmission of social forces, Haldin's claim to be representing the nation entails figuring a *transcendence* of national spirit, one that supervenes his own corporeal life. In this sense, his sentiments evoke Stepniak's depiction of the 'Terrorist' as combining the sublimities of the hero and martyr in order to attain a hyper-materiality, an 'immortality' of limbs. But if the Russian soul is not grounded in any particular body or regime, then the act of assassination itself must be of questionable efficacy.

Haldin's dilemma also stands in stark contrast to the Professor's in *The Secret Agent*. Rather than trying to embody absolute hostility towards the masses by becoming death incarnate, Haldin pictures his own martyrdom as acting on behalf of a national community. Egor Sazonov, the SR member responsible for assassinating Plehve, claimed as much in a letter to his mother:

My Socialist-Revolutionary beliefs merged with religion. . . . we, the socialists, continue the work of Christ, who preached brotherly love among the people . . . and died as a political criminal. . . . Christ's demands are clear. . . . We, the socialists, want to carry them out, we want the kingdom of Christ to come to earth.[133]

As soon as terrorism and political kinship become synonymous, the first person plural becomes a call to violence. Like Kojukhov in Stepniak's *The Career of a Nihilist*, Vladimir Burtsev, another militant revolutionary, also viewed systematic terror as a way of overcoming individual differences so as to produce political solidarity:

Political terror has such decisive importance for the life of our motherland, its influence is so profound and all-encompassing, that all disagreements among terrorists *must disappear* before it. Political terror must become the dominating factor in establishing relations among the groups that recognize its great significance. All supporters of political terror should feel like the members of a single family . . .[134]

These sentiments, along with the depiction of Haldin's, contradict the view promulgated by the British media that Russian politics as a whole was governed 'not by realities but by phantasms'. Violence and terrorism may be offered as acting in the name of a higher national spirit, but this spirit is not realized—recognized and made real—

---

[133] Quoted in Geifman, *Thou Shalt Kill*, 49.   [134] Ibid., 181, Burtsev's emphasis.

without the act of violence itself. Accordingly, if, for Kant, the subject becomes its own 'general' by confronting terror, for terrorists like Burtsev the subject becomes generalized, idealized, by exercising it. For Razumov, the idea of Haldin's terror does not consolidate his resolve so much as infect it. Having agreed to arrange the means of Haldin's escape by contacting a cab-driver, Ziemianitch, the more Razumov is incensed at the terrorist's passions, the less he is capable of controlling his own. After viciously beating Ziemianitch on finding him drunk, he begins to ponder how, short of suicide, he might effect a complete 'annihilation' of Haldin from his life. The possibility of salvation then appears to him through a hallucinatory vision:

> Razumov received an almost physical impression of endless space and of countless millions.
> He responded to it with the readiness of a Russian who is born to an inheritance of space and numbers. Under the sumptuous immensity of sky, the snow covered the endless forests, the frozen rivers, the plains of an immense country, obliterating the landmarks, the accidents of the ground, levelling everything like a monstrous blank page awaiting the record of an inconceivable history. . . .
> It was a sort of sacred inertia. Razumov felt a respect for it. A voice seemed to cry within him, 'Don't touch it.' It was a guarantee of duration, of safety, while the travail of maturing destiny went on—a work not of revolutions with their passionate levity of action and their shifting impulses—but of peace. What it needed was not the conflicting aspirations of a people, but a will strong and one: it wanted not the babble of many voices, but a man—strong and one!   (*UWE*, 78-9)

The same form of schizophrenia that emerged in Haldin's discourse is evident here, as the hope of an immutable, united Russian realm appears only through transcendence. The command 'Don't touch it' that Razumov hears is no different from the voice which Haldin recognized had nothing to do with an 'I'; both speak as a higher power, and throughout the passage a tone of impersonality resonates in the reiteration of the indefinite article. Everything is held in suspense, for if the sanctity of this spirit depends on negating the contingencies of history and locality, its very *appearance* must necessarily be 'inconceivable' and 'monstrous'. Just as for Kant 'we find no territory' of reason's 'Ideas' (*CJ*, 13), so Razumov's ideal of Russia must erase its own terrain. In this sense, too, the proscription against being or writing a character on the page of this national essence echoes Kant's objection to representing Ideas: 'Perhaps there is no sublimer passage in the Jewish Law than the command, *Thou shalt not make to thyself any graven image . . .' (CJ*, 138, Kant's emphasis). The 'sacred inertia' of Razumov's vision remains fragile, though. Its transcendence calls for 'a man—strong and one!' to guard its sanctity from the corruption of the 'many voices', precisely because its separation from the times and 'accidents of the ground' weakens its own sovereignty. The problem of envisioning autocracy is thus developed in parallel with Razumov's incapacity to assert his reason. Unable to reconcile himself to the idea of murder, which he thinks would bring stability at the cost of a 'false memory', he is faced shortly afterwards with a counter vision:

Suddenly on the snow, stretched on his back right across his path, he saw Haldin, solid, distinct, real, with his inverted hands over his eyes, clad in a brown close-fitting coat and long boots. He was lying out of the way a little, as though he had selected that place on purpose. The snow round him was untrodden.

This hallucination had such a solidity of aspect that the first movement of Razumov was to reach for his pocket to assure himself that the key of his rooms was there.[135]   (*UWE*, 81)

Appearing as if out of the 'untrodden' snow like the first written character on the 'monstrous page of inconceivable history', the image of Haldin marks the pollution of Razumov's ideal. The terrorist's infiltration is symptomatic of Razumov's own desire to represent the unrepresentable, which would in itself be against the letter of the law. The phantom of the sublime is also lurking here as the point where politics and aesthetics overlap. As Sandra Dodson has argued, Conrad was undoubtedly familiar with theories of the sublime; discussing his work in relation to Kant, she writes that 'for both writers the ideology of Nature is inseparable from the nature of Ideology, complex topographies of human morality, thought and history'.[136] Certainly in *The Critique of Judgement*, the 'boundlessness' of the sublime is specifically related to spectacles of 'rude nature'—for example, hur-

---

[135] This is similar to Nietzsche's portrayal of the 'sublime man' as one who has not yet grasped the sense of his actions: 'His countenance is still dark; his hand's shadow plays upon it. The sense of his eyes, too, is overshadowed. His deed is still the shadow upon him: the hand darkens the doer. He has still not overcome his deed' (*Thus Spake Zarathustra*, 140).

[136] Sandra Dodson, 'Conrad and the Politics of the Sublime', in *Conrad and Theory*, ed. by Andrew Gibson and Robert Hampson (Amsterdam: Rodopi, 1998), 7. Dodson argues that Conrad initially came into contact with the sublime through Polish Romantic playwrights such as Adam Mickiewicz, Juliusz Slowacki, and Zygmunt Krasinski. Goethe and Schiller were also popular among Polish aesthetic circles at the time.

ricanes, mountain ranges, and the ocean—which force the mind 'to think the unattainability of nature regarded as a presentation of Ideas' (*CJ*, 134). Subjective freedom is thus predicated on determining an autonomous rule of reason—a rational autocracy—as natural law. Yet in so far as reason claims its power by defining itself in opposition to appearance, it ends up forbidding its own presentation. For Kant, the freedom of the subject is the 'goddess' of reason's 'moral law', a law which can only speak its transcendence. Thus, 'when we are listening, we are in doubt whether it comes from man, from the perfected power of his own reason, or whether it comes from an other, whose nature is unknown to us and speaks to man through his own reason'.[137] As soon as the law of the subject is instituted, then, the subject loses the capacity to judge. This is Razumov's confusion: as his image of autocratic reason becomes infected with its own perversion, Haldin's phantom emerges 'Exactly as if alive!' (*UWE*, 82) from out of the 'sacred' image of the landscape itself. Razumov's notion of a stable, national substance is as open to accident and anarchy as his own faculty of judgement is to hallucination.

In *The Critique of Judgement,* a similar amalgamation of ideality and sensation is presented by the faculty of imagination as 'aesthetic Ideas'. Borrowing from 'actual nature', the imagination produces a 'second nature' by associating the 'material' (*Stoff*) of experience with other images.[138] Ideas of reason are *concepts* of an unpresentable object; aesthetic Ideas are *presentations* of what exceeds thought in an object. Yet the imagination's Ideas do not just adumbrate raw experience. Because Kant declares reason's Ideas themselves to be supersensible—and therefore unpresentable—they too must be supplemented by aesthetic Ideas if they are to be incorporated into the subject's experience. The depiction of Jupiter's almighty power using an image of an eagle with lightning in its claws, Kant writes, will be an 'incentive to thought to spread its wings over a whole host of kindred representations' (*CJ*, 177). But in this case—and as the continuation of the 'wings' metaphor suggests—the determination of

---

[137] Immanuel Kant, 'On a Newly Raised Superior Tone in Philosophy', trans. by Peter Fenves, in *On the Rise of Tone in Philosophy: Kant and Derrida*, ed. by Peter Fenves (Baltimore: Johns Hopkins University Press, 1992), 405.

[138] Jean-François Lyotard discusses Kant's aesthetic Idea at length in *Lessons on the Analytic of the Sublime*, trans. by Elizabeth Rottenberg (Stanford: Stanford University Press, 1994), 64–8, 73–4.

reason's omnipotence *is itself an aesthetic Idea*.[139] It can only be present for the subject as such. If rationality is possible only by being formed with the 'material' and objects of experience, though, what is there to stop thought or experience from taking on its own distinct corporeality?

This increasingly becomes Razumov's dilemma when he returns to Haldin after informing on him to his father, Prince K——, and to General T——. Having listened to the terrorist praising the virtues of his own powers of resistance—'They can kill my body but they cannot exile my soul from the world' (*UWE*, 98)—Razumov attempts to repress any feelings of guilt or anger by keeping up the dialogue, but cannot prevent himself from remonstrating:

'Yes. Eternity, of course. I, too, can't very well represent it to myself . . . I imagine it, however, as something quiet and dull. There would be nothing unexpected—don't you see? The element of time would be wanting. . . .

'And unfathomable mysteries! Can you conceive secret places in Eternity? Impossible. Whereas life is full of them. . . . A man's most open actions have a secret side to them. . . . The most unlikely things have a power over one's thoughts—the grey whiskers of a particular person—the goggle eyes of another.'

Razumov's forehead was moist.   (*UWE*, 98–9)

As he is indeed being haunted by images of General T——'s 'goggle eyes' and his father's 'grey whiskers', defending time against eternity only further increases the effects of Haldin's unexpected trespass onto Razumov's vision of eternal national spirit. And the less Razumov is capable of separating his political philosophy from Haldin's, the less he is able to distinguish between the relative forces of 'reality' and 'phantasm'—as when he subsequently contemplates Haldin lying in his bedroom: 'This body seemed to have less substance than its own phantom walked over by Razumov in the street white with snow. It was more alarming in its shadowy, persistent reality than the distinct but vanishing illusion' (*UWE*, 96). The crisis for Razumov is not just one of deciding between autocracy and terrorism, then, but of grasping the very *sense* of politics and terror in both meanings of the word.

In Burke's *Enquiry*, the volatility of 'sense'—as meaning and sensation—appears specifically in relation to language. On the one hand,

---

[139] Gilles Deleuze thus argues that 'The aesthetic Idea is really the same thing as the rational Idea: it expresses what is inexpressible in the latter' (*Kant's Critical Philosophy: The Doctrine of the Faculties*, trans. by Hugh Tomlinson and Barbara Habberjam [1963; Minneapolis: University of Minnesota Press, 1984], 57).

he argues, words are the most potent form of artistic expression because they have a closer proximity to concepts than the materials of painting or music. But because they are nevertheless external, and irreducible, to concepts, words can fashion new 'combinations' of meaning. Moreover, their potential for communication is heightened by their extra-conceptual elements: 'a moving tone of voice', 'an impassioned countenance, an agitated gesture', writes Burke, all produce effects 'independently of the thing about which they are exerted' (*Enquiry*, 175). Words, in harnessing this power, are capable of causing a 'contagion of our passions', whereby 'we catch a fire already kindled in another, which probably might never have been struck out by the object described' (*Enquiry*, 176). For Burke, far from simply mediating violent affects, language can augment their transmission.[140] So too, for Razumov, after receiving a letter from General T— requesting another interview, he is seized with fear at being thought a suspect and then has 'a vision of General T—'s goggle eyes waiting for him—the embodied power of autocracy, grotesque and terrible' (*UWE*, 118). Asking himself 'what can he want with me precisely—I wonder' (*UWE*, 119), the question conjures up 'the familiar phantom' of Haldin in 'extraordinary completeness of detail' (*UWE*, 119). Rather than terror and imagination being supervened by reason, then, for Razumov they appear to have taken on a life of their own.

Burke comments on the possibility of a similarly errant force of sublimity in the *Enquiry*: 'The senses strongly affected in some one manner, cannot quickly change their tenor, or adapt themselves to other things; but they continue in their old channel' (*Enquiry*, 74). The regime of Terror between 1793 and 1794 in the aftermath of the French Revolution is a case in point for him. Instead of being transformed into rational power, the events produced only a more insistent and phantasmic terror:

Out of the tomb of the murdered monarchy in France has arisen a vast, tremendous, unformed spectre, in a far more terrific guise than any which yet overpowered the imagination, and subdued the fortitude of man. Going straight forward to its end . . . that hideous phantom overpowered those who could not believe it was possible she could exist . . .[141]

---

[140] Regarding this point, Peter de Bolla comments: 'the power of sublimity is not a simple reflection of the power in the world, but a discursive *techne*, it articulates the technology of the sublime . . .' (*The Discourse of the Sublime: Readings in History, Aesthetics and the Subject* [Oxford: Blackwell, 1989], 69).

[141] Edmund Burke, *Letters on a Regicide Peace* (1796), in *The Works of the Right Honourable Edmund Burke*, 5 vols. (London: Rivington, 1877–84), v: 155.

Burke's description is clearly similar to Conrad's characterization of Russia as a 'dreaded and strange apparation'—except that for Conrad, the spectrality is related to the terrors of autocracy rather than revolution. For Razumov, however, the difference between these continues to become increasingly unclear. In his second meeting with the authorities—this time with Councillor Mikulin—Razumov accuses them of considering him a suspect and is promptly faced with a hallucination of 'his own brain suffering on the rack—a long, pale figure drawn asunder horizontally with terrific force in the darkness of a vault, whose face he failed to see' (*UWE*, 121). As Razumov is turned inside-out by his psychological anguish, so too are the dynamics of sublimity: instead of terror being provoked by a violent spectacle, terror itself begins to cause violent affects. The predicament worsens for Razumov when he is informed of Haldin's imminent execution. Far from diminishing his anxiety, the news causes him to launch into a fresh tirade against the terrorist:

'He was a wretch from my point of view, because to keep alive a false idea is a greater crime than to kill a man. . . . I did not hate him because he had committed the crime of murder. Abhorrence is not hate. I hated him simply because I am sane. It is in that character that he outraged me. His death . . .'

Razumov felt his voice growing thick in his throat. . . .

'Indeed', he pursued, pronouncing each word carefully, 'what is his death to me? If he were lying here on the floor I could walk over his breast . . . The fellow is a mere phantom . . .'   (*UWE*, 127)

Because Razumov defines his own sanity through negation, Haldin is already a *néant* for him and already incorporated into his own idea of reason. Haldin's earlier assertion that his 'spirit shall go on warring in some Russian body . . .' (*UWE*, 70) is thus confirmed, ironically, by Razumov himself. Moreover, in continuing to be haunted by the terrorist's phantom, Razumov is as guilty as Haldin of keeping a 'false idea'—at least in his own mind—and therefore of committing a crime greater than murder.

By the end of Part I, the focus of the novel has shifted from the impact of violence to the psychological force of terror. In presenting a complex interaction of the two, Conrad's novel can thus be used to problematize the sort of assertions made by terrorologists cited in my Introduction: namely, that terrorism's violence and terror are split like its 'reality' and its representations; or that any one of these must be taken as the basis for an aetiology of terrorism; or that mediation simply diminishes the effects of terror and violence by transforming it into anodyne images. Certainly, the possibility of exchanges between pain and terror occurring has always been of interest to writers on the sublime, as is evident from Burke:

The only difference between pain and terror, is that things which cause pain operate on the mind, by the intervention of the body; whereas things that cause terror generally affect the bodily organs by the operation of the mind suggesting danger; but both agreeing, either primarily or secondarily, in producing a tension, a contraction, or violent emotion of the nerves, they agree likewise in everything else.   (*Enquiry*, 132)

Both pain and terror are inherently transformational, for Burke, and their metaphorization is itself intrinsically violent. In Conrad's novel, this metaphorization is linked specifically to spectrality with the continuing persecution of Razumov by Haldin's phantom. Appearing as a tension between the 'real' and imaginary, pain and terror, self and other, spectrality becomes an example of how representation, psychology, and violence can become confused in the reactions to terrorism's effects—particularly in the attempt to repress them. And with the entrance of the female characters in Part II of the novel, the consequences of this are complicated further.

With Razumov's fate left hanging in suspense, Part II first turns back to events that precede those of Part I. After reiterating his narrative 'artlessness', the narrator recounts his stay in Geneva where he happened to become acquainted with Haldin's mother, Mrs Haldin, and his sister, Nathalie Haldin. The latter has been educated in Russia at a 'Superior School for Women', but Mrs Haldin asks the narrator if he might teach her English because she thinks 'all knowledge' in Russia 'was tainted by falsehood' (*UWE*, 132). Accepting the task, the narrator is immediately struck by Nathalie's masculine charm:

I became aware, notwithstanding my years, how attractive physically her personality could be to a man capable of appreciating in a woman something else than the mere grace of femininity. Her glance was as direct and trustful as that of a young man yet unspoiled by the world's wide lessons.   (*UWE*, 132–3)

Her attraction for him is that of a virgin virago, for it is her purity that he finds potently alluring: 'she had never known deception as yet because obviously she had never fallen under the sway of passion' (*UWE*, 133). But when the narrator comes across an article in *The Standard* on Haldin's execution, and subsequently informs the two women, he revises her appeal: 'At that moment her indefinable charm was revealed to me in the conjunction of passion and stoicism. I imagined what her life was likely to be by the side of Mrs Haldin's terrible immobility, inhabited by that fixed idea' (*UWE*, 144). It is not so much her lack of passion as her suppression of it that suscitates the narrator's ardour for her. On leaving the scene, he is literally gripped by 'the seductive frankness', the 'sort of exquisite virility' of her hand-shake, and we are later told that she has a voice to match: 'slightly harsh, but fascinating with its masculine and bird-like quality' (*UWE*, 163). The same merging of sublimity and beauty ascribed to female terrorists in the popular novels is evident here—perhaps suggesting that it is not only the character Nikita whom Conrad professedly drew from 'sensational novels' (*UWE*, 51).[142] And just as these novels involved uncanny political and aesthetic fusions, so does the narra-tor's encounter with Nathalie. Like Burke seeing a danger in beauty because it can draw the eye into a 'deceitful maze', the narrator de-nies being aroused by Nathalie's suffering because, for him, 'the sway of passion' leads to 'deception'. Rather than admit to her affecting him in ways he cannot understand, he emphasizes her own foreign-ness: 'my concern was reduced to silence by my ignorance of her modes of feeling. Difference of nationality is a terrible obstacle for our complex Western natures' (*UWE*, 144). Like Verloc drawing the blind after witnessing the spectre of Mr Vladimir, the narrator draws a line between East and West to occlude the subliminal crossings that have already taken place. In this sense, the distinctions between England and Russia, disinterested realism and imaginative writing, that he seeks to maintain are entangled in sublimity no less than Razumov's autocratic idealism.

The politics of female sublimity is explored more explicitly when we are introduced to Peter Ivanovitch, a feminist revolutionary, whom Thomas Moser sees as being based on Stepniak.[143] In Russia, Ivanovitch tells the narrator, it is not class-war but sex-war that will

---

[142] Thomas C. Moser, in 'An English Context for Conrad's Russian Characters: Sergey Stepniak and the diary of Olive Garnett', *Journal of Modern Literature* 11: 1 (March, 1984): 3–44, notes the similarity between Nathalie Haldin and the heroine of Stepniak's *The Ca-reer of a Nihilist*, Varvara Alexneva Voinova (33).

[143] See Moser, 'An English Context for Conrad's Russian Characters'. Moser also cites David Garnett who thought Stepniak's commitment to terrorism may have had revenge-ful motives: 'two girls whom young Kravtchinsky had known personally were stripped half-naked and flogged by the orders of a certain General Mesentzov' (19)—the General whom Stepniak later assassinated. Stepniak was friends with the Garnetts when Conrad knew them, as John Batchelor points out in *The Life of Joseph Conrad*, 178–80.

lead to revolution: 'The greatest part of our hopes rests on women' (*UWE*, 146). After overcoming his initial annoyance at finding Ivanovitch in Nathalie's rooms on one occasion, the narrator goes on to give an account of the revolutionary's memoirs. Having become rebellious after the death of a 'society woman' he was about to marry, Ivanovitch had been imprisoned but managed to escape, still dragging his fetters. His flight was made easier when he was offered a file by a young woman who had just discovered her lover had died—after she had walked across half of Russia in search of him. Managing only to free one leg before losing the file, Ivanovitch resolved to struggle on for the sake of the 'heroic girl':

She had selected him for the gift of liberty and he must show himself worthy of the favour conferred by her feminine, indomitable soul. It appeared to be a sacred trust. To fail would have been a sort of treason against the sacredness of self-sacrifice and womanly love.

There are in his book whole pages of self-analysis whence emerges like a white figure from a dark confused sea the conviction of women's spiritual superiority—his new faith confessed since in several volumes. (*UWE*, 148)

Like an inverse image of Haldin's appearance in the snow, the girl's 'self-sacrifice' is in part exalted for being a deference to men. For Ivanovitch, the memory of the girl inspires a revolutionary awakening and a desire to fight for feminism. Yet some of the violent feelings women provoke in Ivanovitch are also directed at them. Tekla, the *dame de compagnie* of his mentor, Madame de S——, provides Nathalie with a glimpse 'behind the scenes':

'After taking down Peter Ivanovitch from dictation for two years, it is difficult for me to be anything. First of all, you have to sit perfectly motionless. The slightest movement you make puts to flight the ideas of Peter Ivanovitch. You hardly dare to breathe. And as to the coughing—God forbid. Peter Ivanovitch changed the position of the table to the wall because at first I could not help raising my eyes to look out of the window, while waiting for him to go on with his dictation. That was not allowed. He said I stared so stupidly. I was likewise not permitted to look at him over my shoulder. Instantly Peter Ivanovitch stamped his foot, and would roar, "Look down on the paper!" It seems my expression, my face put him off.' (*UWE*, 168)

Erasing Tekla of all agency and presence so that his words can be transcribed without contamination, his ideas are conceived only by turning her into a phantasmic medium. Consequently, the dictated division of speech and writing also structures a sexual difference. The supposed purity of writing is based on an enforced suppression of Otherness which becomes a form of violence in itself.

On arriving in Geneva in Part III, Razumov swiftly makes his distaste for feminism apparent.[144] The reason for his stay, as we learn later, is to act as a double-agent for Councillor Mikulin, informing him of revolutionary activity. Subsequently indicted at a state trial for 'unsuspected intrigues', Mikulin has been successful bureaucratically because of his 'almost sublime contempt for the truth' (*UWE*, 291). For Razumov, however, the strain of pretending to be what he is not produces an unbearable tension, and on meeting Ivanovitch and Madame de S— he informs them that he has no intention of 'spend[ing] my time in spiritual ecstacies or sublime meditations upon the gospel of feminism. . . . I made my way here for action . . .' (*UWE*, 229). But this is itself a falsehood—he is certainly not there to perform as a terrorist—and so his declamation of their 'sublime' capers begings to mirror the sublimity of Mikulin's 'contempt for the truth'. The narrator thus comments that Razumov's diary account of the meeting is coloured by the youth's awareness of the increasing degeneration of his ideals:

Mr Razumov looked at it, I suppose, as a man looks at himself in a mirror, with wonder, perhaps with anguish, with anger or despair. Yes, as a threatened man may look fearfully at his own face in the glass, formulating to himself reassuring excuses for his appearance marked by the taint of some insidious hereditary disease. (*UWE*, 220)

This is clearly not the prose of a writer without 'artistry'. Although he states that Razumov's diary 'could not have been meant for any one's eyes but his own' (*UWE*, 220), this assertion of difference is what calls for the narrator to imagine the 'anguish' of Razumov's feelings for himself. The blending of their vision is made explicit in the narrator's subsequent use of free indirect discourse to recount Razumov's encounter with Madame de S—: 'A witch in Parisian clothes, he thought. A portent! He actually hesitated in his advance, and did not even comprehend, at first, what the rasping voice was saying' (*UWE*, 220). The moribundity of the previous mirror scene is now associated with her visage; heavily made-up with rouge she is likened to a 'grin-

---

[144] Paul Kirschner found records in the Geneva Bibliothèque Publique et Universitaire of 'Rasoumoffs' residing in Switzerland in 1907. One of them, Stéphane Rasoumoff, was arrested with two Russian friends for pistol shooting ('Topodialogical Narrative in *Under Western Eyes* and the Rasoumoffs of "La Petite Russie" ', in *Conrad's Cities: Essays for Hans Van Marle*, ed. by Gene M. Moore [Amsterdam: Rodopi, 1985], 253).

ning skull', a 'galvanized corpse out of some Hoffman's tale', and an 'ancient, painted mummy with unfathomable eyes' (*UWE*, 221). The force of repulsion makes it impossible to decide whether the hatred of Madame de S— is Razumov's or the narrator's, for the latter expresses a similar disgust for her earlier: 'I had a positive abhorrence for the painted, bedizened, dead-faced, glassy-eyed Egeria of Peter Ivanovitch' (*UWE*, 179). Justifying his asperity on moral grounds by declaring her a revolutionary 'charlatan', the narrator then denies being capable of painting her in a biased fashion: 'Art is great! But I have no art, and not having invented Madame de S— . . .' (*UWE*, 179). Clearly, though, his talent for embellishing others' experience is already evident.

Familiar and foreign; this is how Freud characterizes the 'uncanny' (*Unheimlich*), attributing its 'terrible' prospect to unnatural mixtures.[145] Things that appear both living and dead, such as 'artificial dolls and automatons', doppelgängers, or the vision of oneself in a mirror, are offered by him as examples.[146] With Madame de S—, though, the admixture of her 'vivid lips' and 'death-like immobility' is not only complicated by the blending of the narrator's and Razumov's gaze, but also because her appearance is coloured by their hatred of her politics. And as Razumov's 'nausea' and taciturnity increase, so does the intensity of her fervour for insurgency. After calling for an 'outrage' to incite the Russian people, she lapses suddenly into a strange lassitude: 'All her angular and lifeless movements seemed completely automatic now that her eyes were closed' (*UWE*, 224). As a result, it becomes unclear whether it is terrorists or marionettes and fetish objects that Razumov finds more terrifying, for his hatred of Madame de S—, we are told, is 'more like that abhorrence caused by a wooden or plaster figure of a repulsive kind' (*UWE*, 228)—examples of which are later encountered by him in a shop 'stocked with cheap wood carvings', owned by a woman 'with a sickly face' (*UWE*, 299).[147] The more he suppresses Madame de S—'s

[145] Sigmund Freud, 'The Uncanny' (1919), in *The Standard Edition of the Complete Psychological Works of Sigmund Freud*, ed. and trans. James Strachey, 24 vols. (London: Hogarth Press and the Institute of Psycho-analysis, 1955), xvii: 224.

[146] Ibid., 378.

[147] Slavoj Žižek writes of the complicity between the fetish, the commodity-form, and Kantian transcendent subject in *The Sublime Object of Ideology* (London: Verso, 1989), though he views the commodity-form as the primary term, 'offer[ing] a kind of matrix enabling us to generate all other forms of the "fetishistic inversion". . . . [I]n the structure of the commodity-form it is possible to find the transcendental subject . . .' (16).

Otherness, the more it is associated with other scenes, and the more he conceals his revulsion, the more he fashions himself into his own false idol:

> Her shiny eyes had a dry intense stare, which, missing Razumov, gave him an absurd notion that she was looking at something which was visible to her behind him. He cursed himself for an impressionable fool, and asked with forced calmness—
> 'What is it you see? Anything resembling me?'
> She moved her rigidly set face from left to right, negatively.
> 'Some sort of phantom in my image?' pursued Razumov slowly. 'For, I suppose, a soul when it is seen is just that. A vain thing. There are phantoms of the living as well as of the dead.'
> The tenseness of Madame de S——'s stare had relaxed, and now she looked at Razumov in a silence that had become disconcerting.
> 'I myself have had an experience', he stammered out, as if compelled. 'I've seen a phantom once.'
> The unnaturally red lips moved to frame a question harshly.
> 'Of a dead person?'
> 'No. Living.'
> 'A friend?'
> 'No.'
> 'An enemy?'
> 'I hated him.'
> 'Ah! It was not a woman, then?'
> 'A woman!' repeated Razumov, his eyes looking straight into the eyes of Madame de S——. 'Why should it have been a woman? And why this conclusion? Why should I not be able to hate a woman?' (*UWE*, 227–8)

As we have seen, for Burke the contaminating effects of terror necessitate that it be 'modified' and simulated. But for Razumov here, repressing his terror only exacerbates it. Attempting to control his feelings by making Madame de S—— all the more Other to him only increases the tangible force of her difference. The image that Razumov fashions of her thus operates in a similar way to Kant's 'aesthetic Idea', which presents what exceeds thought in an object. But whereas for Kant this presentation was still resolutely imaginary and subjective, for Razumov, the images he is presented with are *composites* of subjectivity and objectivity; distinct bodies of sensation irreducible to the perceiver or perceived. This is their spectrality.

In *The Secret Agent*, phantasmal transferences of energy were relatively anonymous and general, even though it affected characters individually. In *Under Western Eyes*, Conrad explores spectrality in all its diversity, showing how it manifests particular 'figures' of transference (Haldin, Madame de S——, General T——, Nathalie Haldin) that are not reducible to metaphor, metonymy, or symbol, for example, because they incorporate forces of lived experience and manifest a veritable dialogism. Each of the figures is a 'complex' in its own right. And in this sense, the novel certainly offers a more radical and sophisticated portrait of idealism and nationalism than the one Conrad paints of Russianness in 'Autocracy and War'. In addition, the novel's examination of haunting is a further honing of Conrad's critique of terrorism, for Anarchism and spectrality were closely tied as far back as Max Stirner. In *Einzige und Sein Eigentum* (1844)—translated into English in 1907 as *The Ego and its Own*—Stirner argues that through positing the essence of life as a higher existence, metaphysics has turned the world into a ghostly being: 'Yes, the whole world is haunted! Only *is* haunted? Indeed, it itself "walks," it is uncanny through and through, it is the wandering seeming-body [*Scheinleib*] of a spirit, it is a spook.'[148] As all state authority is also spectral, he argues, the individual must destroy it in order to be liberated:

In the time of spirits thoughts grew until they overtopped my head, whose offspring they yet were; they hovered about me and convulsed. The thoughts had become *corporeal* on their own account, were ghosts, such as God, emperor, fatherland, etc. If I destroy their corporeity, then I take back into mine and say 'I alone am corporeal.'[149]

The rapidity with which Stirner completely reduces spirit and thought to conveniently destroyable bodies weakens the argument, as Marx noted.[150] Furthermore, the temporal flux which Stirner sees as extirpating spectrality for the ego engenders its own phantoms elsewhere in his book: 'Over each minute of your existence a fresh minute of the future beckons to you, and, developing yourself, you get away "from yourself," that is, from the self that was at that moment.'[151] As Bergson would argue, though, the past that passes is also passed on. Only by breaking time or ceasing to live in it could Stirner's anarchic ego finally be free of its ghostly selves. For this reason, Emmanuel Lévinas has argued that the experience of time is

---

[148] Max Stirner, *The Ego and Its Own*, trans. by David Leopold (Cambridge: Cambridge University Press, 1995), Stirner's emphasis, 36.

[149] Ibid., 17, Stirner's emphasis.

[150] See the section 'Saint Max', in Karl Marx, *The German Ideology*, trans. by C. P. Magill (London: Lawrence and Wishart, 1940).

[151] Stirner, *The Ego and Its Own*, 38.

itself 'an-archic' in so far as the subject finds itself split internally by duration: 'This being torn up from oneself in the core of one's unity, this absolute non-coinciding, this diachrony of the instant, signifies in the form of one-penetrated-by-another.'[152] Accordingly, for Lévinas, 'A subject is a hostage.'[153]

By Part IV of *Under Western Eyes*, there is little doubt in Razumov's mind that his subjectivity has been taken hostage by Haldin. Feeling increasingly spectral himself, the terrorist's haunting of him begins to appear indistinct from his own persecuting conscience: 'everywhere Haldin: a moral spectre infinitely more effective than any visible apparition of the dead' (*UWE*, 286). Unable to vanquish it from his mind, it eventually leads him to confess his guilt to Nathalie Haldin: ' "It's myself whom I have given up to destruction", thought Razumov. "He has induced me to do it. I can't shake him off" ' (*UWE*, 318). For Jacques Derrida, such confusing spectral effects mean that 'the subject that haunts is not identifiable, one cannot see, localize, fix any form, one cannot decide between hallucination and perception . . .'.[154] Spectrality, he argues, thus 'hesitates between the singular "who" of the ghost and the general "what" of the simulacrum.'[155] But in *Under Western Eyes*, although the phantasmal is similarly ambivalent, it is also affected by the 'who' of living bodies and the 'what' of specific places. For Razumov, 'It was only the room through which that man [Haldin] had blundered on his way from crime to death that his spectre did not seem able to haunt' (*UWE*, 286). In contrast, the hallway of Madame de S——'s house contains a spectral surveillance all of its own: 'its chequered floor of black and white seemed absurdly large and like some public space where a great power of resonance awaits the provocation of footfalls and voices' (*UWE*, 229). Having heard his own words echoed in it, this uneasiness becomes more pronounced: 'He felt, bizarre as it may seem, as though another self, an independent sharer of his mind, had been able to view his body very distinctly' (*UWE*, 232). In contrast to the 'monstrous blank page' of Russia's 'endless space' and 'spirit', the novel's interior spaces present a mutable dialogism of spectrality.

---

[152] Emanuel Lévinas, in *Otherwise than Being; or, Beyond Essence*, trans. by Alphonso Lingis (1974; Dordrecht: Kluwer, 1991), 49.

[153] Ibid., 112.

[154] Jacques Derrida, *Specters of Marx: The State of Debt, the Work of Mourning, and the New International*, trans. by Peggy Kamuf (London: Routledge, 1994), 110.

[155] Ibid., 169.

As with *The Secret Agent*, *Under Western Eyes* clearly manifested its own force of contagion for Conrad. Having been suffering from impecuniousness and general stress while composing the novel, on submitting the typed but uncorrected manuscript to his publisher he promptly had a nervous breakdown. A letter from his wife, Jessie, to David Meldrum suggests that Conrad himself had fallen victim to the novel's spectrality: 'Poor Conrad is very ill and Dr Hackney says it will be a long time before he is fit for anything requiring mental exertion . . . he lives mixed up in the scenes and holds converse with the characters.'[156] By showing how the spectral involves specularity, transference, and textuality simultaneously, *Under Western Eyes* indicates how the relations of violence, terror, and representation that are intrinsic to the sublime can be embodied differently. And in this respect, it amounts to a rigorous and novel critique of terrorism's impact—especially regarding its mediation. Whereas *The Secret Agent* focused more on the impact of *violence* and its politicization, *Under Western Eyes* is clearly more concerned with how the effects of *terror* can be figured and fought—although in neither of the novels is there a simple separation of the two. As we saw from the statements of various terrorologists in my Introduction, however, outlining a theory of terrorism's status *has* often meant positing a separation between its violence and its terror, as well as between its facts and fictions. Through such divisions, structural aetiologies of terrorism have been presented in order to etiolate its socio-political impact, and also to enforce a distanced empiricism. The efficacy of such separations is what *Under Western Eyes* explores at length through the reactions of Razumov and the narrator.

That the narrator's judgement is affected as much as Razumov's by his efforts to suppress certain feelings is evident from a number of passages. On recalling Razumov staring down at the swift current of a river in Geneva, for example, the narrator comments on his own fear of sublime spectacles: 'I myself can never look at it for any length of time without experiencing a dread of being snatched away by its destructive force. Some brains cannot resist the suggestion of irresistible power and headlong motion' (*UWE*, 206). But strenuously detaching himself from events produces its own anxiety and spectrality for him, as when he witnesses Ivanovitch's intimacy with Nathalie Haldin:

---

[156] Jessie Conrad to Meldrum (6 February 1910), quoted in Najder, *Joseph Conrad*, 357.

I did not like to see him sitting there. I trust that an unbecoming jealousy of my privileged position had nothing to do with it. . . . Removed by the difference of age and nationality as if into the sphere of another existence, I produced, even upon myself, the effect of a dumb and helpless ghost, of an anxious immaterial thing that could only hover about without the power to protect or guide by as much as a whisper. (*UWE*, 151–2)

Just as when he faced Nathalie Haldin's 'indefinable charm', rather than admit to being affected by the situation the narrator invokes foreignness as a way of extricating himself from the scene. Consequently, the only way he can maintain an insight into the situation is by embodying a quasi-relation and quasi-reality of ghostliness. In the same way that the professedly detached 'realism' of his writing combines reportage and flights of fancy, so the narrator's relation to the other characters frequently combines the sort of intimacy and detached surveillance involved in Razumov's role as double-agent. Derrida identifies a similarly uncanny production of 'spectrality' in modern media reports which 'both invent *and* bring up to date, inaugurate *and* reveal, cause to come about *and* bring to light *at the same time* . . .'.[157] To the extent that spectrality in *Under Western Eyes* also draws the relative performativities of physical violence and psychological terror into confrontation, the potential volatility of such immediation becomes wide-ranging.

By the end of the novel, the spectral also occasions a new vision of enlightenment for Razumov. His last action is to reveal his identity to the revolutionaries, for which he is deafened by the terrorist Nikita. Stumbling along the street afterwards, he is then run over by a tram and crippled. Prior to the scene of this injury, though, the narrator cites Razumov's final diary entries which recount his spiritual regeneration through Nathalie Haldin. After a 'page and a half of incoherent writing', Razumov

express[es] in broken sentences, full of wonder and awe, the sovereign (he uses that very word) power of her person over his imagination, in which lay the dormant seed of her brother's words.
'. . . The most trustful eyes in the world—your brother said of you when he was as well as a dead man already. And when you stood before me with your hand extended, I remembered the very sound of his voice, and I looked into your eyes—and that was enough.' (*UWE*, 330–1)

---

[157] Derrida, *Specters of Marx*, 79, Derrida's emphases.

If the image of Haldin on the snow marked the failure of Razumov's reason, Nathalie embodies the power of his imagination—the 'seed' of which was planted by Haldin himself. Her 'sovereign power' is a new conception of moral exchange: 'To save me, your trustful eyes had to entice my thought to the very edge of the blackest treachery. I could see them constantly looking at me with the confidence of your pure heart which had not been touched by evil things' (*UWE*, 331). But this purity is problematic, for it has already been exchanged into a memory of Haldin. The sublime object of Razumov's ideology is simultaneously affirmed and negated, real and ideal; in short, spectralized. Like Kant conceiving the supersensibility of the 'moral law' as a 'veiled Isis', Razumov fashions his own shrouded goddess to oversee his psyche. For Kant, though, conceiving the transcendent in this way has its own dangers: 'the procedure whereby the law is personified and reason's moral bidding is made into a veiled Isis . . . is an *aesthetic* mode of representing . . . [and] always runs the danger of falling into an exalting vision which is the death of all philosophy'.[158] As far as Kant is concerned, the imagination can only produce degraded representations of reason's law and ideas; it is a mere supplement. In *Under Western Eyes*, though, the spectre as an aesthetic Idea combines complex interactions between subjects as a single dynamic figure. It does not simply offer an abstract conception or image of how, for example, objects and subjects, violence and terror, past and present relate; rather, it *incorporates* these relations. Together with *The Secret Agent*, Conrad thus uses terrorism as a subject with which to explore the relation of literature to transformations of force more generally.

As Charles Altieri has argued, this issue of force is a common interest among many modernist writers who were concerned with advancing literature's agency in the face of scientific and more general cultural developments.[159] As we have seen, Conrad's own engagement with science was fundamentally a matter of critique, no less than his depictions of Anarchism, Nihilism, or the sublime. In each case, his figuration of a novel, cultural complex arises from producing a dialogism of issues that feeds the force of literature itself. For Altieri, this conception of modernist force is particularly important

---

[158] Kant, 'On a Newly Raised Superior Tone in Philosophy', 405.
[159] Charles Altieri, 'The Concept of Force as Modernist Response to the Authority of Science', *Modernism/Modernity* 5: 2 (April 1998): 77–93.

for avant-garde movements such as Imagism, Futurism, and Vorticism. Accordingly, in the following chapter, I shall compare the Futurists' and Vorticists' notions of literary force before going on to examine how Wyndham Lewis attempts to develop an avant-gardisme that becomes increasingly terroristic.

2. Wyndham Lewis: Literary 'Strikes' and Allegorical Assaults

Refiguring the Avant-Garde: Vorticism's Syndicalism

If Conrad's *The Secret Agent* gestures towards a politically engaged style of literature, it is the avant-garde movements and periodicals which flourished throughout Europe in the early twentieth century that attempt to turn such gestures into a punch. As Renato Poggioli writes in *The Theory of the Avant-Garde* (1968), these movements were closely affiliated with military vanguards from the outset. Only after the Paris Commune in 1871, he argues, did the term 'begin to designate separately the cultural artistic avant-garde while still designating, in a wider and more distinct context, the socio-political avant-garde'.[1] In contrast to the nineteenth-century periodical, which functioned largely as a liberal 'organ of opinion', the avant-garde periodical, Poggioli argues, was 'an independent and isolated military unit, completely and sharply detached from the public, quick to act, not only to explore but also to battle, conquer and adventure on its own'.[2] Avant-garde groups explicitly presented their aesthetic stances in terms of militancy, as is evident from journals such as *Die Aktion* ('Action') and *Der Stürm* ('Storm') in Germany, *Vzorval* ('Explodidity') in Russia, and literary works such as Gian Pietro Lucini's book of poems, *Revolverate* (1909). Nowhere is the terroristic affinity of avant-gardisme more clearly voiced than in André Breton's declaration that the Surrealist act *par excellence* is to fire 'a volley shot into a crowd'.

In the early part of the twentieth century, though, the movement which advocated violence most ardently was undoubtedly Italian Futurism, led by Filippo Tommaso Marinetti. In 'The Founding and Manifesto of Futurism', published in *Le Figaro* in 1909, a new form of culturally violent literature is heralded. Poetry, Marinetti writes, 'must be conceived as a violent attack on unknown forces, to reduce

---

[1] Renato Poggioli, *The Theory of the Avant-Garde*, trans. by Gerald Fitzgerald (Cambridge, Mass.: Harvard University Press, 1968), 10.
[2] Ibid., 23.

and prostrate them before man'.[3] As a weapon in itself, Futurist aesthetics is also imagined as aiding the spread of violence more generally by singing the praises of 'polyphonic tides of revolutions in capitals', and glorifying war, 'the world's only hygiene'.[4] But rather than struggling against contemporary culture, the ethos of the Futurists was a wholesale affirmation of capitalist modernization:

Multicoloured billboards on the green fields, iron bridges that chain the hills together, surgical trains that pierce the blue belly of the mountains, enormous turbine pipes, new muscles of the earth, may you be praised by the Futurist poets, since you destroy the old sickly cooing sensitivity of the earth.[5]

The technology of mass production is seen as turning the categories of time and space into anachronisms. In their place, Marinetti states, a 'new aesthetic of speed' is emerging that will precipitate the 'ubiquity of multiplied man'.[6] Avant-gardism and political revolution are thus seen as feeding off the same energy: politics becomes a matter of aesthetics, just as the literary work becomes expressive of a universal, mechanized 'will'.[7] And because there are no longer any natural 'categories of images, noble or gross or vulgar', he argues, we must 'destroy syntax' accordingly. The Futurist style is to be composed of 'nouns scattered at random', onomatopoeia, and infinitives—'because they adapt themselves elastically to nouns and don't subordinate themselves to the writer's *I* that observes or imagines. Alone the infinitive can provide a sense of the continuity of life.'[8] As the infinitive in Italian can also be an imperative or a present participle, it stands, for Marinetti, as an exhortation to mass action.[9] However, by affirming a contiguity of Futurist practice and mass-modernizing, Futurism's capacity to maintain an independent agency becomes questionable. The tension is manifest in Marinetti's pronouncements on 'will'. In his 'Futurist Speech to the English', delivered at the Lyceum Club in London in 1910, he invokes an ideal future scenario in which 'man will be able to externalize his will and make it into a huge in-

---

[3] In Filippo Tommaso Marinetti, *Let's Murder the Moonshine: Selected Writings*, trans. by R. W. Flint and Arthur A. Coppatelli (Los Angeles: Sun and Moon, 1991), 49, hereafter cited as *LMM*.

[4] Ibid., 50.   [5] Marinetti, 'War, the World's only Hygiene', in *LMM*, 76.

[6] Marinetti, 'The Birth of a Futurist Aesthetic', in *LMM*, 89.

[7] Marinetti, 'Futurist Speech to the English', in *LMM*, 99.

[8] Marinetti, 'Technical Manifesto of Futurist Literature', in *LMM*, 92, Marinetti's emphasis.

[9] On Futurist style and action more generally see Lawrence Rainey, 'Taking Dictation: Collage Poetics, Pathology, and Politics', *Modernism/Modernity* 5: 2 (April 1998): 142–8.

visible arm. Dream and Desire, which are empty words today, will master and reign over space and time.'[10] But this will is efficiently violent only in so far as it is dehumanized: 'This nonhuman and mechanical being, constructed for an omnipresent velocity, will be naturally cruel, omniscient and combative.'[11] Thus, the more Futurism aligns itself with a general, technologizing social process, the more it risks turning its impact into a mass-produced phenomenon.

The problematic emerging here is one that Peter Bürger identifies in *The Theory of the Avant-Garde* (1984) as exemplifying the avant-garde's relation to mass culture and modernity in general. Aestheticism, he argues, becomes a distinct entity only with the development of bourgeois life. Avant-garde separatism thus has its roots in the nineteenth-century aesthetics of 'art for art's sake':

Only after art has in fact wholly detached itself from everything that is the praxis of life can two things be seen to make up the principle development of art in bourgeois society: the progressive detachment of art from real life contexts, and the correlative crystallisation of a distinctive sphere of experience, i.e., the aesthetic.[12]

Despite appearing to apportion the aesthetic a degree of autonomy in this passage, Bürger is generally unequivocal about stating that the avant-garde's secession is institutionally and socially 'conditioned'— the 'precarious product of overall social development' (*TA-G*, 24). But the schism of praxis and aesthetics he outlines is ambivalent. One of the results of the division, he states, is that the avant-garde work can free itself from historical strictures and so draw on a range of styles: 'Up to this period in the development of art, the use of artistic means had been limited by the period style' (*TA-G*, 18). Instead of having an 'organic' relation to society, the avant-garde is decidedly 'inorganic' in its detachment. The resulting autonomy endows it with a distinct agency. Moreover, writes Bürger, the withdrawal from the social process facilitates both critique and 'engagement': 'the structural principle of the non-organic is emancipatory in itself, because it permits the break-up of an ideology that is increasingly congealing into a system' (*TA-G*, 91). Yet Bürger still strives to maintain that the avant-garde is incapable of freeing itself from the determinations of a separate economic base. The avant-garde work cannot form its own

---

[10] Marinetti, 'Futurist Speech to the English', in *LMM*, 99.   [11] Ibid.

[12] Peter Bürger, *Theory of the Avant-Garde*, trans. by Michael Shaw (Minneapolis: University of Minnesota Press, 1984), 23, hereafter cited as *TA-G*.

political 'content' (*Gehalt*), he argues, for while its autonomy emerges from bourgeois fetishism and commodification, it also precludes it from having any real relation to political 'praxis'. Behind the action of the avant-gardist there is, for Bürger, always an institution that has pre-determined its status in the first place: 'it is art as an institution that determines the measure of political effect avant-garde works can have', which is why they remain 'distinct from the praxis of life' (*TA-G*, 92).[13]

This theory of avant-garde practice thus remains caught within the same double-bind that problematizes Futurism's potential for cultural assault. An art that is no longer distinct from life, Bürger argues, 'loses the capacity to criticise it' (*TA-G*, 50). Yet in being wrested from the social body, the avant-garde's relation to the 'practical'—which it desires to 'direct itself toward' (*TA-G*, 34)—remains mere metaphor. The same conclusion is drawn by several other critics. For Poggioli, the 'withdrawal' into a select circle is '*like* the gestures of plebeian, anarchistic, and terroristic revolt';[14] essentially, the equivalence between artistic and political revolution is 'no more than purely rhetorical'.[15] Marjorie Perloff also concurs, stating that in 'conferring primacy on the language' in their violent pronouncements, the Futurists 'merely perpetuated the split between ideas and praxis',[16] thereby frustrating the possibility of real revolution.

For Marinetti, though, emphasizing a contiguity of Futurist aesthetics and modernization harboured the potential for a new 'synthetic violence':

The plainest, the most violent of Futurist symbols, comes to us from the Far East. . . . In Japan they carry on the strangest of trades: the sale of coal made from human bones. All their powderworks are engaged in producing a new explosive substance more lethal than any yet known. . . . For this reason countless Japanese merchants are exploring the corpse-stuffed Manchurian battlefields. . . . Glory to the indomitable ashes of man, that come to life

---

[13] For Josephine Guy, in *The British Avant-Garde: The Theory and Politics of Tradition* (London: Harvester Wheatsheaf, 1991), 'Bürger's proposal has the effect of erasing the artist from the picture' (35). Similarly, for Richard Murphy, 'Bürger's own ambiguity in attempting to distinguish the avant-garde's position on autonomy is . . . the central weakness that affects the main concepts throughout his analysis' (*Theorizing the Avant-Garde: Modernism, Expressionism, and the Problem of Postmodernity* [Cambridge: Cambridge University Press, 1998], 28).

[14] Poggioli, *The Theory of the Avant-Garde*, 99, my emphasis.   [15] Ibid., 96.

[16] Marjorie Perloff, *The Futurist Moment: Avant-Garde, Avant-Guerre, and the Language of Rupture* (Chicago: Chicago University Press, 1986), 33.

in cannons! My friends, let us applaud this noble example of synthetic violence.[17]

War and capitalism are fully meshed around the issue of reproduction here, forming a continuous process that turns every moment of crisis into one of synthesis. Rupture and catastrophe are already commodified, incorporated into the movements of corporations. Returning to the problem of separatist agency, we can see that this 'symbol' complicates the issue of avant-garde violence theorized so far. For Bürger, the avant-garde's separatism involves 'killing the "life" of [its] material' by 'tearing it out of its functional context' (*TA-G*, 70). This process is symptomatic of the avant-garde's 'inorganic' relation to socio-political life, he argues, and is another factor in preventing it from becoming a real mode of praxis. In Marinetti's symbol, though, the extent to which the inorganic no longer affects organic 'life' is problematic, as the ability to obviate distinctions between life and death, material and product, production and reproduction, are viewed as being inherent to the whole war-commerce process. Consequently, the 'synthetic violence' is also potentially aesthetic; just as the human bones are synthesized with explosivity, so 'symbol' is incorporated into the material transformations.

This is not to suggest, as Andrew Hewitt does in his reading of the symbol, that the result is a 'negation of materiality'.[18] The collocation of sign, commodity, and event involved in the synthetic violence is also an overturning of the opposition between aesthetics and praxis. Hewitt does acknowledge this elsewhere in his analysis when he proposes a notion of 'Fascist theatricality'. The political work of Futurism, he writes, is evident in the textual dynamics of the manifestos themselves in so far as 'the *practice* of the manifesto is the practice of the text itself' (*FM*, 130, Hewitt's emphasis). By this he means that the manifesto is attempting to precipitate what it is declaring. Its temporality thus re-constitutes the text through each reading/performance—a phenomenon Hewitt terms the 'manifest': 'The fusion of representation and production that I have termed the "manifest" serves in the performance to mark the temporal act of enunciation itself' (*FM*, 130).[19] The merging of production and reproduction that

---

[17] Marinetti, 'The Birth of a Futurist Aesthetic', in *LMM*, 91.

[18] Andrew Hewitt, *Fascist Modernism: Aesthetics, Politics, and the Avant-Garde* (Stanford: Stanford University Press, 1993), 157, hereafter cited as *FM*.

[19] Janet Lyon discusses this iterativeness of the manifesto in terms of its attempt to constitute a collective authority and audience in *Manifestoes: Provocations of the Modern* (Ithaca: Cornell University Press, 1999), ch. 1.

characterizes the capitalist process is developed in the Futurist text as its own event. So rather than being subsumed into the process in general, the iteration of the manifesto presents its own agency. What is 'immediately present' in the manifesto, states Hewitt, is 'the act of mediation' itself. Contrary to Bürger's assertions, then, the manifest is in no way prevented from forming a political content or praxis:

Fascist theatricality—and I would contend, the performative shift in the avant-garde toward the aesthetics and politics of the manifest—might, indeed, be taken as an attack on the bourgeois system of mediated representation. Its particular form of totalitarianism might be understood as an immanentism, an absolutism, in which the conflation of signifier and signified, the conflation of power and its representation has been completed. (*FM*, 180)

Given the particularity of Futurist practice, this is a convincing argument. Yet the issue of whether it is possible to produce a politics of *dissent* when harnessing aesthetic practice to mass modernization remains. The extent to which the manifest can 'attack' bourgeois mediation by affirming an immanence of commercialism and aesthetics, as Marinetti does, is clearly questionable. For both Bürger and Hewitt, the totalizing tendencies of capitalism and Fascism are used respectively as a way of offering a holistic theory of avant-garde modernism. In both cases, the potential 'separatism' of the avant-garde is compromised by larger structures of power. Is there an alternative position? Two questions need to be raised in response to this. First: to what extent was capitalism in this period a hegemonic system overdetermining socio-political reproduction? And second: can the avant-gardism of this period be characterized as having general, structural tendencies that are common to the various movements?

These issues are ones that the writer and artist Wyndham Lewis can be seen as having explored from within the ranks of the avant-garde at the time. 'Vorticism', the movement he developed with Ezra Pound, Henri Gaudier-Brzeska, and other aesthetes in the two issues of the journal *Blast* published in June 1914 and July 1915, was nothing if not antagonistic. In the course of its short life, *Blast* brought together an international cast of writers and artists, including Jessica Dismorr, Jacob Epstein, T. S. Eliot, Rebecca West, Helen Saunders, and Ford Maddox Hueffer (later Ford). For Lewis, though, it was clearly his own affair; the advertisement in *The Egoist* (1 April 1914) for the first issue of *Blast* pronounced in large, bold type that it was 'edited by Wyndham Lewis', and Lewis himself was quick to correct dissenting views in subsequent years.[20] Expounding the Vorticist ethos in 'Our Vortex', Lewis places the movement in blatant opposition to the central tenets of Marinetti's Futurism.[21] Speed and the flux of the present are denounced in favour of discrete, resistant forces: 'The vorticist is at his maximum point of energy when stillest'.[22] Instead of worshipping processes of modernization and the 'continuity of life', the Vorticist labours to foster interruptions so as to restitute autonomy from the social machine. 'Our vortex depends on water-tight compartments' (*B1*, 147), declared Lewis.[23] Rejecting any links with mass production, *Blast* attempts to promulgate intervention in popular culture on behalf of 'THE INDIVIDUAL': '*Blast* will be popular, essentially', we are told, in 'Long Live the Vortex', 'But it is nothing to do with the People' (*B1*, 7). Rather than fold the individual into the masses, Lewis calls for a suspension of relations between the socius and its members. Vorticism is to be its own discontinuous zone: 'Between action and reaction we would establish ourselves' (*B1*, 2).

Two books that Lewis wrote between 1918 and 1926, *The Art of Being Ruled* (1926), and *Time and Western Man* (1927), expand these ideas further. The first is a sustained critique of liberal democracy and other forms of state governance, in which Marinetti, among a host of others, is lambasted for being a capitalist puppet. If one is a true revolutionary, states Lewis,

A propagandist of the vulgarest capitalism, such as Marinetti was or is, will in consequence not please you much. All that absurd and violent

[20] In 1949 Lewis wrote to the editor of *Partisan Review* who had claimed that *Blast*'s inception was Pound's responsibility: '*Blast* was my idea . . . I was the editor . . . in short the whole affair was mine . . .' (*The Letters of Wyndham Lewis*, ed. by W. K. Rose [London: Methuen, 1963], 492). For a discussion of *Blast*'s promotion in relation to advertising and popular culture, see Paige Reynolds, ' "Chaos Invading Concept": *Blast* as a Native Theory of Promotional Culture', *Twentieth Century Literature* 46: 2 (Summer 2000): 238–67.

[21] For a general consideration of the Vorticists' relation to the Futurists, see Paul Peppis, *Literature, Politics, and the English Avant-Garde: Nation and Empire, 1901–18* (Cambridge: Cambridge University Press), ch. 3; and William C. Wees, *Vorticism and the English Avant-Garde* (Manchester: Manchester University Press, 1972), chs. 6 and 7.

[22] Wyndham Lewis, 'Our Vortex', *Blast: Review of the Great English Vortex*, ed. by Wyndham Lewis, 1 (June 1914; Santa Rosa: Black Sparrow, 1997), 148, hereafter cited as *B1*.

[23] The difference in aesthetic concerns between Vorticism and Futurism mirrors the distinction T. E. Hulme makes between geometric and vitalist art, respectively. Hulme argues that whereas geometric art such as cubism engenders a 'feeling of separation in the face of outside nature', vitalist art tends to elicit a feeling of 'empathy' and 'organicism' ('Modern Art and its Philosophy', in *Speculations: Essays on Humanism and the Philosophy of Art*, ed. by Herbert Read [1924; London: Routledge & Kegan Paul, 1987], 85). He also argues that 'the use of mechanical lines in the new [geometric] art is in no sense merely a reflection of a mechanical environment' (77).

propaganda of *actuality*, stinking of the optimism of the hoardings and the smugness of the motoring millionaire, disguising the squalor of the capitalist factory beneath an epileptic rhetoric of *action*, will not stir you to sympathetic yawps.[24]

Futurism, for Lewis, is unacceptable not only because he views it as having no critical relation to mass modernization, but also because he perceives a hypocrisy in being rhetorical about action. This is elaborated into a wider diatribe in *Time and Western Man*, where Lewis connects Futurism to the tyranny of what he calls the 'Time-cult'. The 'inner meaning' of time philosophy, he contends, is 'the doctrine of a mechanistic universe: periodic, timeless, or nothing but "time", whichever you prefer, and essentially *dead*.'[25] Identifying its main proponents as Samuel Alexander, Bergson, Alfred North Whitehead, and Oswald Spengler, Lewis argues that the avatar of the Time-cult is the 'man of action', a similarly 'mechanical, functional creature' (*TWM*, 20). Against this figure, Lewis calls for the development of artistic techniques that might resist the technologization:

the identity of philosophy or of speculative thought with politics is largely owing to the fact that both depend more and more absolutely upon machines of greater and greater precision, on machines so wonderfully complex and powerful that they usurp to a great extent the functions of independent life.   (*TWM*, 156)

Yet Lewis's call for an alternative avant-garde movement is not without its own internal contradictions. In *Blast*, for example, there are a number of instances where the purported distinctions between Vorticism and Futurism appear blurred; the manifesto is its main form of assertive militancy, and the experiments with typography and *mise-en-page* are strikingly similar, as is the occasional alignment of textual militancy with physical violence. Among the list of people and things that the journal 'Blesses' rather than 'Blasts', for example, are popular boxers of the time such as Dick Burge, 'Petty Officer Curran', and 'Bandsman Rice', along with Charlotte Corday (Marat's assassin), Oliver Cromwell, and the Irish Unionists Edward Carson and Captain James Craig, who were leading the fight against Irish Home Rule (*B1*, 28). Moreover, the most intense aesthetic experience is imagined

---

[24] Wyndham Lewis, *The Art of Being Ruled* (London: Chatto & Windus, 1926), 154, Lewis's emphases, hereafter cited as *ABR*.

[25] Wyndham Lewis, *Time and Western Man* (Santa Rosa: Black Sparrow, 1993), 91, Lewis's emphasis, hereafter cited as *TWM*.

in 'Futurism, Magic and Life' as being murder: 'Killing somebody must be the greatest pleasure in existence: either like killing yourself without being interfered with by the instinct of self-preservation—or exterminating the instinct of self-preservation itself!' (*Bi*, 133). The metaphorizing of violence here is certainly no less extreme than Marinetti's 'symbol' of the explosive ashes of man.

In *The Art of Being Ruled*, though, Lewis advocates a violence of ideas which he contrasts with physical violence. A quotation from the French Syndicalist writer Georges Sorel is offered as an authoritative precedent:

Historians attach an exaggerated importance to the acts of violence. . . . The description of these events relieves them of the necessity for seeking out the causes of the change that has occurred. . . . What is really essential is the transformation occurring in the *ideas of the community*. (*ABR*, 6, Lewis's emphasis)

Announcing Sorel to be the 'key to all contemporary political thought' (*ABR*, 128), the Syndicalists' theory of the 'General Strike' is viewed by Lewis as exemplifying this force of ideas. The central concern of Sorel's Syndicalism is that of critiquing the notion that liberal democracy is an emancipatory form of statehood: 'Never has anyone tried to justify the singular paradox according to which the rule of a chaotic majority leads to the appearance of what Rousseau called a General Will which could not err.'[26] A vote is an 'abdication' of power rather than a means of self-assertion, states Sorel, because it implies investing power in a state that has already made it impossible for real social change to take place. As he argues in his central work *Reflections on Violence* (1906), this is largely an outcome of the collaboration between the press and the liberalist governing powers. There is, he writes,

a great resemblance between the electoral democracy and the Stock Exchange; in one case as in the other it is necessary to work upon the simplicity of the masses, to buy the cooperation of the most important papers, and to assist chance by infinite trickery.[27]

The democracy that appears to be representing individual freedom is actually a form of covert 'scattered violence', Sorel contends, one that

---

[26] Georges Sorel, *L'Avenir Socialiste des Syndicats* (Paris: Librairie de l'art Sociale, 1898), 118.

[27] Georges Sorel, *Reflections on Violence*, trans. by T. E. Hulme (New York: Collier, 1961), 222, hereafter cited as *RV*.

'acts through economic conditions' (*RV*, 172) to expropriate workers from the power base. In opposition to this 'organized force' of the state, he proposes a 'proletarian violence' that would destroy the hegemony of capital and the bourgoisie. Labour strikes are advocated as the most effective form of violence because they directly attack the state's main source for accumulating power—and certainly by 1900 strikes had become the Syndicalists' primary weapon.[28] The resulting anti-parliamentarianism was declared to be anti-political by the Syndicalist executive body, the *Confédération Générale du Travail* (CGT), which declared political neutrality in its charter of 1906.[29] However, this neutrality was also offered as an active hijacking of liberal democracy: Léon Jouhaux, the CGT secretary, declared in 1909 that autonomy would enable the Syndicalists to 'subordinate political action to trade union action'.[30] The policy of neutrality thus became, in effect, an alternative politics.

Separation from the sphere of production is a form of militancy in itself for Sorel: 'The proletariat organises itself for battle, separating itself from the other parts of the nation, and regarding itself as the great motive power of history' (*RV*, 167). But this is not to say that Syndicalists did not also adopt more blatantly combative methods. At various points in the *Reflections on Violence* Sorel calls for strikes to be 'accompanied by violence', and this accompaniment did frequently materialize in France. Sabotage of production lines was inaugurated as a Syndicalist policy in 1898 by Émile Pouget at a conference in Rennes, and this was follwed by concerted attacks on shops and on lines of communication and transport. By 1913, Sorel defended such actions in an appendix to *Reflections on Violence*, arguing that 'The strike is a phenomenon of war'; 'there is something terrifying in this which will appear more and more terrifying as violence takes a greater place in the mind of the proletariat' (*RV*, 274, 275). One of the results of this incendiarism was that Syndicalist activism was seen by some as amounting to terrorism. For many Syndicalists, though, violence was rather an adjunct to the more primary work of the strike as radical inaction.

[28] See Barbara Mitchell, 'French Syndicalism: An Experiment in Practical Anarchism', in *Revolutionary Syndicalism: An International Perspective*, ed. by Marcel van der Linden and Wayne Thorpe (Aldershot: Scolar, 1990), 26–9.

[29] See F. F. Ridley, *Revolutionary Syndicalism in France: The Direct Action of its Time* (Cambridge: Cambridge University Press, 1970), 95–7.

[30] Quoted in Marcel Linden and Wayne Thorpe, 'The Rise and Fall of Revolutionary Syndicalism', in van der Linden and Thorpe, *Revolutionary Syndicalism*, 3.

The strike's performativity can thus be used to question the notion of separatist autonomy and engagement theorized by Poggioli and Bürger. Withdrawal, for Sorel, in no way signifies a move into abstraction or a mere metaphorizing of agency. When he uses imagery of battle and revolution it is because the (anti-)activity of the strike is asserted to be the most potent means of interfering with state power. Attacking the democratic system through non-participation, the strike presents a form of disruption that resists assimilation by capitalism or the state. Moreover, the 'language of strikes', for Sorel, is also a strike involving language itself, as is evident from his discussion of the 'myth' of the general strike. This myth, he states, is a 'body of images' that provokes revolutionary instincts and corresponds to all the 'different manifestations of the war undertaken by Socialism against modern society' (*RV*, 127). In parallel with actual labour strikes, which enable the proletariat to maintain a separate autonomy, the myth is accorded its own inexhaustible energy:

The myth must be judged as a means of acting on the present; any attempt to discuss how far it can be taken literally as future history is devoid of sense. *It is the myth in its entirety which alone is important*: its parts are only of interest in so far as they may bring out the main idea. No useful purpose is served, therefore, in arguing about the incidents which may occur in the social war, and about the decisive conflicts which may give victory to the proletariat . . . (*RV*, 126, Sorel's emphasis)

For Lewis, who first encountered Sorel's writings when living in Paris between 1903 and 1908, the strike and its myth offered new possibilities of revolution.[31] With 1,026 labour stoppages in France in 1904 alone, it would have been impossible to have remained unaware of the Syndicalists' impact.[32] Seeing in Sorel's works the potential for a new mode of literary combat, Lewis set about putting it into practice.[33] In England, *Reflections on Violence* was translated by T. E. Hulme, Lewis's friend and aesthetic associate, and was finally published in 1916. Hulme's Frith Street Circle, an intellectual group in which Lewis and Ezra Pound were active, also attracted British

[31] In contrast, Vernon Lee, in 'M. Sorel and the "Syndicalist Myth" ', *Fortnightly Review* 96 (October 1911): 664–80, sees the 'myth' of the strike as an idealization.

[32] Jeremy Jennings, *Syndicalism in France: A Study of Ideas* (London: Macmillan, 1990), 7.

[33] On the influence of Sorel's Syndicalism on Vorticism see Rod Mengham, 'From Georges Sorel to *Blast*', in *The Violent Muse: Violence and the Artistic Imagination in Europe, 1910–39*, ed. by Rod Mengham and Jana Howlett (Manchester: Manchester University Press, 1994); and Vincent Sherry, *Ezra Pound, Wyndham Lewis and Radical Modernism* (Oxford: Oxford University Press, 1993), 31–4.

Syndicalist activists such as Jim Larkin, an Irish Liverpudlian who orchestrated the Dublin Strike of 1913, and A. J. Cook, who was rumoured to have co-authored the militant pamphlet 'The Miners' Next Step'.[34] Alfred Orage, another habitué of Hulme's group, had introduced Larkin to Syndicalist writings and also edited *The New Age*, a Socialist journal to which Pound contributed several articles.[35] Furthermore, between 1910 and 1914 Britain was the international centre for Syndicalist activity. The national miners' strike of 1912 was the largest the world had seen, and in 1913, the year before the first issue of *Blast*, strike figures reached their apogee.[36]

Ireland was also a place in which Syndicalism took root. James Connolly, for example, who was instrumental in rousing Irish Republican forces against the British, had studied with Sorelian Syndicalists in France. Together with Padraic Pearse, Connolly advocated a coupling of violence and myth that helped to precipitate the Easter Rising of 1916, in which armed Republicans made an unsuccessful stand against the British Army in Dublin. Conolly's and Pearse's discourse of rebellion also found an adherent in William Butler Yeats. In one of his early plays, 'Where There is Nothing' (1903), Yeats had already shown a fascination for Syndicalist ideas, depicting the protagonist, Paul Rutledge, as rejecting his upper-class background and calling for a liberation of the proletariat: 'Let us send messengers everywhere to tell the people to stop working, and then the world may come to an end.'[37] Having been inspired earlier by William Morris's romantic politics, Yeats came to admire both Connolly and Pearse, and reacted to the British Army's execution of them, along with other leaders of the Easter Rising, by immortalizing them in his poem 'Easter 1916'. The 'terrible beauty' that he proclaims in the poem to be 'born' as a result of the failed insurrection marks a defi-

---

[34] On Hulme's Syndicalist proclivities and his importance for the Vorticist aesthetic, see Miriam Hansen, 'T. E. Hulme, Mercenary Modernism; or, Fragments of Avantgarde Sensibility in Pre-World War 1 Britain', *ELH* 47: 2 (Summer 1980): 355–85.

[35] For a detailed account of Ezra Pound's Syndicalist connections, see David Kadlec, 'Pound, *Blast*, and Syndicalism', *ELH* 60: 4 (Winter 1993): 1015–31.

[36] See Bob Holton, *British Syndicalism 1910–14: Myths and Realities* (London: Pluto, 1980); and John Lovell, 'British Trade Unions 1875–1933', in *British Trade Union and Labour History: A Compendium*, ed. by L. A. Clarkson (London: Macmillan, 1990), 105–15.

[37] W. B. Yeats and Lady Gregory, 'Where There is Nothing', in *'Where There is Nothing' and 'The Unicorn from the Stars'*, ed. by Katherine Worth (Washington, DC: Catholic University of America Press, 1987), 86. Michael Tratner also discusses Syndicalist influences on Yeats in *Modernism and Mass Politics: Joyce, Woolf, Eliot, Yeats* (Stanford: Stanford University Press, 1995), ch. 6.

nite shift in his aesthetics towards seeing violence as having potentially positive political effects. Using the symbol of a stone in a stream,
Yeats praises the leaders of the Rising for having been so rebelliously
resolute:

> Hearts with one purpose alone
> Through summer and winter seem
> Enchanted to a stone
> To trouble the living stream.[38]

As Michael Tratner points out, there is a specific correlation here
with Connolly's attempt to 'enchant' the hearts of Republicans to a
single Syndicalist principle of mass rebellion. Yet as Yeats declares in
the poem: 'Too long a sacrifice / Can make a stone of the heart';
there is a difference between the heart inspired by stony determination and a heart that has turned to stone. Seeing the Rising's leaders
defeated by the British in spite of blind belief, Yeats can only offer the
poem itself as a force acting ongoingly on the present—just like
Sorel's myth of the general strike:

> I write it out in a verse—
> Macdonagh and MacBride
> And Connolly and Pearse
> Now and in time to be,
> Wherever green is worn,
> Are changed, changed utterly:
> A terrible beauty is born.[39]

In contrast, British Syndicalism was initially linked not so much to
nationalism as to left-wing industrial action. The Syndicalists in
France, however, were not without right-wing leanings. By 1910
Sorel, for example, had become increasingly interested in nationalist
monarchism. After 1909, convinced that democratic and French republican forces were working against proletarian combat, he turned
to extreme right-wing figures such as Charles Maurras—whom Lewis
had met in Paris at the *Closérie des Lilas*—and his monarchist movement, *Action Française*, for support. Radical separatism was their common bond. Sorel went so far as to label the 'friends of Maurras' the
new 'avant-garde'[40] in the Italian Syndicalist journal *Il Divenire Sociale*
in 1909, and writers such as Lewis, Pound, Yeats, and T. S. Eliot went

---

[38] W. B. Yeats, 'Easter 1916', in *Collected Poems* (London: Macmillan, 1990), 204.
[39] Ibid., 205.   [40] Quoted in Jennings, *Syndicalism in France*, 105.

on to become interested in the alliance of Socialism and nationalism to varying degrees. These intellectual and political concatenations were further complicated in that monarchists like Edouard Berth and Georges Valois, with whom Sorel formed the journal *L'Independance* (1911–13), were also avid Bergsonians—hardly a position that Lewis was sympathetic to.[41]

Rather than simply fall in line with Syndicalist politics, Lewis used aspects of Syndicalism to form his own individualist avant-garde. Always wary of aligning himself with groups, his first significant act of fractiousness was his break from Roger Fry's art group, the 'Omega Workshop', in October 1913. In opposition to Fry, Lewis founded his own 'Rebel Art Centre'. It is with *Blast*, however, that his avant-garde separatism becomes clearly aligned with the Syndicalist *bourse du travail* as the creation of an avant-garde unit of 'individuals'. Vorticism was bluntly offered in the journal as a militant aesthetics. Lewis himself told a reporter of the *Daily Mail*, that the title, *Blast*, 'means the blowing away of dead ideas and worn out notions'.[42] The journal was not without competition from other areas, though. With problems of Suffragette militancy and Irish Home Rule in addition to widespread labour strikes, some historians have gone so far as to suggest that prior to the outbreak of the Great War, Britain was on the verge of revolution.[43] Indeed, for some commentators at the time the part played by Syndicalist and trade union activism in fomenting such general upheaval was nothing short of terroristic:

Arson, riots and sanguinary encounters with the police and military have occurred in many parts of the kingdom. . . . Our workers must be taught they have the right to strike, but not the right to terrorize, assault, loot and burn. . . . We must prepare for the possibility of revolution.[44]

Considering this prevalence of Syndicalist violence in Britain, the affiliation of Lewis's separatism is clear; as Rod Mengham argues: 'Lewis's attitude towards the avant-garde group as a kind of terrorist cell, engaged in guerrilla warfare against bourgeois philistinism . . . should be seen as having emerged naturally from French [Syndical-

---

[41] See Mark Antliff, *Inventing Bergson: Cultural Politics and the Parisian Avant-Garde* (Princeton: Princeton University Press, 1993), 155–60.

[42] 'Rebel Art in Modern Life', *Daily News* (7 April 1914): 14.

[43] See Lovell, 'British Trade Unions', 110; also George Dangerfield, *The Strange Death of Liberal England* (1935; London: MacGibbon & Kee, 1966), ch. 4.

[44] J. Ellis Barker, 'The Labour Revolt and its Meaning', *Nineteenth Century* 70: 415 (September 1911): 459–60.

ist] thinking about the uses of violence in political life.'[45] And it is within Lewis's 'play' 'Enemy of the Stars', included within the first issue of *Blast*, that Lewis moves from rhetorically aligning Vorticism with terroristic violence to presenting a 'strike' that is essentially literary.

'Enemy of the Stars'

Between 1914 and 1932, when Lewis rewrote and republished 'Enemy of the Stars', he experienced a great deal of political crises. Avowedly, the Great War along with the Great Strike of 1926 were the most significant events in his 'political education'—the war particularly so.[46] Lewis volunteered as a gunner in the Royal Artillery in March 1916, and was posted as a subaltern to a siege battery in Bailleul, France, in May 1917. With a one-month hiatus suffering from trench fever in a military hospital in Étaples, he experienced six months of severe shelling until he was granted emergency leave in November to visit his sick mother. Rather than return to the front when she recovered, he became a war artist.[47] Yet if the war became swiftly incorporated into Lewis's artistic career, it also marked the end of the Vorticists' alliance: both Gaudier-Brzeska and Hulme died in action, and the third and promised issue of *Blast* never materialized.[48]

Of the war's impact on him, Lewis, characteristically, offers differing accounts. 'I started the war a different man to what I ended it' (*Blasting*, 186), he wrote. But it was not so much transformation as distillation that he underwent, as he comments regarding his military training: 'I . . . was being translated from a relaxed system to a far more stringent one: I was experiencing my full share of perplexity at finding myself assisting at the assassination of Democracy' (*Blasting*, 27–8). The drills and discipline of army life were thus in step with the Vorticists' desire for regimented aesthetics—even the violence was, if we believe Lewis's later comments to be sincere: 'War, and especially

[45] Mengham, 'From Georges Sorel to *Blast*', 33.

[46] See Lewis's first autobiography, *Blasting and Bombardiering* (1937; London: Calder & Boyars, 1967), 235, hereafter cited as *Blasting*.

[47] For a detailed account of Lewis's time at the front, see Jeffrey Meyers, *The Enemy: A Biography of Wyndham Lewis* (London: Routledge & Kegan Paul, 1980), ch. 6; also Lewis's letters to Pound in *Pound/Lewis: The Letters of Ezra Pound and Wyndham Lewis*, ed. by Timothy Materer (London: Faber & Faber, 1985), pt. 2.

[48] Regarding *Blast 2*'s critique of the war, see Peppis, *Literature, Politics, and the English Avant-Garde*, ch. 4.

those miles of hideous desert known as "the Line" in Flanders and France, presented me with a subject-matter so consonant with the austerity of that "abstract" vision I had developed, that it was an easy transition.'[49] But the war also became an example for Lewis of how industrialized life spells a death sentence for individualism. As David Ayers argues, whereas before the war he had championed a duality of the self, after the war he increasingly viewed the fragmented subject as a symptom of capitalist culture.[50] And although he continued to eschew any one political allegiance, his sympathies turned distinctly Fascist. I shall not be discussing Lewis's works or politics of the 1930s in this chapter. I shall, however, be addressing the 'turn' evident in his writings from the war period—particularly in relation to his pronouncements on female suffrage and democracy. Referring at points to the both versions of 'Enemy of the Stars' will thus provide an introduction to this distillation of Lewis's increasingly 'enemy' politics.

Bold characters, capitals, and underlining foreground writing as a pre-eminent element at work in the first version of the play. The admixture of contrasting writing styles and typography—advertisement, manifesto, news headline—highlights the disintegration of a uniform, framed space of the page, creating the impression that the individual word-blocks compose the dynamic of the whole. The self-reflexivity is evident in the paronomasia that introduces the cast:

CHARACTERS.
TWO HEATHEN CLOWNS, GRAVE BOOTH ANIMALS
            CYNICAL ATHLETES.   (*Bı*, 55)

The twinning of written and theatrical 'characters', the latter dressed in 'BLACK CLOTH CUT SOMEWHERE, NOWADAYS, ON THE UPPER BALTIC', is reiterated later: '*Type of characters* taken from broad faces where Europe grows arctic, intense, human and universal' (*Bı*, 59, my emphasis). The allusions to the 'Upper Baltic' and 'arctic' are probably a reference to a literary precursor, the Russian Futurist play of Kazimir Malevich and Aleksei Kruchenykh, 'Victory Over the Sun' (1913).[51] As Jo Anna Isaak has pointed out, the

---

[49] Wyndham Lewis, *Rude Assignment: An Intellectual Biography* (1950; Santa Barbara: Black Sparrow, 1984), 138.

[50] David Ayers, *Wyndham Lewis and Western Man* (London: Macmillan, 1992), 3, 217.

[51] Elsewhere in *Blast* such landscape is identified psychologically with England: 'England is just as unkind and inimical to Art as the Arctic zone is to Life. This is the Siberia of the mind' ('The Improvement of Life', *Bı*, 146).

Futurist work presents a number of theatrical and stylistic elements that 'Enemy of the Stars' appears to replicate.[52] In particular, the self-reflexivity of Lewis's 'characters' echoes Malevich and Kruchenykh's notion of the 'autotelic word' which figures language as a law unto itself. The performance of 'Victory' in St Petersburg certainly gave the impression of exuding an internalized force. In his review of the play, Mikhail Matyushin wrote: 'there was such an inner strength in each word . . . the Future people and Strong men conquered the cheap, pretentious sun and lit their own light inside themselves'.[53] For the play's 'Future Men', the creation of mechanized mass violence is tantamount to an assassination attempt against an autocracy symbolized as solar. Having waited with knives for darkness to fall, the new 'Many' carry out the sun's 'slaughter': 'We pulled out the sun by its fresh roots / These fat ones became permeated with arithmetics'.[54] By fostering their own mass production, though, the Future Men also engender homogeneous organicism. Everything collapses into undifferentiated immanence: 'here . . . everything runs without resistance', sing the 'Sportsmen'; 'from everywhere self-propels com icing [sic] / death graves glasses and posters / footsteps are hanged / on signboards / people run down / like tumbling derby hats'.[55] Rather than making language an end in itself, the autotelic word produces its own end of autonomy. The fragmentation has become absorbed into modernization more generally.

In 'Enemy of the Stars', Lewis pieces together a different form of assault. Just as the Russian Future Men were lit by their own interior light, so Lewis's characters are 'BURSTING EVERYWHERE THROUGH HEAVY TIGHT CLOTHES' (*B1*, 55). But they are also presented as conflicting types. The main protagonist, Arghol, we are told, is 'IN IMMENSE COLLAPSE OF CHRONIC PHILOSOPHY. YET HE BULGES ALL OVER, COMPLEX FRUIT, WITH SIMPLE FIRE OF LIFE' (*B1*, 59). Arghol's energy arises from not participating in what Lewis in *Time and Western Man* calls the 'Time-cult'—punningly alluded to here as 'chronic philosophy'. Of the other two characters, one is a 'superintendent' who is 'NO

---

[52] Jo Anna Isaak, *The Ruin of Representation in Modernist Art and Texts* (Ann Arbor: UMI Research Press, 1986), 75–80.

[53] Mikhail Matyushin, 'Futurism in St Petersburg' (1913), reprinted in *The Drama Review* 15: 4 (Fall, 1971): 103.

[54] Aleksei Kruchenykh and Kazimir Malevich, 'Victory Over the Sun', reprinted in *The Drama Review* 15 (Fall 1971): 116.

[55] Ibid., 12.

MORE IMPORTANT THAN LOUNGING STAR OVER-
HEAD' and rushes offstage on entering, and the other, Hanp, is
Arghol's foil, an 'APPALLING "GAMIN", BLACK BOURGEOIS
ASPIRATIONS UNDERMINGING [*sic*] BLATANT VIRTUOS-
ITY OF SELF' (*B1*, 59). With the drama set up along particular po-
litical and ideological lines, the antagonism is complicated by a
reference to the relation between the reader and the text:

'Yet you and me: why not from the English metropolis?'—Listen: it is our
honeymoon. We go abroad for the first scene of our drama. Such a strange
thing as our coming together requires a strange place for initial stages of our
intimate ceremonious acquaintance. (*B1*, 59)

Already the initial 'advertisement' has declared the drama to be
'VERY WELL ACTED BY YOU AND ME' (*B1*, 55). Thus, it becomes clear that the text is not, in fact, meant to be staged in the usual
manner. Instead, the very transaction of writing and reading has
been staked out as the agonistic space.

This space is further outlined in the 'stage arrangements' describ-
ing the two scenes: the first is an arena littered with 'OVER-
TURNED CASES AND OTHER IMPEDIMENTA'; the other, a
hut that is also overturned and has a 'SHAFT LEADING DOWN
INTO MINES QUARTERS' (*B1*, 60).[56] That the hut is a veritable
'vortex' is 'only too plain', we are told in the play's second version:
'*into its dark mouth all that is in movement in the visible world tends to be en-
gulfed*'.[57] Despite appearances it is an anti-mine. Instead of being extracted from, the hut is like a black hole, absorbing movement into
itself, feeding on speed. This agency of inertia is also attributed to
Arghol, whom we find fighting against an 'INVESTMENT OF RED
UNIVERSE' (*B1*, 61). The demarcation of an avant-garde zone thus
arises from figuring a disjunction between the individual and the industry of capitalism. This is complicated, however, by the fact that
mechanization seems to have become its own natural system. Even
before the action proper commences we are told that the 'WALLS
OF THE UNIVERSE' close in on Arghol and the cast producing an
'ATMOSPHERE OF TERROR' (*B1*, 61) that causes their death.

---

[56] 'Mines' here was erroneously printed as 'Mimes' originally, as Lewis indicates in his
list of *errata* for the play (*B1*, 4). It is corrected in the text in the Black Sparrow Press edition
from which I am quoting.

[57] Wyndham Lewis, 'Enemy of the Stars' (1932 version), in *Wyndham Lewis: Collected
Poems and Plays*, ed. by Alan Munton (Manchester: Carcanet, 1979), 160, Lewis's emphases.
Hereafter cited as 'Enemy 2'.

With the 'EXECUTION' over, the universe counts its profits: 'THE BOX OFFICE RECEIPTS HAVE BEEN ENORMOUS' (*B1*, 61). But because the system needs Arghol in order to show its opposition, his demise sabotages its sovereignty. The power arrangement must be resuscitated. Consequently the theatrical space of the vortex re-opens in the no-man's land that arises from the conflict's irresolution.

With the 'granite flower' of the earth having 'burst' to reveal the scene—'a wheelwright's yard' (*B1*, 62)—we are suddenly presented with a violent assault by the superintendent on Arghol:

> At each blow, in muscular spasm, he made the pain pass out. . . .
> The boot, and heavy shadow above it, went. The self-centred and ele-
> mental shadow, with whistling noise peculiar to it, passed softly and sickly
> into a doorway's brown light.   (*B1*, 63)

Arghol is part of an industry of violence meted out by the 'Super' who manages the mine and is also Arghol's 'uncle'. The avuncular nature of their relationship expresses its inherent ambiguity. Arghol is not the direct offspring of this industry, which is why he tells Hanp in their ensuing discussion that he will not 'kill' the Super: 'my uncle is very little of a relation' (*B1*, 66). As far as Arghol is concerned, though, industry and vitalism have formed a conglomerate, for the Super embodies 'the will of the universe manifested with directness and per-sistence' (*B1*, 66). Lewis's view that the Bergsonian *élan vital* is tanta-mount to social mechanization thus makes an entrance here. For Lewis, Bergson's thesis that the flux of *durée* blends individual times with a universal time amounts to organic mass production.[58] Amongst Bergsonians themselves, the idea that cycles of industry are indeed linked to the *élan vital* did not gain much currency. In fact, for a number of commentators it was Syndicalism and not capitalism that exemplified Bergson's thinking.[59] Not for Lewis, though. In 'Enemy of the Stars' the cycle of violence produces its own counter-strike as the Super's attack on Arghol is echoed by another: 'the sec-ond attack, pain left by first shadow, lashing him, was worse. He lost consciousness' (*B1*, 63). Whereas the initial kick aims at enforcing an

---

[58] Georges Simmel, in *The Conflict of Modern Life* (1918), expressed similar sentiments, see-ing modern capitalist industrialism as a 'product' of Bergsonian 'Life'—see Antliff, *Invent-ing Bergson*, 172.

[59] See John Hunter Harley, 'Syndicalism and Labour Unrest', *Contemporary Review* 101 (March 1912): 348–57; and Arthur Oncken Lovejoy, 'The Practical Tendencies of Bergson-ism', *International Journal of Ethics* 23 (July 1913): 429–43. Lewis himself later declares Sorel a Bergson 'disciple' in *TWM*, 201.

industry of control, this second attack is broken off, abstracted like a surplus value. In the second version, the distinction is presented more blatantly: '*The second attack, in its absence—the pain that is, left by the first shadow, lashing him—is worse. He loses consciousness, at this empty repetition— the recollection—the rankling—of the blackened flesh*' ('Enemy 2', 147, Lewis's emphasis). Alienating Arghol even more effectively from the Super's power, the secondary 'recollection' of 'pain' ironically comes to be associated with Arghol's autonomy and detachment. A contrapuntal dynamic of alienation in the classic Marxist sense is emerging.[60] Instead of a rhythm of continuity that garners disruption into its own flow, as in Marinetti's explosive 'symbol', industrialization in 'Enemy of the Stars' produces two parallel but opposing forces. And because the power of the Super is predicated on subordinating Arghol, his violence is also an investment in maintaining the antagonism; the kick must be dealt 'every day . . . in the same spot'. As Arghol himself comments: 'a superstition—a habit is there, curbing him mathematically: that of not killing me' ('Enemy 2', 164). Absolute supervention can never be attained.

Manifesting a force of re-presentation and abstraction, the secondary attack of pain points the way for the development of a 'literary strike'. After the scene of the beating, Arghol finds himself being accosted by words:

Fungi of sullen violent thoughts, investing primitive vegetation. Hot words drummed on his ear every evening: abuse: question. Groping hands strummed toppling Byzantine organ of his mind, producing monotonous black fugue. . . .

His mind unlocked, free to this violent hand. (*B1*, 65)

The conflict between Arghol and the Super has shifted to a general antagonism in which thoughts and things, mind and body, word and action, are drawn into a general mêlée. Thus, in the tattoo beaten by this linguistic 'strike' there is inscribed a force of disjunction that potentially grows in interstices everywhere. Once again, antagonism produces beneficial separations for Arghol: 'His body was quite strong again and vivacious. Words acted on it as rain on a plant. It got a stormy neat brilliance in this soft shower' (*B1*, 66). And just as

---

[60] Marx argues, for example, that: 'The labour which stands opposite capital is *alien* [*fremde*] labour, and the capital which stands opposite labour is *alien* capital. The extremes which stand opposite one another are *specifically* different' (*Grundrisse: Foundations of the Critique of Political Economy*, trans. by Martin Nicholaus [Harmondsworth: Penguin, 1987], 266, Marx's emphases).

Arghol finds his agency rejuvenated from the conflict, so we find the play's language resolving itself into discrete syntactic units. Lewis's frequent use of parataxis, for example, disrupts the flow of meaning between and within the sentences:

> Mastodons, placid in electric atmosphere, white rivers of power. They stood in eternal black sunlight.
>
> Tigers are beautiful imperfect brutes.
>
> Throats iron eternities, drinking heavy radiance, limbs towers of blatant light, the stars poised, immensely distant, with their metal sides, pantheistic machines. (*B1*, 64)

In order for a relation to exist between two or more entities there must, of necessity, first be a separation. This is what the Vorticist wants to claim for their 'water-tight compartments' and 'adolescent clearness' of extremes. As Pound declares in 'Vortex': 'The vorticist relies not upon similarity or analogy, not upon likeness or mimicry' (*B1*, 154). In the passage above the copula and conjunction have thus become virtually extinct: instead, separation engenders its own aphoristic sense.[61] We can no longer be sure, for example, of stating that 'Mastodons' are being metaphorized into white rivers of power. Both terms are retained as discrete while being held in relation through the interruption of the middle phrase, 'placid in electric atmosphere'. The infinite exchange of values associated with the Futurists' war-commerce process is therefore resisted. This is not to say that the 'pantheistic machines' of the stars are not linked to the universe as a whole, though. The point is that we are offered a production of mass by fragments, rather than mass-produced fragmentation, and there is a world of difference between the two. By granting the breaks their own determinacy, viewing the stars as merely metonymic emanations of the whole is also problematic. In contrast to the relations implicated in metonymy, metaphor, and the basic sentence unit, then, Lewis offers us a syntax of collage instead.[62]

---

[61] Jacques Derrida, in 'Aphorism Countertime', in *Acts of Literature*, trans. by Nicholas Royle, ed. by Derek Attridge (London: Routledge, 1992), writes of the aphorism as an expression of disjunction: 'As its name indicates, aphorism separates, it marks dissociation (*apo*), it terminates, delimits, arrests (*horizó*). It brings to an end by separating, it separates in order to end—and to define [*finir et définir*]' (416).

[62] For Scott Klein, such stylistic avant-gardisme backfires in the play because a phrase like 'throats iron eternities' has no 'objective correlative' ('The Experiment of Vorticist Drama: Wyndham Lewis and "Enemy of the Stars" ', *Twentieth Century Literature* 37: 2 [1991]: 234). Similarly, Reed Way Dasenbrock, in *The Literary Vorticism of Ezra Pound and Wyndham Lewis: Towards the Condition of Painting* (Baltimore: The Johns Hopkins University

The drama of disjunction is developed further through a confrontation between Arghol and Hanp. By now, Arghol's separatism is
becoming supercilious: 'Anything I possess is drunk up here on the
world's brink, by big stars, and returned to me in the shape of thought
heavy as a meteorite' (*B1*, 70), he claims. Hanp, the 'serf of capital',
counters by telling him that his ideas are merely 'buried in yourself',
to which Arghol immediately rejoins: 'A thought weighs less in a million brains than in one. No one is conjuror enough to prevent spilling.
Rather the bastard form infects the original' (*B1*, 70). Like Razumov
in relation to Haldin, rather than acknowledge the metaphysical contradictions in his philosophizing, Arghol transfers the responsibility
for the 'souillure' (soiling) of the soul onto the 'process and condition
of life' (*B1*, 70)—and, more specifically, Hanp. From the accretions of
social frottage, a social 'Self' builds up around the soul. This self,
states Arghol, is 'like murder on my face and hands' (*B1*, 70). An authentic individual soul thus becomes 'the one piece of property all
communities have agreed it is illegal to possess' (*B1*, 66). But having
formed his self-image in relation to the 'Not-self' of Hanp, Arghol realizes that the negativity of their coupling remains an exchange for all
that. As a result, he attempts to transform Hanp into his own mirror
image: 'Every man who wants to make another HIMSELF, is seeking a companion for his detached ailment of a self' (*B1*, 73). But of
course this subjectivity that Arghol seeks to replicate in Hanp has already been subject to social contagion.

Focusing on the relation of individual and collective identity in this
way, the play thus draws Syndicalist detachment into the drama of
forming a Vorticist movement. The sort of truculent detachment that
Lewis later adopted in relation to fellow Vorticists like Pound is reflected in Arghol's growing rejection of Hanp.[63] Unlike Pound, however, Hanp chooses to respond to the breakdown in communication

Press, 1985), argues that the play's stylistics remain entrenched in Futurism, 'Innovating
simply to be modern' (131). My view, however, is that such criticisms fail to take into account the importance of Syndicalist disjunction for Lewis. For responses that do affirm the
play's stylistic/performative difference, see Toby Avard Foshay, 'Wyndham Lewis's Vorticist Metaphysic', *Ariel* 24: 2 (April 1993): 50; and David Graver, 'Vorticist Performance and
Aesthetic Turbulence in *Enemy of the Stars*', *PMLA* 107: 3 (May 1992): 482–96.

[63] In *Blasting and Bombardiering*, Lewis writes: 'It has not to this day, I think, occurred to
Ezra Pound that the authentic revolutionary (not the revolutionary when everyone else is
a revolutionary, but the really sinister and uncommon fellow) will rebel against everything—not least rebellion' (272). In *Rude Assignment*, Lewis also states that he found Pound's
poetic contributions to *Blast* 'compromising': 'I wanted a battering ram that was all metal.
A good deal of what got in seemed to me soft and impure' (138).

with physical violence. But the more Arghol absorbs Hanp's blows, the more he becomes detached, leaving Hanp to fight his own hatred:

> Hanp's punch wore itself out, soon, on herculean clouds, at mad rudder of boat on Arghol. . . .
> Arghol did not hit hard. Like something inanimate, only striking as rebound and as attacked. . . .
> He became part of responsive landscape: his friend's active punch key of the commotion.
> Hanp fell somewhere in the shadow: there lay. *(B1*, 75–6)

Investing his opponent with power by attacking him, Hanp turns Arghol into a vortex of passive resistance. In this way, the play figures a distinct parallel with the transport and industry strikes that gripped Britain between 1911 and 1914. For it was not just the use of violence by Syndicalists that was declared 'terroristic'; the inactivity of strike action was itself seen as a form of indiscriminate warfare. According to *The Spectator*, for example, 'all [the Syndicalists'] recent tactics are essentially a question of war. The Syndicalist workman wants to hit someone or something and does not much care whom or what he hits.'[64] The British government held the same view and frequently suppressed Syndicalist activity by mobilizing the army.[65] As government militancy only increased the resolve of workers to bring about a general strike, though, the potential for workers to paralyse the nation became a very real fear. Similarly, in Lewis's play mass action is explored on an individual level as the impact of Arghol's withdrawal is magnified the more Hanp opposes it. The later version makes this explicit:

> *The Enemy of the Stars has of a sudden become solidary with the massive landscape. Its springs have become his springs, it is he who is now at the heart of its occult resistances. The key to the commotion, the frantic fist of Hanp, drums and taps more erratically upon this elasticated mass he has attacked.* ('Enemy 2', 180, Lewis's emphasis)

At this point, the reader is confronted with a double peripeteia, as both protagonists are repositioned in relation to all of the preceding conflict. While Hanp is knocked unconscious, Arghol returns to the

---

[64] 'Anarchy and Industry', *The Spectator* 4464 (17 January 1914): 174. For other statements on strikes as terrorism, see Harold Cox, 'Holding a Nation to Ransom', *Nineteenth Century* 71 March 1912): 402; W. S. Lilly, 'The Philosophy of Strikes', *Nineteenth Century* 70 (October 1911): 638; 'The Recent Strikes', *Quarterly Review* 215 (November 1912): 578, 592; and 'G.', 'Strikes', *Fortnightly Review* 96 (February 1912): 239.

[65] See Barbara Weinberger, *Keeping the Peace?: Policing Strikes in Britain, 1906–26* (New York: Berg, 1991).

previous events in a dream and revises his understanding of their significance. The scene suddenly shifts to a student room in which there
lies a copy of Stirner's *The Ego and Its Own*.[66] The image reiterates
Arghol's earlier opinion that radical individuality is attained by destroying one's Otherness. More importantly, though, it acknowledges
that this view is someone else's thought. This becomes clear to Arghol
when Stirner himself appears as Hanp. Arghol's reaction is to pay
him to leave and then to throw the books out of the window after a
'scrap' ensues. 'These books are all parasites', he declares, 'eternal
prostitutes' (*B1*, 77). The thoughts which he had believed were
heaven-born now appear to be Other themselves. Arghol's solution is
to try and rid himself of the relation to this other self to the point of
refusing to acknowledge a friend's greeting: 'I am not Arghol', he
replies. But this does not prevent him from seeing that his friend was
'himself', and in recognizing his own difference he arrives at a 'new
state of mind':

> 'I am Arghol'.
> He repeated his name—like sinister word invented to launch a new Soap,
> in gigantic advertisement—toilet-necessity, he, to scrub the soul.
> He had ventured in his solitude and failed. Arghol he had imagined left in
> the city.—Suddenly he had discovered Arghol who had followed him, in
> Hanp. Always a deux [*sic*]! (*B1*, 80).

Arghol's inability to become a hermetically sealed individual is now
viewed as a means of escaping society's totalizing effects. The Otherness he acknowledges in himself is matched by his relation to the perceived autonomy of his own name. Thus, the re-production of egoism
that Arghol grappled with before has been replaced by a notion of
performative iteration in which he retains his own mediating
agency—just as the preceding drama has been re-fashioned through
dream-work.[67]

The entire dream episode is also a reworking of the Vorticist's relation to group mentality. The entrance of Stirner and his text can be
seen as a direct allusion to the ideas set out in the anti-Suffragist jour-

---

[66] Translated into English in 1907, Stirner's book enjoyed a renaissance in Britain
around this time. See Paul Carus, 'Max Stirner, the Predecessor of Nietzsche', *The Monist*
21: 3 (July 1911): 376–97.

[67] In 'Vortex No.1', *Blast 2: War Number*, ed. by Wyndham Lewis (July 1915; Santa Rosa:
Black Sparrow, 1993), Lewis reiterates the need for individual dualism: 'You must talk with
two tongues. . . . You must be a duet in everything. . . . Why try and give the impression
of a consistent and indivisible personality?' (91). *Blast 2* hereafter cited as *B2*.

nal *The Egoist*, which, as I have already stated, carried an advertisement for *Blast* in April 1914. Founded as *The Freewoman* in 1911 by Dora Marsden, it became *The New Freewoman* in 1913, attracting adherents such as Harriet Shaw Weaver and Pound, both of whom helped it to evolve into *The Egoist*. Many of the views espoused in Marsden's journal were close to Lewis's own position. Individuality, for example, is at all times placed above the values of race, nation, and groups generally. Moreover, Stirner's notion of the 'ragamuffin' is offered as the 'ideal citizen' because he is 'devoid of property' and has 'no objections to so being'.[68] In spite of the affirmations of separatism though, *The Egoist* was by no means sympathetic to Syndicalism. Unionism and guilds are denigrated for being as inimical to individual freedom as the state, and strike action also comes under attack, being labelled 'a truly tragic misnomer' because 'hitting' is precisely what it does not do: 'except in the inverted sense—it is the strikers who are hit.'[69] In some respects, Lewis's rejection of group solidarity is no less anti-Syndicalist. Despite recognizing diversity, Arghol still fashions a separatism based on individualism rather than collectivity. But in contrast to *The Egoist* which attacks strike action in general, Lewis sees the strike as a way of figuring a disruptive power for the individual in particular.

Returning to Lewis's play, whereas Arghol revises his earlier position, Hanp, in contrast, awakes with a more furibund resentment—'at Arghol ACTING, he who had not the right to act' (*B1*, 80). Beaten at his own game, the catalyst for Hanp's decision to murder Arghol is the sight of him sleeping and the sound of his 'Bluebottle' snore:

Arghol was glutted with others, in coma of energy.
He had just been feeding on him—Hanp!
He REFUSED to act, almost avowedly to infuriate: prurient contempt.
His physical strength was obnoxious: muscles affecting as flabby fat would in another.
Energetic through self indulgence. (*B1*, 81)

On Hanp's part, there is no understanding that Arghol's individuality is not a negation of his own. While Arghol ends up accepting difference, Hanp's last act is to rid himself of any intimacy by stabbing his Syndicalist foe: 'He could hardly help plunging it in himself, the

[68] 'Views and Comments', *The New Freewoman: An Individualist Review* 6: 1 (1 September 1913): 104.
[69] 'Views and Comments', *The New Freewoman* 8: 1 (15 October 1913): 163–4.

nearest flesh to him' (*B1*, 118). The agency of the action is ambiguous here: rather than finally striking a blow for difference, Hanp kills himself *as* Arghol and is then forced to follow through by committing suicide: 'He sprang from the bridge clumsily . . . his heart a sagging weight of stagnant hatred' (*B1*, 85). The same denouement is retained in the second version: 'Immense relief throughout of the starry universe—congratulating itself heartily upon the news of this political assassination of first-class importance' ('Enemy 2', 191). Thus the antagonism between individualism and social production has become part of a universal conspiracy, a form of systematic terrorism, reflecting Lewis's increasing pessimism over contemporary political life. Indeed, by the beginning of the 1930s he was arguing that 'the truth of the matter is that there is no place to-day for any *individual*, politically, at all, either upon the Right or upon the Left. The *person* is a thing of the past, in public life, as much as in commercial or military life.'[70]

In light of the intricacies of the conflict, and the development of two opposed economies of violence, Klein's concluding summations on the play are problematic in so far as he argues that

by insisting upon its own programmatic unperformability, [it] exposes the degree to which the stylistic experimentation of vorticism is its own unperformable act, containing within itself the failure of its own transcendence— of language, self, and narrative genre.[71]

Certainly, the play does resist traditional performance, but as I have argued, its performativity can also be seen as shifting to a drama between text and reader. Moreover, a large part of the play is precisely about *not working*—being on strike. Viewing the play as a contest between activity (Hanp) and inactivity (Arghol) thus allows us to see Vorticist praxis as being distinct from the type of Futurist agonism that Poggioli and Perloff identify as limiting avant-gardisme to mere rhetorical analogies with physical violence. For Lewis, the detachment of the Vorticist is a violence *of* withdrawal, a terroristic disruption performed by the text, and one that is envisaged as boring spaces of contestation into mass culture. In this sense, the performative separatism of 'Enemy of the Stars' stands in marked contrast to the 'manifest' performativity of the Futurist manifesto which Hewitt views as making capitalist processes inhere in textual production.

---

[70] Wyndham Lewis, *The Diabolical Principle and the Dithyrambic Spectator* (London: Chatto & Windus, 1931), 142, Lewis's emphases.

[71] Klein, 'The Experiment of Vorticist Drama', 238.

Poggioli disagrees, stating that Lewis's Vorticist aesthetic bears the same 'agonism' and 'nihilism' that the Futurists advance.[72] Indeed, Futurism, he argues, is exemplary of the avant-garde's 'self-destructive' tendencies in general; its praxis is essentially 'tragic'.[73] But in 'Enemy of the Stars' it is Hanp who finds himself in a tragedy in which Arghol is refusing to take part. Arghol's arrogation of autonomy elicits in Hanp, the 'serf of capital', his own downfall.

Despite its textual militancy, *Blast*'s publication was received by many critics as more of a fizzle than a bang.[74] But its 'mine-shaft' also tunnelled into the political unconscious—if we can believe Lewis when later recounting Prime Minister Asquith's reaction:

> He smelled politics beneath this revolutionary artistic technique. . . . That it should be suspected that an infernal machine was hidden in the midst of the light-hearted mockery of my propaganda was to me fantastic. I was cross-questioned at length about my principles. I remember especially that he asked me 'whether I was in touch with people of similar views in other countries'. Yes, I admitted, I had corresponded with continental painters, critics and men of letters. . . . It obviously gave him food for thought. Here was a movement making itself beneath the harmless trappings of the fine arts, and camouflaged as a fashionable stunt of the studios, but with wide ramifications in all countries, and with unavowed political objectives. (*Blasting*, 51)

Lewis's incredulity at Asquith's reaction may be more 'light-hearted mockery', but *Blast* itself took satire and humour very seriously, 'English Humour' being simultaneously 'Blessed' and 'Blasted' in the first issue, which also announced in the 'Manifesto' that 'We only want tragedy if it can clench its side muscles like hands on its belly, and bring to the surface a laugh like a bomb' (*B1*, 31). Arghol's snoring is a somnolent form of this laughter: 'terrible, distant, and eccentric', for Hanp it is the epitome of antagonistic inactivity, a form of *actio in distans*: 'Every time [the snoring] rose he gasped, pressing back a clap of laughter' (*B1*, 84). As I have already pointed out, incendiarism was indeed *Blast*'s intended effect for Lewis at the time. In a later comment

---

[72] Poggioli, *Theory of the Avant-Garde*, 74.   [73] Ibid., 69.

[74] The *New York Times*, for example, described the magazine as 'merely a rather dull imitation of Signor Marinetti and his Futurists' ('Vorticism, the Latest Cult of Rebel Artists' [9 August 1914]: 10). R. A. Scott-James in 'Blast', *New Weekly* 2 (4 July 1914), was not so dismissive: 'what is really new about the Vorticists is that whilst they expect you to take them seriously, they engage in propagandism with the combined earnestness and lightheartedness of sportsmen' (88).

on the importance of 'Enemy of the Stars', he claims in no uncertain terms that it had also been revolutionary for modernist practice:

The explosive technique employed, together with the economy of statement, is certainly suggestive of the stage directions in the Walpurgis Nacht fantasia of Mr Joyce. . . . this play of Mr Wyndham Lewis's [*sic*], written and published in 1914, marks, in English letters, together with his novel *Tarr* (pub. 1918) the opening of an epoch.[75]

On another occasion, Lewis informed Ford Madox Ford that such technical warfare undermined all that had gone before it: 'You and Mr Conrad and Mr James and all those fellows are done. . . . Exploded!'[76] But such convictions about his literary impact contrast with Lewis's increasingly jaundiced view about the effects his writings had produced: ' "Kill John Bull with Art!!" I shouted. And John and Mrs Bull leapt for joy, in a cynical convulsion. For they felt safe as houses. So did I' (*Blasting*, 36). As the second version of 'Enemy of the Stars' testifies, though, Lewis did not reject separatist individualism in the face of this impasse; rather, he insisted on it all the more vehemently. What *Blast* failed to achieve in violent upheaval, the war achieved. But Lewis had never wanted actual war or revolution. He wanted a space of individualism because he saw this to be the only form of radical politics left. And in this respect, Asquith's reported comments only confirmed Lewis's contention: to be a real social outsider is itself potentially terroristic.

In the last chapter, I argued that Conrad's entropolitics and spectrality problematize the rigid, structural relations between terror, violence, and mediation that many terrorologists have been invested in defending. But containing the complexity of terrorism by figuring it essentially as a fiction, media event, or propaganda can also increase the impact of its perceived 'Otherness', and certainly does not mean that the mediated images and discourses do not carry their own exacerbating affects. The creation of a violence that is not merely a metaphoric gesture but has material consequences is precisely what Lewis's literary strike is about. Whereas Conrad figures phantasmal 'immediations' in which violence and terror, physicality and psychology, are subject to mutual contagion, Lewis wants a disjunctive textuality as a form of violence in itself. And as he becomes more

---

[75] Quoted in Munton, *Wyndham Lewis*, 221–2n.
[76] Quoted in Jeffrey Myers, *The Enemy* (London: Routledge & Kegan Paul, 1980), 29.

convinced of the individual's opposition to society in general, so his avant-gardisme becomes increasingly terroristic.

Vorticism and Suffragette Violence

While the 'literary strike' was aimed at resisting the production of social masses, Lewis gradually boils down his 'enemy' aesthetics into a confrontation between the individual artist and the mob. Instead of affirming a Syndicalist 'horizontal diversity' between specific groups or social discourses, he begins to figure society as a single, inert mass so that he stands out more violently in his detachment. The result is a duplicitous allegorizing. On the one hand, Lewis relates the production of the social mass to a disparate assortment of things and concepts: democracy, time, nature, matter, automation. Yet on the other hand, all of these elements are rolled into one generalized figure that is presented as having no intellectual or political agency at all: the mass-female. The body-politic is thus figuratively gathered into vassalage and contrasted with the avant-gardist's regal detachment. This strategy is already evident in *Blast 2*, in which Vorticism, surrounded by the war's 'multitude of other Blasts',[77] turns up the nationalist heat. 'The universal artist, in fact, is in the exactest sense national', argues Lewis in the 'Editorial': 'He gathers into one all the types of humanity at large that each country contains' *(B2, 5)*. Rather than representing the national spirit, for Lewis the true avant-gardist takes possession of it. Just as Sorel had moved towards a proto-Fascist nationalism, then, so does Lewis. Moreover, asserting a 'hierarchy of power and vitality' is directly linked by him in *Blast 2* to en-gendering fundamental divisions—for example, between the individual artist and the 'suburban Matron' of 'Nature' *(B2, 70)*. Similarly, in *Time and Western Man*, the very distinction between time and space is translated into a domestic squabble: 'the wedding of these two abstractions result, as we believe (as a triumphant feminism would result not in equality but in feminine ascendancy) in the ascendency of Time (which also happens to be the feminine principle in this partnership)' *(TWM, 417)*.[78]

---

[77] Lewis, 'Editorial', *B2*, 5.

[78] In *The Art of Being Ruled*, Lewis also asserts that power and class distinctions are based on sexual difference: 'The divisions between rulers and ruled partakes of a sexual division; or rather the contrast between one class and the other is more like that between the sexes than anything else. The ruled are the females and the rulers the males . . .' *(ABR, 95)*.

Lewis's allegorizing, true to the term's etymology, is fundamentally a matter of *making other* (*allos agoruein* in Greek means 'saying other'). Yet his use of the figure is complex in its reductiveness. By configuring a disparate set of elements into one mass, the enemy is made both impersonal, generalized, *and* interpersonal—involving a single Other. All of the social progeny Lewis traduces thus become orphaned manifestations of a higher power-matrix, which is in turn reduced to a single figurative concept. When writing of feminism and homosexuality, for example, Lewis asks: 'Is it not the same old hag that in a "morality" would be labelled Power . . . who has pupped this batch of fashions?' (*ABR*, 241). Comments like these draw together two forms of violence, rhetorical and critical, that have been attributed to allegory by literary critics. For John Crowe Ransom, allegory's categorizing makes it 'militant, always sciencing and devouring',[79] a point that is reiterated by Julie Ellison: 'Overly organized reductive meaning is . . . the source of [its] aggressiveness.'[80] In contrast, Walter Benjamin in *The Origin of German Tragic Drama* (written during the Great War) associates it with a critical capacity for figuring historical rupture because it presents disjunctions between characters and what they represent: 'Whereas in symbol, destruction is idealized and the transfigured face of nature is fleetingly revealed in the light of redemption, in allegory the observer is confronted by . . . history as petrified primordial landscape'.[81] With Lewis, then, not only is allegory presented as a form of descriptive critique, it also offered as proactive rhetorical attack.

As far as Fredric Jameson is concerned, Lewis's use of the figure is an attempt to depict a 'more complicated allegorical system' that can respond to capitalism's suffusion of the nation-state.[82] But the ultimate force acting on the body-politic is frequently made ambiguous by Lewis. Presenting either a grouping or a dispersal of power, the dual nature of his allegorizing enables him to fight his foe(s) on at least two fronts. In *The Art of Being Ruled*, for example, Lewis attacks the idea that the social body is controlled by a higher power: 'often things are put down to some alien natural force of fatal *growth* which are really less anonymous' (*ABR*, 37, Lewis's emphasis). Similarly, in *Time*

[79] John Crowe Ransom, 'Poetry: A Note in Ontology', in *Critical Theory Since Plato*, ed. by Hazard Adams (New York: Harcourt, 1971), 87.

[80] Julie Ellison, 'Aggressive Allegory', *Raritan* 3: 3 (Winter 1984): 104.

[81] Walter Benjamin, *The Origin of German Tragic Drama*, trans. by John Osborne (London: Verso, 1990), 166.

[82] See Fredric Jameson, *Fables of Aggression: Wyndham Lewis, the Modernist as Fascist* (Berkeley: University of California Press, 1979), 90–4.

and Western Man, he argues that if 'Will' is transcendent it is ridiculous to claim that it 'produces Charlie Chaplin, the League of Nations, wireless, feminism, Rockefeller . . . [and] millions of women to drift in front of, and swarm inside, gigantic clothes shops in every great capital . . .' (*TWM*, 312). At other points, though, social life in general is enveloped within abstraction, as when he argues that the 'Great war', the 'class war', and the 'sex war' are all instances of social bodies struggling after a power of 'freedom', which, he claims, is a 'feminine conception' (*ABR*, 269). Asserting that the diversity of strife operates *as* a process of allegorizing, he can thus claim a real power of mediation for the writer.

Lewis's own conception of allegory as cultural violation is made explicit by him in an essay, 'The Foxes' Case', in which a hypothetical confrontation of writer and society is depicted as a rape:

> The meeting would end in a barren police-court outrage. A kind of free fight would occur, accompanied by a discharge; armed with contraceptives, the world would remain triumphantly sterile, and with her mighty female fist hurl the impossible creator back into chaos. . . . the creator is either gloriously acquitted of humbug and rape, and pronounced by posterity a most fertile person, and his methods dignified as acts of necessary violence, or legitimate coyness; or (under a battery of microscopes) his seed is found wanting, he is branded as an impostor, his effigy is publicly burnt, his books perish, his squirrel-like methods are pronounced an unpardonable bluff, and that is the end of him.[83]

Like the scene between Peter Ivanovitch and Tekla in *Under Western Eyes*, Lewis predicates the male writer's power on his creation of a sterile, female addressee, but in a much more extreme fashion. Terroristic violence and sexual assault have become indistinguishable, and it is the writer, supposedly, who authorizes the conjunction. The index of authentic violence is not physical force, then, so much as the degree of an individual's detachment from the mob. This is what Lewis, in *Blast 1*, argued that the militant Suffragettes, who were at the time destroying a range of cultural property, had not yet grasped:

---

[83] Lewis, 'The Foxes' Case', in Wyndham Lewis, *Creatures of Habit and Creatures of Change: Essays on Art, Literature and Society, 1914–1956*, ed. by Paul Edwards (Santa Rosa: Black Sparrow, 1989), 123.

TO SUFFRAGETTES.

A WORD OF ADVICE.

IN DESTRUCTION, AS IN OTHER THINGS,

stick to what you understand.

WE MAKE YOU A PRESENT OF OUR VOTES.

ONLY LEAVE WORKS OF ART ALONE.

YOU MIGHT SOME DAY DESTROY A

GOOD PICTURE BY ACCIDENT.

THEN!—

MAIS SOYEZ BONNES FILLES!

NOUS VOUS AIMONS!

WE ADMIRE YOUR ENERGY. YOU AND ARTISTS

ARE THE ONLY THINGS (YOU DON'T MIND

BEING CALLED THINGS?) LEFT IN ENGLAND

WITH A LITTLE LIFE IN THEM.

IF YOU DESTROY A GREAT WORK OF ART you

are destroying a greater soul than if you

annihilated a whole district of London.

LEAVE ART ALONE BRAVE COMRADES!   (B1, 151–2)

The fear of paintings being damaged is not the main thing voiced here; rather, it is the fear that the Suffragettes' militancy might be doing a better job of avant-garde activism than the Vorticists'. The patronizing offer of 'our votes' is effectively a denial of access to avant-garde citizenship, allowing the Suffragettes to become absorbed into the masses that the Vorticist scorns. Art would thus be retained for the select few who would also secure the rights to authentic political representation. Allowing that the great 'soul' of art is linked to its materiality, however, only lends credibility to the effectiveness of the Suffragettes' 'energy'. The Vorticists' address thus produces its own confusion, hovering between admiration and derision.

To what extent can the Suffragettes be seen as a competing avant-garde movement, then? Do they share with the Vorticists a common militant 'energy'?

It was certainly the case that the Suffragettes combined attacks on injustices of political representation with assaults on representation more generally. Militancy was inaugurated as a Suffragette tactic in 1905 after Christabel Pankhurst and Annie Kenney, members of the 'Women's Social and Political Union' (WSPU), were thrown out of the Manchester Free Trade Hall by Liberal Party stewards after refusing to leave until their demands for female suffrage were heard.[84] Once outside the hall, Pankhurst ensured her arrest by spitting on a policeman. It was the first move towards the campaign of 'propaganda by deed' through which the Suffragettes distinguished themselves from the female 'Suffragists' who were opposed to the use of physical force. In the years following, Asquith's Liberal government flirted with limited female suffrage but prevented any Bills extending the franchise to women from being passed. The Conciliation Bill, which would have introduced political representation for some women, was 'torpedoed' in March 1912 by the Prime Minister, who announced that it would be appended to another male Franchise Bill—knowing that such a general increase would never be countenanced by parliament.[85] Consequently, Suffragette militancy began in earnest. From her exile in Paris, Christabel Pankhurst ordered a protracted campaign of bombing, arson, and general sabotage.

By restricting their targets to property, the Suffragettes were, in effect, attacking their own perceived position as chattels of a male-dominated state. As a member of the WSPU explained to the jury when being prosecuted for attacking letterboxes: 'This is a women's war, in which we hold human life dear and property cheap. . . . Attack man's god of property if that is the last resource to rouse him to think and act on behalf of the oppressed women of this country.'[86] Intensive window smashing commenced in London on 1 March 1912 after which havoc was wreaked around the country—all of which was assiduously recorded in the 'Militancy This Week' sections of the WSPU journal, *The Suffragette*. The palaces of Hampton Court, Kew, Kensington, and Holyrood were attacked; bombs were discovered outside the Bank of England and Wheatley Hall in Doncaster; Prime Minister Asquith's country home was set fire to; telegraph wires were cut; acid was poured into letter-boxes; and golf greens were vandalized with messages such as 'Votes or War' burned into the turf.[87] By

---

[84] See Susan Kingly Kent, *Sex and Suffrage in Britain, 1860-1914* (Princeton: Princeton University Press, 1987), 170-3.

[85] Before the war, only 60 per cent of adult males were on the parliamentary register. Regarding electoral legislation, see Dangerfield, *The Strange Death of Liberal England*, 145-53; Antonia Raeburn, *The Militant Suffragettes* (London: Joseph, 1973), 161-4; and Sandra Stanley Holton, *Feminism and Democracy: Women's Suffrage and Reform Politics in Britain, 1900-18* (Cambridge: Cambridge University Press, 1986), 70-6.

[86] Quoted in 'Pillar Box Trial at the Old Bailey', *The Suffragette*, ed. by Christabel Pankhurst, 1: 13 (10 January 1913): 184.

[87] See Brian Harrison, 'The Act of Militancy, Violence and the Suffragettes, 1904-14', in *Peaceable Kingdom: Stability and Change in Modern Britain* (Oxford: Clarendon, 1982), 26-81;

the end of 1913 over £500,000 worth of damage had been caused by arson alone.[88] For all its devastating impact, though, Suffragette militancy exploded onto the national scene into a cloud of legal and political ambivalence. This was in part a result of the Suffragettes' own equivocation as to the status of their acts. In demanding to be recognized as political offenders, they actively compared their actions to the militancy of those defending Irish Home Rule: 'Even the armed rebels of Ulster do not expect to defeat the British army in open combat. What they do expect is to create a most unpleasant situation. Surely women can do that!'[89] Militant suffragism was thus declared to be the 'advance-guard of the new womanhood' by Christabel Pankhurst, a 'guerrilla warfare' of systematic terrorizing.[90] The women involved in arson attacks, she stated, 'must escape from the scene of outrage unnoticed; fires, rising at unexpected moments and in unlikely places, must produce the effect of a secret and healthy terror.'[91]

Comparing their tactics to the violence in Ireland was of strategic importance because the Irish movement was frequently viewed as having a more manifest political content.[92] *The Suffragette*, for example, quotes Lord Robert Cecil as arguing that: 'The members of the Women's Social and Political Union are fond of comparing themselves to rebels. But they forget that rebellion and terrorism are entirely distinct.'[93] He elaborates the distinction by contrasting Suffragettes to the 'Ulstermen' who, he says, 'mean to get some form of Government in North-East Ireland independent of Home Rule, and are certainly not less careful to maintain law and order'.[94] At-

---

also Dangerfield, *The Strange Death of Liberal England*, 153–63; and Raeburn, *The Militant Suffragettes*, 184–90.

[88] Dangerfield, *The Strange Death of Liberal England*, 172.

[89] Christabel Pankhurst, 'Militancy: A Virtue', *The Suffragette* 1: 13 (10 January 1913): 186. Regarding the legal and political problems faced by the Suffragettes as compared to the nineteenth-century Fenians, see Radzinowicz and Hood, *A History of English Criminal Law*, 439–61.

[90] See 'Foreword', *The Suffragette* 1: 1 (18 October 1912): 1.

[91] Quoted in Dangerfield, *The Strange Death of Liberal England*, 153.

[92] In her autobiography, *Unshackled: The Story of How We Won the Vote* (London: Hutchinson, 1959), Christabel Pankhurst makes explicit the motivations behind drawing a parallel between the movements: 'It was not that we were concerned to question or assert the moral justification of Ulster's militancy, actual or prospective, but we did claim the same immunity from prosecution and imprisonment for militant women whose grievance was at least equal and whose militancy was far milder' (216).

[93] Quoted in Christabel Pankhurst, 'Standards of Morality', *The Suffragette* 1: 25 (4 April 1913): 404.

[94] Ibid.

tacking the power of the parliament in which they had no share, the militancy of the Suffragettes could thus be interpreted as anti-political and therefore 'terrorist'. Furthermore, while the Irish Home Rule insurgents had also been denied political status, the fact that they attacked *people* led to their tactics being recognized as proper *political* warfare.' In *The English Review*, for example, a commentator using the pseudonym 'Cornelia' criticized the Suffragettes for not attacking bodies: '*À la guerre, comme à la guerre*. Blood for blood. That would at least be militancy, though, of course, indescribably silly because impotent.'[95] Reactions like these subsequently provoked Christabel Pankhurst to reject comparisons to the campaign in Ireland—precisely because Home Rule militancy both in its masculinity and its methods was more readily coded into a parliamentary platform. By resolving not to attack bodies, though, the Suffragettes highlighted the problem of their own status within the body-politic all the more effectively. The outlaw status they acquired was also viewed as legitimating further activism. 'As well they might argue with Nature and her laws', wrote Christabel Pankhurst of the government's declamations: 'Militant Suffragists owe no allegiances to public opinion; our task is to alter public opinion.'[96] Alienating the WSPU thus had the effect of endowing it with the sort of independence that Lewis himself wished to possess: 'The Suffragettes as the fighting force—the advance guard—necessarily stand alone. Theirs is a glorious isolation—the splendour of independent strength.'[97] And *Blast* certainly never attained the outlaw status that *The Suffragette* did when the British government called for its suppression in 1913 and then incarcerated some of those involved in its production as 'conspirators'.[98]

The ambivalence and tension involved in repressing the force of Suffragette activities is particularly evident in press commentary of the time. *Punch* in 1913 allegorized the campaign as a matter of household disorganization, representing it variously as a female arsonist who has mislaid her matches, or whose kitchen fire will not light.[99] Like the Vorticists' condescension, *Punch* ridicules the Suffragettes'

[95] 'Cornelia', 'Epidemic Hysteria', *The English Review* 17 (July 1914): 500.
[96] Christabel Pankhurst, 'Militant Methods' (1909), in *Suffrage and the Pankhursts*, ed. by Jane Marcus (London: Routledge & Kegan Paul, 1987), 123.
[97] 'The Inner Policy of the W.S.P.U.', *The Suffragette* 2: 68 (30 January 1914): 353.
[98] The trial provoked a rally of 30,000 to demonstrate for free speech in Trafalgar Square—see Raeburn, *The Militant Suffragettes*, 199–203.
[99] See Lisa Tickner, *The Spectacle of Women: Imagery of the Suffrage Campaign, 1907–14* (London: Chatto & Windus, 1987): 205–6.

activism by incarcerating it within a domestic space and so sealing it off from the political arena. In contrast to such trivializing, however, there were also assertions of Suffragette actions as being totally trans-gressive—particularly when they involved valuable cultural artefacts. The attacks on art that Lewis abjured were certainly intended by Suf-fragettes to be spectacular forms of violence: thirteen paintings were slashed in the Manchester Art Gallery on 1 April 1913; Sargent's por-trait of Henry James hanging at the Royal Academy was attacked on 4 May 1914; five more in the Venetian Room of the National Gallery were damaged on 21 May, as was Richard Clausen's 'Primavera' at the Royal Academy.[100] But it was Mary Richardson's attack on Velazquez's 'Rokeby Venus' that drew the most incensed response: 'Perhaps no other act of militancy has ever caused so much comment in the press and amongst the public',[101] declared *The Suffragette*. For Richardson this attack on cultural capital was a direct action against 'Justice' itself:

Justice is an element of beauty as much as colour and outline on canvas . . . if there is an outcry at my deed, let everyone remember that such an outcry is an hypocrisy as long as they allow the destruction of Mrs Pankhurst and other beautiful living women . . . [102]

Richardson's anger is directed against the policy of forcible feeding that the government supported in dealing with gaoled Suffragettes who went on hunger strike.[103] By asserting that the state's relation to the bodies inhabiting it is analogous to the artwork's relation to its constitutive materiality, Richardson sees her act as challenging the government's ability to remain impervious to physical force. In this sense, the slashing of Venus for her becomes an allegorical refiguring, an attack on the state's perceived conception of its female subjects as objects.

That Richardson was sentenced to six months' imprisonment, the maximum for attacking art, as opposed to eighteen months for de-stroying property, shows the extent to which her attack was difficult

---

[100] See *The Annual Register 1913: A Review of Public Events at Home and Abroad* (London: Longman's, 1914), 55, and *The Annual Register 1914* (London: Longman's, 1915), 13, 15, 113.
[101] 'Retribution', *The Suffragette* 2: 74 (13 March 1914): 491.
[102] Ibid. See also Mary Richardson's account of the attack in her *Laugh a Defiance* (London: George Weidenfeld & Nicolson, 1953), ch. 53.
[103] For an account of forcible feeding and the government's general reaction to the Suf-fragettes' hunger-striking, see Sylvia Pankhurst, *The Suffragette Movement: An Intimate Account of Persons and Ideals* (1931; London: Virago, 1977), 300–20, 438–54, 471–91.

for the law to judge. As far as *The Times* was concerned, the symbolic value of the painting only made the crime more viscerally brutal: 'What is described by one who afterwards saw the damaged masterpiece as probably the most serious blow has caused a cruel blow to the neck. . . . The other cuts are cleanly made in the region of the waist.'[104] The attack on a figure of supreme beauty is thus imagined as an act of supreme violence. Far from demonstrating that women were incapable of exercising real force, then, the attacks on art showed the degree to which destroying cultural capital could indeed be a way of striking out for justice. As the Suffragette Maud Arncliff-Sennet commented, the fight for the right to allegorize was essential for the determination of the movement: '*More Allegories!!* They label Women—Liberty, Justice, Humanity & rob her of every power in these abstract names.'[105] As Benjamin writes on allegory's division of power: 'For the thing possessed, representation is secondary; it does not have prior existence as something representing itself.'[106] This is what many women's Suffragist groups attempted to correct by reclaiming a variety of mythic and allegorical female figures—Athena, Boadicea, and Justice featuring prominently. WSPU rallies were also frequently led by women dressed as Joan of Arc, whom Christabel Pankhurst declared to be the movement's 'patron saint', and *The Suffragette* offered its own fighting figure: 'Justice herself is become a Suffragette and leaving judges and legislators, her accustomed ministers, in the lurch, she befriends the militants.'[107] As Lisa Tickner argues, 'The task for suffrage art and rhetoric . . . was to reinhabit the empty body of female allegory, to reclaim its meanings on behalf of the female sex.'[108] Much of the militant rhetoric also sought to defend woman's sacred status. A group calling themselves 'The New Crusaders' wore royal purple mantles and claimed to symbolize 'the militant and idealistic organization of women in a Holy war, to reassert the rights to possess the Sacred Places'.[109] In contrast, the 'National Union of Women's Suffrage Societies' (NUWSS), a moderate Suffragist group that opposed militancy, offered their 'Bugler Girl' as an

---

[104] 'National Gallery Outrage', *The Times* (11 March 1914): 9. The description of the damage done to Henry James's portrait is similar in tone: 'The picture, which was covered by glass, was badly cut in three places, on the left side of the head, on the right side of the mouth, and below the right shoulder' ('Academy Outrage', *The Times* [5 May 1914]: 8).

[105] Quoted in Tickner, *The Spectacle of Women*, 205, Sennet's emphasis.

[106] Benjamin, *Origins of Tragic Drama*, 29.

[107] 'The Majesty of the Law', *The Suffragette* 1: 22 (14 March 1913): 341.

[108] Tickner, *The Spectacle of Women*, 209.   [109] Quoted ibid., 25.

alternative. Inspired by Elizabeth Barrett Browning's poem 'Now Press The Clarion to Thy Woman's Lip', as Tickner points out, 'Bugler Girl' is a paragon of womanly virtue:

> Does she represent Joan of Arc? No—except as far as Joan of Arc herself embodies for women the spirit of courage and love . . . our Bugler Girl carries her bugle and her banner; her sword is sheathed by her side; it is there but not drawn, and if it were drawn it would not be the sword of the flesh but of the spirit.[110]

So while both militant and non-militant groups used allegorizing to assert their collective agency, there were marked differences in how they linked it to political stances.[111]

For Lewis, the Suffragettes are to be dismissed because all of their radicalism is nevertheless an investment in liberal democracy. Between the Vorticists' and the Suffragettes' allegories there is thus a conflict of interests. Suffragette militancy was seeking to attack the parliamentary control of discourse which ensured that their speeches and actions bore no socio-political significance. In contrast, Lewis's avant-garde militancy affirms such a state of affairs: the only significant socio-political force is aesthetic, and the only significant aesthete is the Vorticist. Janet Lyon's reading of the relation between the Vorticists and Suffragettes is thus problematic in so far as the distinction she draws between them becomes reducible to an opposition of rhetoric and action, respectively. For Lyon, this opposition was foregrounded by the press, which commonly represented avant-gardism as 'frustrating and distressing', and Suffragette militancy as 'positively dangerous'.[112] But this does not account for the press's concerted trivializing of the Suffragettes, or for the extent to which Suffragism had to fight representation more generally. As Susan Kingly Kent has argued:

> The effectiveness of [the Suffragettes'] militant propaganda had at some point to be determined by the extent to which it could retain its status as *political* representation and activity, and not be reduced—the cause and the adherents along with it—to the category of feminine hysteria.[113]

---

[110] Quoted in Tickner, *The Spectacle of Women*, 210.
[111] Concerning the diverse arguments used by anti-Suffragists to support political divisiveness between the sexes, see Brian Harrison, *Separate Spheres: The Opposition to Women's Suffrage in Britain* (London: Croom Helm, 1978).
[112] Lyon, *Manifestoes*, 104.
[113] Kent, *Sex and Suffrage in Britain*, 200, Kent's emphasis.

In arguing that 'the WSPU's militant speech acts took as their referents the bodies of WSPU members' by inciting action whereas 'the militant discourse of Lewis and Pound was confined mostly to the page',[114] Lyon obscures the more general power struggle involved in the right to allegorize. Moreover, as Lewis's writerly rape in 'The Foxes' Case' suggests, his own ideas of avant-gardism did not rule out assaults on bodies. Indeed, at points in *Blast 2* the referents of his barbs are figured as the bodies of Suffragists in general.

'The Crowd Master'

Lewis's 'The Crowd Master', first published in *Blast 2* and then rewritten in *Blasting and Bombardiering*, stages confrontations between militancy and mass production, physical and discursive violence, explicitly around the issue of suffrage. In the *Blast 2* version the scene opens in London in July 1914 with the spectacle of an immense mob gathering—the mobilization for war:

THE POLICE with distant icy contempt herd London. They shift it in lumps here and there, touching and shaping with heavy delicate professional fingers. Their attitude is as though these universal crowds wanted some new vague Suffrage. (*B2*, 94)

The mass grouping here is aligned with political passivity; the crowd waits for power to be donated: 'Some tiny grain of suffrage will perhaps be thrown to the millions in the street or taken away (*B2*, 94). If 'THE CROWD is the first mobilisation of a country' (*B2*, 94), then this mobilization is also a nationalized division of power. Lewis's portrayal of the event thus herds a number of issues together. First, in comparing the individuals mobilized for war with Suffragist demonstrations, Lewis refuses to acknowledge the essential political difference between them. Suffrage demonstrations by women—involving the largest crowds recorded in history up to that point—were necessary because one of the reasons cited for not granting women political representation was that they would be incapable of physically enforcing laws.[115] In contrast, the fighting ability of soldiers was viewed as a reason for giving them more rights—as when demands

---

[114] Lyon, *Manifestoes*, 105.

[115] Regarding Suffragist crowd sizes, see Raeburn, *The Militant Suffragettes*, 200. On physical force and the legitimate right to representation, see Martin Pugh, *Electoral Reform in War and Peace, 1906–18* (London: Routledge & Kegan Paul, 1978), 140–53; Kent, *Sex and Suffrage in Britain*, 174–82; and Harrison, *Separate Spheres*, 34–60.

were made in parliament to extend the franchise to individuals who had fought for their country.[116] But Lewis's strategy is to diminish the spectacles of both mobilization and Suffragism by presenting them as equally mass-produced and passive. Authentic national representation is thus figured as being policed over by the Vorticist himself. As Lewis contends in *Blast 1*: 'In France no Artist is as good as "the Policeman" . . . the Artist in England has the advantages and gifts possessed by the Policeman in France' (*B1*, 137). It is the Vorticist himself, then, who is supposedly behind the 'touching and shaping' of the crowd, feeding off the difference: 'There is Yourself and there is the Exterior World, that fat mass you browse on. You knead it into an amorphous representation of yourself inside yourself.'[117]

In 'The Crowd Master', though, the Vorticist's single-handed attempt at crowd control is in competition with that of the press:

THE NEWSPAPERS already smell carrion. They allow themselves almost BLAST type already.

Prussia was invented for Newspaper proprietors. Her theatrical instinct has saved the crowd from breaking up for twenty years.   (*B2*, 94)

In this sense, there is a reversal; the war has been mobilized by the press for the crowd. Consequently, the slaughter of war is seen as being secondary to the violence involved in mashing the individual into a mass. Despite the fact that the crowd seems to be 'an immense anaesthetic towards death', 'Death is . . . only a form of crowd' (*B2*, 94), we are told. And the more disaster is commodified, the more it becomes simply a form of popular entertainment. Having made the initial 'dramatic Suffragette analogy', Lewis then declares the 'crude violet lettering' of posters announcing popular events to be a 'distillation of 1905–1915: Suffragism. H. G. Wells. Morpeth Olympiads' (*B2*, 95). In this sense, Suffragism is imagined as having become a form of mass seduction. 'Are the crowds female?' asks Lewis in the second version—the answer is given categorically when he allegorizes a confrontation between 'The Bachelor' individual and 'the Husband Crowd' (*B2*, 94). The second version gives a fuller account of the disparity, in which the story's protagonist, Cantleman, (called 'Blenner' in the first version) immerses himself in the throng:

Suddenly he experienced a distinct and he believed *authentic shock*. It could only come from the crowd! Evidently he had penetrated its mind—the cer-

---

[116] Pugh, *Electoral Reform in War and Peace*, 145.   [117] Lewis, 'Vortex No. 1', *B2*, 91.

ebration of this jelly fish! Hence the sting! He had received his first novel sensation. What was it exactly—could he define it? Well, it seemed to be that he was a *married man.*

Unquestionably he possessed, and with extreme suddenness at that, *that married feeling.* . . . He immediately withdrew from the crowd. (*Blasting,* 81, Lewis's emphases)

Cantleman cannot ascribe his own sense of detachment to others, for this would mean having to accept that the crowd itself is made up of individuals—rather than being an agglomeration of jellyfish incapable of distinguishing themselves from sea. He is therefore caught in a double-bind of having to receive his own 'shock' as Other, coming 'from the crowd', while nevertheless resisting any transference of experience. It is the staging of a mystical writing pad as a national event. The analogy is made by Lewis in the second version: 'He interpreted the [crowd's] messages. Like the spirit writing of the planchette pencil, they were exceedingly stupid' (*Blasting,* 80). The writing of a planchette is dictated: consisting of a small board on coasters that holds a pencil over a sheet of paper, the planchette was designed to be held by one or two spiritual mediums, thereby making it responsive to any tremor from the other world.[118] For Lewis, the crowd is a medium that has no real hand in determining its messages; the 'stupid' writing that Cantleman interprets has already been dictated by the newspapers. But in placing himself as a medium in relation to the crowd, this writing is inevitably inscribed in his own consciousness. The amorphous 'character' of the unconscious 'exterior' is thus recognized because it is internalized.

Freud, in his 'Note on the Mystic Writing Pad' (1925), also argues that the purity of perception depends on its being separable from the unconscious. Using the mystic writing pad as an analogy for the psychology of the subject, he sketches a one-way system. Consisting of one layer of celluloid (perception) and one of wax-paper (consciousness) both of which cover a slab of wax (the unconscious), the wax-paper can receive impressions through the celluloid when it is in contact with the wax, but if the paper is lifted off with the celluloid, 'the writing vanishes and . . . does not appear again'.[119] What Freud

[118] Rainey discusses the planchette in relation to automatic writing, psychical research, Futurism, and Mussolini, in 'Taking Dictation', 128–48.

[119] Sigmund Freud, 'A Note upon the "Mystic Writing Pad" ', in *The Standard Edition of the Complete Psychological Works of Sigmund Freud,* trans. by James Strachey, 24 vols. (London: Hogarth and the Institute of Pschoanalysis, 1961), xix: 227.

does not acknowledge is that the consciousness of an impression can thus only arise when it is contiguous with, and conserved in, the unconscious.[120] Cantleman's interpretation of the planchette pencil is just as problematic. According to Lewis elsewhere, authentic consciousness depends on its detachment, for it is 'in our "Unconscious" that we live in a state of common humanity' (*TWM*, 301). Yet in *Blast 1* he also opines that: 'WE NEED THE UNCONSCIOUSNESS OF HUMANITY—their stupidity, animalism and dreams.'[121] In 'The Crowd Master' we are thus offered a vacillation between an experience of separation and the splitting of experience itself: 'The Crowd surged into him from these sheets of inconceivable news. . . . You seemed to swim in it outside' (*B2*, 99). Lewis, though, naturally inclines towards the separatism; it is the masses who lack conscious will: 'Great National events are always preparing, the Crowd is in its habitual childish sleep. It rises to meet the crash half awake . . . struggling, with voluptuous and violent movements' (*B2*, 98). The second version is more explicit: 'It is the Rape of the Crowd' (*Blasting*, 77). The Vorticist with his prophylactic consciousness is thus the only person capable of critique. Pretending to be as inactive as the medium holding the planchette, he secretly exerts all his force in scrawling violation over everyone.

For Lewis, the crowd's impotence lies in its incapacity to allegorize a separation between self and Other. All it can produce is a sense of conjugality: 'The Married Man is the Symbol of the Crowd' (*B2*, 94). But in spite of Lewis's insistence on individualist originality, all of this general categorizing is a close replication of Gustave Le Bon's foray into mass psychology that he presents in *The Crowd: A Study of the Popular Mind* (1896). Like Lewis, Le Bon also associates crowds with contagious unconsciousness, the sacrifice of individual agency, and the sort of general behaviour that belongs to 'inferior forms of evolution—in women, in savages, and children, for instance'.[122] Furthermore, Lewis's portrayal of the feminized crowd as being unable to distinguish between actual events and the hysteria of headlines also

---

[120] See also Jacques Derrida's analysis of Freud's essay in 'Freud and the Scene of Writing', in *Writing and Difference*, trans. by Alan Bass (Chicago: University of Chicago Press, 1978), 221–31.

[121] Lewis, 'Long Live the Vortex!', *B1*, 7.

[122] Gustave Le Bon, *The Crowd: A Study of the Popular Mind*, trans. by Robert K. Merton (New York: Penguin, 1977), 16. On Freud's relation to Le Bon in terms of subjectivity and politics, see Mikkel Borch-Jacobsen, *The Freudian Subject* (1982; Basingstoke: Macmillan, 1989), 137–46.

has a precedent in the work of Maurras, who, in *The Future Intelligence* (1905), declares that 'It is a womanly pleasure to handle words like material.'[123] Such misogyny in the name of progressive modernism was a position also adopted by the Futurists, although Marinetti himself seized the opportunity to take part in mass disturbance in March 1912 by marching with the Suffragettes in London.[124] So far as the Suffragettes were concerned, though, treating words like material could be decidedly subversive, as they attempted to show in their attacks on the public's mail: 'Letters a conglomerated Mass', declared a headline in *The Suffragette* after a series of assaults on letter-boxes.[125] In contrast, for Lewis, linking writing's impact to detachment and abstraction makes it *megaphonic*. Once the clamour of crowds has been reduced to a general babble, only the voice of the Vorticist remains to be heard distinctly.

The correlation of writing and crowd control is made further apparent in the first version of 'The Crowd Master' when Blenner recalls buying a book called 'The Crowd Master' by an American, 'Brown Bryan Multum', from 'The Bomb Shop' in Charing Cross Road. The book's title suggests to Blenner a new revolutionary mindset: 'An opposition of and welding of the two heaviest words that stand for the multitude on the one hand, the Ego on the other' (*B2*, 99). Having posed the question of whether this meant 'a possessive domination by the individual', we are then given a brief outline of the text's ideology:

> This American book spoke of the 'soft conservatisms' of England as the really barbarous things, 'the anarchy and confusion of Past-Living'. It opposed to the English tory, a sort of Red Indian machine, with a soul like Walt Whitman . . .[126] (*B2*, 100)

Sympathetic to this cultural critique, Blenner is nevertheless hesitant about accepting it from an American: 'An American was—well, we

---

[123] Charles Maurras, *L'Avenir de l'intelligence* (1905; Paris: Flammarion, 1927), 214. See also Peter Nicholls, 'Futurism, Gender, and Theories of Postmodernity', *Textual Practice* 3: 2 (Summer 1989): 202–21.

[124] In Lewis's later version of 'The Crowd Master' he declares that Cantleman himself is essentially 'a suffragette' before explaining that: 'I've just put this in. The editor of *Blast* would never have admitted he was a suffragette. I've had to put a lot more in, too. I've toned him down' (*Blasting*, 66).

[125] 'Letters a Conglomerated Mass', *The Suffragette* 1: 12 (3 January 1913): 177.

[126] Elsewhere in *Blast 2* Lewis states that American art 'when it comes . . . will be Mongol, inhuman, optimistic . . .' ('History of the Largest Independent Society in England', *B2*, 82).

all know what an American is' (*B2*, 100). On meeting 'the American poet', though, Blenner forges an ongoing alliance, 'sacrificing his antagonisms at each meeting . . .' (*B2*, 102)—as Lewis professedly saw himself doing with Pound at the time. In contrast to the crowd's husbandry, though, this Vorticist alliance is based on an acknowledgement of detachment that mitigates the sacrifice of antagonism; the pleasure Blenner derives from Multum's text is attributed to its insulting tone. Not that he reads it; instead, the book literally begins to 'praise itself' to him:

> 'I am so huge and have no past. I am like all your Pasts and the Present dumped into one age together. Just so: what is the matter with you is the matter with me, only more so. But I shall absorb my elements because I am all living, whereas you are 80 per cent. dead.
>
> Yah! Booh! I can only put my tongue out now. But I shall have an artisitic snaky visiting card some day.
>
> I am the vulgarest thing on Earth. Amen.'   (*B2*, 100)

The text is thus a vortex combining an absorptive space and an audible belligerence as the one *volume*. In contrast to the 'stupid' contagion of the crowd's writing, Multum's text manifests self-regard and keeps its contents in reserve.

The conjunction of artistic and political representation that Lewis dramatizes in 'The Crowd Master' is one that Gordon Teskey in *Allegory and Violence* (1996) relates specifically to allegory. The political implications of allegory are evident in its etymology, he argues, which also connotes a gathering (*ageiro*) of others (*allos*) through speech: 'Allegory speaks in the agora, the gathering place, but in an "other" way, mysteriously, disclosing a secret to the initiated while keeping away the profane.'[127] 'The Crowd Master' is an extreme performance of this, initiating itself into its own separatism by alienating everyone. Moreover, the story's figuring of the gathering as a *corporeal* mass is another feature that Teskey links to the allegorical:

> As a gathering of bodies with interiors, the agora is a corporeal manifold, a space containing spaces that are nevertheless external to it. Only when voice is denied them do bodies in the agora lose this interiority, becoming an indifferent substance ready to be imprinted with ideology.[128]

Thus, in the second version, when Cantlemen hears the 'Hoarse voices' of the crowd dissolve into 'muttering all around him', he finds

---

[127]   Gordon Teskey, *Allegory and Violence* (Ithaca: Cornell University Press, 1996), 123.
[128]   Ibid., 124.

himself 'losing ground' until he manages to place himself out of earshot on a pedestal: 'Upon the plinth of the Nelson Column [in Trafalgar Square] he strained for a distinct sensation. . . . Nothing came at all. . . . He felt as detached as the stone Nelson' (*Blasting*, 82). The implication is that the Vorticist becomes the true national leader, but only to the extent that the masses can be made inert. Similarly, elsewhere in *Blast 2* we find Lewis pondering a programme of genocide even more extensive than the one that was to take place in World War II: 'We might eventually arrive at such a point of excellence that two-thirds of the population of the world could be exterminated with mathematical precision in a fortnight. War might be treated on the same basis as agriculture.'[129] After experiencing war first-hand, however, Lewis came to reject such views: 'There is for me no good war (*la bonne guerre*) and bad war. There is only *bad* war' (*ABR*, 115, Lewis's emphasis). This change of stance is also evident in another of Lewis's short stories, 'Cantleman's Spring Mate', which despite its deliberately distasteful narrative is critical of the perceived intimacy of industry, war, and nature.

'Cantleman's Spring Mate'

First appearing in *The Little Review* in October 1917, 'Cantleman's Spring Mate' returns to the issue of whether or not there is a general enemy 'Will' operating behind socio-political lines. Instead of figuring the masses as a single person, the concern is now to question the individual's relation to an enemy 'Nature'. The story describes the newly-enlisted Cantleman joining the camp of his battalion somewhere in the English countryside. After reading Hardy's *The Trumpet Major*, which he steals from one of the officers in his room, he is suffused with the desire to see a country girl, Stella ('star' in Latin) again. The part played by the text in fostering his romantic frame of mind is rapidly forgotten, though, as Nature itself begins to appear as author of all things:

In the factory town ten miles away to the right, whose smoke could be seen, life was just as dangerous for the poor, and as uncomfortable, as for the soldier in his trench. The hypocrisy of Nature and the hypocrisy of War were the same. . . . He, Cantleman, did not want to owe anything to life or enter into league or understanding with her. The thing was either to go out of

[129] Lewis, 'A Super-Krupp—Or War's End', *B2*, 13.

existence: or, failing that, remain in it unreconciled, indifferent to Nature's threat, consorting openly with her enemies, making war within her war upon her servants. (*Blasting*, 309–10)

For Cantleman there is no life-form that the figure of Nature has not already taken hostage. Resolving to take the terroristic course of resistance, on meeting Stella he cannot prevent himself from seeing her as one of Nature's secret agents: 'she was a sort of Whizzbang. With a treachery worthy of a Hun, Nature tempted him towards her . . . considered as an unconscious agent, all women were contaminated with Nature's hostile power and might be treated as spies or enemies' (*Blasting*, 310).[130] Rather than consider Stella as having a similarly complex relation to Nature, Cantleman's response is to enforce and then combat her allegorical status with an act of rape:

He bore down on her as though he wished to mix her body into the soil, and pour his seed into a more methodless matter, the brown phalanges of floury land. As their two bodies shook and melted together, he felt that he was raiding the bowels of Nature: he was proud that he could remain deliberately aloof, and gaze bravely, like a minute insect, up at the immense and melancholy night . . . (*Blasting*, 310–11).

Stella is violently transformed into Nature, while Cantleman's violence takes on cataclysmic proportions in supposedly violating the world. The vile double-movement of the action reflects Cantleman's confusion, for his own violence is attributed the same contaminated agency—'Nature tempted him towards her'—as Stella. His allegorical assault thus involves trying to impose a series of contradictory propositions: Stella is extraneous to Nature; Stella is Nature; Nature consents to Stella's rape—'consent flowed up into her body from all the veins of the landscape' (*Blasting*, 310); Nature itself provokes the rape. As an attempt to link the allegorical figure to a particular body, Cantleman's action becomes a battle for his own grand narrative. Stella's body is given no voice, and nor are the German soldiers whom Cantleman subsequently encounters: 'when he beat a German's brains out it was with the same impartial malignity that he had displayed in the English night with his Spring-mate' (*Blasting*, 311). Considering Lewis's presentation of rape in 'The Foxes' Case' as ex-

---

[130] Lewis also posits an intimacy of war and sexual reproduction in *Blast 2*: 'Women's function [is] the manufacturing of children (even more important than cartridges and khaki suits. . . . It takes the deft women from twelve to sixteen years to fill and polish these human cartridges . . .' ('A Super-Krupp—or War's End', *B2*, 16).

emplifying what the writer does, the mixture of violence and violation is undoubtedly intended to shock. But Lewis also signals that Cantleman's actions show that he is incapable of forming any proper ethical understanding. Regarding his killing of the soldiers, for example, the narrator concludes that '[Cantleman] considered there too that he was in some way outwitting Nature, and had no adequate realization of the extent to which the death of a Hun was to the advantage of the world' (*Blasting*, 311). The paranoid politics of conspiracy theory is thus acknowledged as being in need of some serious therapy and critique.

On another level, like 'Enemy of the Stars' 'Cantleman's Spring Mate' is a dramatization of Lewis's textual politicking in relation to the publishing world. Pound wanted *The Little Review*, in which 'Cantleman's Spring Mate' appeared, to be affiliated to *The Egoist*. Founded by Margaret Anderson, Pound became *The Little Review*'s literary editor, stating in an early editorial that he wanted the journal to 'aid and abet *The Egoist* in its work'.[131] It was certainly marketed with a similar antipathy towards mass-culture, declaring itself to be 'MAKING NO COMPROMISE WITH PUBLIC TASTE'. As Geoff Gilbert has pointed out, the journal's literary detachment was manifest in the scant interest the journal took in responding to the war crisis.[132] Lewis's story can thus be seen partly as a dissenting piece grappling with the detachment of the publication in which it appears. Yet the force of the story's critique is diminished in that ultimately it offers no alternative to Cantleman's confused actions. The effect of Lewis's rape narrative thus echoes the writer's attempted rape of the world described in 'The Foxes' Case'. The United States at least attempted to 'remain triumphantly sterile' in the face of his assault; under Section 211 of the US Criminal Code, which banned the distribution of obscene material, the US Post Office seized the copies of *The Little Review* carrying the story.[133] Perhaps ironically, the

---

[131] Ezra Pound, 'Editorial', *The Little Review* 4: 1 (May 1917): 5. See also Thomas L. Scott (ed.), *Pound/The Little Review: The Letters of Ezra Pound to Margaret Anderson* (London: Faber, 1988).

[132] See Geoff Gilbert, 'A Career in Modernism: Wyndham Lewis, 1909–31', Ph.D. thesis (University of Cambridge, 1995), 95–100.

[133] The summation of the judge, Augustus N. Hand, was later quoted in Margaret Anderson, 'Judicial Opinion (Our Suppressed October Issue)', *The Little Review* 4: 8 (December 1917): 47–8, and included his synopsis of the story: 'In his revolt at the confusion and injustice of the war he [Cantleman] feels justification at having wreaked his will and obtained his satisfaction—thus, as he says, outwitting nature' (47).

section of the Code also included a ban on 'anything for preventing conception or producing abortion'.[134] Lewis's literary assault was to some extent successful, then, in so far as he gained legal recognition of his writing's impact. The story had not simply ended in a 'barren police-court outrage'; indeed, some of the figures involved with *The Little Review* saw the whole affair as a real advance. In a letter to Margaret Anderson, Pound reported Yeats's pleasure on hearing of the ban: 'Yeats says suppression of October number is great luck, and ought to be the making of the magazine.'[135] In another sense, though, the allegorical assaults that Cantleman performs mark a shift in Lewis's aesthetics from the avant-garde separatism of the 'literary strike' towards a pessimism about literary praxis. It was not a Vorticist force of detachment or individualism that provoked the proscription of 'Cantleman's Spring Mate' but rather its depiction of highly distasteful actions. The laughing snore that Arghol finally emits does indeed appear to have culminated in a nihilistic tragedy of impasse for Lewis, for the enemy of Stella is no enemy of the stars. Whereas Arghol's withdrawal becomes a form of violent resistance in itself, Cantleman needs violence to enforce his detachment in the first place.

I argued earlier that Lewis's literary Syndicalism is problematic for some of the theories advanced in terrorism studies because it exemplifies the way in which, far from being structurally rigid, relations between violence and discourse have been actively contested. The ways that a text can embody its own disruptive cultural force are obviously a problem that a range of avant-garde writers and theorists have grappled with. Lewis's 'allegorical assaults' are pertinent to terrorism studies precisely because they show how political and figurative representation have clashed and been drawn into specific historical crises. In addition, the allegorical assault presents its own complexities in as much as it is an attempt to make violence textual while keeping the body politic in its sights.

As a deed by propaganda, Lewis's hyperbolizing of violence is also particularly relevant to some of the conspiracy theories advanced by certain terrorist groups and terrorism scholars alike. Timothy McVeigh, for example, who was executed in 2001 for his bombing of

---

[134] Pound cited the Code at length in 'The Classics "Escape" ', *The Little Review* 4: 11 (March 1918): 32–4.
[135] Scott, *Pound/The Little Review*, 167.

the Murrah Federal Building in Oklahoma City that killed 167 people, reportedly declared that the US Army had implanted a computer chip in one of his buttocks in order to control him.[136] His belief in an endemic conspiracy of Federal government forces thus ended up bolstering his conviction that the bombing had to be of massive proportions. Such a belief may indicate clinical paranoia in McVeigh's case, but it is not far removed from the type of conspiracy theory advanced in Claire Sterling's book, *The Terror Network: The Secret War of International Terrorism* (1981). 'This is not a book of fiction. It deals with facts',[137] we are told in the prologue; 'facts' outlining the Soviet Union's purported orchestration of terrorist organizations worldwide, from the Basque ETA to the IRA. As Joseba Zulaika and William Douglass point out, the book was widely read and praised by President Reagan and his administration—only for them to discover that it was founded on 'CIA disinformation "blown back" '.[138] Of course, terrorist groups *are* in some cases supported by other larger political or financial bodies. But the point is that on occasions, presenting the 'facts' about hidden terror networks has also involved no less allegorizing and 'making Other' than Lewis's fictions, thereby confusing the difference between terrorism and its fabulation, as well as between its violence and its terror.

As I have argued, for Lewis the allegorizing he uses to lump his enemies together also becomes identified as a process employed by the enemies themselves. Just as his portrayals of the female-mob were concerned with herding a disparate assortment of hates together, in several of his 1920s and 1930s writings he sought to present another figure as being behind the conglomerations of power: the Jew. In Lewis's political tract, *Count Your Dead: They Are Alive!* (1937) for example, he suggests that the British government is a puppet of Jewish financiers and secret Semitic forces which 'do not necessarily belong to us, but . . . are *with* us'.[139] The fashioning of this scapegoat is evident as far back as the 'Imaginary Letters' which Lewis published between

[136] See Timothy Melley, *Empire of Conspiracy: The Culture of Paranoia in Postwar America* (Ithaca: Cornell University Press, 2000), 37.

[137] Claire Sterling, *The Terror Network: The Secret War of International Terrorism* (London: Weidenfeld & Nicolson, 1981), iv.

[138] Joseba Zulaika and William Douglass, *Terror and Taboo: The Follies, Fables, and Faces of Terrorism* (London: Routledge, 1996), 14. See also Edward Herman and Gerry O'Sullivan, *The 'Terror' Industry: The Experts and Institutions that Shape Our View of Terror* (New York: Pantheon, 1989), 171.

[139] Wyndham Lewis, *Count Your Dead: They Are Alive!* (London: Lovat Dickson, 1937), 16, Lewis's emphasis.

May 1917 and April 1918 in *The Little Review*. Dated from 7 January to 20 May 1917, the seven fictional letters are from William Bland Burn in St Petersburg to his wife, Lydia, in London. According to Burn, the Jews are responsible both for Germany's declaration of war and the revolution taking place in Russia:

The Revolution here is on a par with all other contemporary events. I am afraid it will make the War more interminable than ever. All the Jews are mobilized. They march about in huge tribes with banners. They have formed themselves into a sort of Parliament, getting elected all over the place or electing themselves.[140]

Lewis was not alone in expressing such views; they gained currency in Russia and elsewhere largely on account of the conspiracy text *Protocols of the Elders of Zion*, millions of copies of which circulated internationally during the 1920s and 1930s.[141] Confected by Russian anti-Semites in the late nineteenth century, it linked Anarchists to Jewish secret societies that were supposedly plotting world domination. Along with similarly racist texts like Hillaire Belloc's *The Jews* (1922) and Alfred Rosenberg's *The Myth of the Twentieth Century* (1920), the *Protocols* helped turn anti-Semitism into its own terror industry.[142] Writing of the text in *Mein Kampf*, Hitler argued that Jewish claims that the *Protocols* was a forgery was 'the best proof that they are authentic'.[143] After being encomiastic in *Hitler* (1931) about the eponymous dictator, Lewis rescinded his approval in *The Hitler Cult* (1939) on realizing the inevitability of a second World War. Similarly, in *The Jews, Are They Human?* (1939), he proceeded to denounce anti-Semitism in general. The same cannot be said for Pound. Developing a taste for anti-Semitic ideology in the 1930s, Pound turned it into a cornerstone for his aesthetics and ideas on culture on emigrating to Mussolini's Italy. By the 1950s, Lewis himself was berating him for it. In the following chapter, I shall address how Pound develops his ideas on 'Jew usury' in relation to specific acts of terrorist violence.

---

[140] Wyndham Lewis, 'Imaginary Letters, IX', *The Little Review* 4: 6 (April 1918): 51.

[141] See Norman Cohn, *Warrant for Genocide: The Myth of the Jewish World-Conspiracy and the Protocols of the Elders of Zion* (1969; Chico, Calif.: Scholars, 1981).

[142] Regarding the growth of anti-Semitism in Britain at this time, see Gisela C. Lebzeltzer, *Political Anti-Semitism in England, 1918–1939* (London: Macmillan, 1979).

[143] Quoted in George Johnson, *Architects of Fear: Conspiracy Theories and Paranoia in American Politics* (Los Angeles: Torcher, 1983), 110.

3. Ezra Pound: Anti-Semitism, Segregationism, and the 'Arsenal of Live Thought'

Radio Assassination

'[I]t is not merely political, it is molecular or atomic. It destroys all scale and all sense of proportionate values. . . . It profanes. It soils, it is greasy and acid. . . . it entangles the clean, it entangles them because of their inconsequentiality, their incapacity to see the connection between one thing and another.'[1] Ezra Pound, broadcasting for the Italian Fascists on Radio Roma in 1943 to Britain and the USA, is waging war against a 'new INTERNATIONAL empire', the cause of cultural disintegration in general. The culprit, he says, is 'Jew usury'. World War II, in truth, has its origins in 1696 with the founding of the Bank of England, 'when the virus of death, the invisible silent virus, more deadly than syphilis, was shot into the English people. Bank of England, makin' money from the VACUUM.'[2] The real danger of this foe is its capacity to become an entire system of exchange: 'The ENEMY is Das Leihkapital.'[3] Production of interest accruing from borrowed capital, and the proliferation of Jewishness are posited, by Pound, as being two sides of the same coin. This alien-event threatens facticity itself. 'It' no longer even depends on material existence; instead, it reproduces itself spectrally, transmogrifying values, constantly extending its limits, paying obeisance to no national borders.

---

[1] Pound, 'Toward Veracity' (7 March 1943), in *'Ezra Pound Speaking': Radio Speeches of World War II*, ed. by Leonard Doob (Westport: Greenwood, 1978), 239. *'Ezra Pound Speaking'* hereafter cited as *EPS*.

[2] Pound, 'The Pattern' (30 March 1942), in *EPS*, 78.

[3] Pound, 'Gold: England' (8 March 1942), in *EPS*, 55.

Elucidating this is the first step in countering it: 'My function is to arouse a little curiosity about a PROCESS. War is part of a process. Some men would want to know what part of a process it is part OF.'[4] But how can you dissect this genitive, when the enemy originates as the capacity for incessant *re*-production and so confounds the very notion of location? 'I lose my way sometimes. So much that I can't count on anyone's knowing. Thread, as they call it, of discourse.'[5] Attempting to confront this ambiguity, Pound's speech-attacks, like Lewis's allegorizing, fight on two fronts. On the one hand, he pinions responsibility for the 'process' on the Jewish race and specific Jews. On the other hand, the force of his foe is a *hyper*-insidiousness, by virtue of which anyone can become Jewish. England is now 'anglo-judaea', the 'Archbishopry of England' is 'kiker', President Roosevelt is really 'Jewsfeldt', and democracy has become a 'judaeocracy'. The enemy's ambiguity has facilitated a double strategy: its iniquity is made a hypostasized evil, which can in turn be linked to a specific racial body. Thus Pound makes the figure of the 'Jew usurer' embody political and discursive schisms generally, just as for Lewis it was the Jew who was the culprit working behind the enemy lines.

If hunting this enemy means following it in its tracks, radio, for Pound, provides the ideal means for doing so. Bypassing the more material forms of media—which he viewed as Jew-controlled anyway—Pound can transmit himself across the seas, offer himself as household phantasm to exorcize those propagated by his foe: 'The phantom that the Anglo-Jew world is fighting' is a 'Jew usurer instigation'.[6] Because the terrorizing force of 'Jew usury', for Pound, is linked both to its power to engender an army of phantoms *and* to its capacity to take material possession of states, so he must view his air-wave vitriol as a potential assassination in itself. Not only do the speeches invoke pogroms and selective killings—'I think it might be a good idea to hang Roosevelt and a few hundred yidds. IF you can do it by due legal process'[7]—he also declares his wish for a purge *by* radio to the Italian Fascist writer, Camillo Pellizzi, pondering 'How to slip over something that wd/ be equivalent to killing Morgenthau

---

[4] Pound, 'Debt' (5 June 1943), in *EPS*, 334.

[5] Pound, 'Gold: England', 57.

[6] Pound, 'With Phantoms' (18 May 1942), in *EPS*, 137.

[7] Pound, 'On Retiring' (27 April 1943), in *EPS*, 289. See also in *EPS*: 'England' (15 March, 1942), 62; 'With Phantoms', 140; 'More Homely' (18 February 1943), 221; 'Serviti' (21 February 1943), 229; 'Pogrom' (21 March 1943), 255; and 'Administration' (16 May 1943), 311.

[the US treasurer] and the god damn kike agents, and leading Jews-feldt to gawd or an honest life.'[8] Equivalent—which also implies something that remains distinct. A simulacrum that is both absolutely identical to *and* different from what it copies is what is being called for. Turning himself into a form of his foe, Pound can claim that the Jewish mind is responsible for his own confusion—moreover, that his confusion *is* Jewish, for the Jew usurer is the cause of simulacra in the first place.

Pound's call for violence, coupled with the violence of the call, is offered by him as a new mode of cultural and political counter-attack. Indeed, it is not simply cultural value that needs to be reinstituted but political violence itself, for Pound sees the practice of it as having gone very much astray. This is particularly so in the USA, he argues, where it is needed most:

American lynch-law had its origins in the Jewish ruins of the American South. . . . The Ku Klux Klan once had a reason. Today the survival of lynch-law appears, at least from Europe, to be a sheer manifestation of COWARDICE. . . . You lynch the Negro, glory in the manhunt, but you are incapable of political violence.[9]

Simply murdering the enemy is not enough. The Negro in this instance is merely the scapegoat of a more invidious force—even though Pound also implies there was a legitimacy of lynching to the extent that the Ku Klux Klan might originally have been fighting Jewishness!

Clearly, an efficient political programme of engagement is indissociable, for Pound, from determining the very dynamics between discourse and action, value and exchange. This is why the relation of his political beliefs to his modernism cannot be posed without addressing how he figures relations between politics, race, and economics more generally. This does not mean that judging the spirit of Pound's anti-Semitism is ultimately a matter of aesthetics. The degree to which a mode of representation can be defined politically or racially, and the extent to which a political stance necessitates specific aesthetic dynamics, are precisely the questions Pound is grappling with. For this reason, Daniel Tiffany's discussion of the radio speeches, in *Radio*

---

[8] Pound, letter to Camillo Pellizi, 15 February 1941, quoted in Tim Redman, *Ezra Pound and Italian Fascism* (Cambridge: Cambridge University Press, 1991), 209. *Ezra Pound and Italian Fascism* hereafter cited as *EPIF*.

[9] Pound, 'Violence' (15 June 1942), in *EPS*, 171.

Corpse (1995), is problematic, for he attributes all Pound's contradictions and confusion in the broadcasts to his modernism: 'Oscillating
between inscription and transmission, phonography and telephony,
the production of Pound's radio speeches replicates in a technical
medium the oscillation of the modernist Image between positivism
and hermeneutics . . .'.[10] For Tiffany, the 'oscillations' of the speeches
seem to take place automatically; the radio itself 'replicates' a more
originary modernist aesthetic.[11] And so too does the political content
of the broadcasts, for according to Tiffany radio, for Pound, is 'at
once the essence of fascism and the mediumistic equivalent of the
Jew'.[12] The politics of anti-Semitism has thus become an automated
drama, eliding the possibility of Pound's performative strategizing.
William Chace supports a similar elision of Pound's agency when he
writes that 'Pound's anti-semitism and the literary uses to which he
repeatedly puts it may be evaluated most productively as an alto-
gether logical corollary to his philosophical and aesthetic principle,
not as an inexplicable divergence from them.'[13] From this perspective, Pound's hate-speech can only signify as aesthetics; the possibility that the poet might have viewed his aesthetics as developing a
more potent form of cultural activism is discounted in advance.

Admittedly, it is not as if Pound himself does not at times declare
that anti-Semitism is fundamentally a theological or philosophical
problem: 'Semitophobia is better explainable as semi-conscious re-
venge on the race that has brought monotheism in European circulation than by any other single or complex set of reasons . . .'.[14] But
whatever the reason behind it, Pound still sees Jew usury and the battle against it as involving concrete cultural values and affairs, not to
mention lived experience. Safeguarding authentic culture might
mean fighting for a control of ontology, but that is because ontology,
for Pound, is wholly linked to the body-politic. Nowhere is this made

---

[10] Daniel Tiffany, *Radio Corpse: Imagism and the Cryptaesthetic of Ezra Pound* (Cambridge,
Mass.: Harvard University Press, 1995), 230.

[11] For alternative viewpoints—including those of Marinetti and Antonin Artaud—on
the relations between radio, poetry, and the avant-garde, see *Wireless Imagination: Sound
Radio, and the Avant-Garde*, ed. by Douglas Kahn and Gregory Whitehead (Cambridge,
Mass.: MIT Press, 1992).

[12] Tiffany, *Radio Corpse*, 236.

[13] William M. Chace, *The Political Identities of Ezra Pound and T. S. Eliot* (Stanford, Calif.:
Stanford University Press, 1973), 81.

[14] Pound, 'Convenit esse Deos' (1940–2), in *Machine Art & Other Writings: The Lost Thought
of the Italian Years: Ezra Pound*, ed. by Maria Luisa Ardizzone (Durham: Duke University
Press, 1996), 135.

clearer for him than in the writings of Confucius which he translated. In turning to these texts as a way of further exploring Pound's own ideas about political ontology, I am not suggesting that Confucius was his sole inspiration. As is evident from Pound's *Cantos* and other writings, in addition to a massive range of aesthetic, economic, and historical sources, he also refers to a variety of philosophers, ranging from Aristotle and the Scholastics through to Leibniz and George Santayana.[15] Moreover, all of these various sources are invariably cited only to be placed in dialogue with each other. While it would be problematic to sum up Pound's aesthetics as simply Confucian, then, the writings of Confucius are nevertheless presented by Pound as being exemplary of an authentic defence of culture, and came to play an increasingly important part in his own political struggles in later years.

In all of the Confucian texts, upholding cultural essence is wholly linked to a pedagogy of limits and measures. In 'The Great Digest', for example, the 'great learning' arises from 'looking straight into one's heart and acting on the result' (*Confucius*, 27). Self-reflection limits oneself to oneself. Value is given before social exchange. Enforcing social values thus entails ordering a series of measures. Setting up 'good government' requires regimenting families, which calls for 'self-discipline', which demands 'precise verbal definitions', which necessitates 'sorting things into organic categories' (*Confucius*, 29).[16] Grasping the Confucian 'luminous principle' thus means acknowledging the categorical imperative that a state must be fundamentally 'totalitarian'.[17] But the essential root of value is subsequently shown to reside in neither institutions nor words but in a 'sovereign' light, an 'inborn nature', which 'heaven has disposed and sealed' (*Confucius*, 99). Unity of the process is thus founded on determining a separation between its essence and its existence. But the resultant ontological divide threatens the stability of the whole; set up as an absolute value, the sovereign light loses the power of absolute control. As a result,

---

[15] Pound links the Confucian 'process' to other writings in *Confucius: The Great Digest and Unwobbling Pivot*, trans. and commentary by Ezra Pound (London: Peter Owen, 1952), hereafter cited as *Confucius*: 'The sun and moon, the total light process, the radiation, reception and reflection of light; hence intelligence. Bright, brightness, shining. Refer to Scotus Erigena, Grosseteste and the notes on light in my *Cavalcanti*' (22).

[16] See also, *Ta Hio: The Great Learning*, trans. by Ezra Pound (1928; Seattle: Folcroft, 1970), 9; and *Confucian Analects*, trans. by Ezra Pound (1933; London: Peter Owen, 1956), 7.

[17] Pound, 'Mang Tsze (The Ethics of Mencius)' (1938), in *Ezra Pound: Selected Prose 1909–65*, ed. by William Cookson (London: Faber, 1973), 99.

Pound is forced to defend contradictory statements: 'The process is not far from man', we are told, 'those who want to institute a process alien to man cannot make it function as an ethical system' (*Confucius*, 119). But as the process must indeed alienate itself from social exchanges in order to remain 'immaculata', this has to be qualified: 'You do not depart from the process. What you do depart from is not the process' (*Confucius*, 101). In his *Guide to Kulchur* (1938), a similarly ambivalent image of money is proferred. Its proper function is linked to enforcing state measures, argues Pound: 'The spartan coin provided a measure. That is the statal adjunct.'[18] Money accedes to state authority: 'it exists not by nature but by custom . . .'. The authority of value must be materially grounded, then, as Maud Ellmann notes: 'Power must be cashed in words or coins to circulate among these currencies, for Pound distrusts potential energy.'[19] But Pound also claims monetary value must be non-negotiable to the point that the coin mints an immutable form, an 'immortal *concetto*': 'the bust outlasts the stone. The coin Tiberius' (*GK*, 152). Faced with this difficulty of defining the nature of just monetarism, Pound searched for contemporary alternatives—Major C. H. Douglas's 'Social Credit' and the economic theory of Silvio Gesell being two that he particularly favoured.

Pound first met Douglas through Alfred Orage, who was also responsible for introducing him, along with Wyndham Lewis, to various union leaders and Syndicalists (see Chapter 2). Both Pound and Douglas wrote extensively on 'Social Credit' theory in Orage's journal, *New English Weekly*, the main feature of the theory being a regulation of capital whereby the state determines the value of currency according to the condition of the economy. Pound moved away from Douglas's ideas in the mid 1930s, however, because he found Douglas's liberalism increasingly hard to reconcile with Fascism.[20] Gesell, on the other hand, had not only proposed a revisioning of money, his theories had also been implemented in Wöergl, Switzerland, in 1932. In his main work, *The Natural Economic Order* (1906–11), Gesell argued

[18] Ezra Pound, *Guide to Kulchur* (1938; London: Peter Owen, 1966), 35, hereafter cited as *GK*.
[19] Maud Ellmann, *The Poetics of Impersonality: T. S. Eliot and Ezra Pound* (Sussex: Harvester, 1987), 164. Pound states as much in 'Towards Orthology', *New English Weekly* 6: 26 (11 April 1935): 'Money and language exist by being current. The acceptance of coin as of value; of words as having meaning, are the essence of currency and of speech' (534).
[20] On this point, see Peter Nicholls, *Ezra Pound: Politics, Economics and Writing: A Study of The Cantos* (London: Macmillan, 1984), 83–9.

that instead of trying to organize a revolution of classes by organizing a proletarian movement, the nature of money itself needed to be changed. In particular, its dominance over commodities must be countered: 'money can be measured only by wares, by the material characteristics of wares'.[21] This, he argued, could be effected by '*Schwundgeld*' (scrip-money) which Pound describes in 'Gold and Work' (1944) when writing of a model community:

they attribute their prosperity to a simple method they have of collecting taxes, or rather, their one tax, which falls on the currency itself. For on every note of 100 monetary units they are obliged, on the first of every month, to affix a stamp worth one unit. And as the government pays its expenses by the issue of new currency, it never needs to impose other taxes.[22] (*SP*, 306)

This was the scheme introduced in Wöergl with some success until the Austrian bank took the village to court—for infringing its monopoly on the issue of currency—and won. For Pound, the stamp-scrip system was the best example of a practical solution to the 'just price' issue, for it aimed at instituting an absolute adequation between money and the goods it represents. Taxing money each month encouraged circulation rather than hoarding, and meant that the currency was as perishable as the commodities themselves. With such a system, declares Pound:

The various degrees of durability, fruit, grain, clothing, houses, wood, stone and machinery, could conceivably (but very cumbrously) be *each* represented by money that should melt at a parallel rate . . . a just proportion between a fixed and a diminishing money *would* equate the value of all goods to the value of available money.[23]

But by effectively turning money into a counterfeit version of what it represents, the possibility of it remaining a detached, determining form is undermined. Pound is caught between wanting to uphold an empiricism of money, whereby it reflects a value inherent to an object, at the same time as wanting values to be determined and guarded by the state—or as Gesell proposed, by a group of educated men who would act 'as a bodyguard, so to speak, to protect the mark from bunglers and swindlers'.[24] The divergence of Pound's economic

---

[21] Silvio Gesell, *The Natural Economic Order*, trans. by Philip Pye (London: Owen, 1958), 202.

[22] Pound, 'Gold and Work' (1944), in *Ezra Pound: Selected Prose*, 306.

[23] Pound, 'The Individual in his Milieu' (1935), in *Ezra Pound: Selected Prose*, 247, Pound's emphasis.

[24] Gesell, *The Natural Economic Order*, 136–7.

theorizing is analogous to the ontological division evident in his Confucian translations. As soon as the Confucian process founds its unity there are two processes, as Pound asserts elsewhere: 'one that divides, shatters, and kills and one that contemplates the unity of the mystery.'[25] The more the process is posed as an absolute power, the more ambivalent and divided it appears. And the more it is made ambivalent, the more it needs someone to fight for its clarity: 'Such are the seeds of movement [*semina motuum* . . .] one word will ruin the business, one man can bring the state to an orderly course' (*Confucius*, 61).

Pound and Italian Fascism

For Pound, bringing the state to an 'orderly course' is precisely what the Fascists in Italy were attempting to do. Formed in November 1921 and led by Mussolini after 1922, the roots of the Fascist party were various, though it was launched as a mass movement primarily as a result of frustrated, petty bourgeoisie being faced with postwar unemployment and depression.[26] Opposing the parliamentary process because they were not assured of sufficient representative power, the 'Populist' bourgeois faction joined forces with the Syndicalist movement.[27] The process of setting up the totalitarian, Fascist regime was termed '*l'inquaramento*', connoting regimentation as well as framing and enclosure. Like Pound's image of the Confucian state, it primarily meant instituting a series of measures and limits.[28] What became increasingly clear, however, was that the creation of state control necessitated a monopoly over all local determination and thus a suppression of the very Syndicalist ideology that had initially been adopted. Between 1925 and 1939, policies were implemented to accelerate the Fascist nationalization of the economy and culture generally.[29] No other political party was allowed to exist, and mem-

---

[25] Pound, 'A Visiting Card' (1942), in *Ezra Pound: Selected Prose*, 277.

[26] For an overview of the development of Fascism in Italy, see Philip Morgan, *Italian Fascism, 1919–45* (London: Macmillan, 1995); and Alexander Del Grand, *Italian Fascism: Its Origins and Developments* (Lincoln: University of Nebraska Press, 1982).

[27] See David Roberts, *The Syndicalist Tradition and Italian Fascism* (Manchester: Manchester University Press, 1979), ch. 1.

[28] Pound argued that writers and artists should belong to specific Fascist syndicates according to their talents: 'There are at least three kinds of people who practise the art of writing: the instinctives, almost unconsciously; the inventors; and the exploiters. They ought to be organised in separate divisions of the Fascist Syndicate, or given separate Syndicates in the Corporation' ('A Visiting Card', 289).

[29] See Morgan, *Italian Fascism*, ch. 4; also Roberts, *The Syndicalist Tradition*, ch. 11.

bership consequently soared. The Press Office of the Council of Ministers regulated the newspapers and then radio, cinema, theatre, and tourism with the creation of a sub-ministry for Press and Propaganda in 1934. From 1935 onwards, a stringent elimination of market forces was also policed over by the newly formed 'Superintendency of Foreign Exchange and Commerce' which established state prices. This became part of the doctrine of 'autarchy' that Mussolini introduced to the nation on 23 March 1936.[30] Tariffs were subsequently imposed, and holders of foreign currency were required to deposit it in the Bank of Italy. Having allied itself to Germany with the Axis Agreement of 1936—which gave formal recognition of Italy's conquest of Ethiopia, and of Germany's pact with Austria—autarchy was presented by Mussolini as heralding a Fascist 'perpetual war'.

Pound, having embraced Syndicalist ideas in his *Blast* years, saw in Fascism the grounds for introducing 'Social Credit' on a national scale. It was all a natural development of his earlier beliefs: 'If I am introducing anybody to Kulchur, let 'em take the two phases, the nineteen teens, Gaudier, Wyndham L. and I as we were in *Blast*, and the next phase the 1920s. The sorting out, the *rappel à l'ordre*, and thirdly the new synthesis, the totalitarian.'[31] On migrating to Italy, he rapidly set about fashioning himself as an expert in economics and began a long correspondence with Odon Por, author of *Guilds and Co-operatives in Italy* (1923) and *Fascism* (1923).[32] The Syndicalist model was argued by both writers to be intrinsic to the Fascist *idea statale*. For Pound, the 'last manifestation of Mussolini's powers of organisation is a great resurrection of guildism, not furnished with William Morris's mediaeval tapestries and upholsteries.'[33] In *Jefferson and/or Mussolini* (1934), he also makes other connections between Italian Fascist ideology and his own intellectual legacy. The 'STRONG ITALY' of the Fascists, he argues, is the 'only possible foundation' for 'the good life of Europe'—as well as being the avatar of Jefferson's 'heritage'.[34] In parallel with this cultural equation, Pound also asserts that Mussolini is effectively making political practice equivalent to aesthetic labour: 'I don't believe any estimate of Mussolini will be

---

[30] See Del Grand, *Italian Fascism*, ch. 7. [31] Pound, *GK*, 95.
[32] See Redman, *EPIF*, ch. 5.
[33] Pound, 'The Italian Score', *New English Weekly* 7: 6 (23 May 1935): 107. Writing on 25 March 1935 to the Social Credit secretariat in London, Por also argued that 'the corporate system now definitely at work is heading straight towards S[ocial] C[redit], or something like it' (quoted in Redman, *EPIF*, 124).
[34] Ezra Pound, *Jefferson and/or Mussolini* (1934; London: Stanley Nott, 1935), 35.

valid unless it *starts* from his passion for construction. Treat him as *artifex* and all the details fall into place. Take him as anything save the artist and you will get muddled with contradictions.'[35] The statement is not without foundation. As Mussolini came to realize, a total organization of political life also meant controlling the media and general cultural practices. Yet whereas in Pound's Confucian vision the real force of construction was 'disposed and sealed' in heaven, for the Fascists state power resided ultimately with Mussolini and his party.

Pound's views on the relation between political practice and aesthetics at this time are also not without their inconsistencies. In *Guide to Kulchur* we are told that 'The history of culture is the history of ideas going into action' (*GK*, 44). In another passage, ideas themselves appear to be at the mercy of specific advancements in media and technology—although these in turn are then supervened by a higher force: 'From sheer force, physical prowess, craft, jaw-house, money-pull, press to radio, government has undergone revolutions of modus and instrument. Ideologies float over this process. Emotions, appetites are focused into political forces' (*GK*, 259). Pound's 'unwobbling pivot' is once more caught in a theoretical vacillation. Social Credit theory needs a Mussolini, yet the 'things still needing to be remedied in the Italian state are due to an Aristotelic residuum left in Mussolini's own mind' (*GK*, 309). (No doubt Pound's decision to send his *Cantos 51–70* to *il Duce* in 1940 was a step towards mutually legitimizing political and aesthetic authority in one blow.[36]) With the consummation of the Mussolini–Jefferson coupling not in evidence, Pound began to make 'Jewusury' increasingly accountable. In 1935 he had criticized the idea of persecuting a Jew on the grounds of race, but by the end of the 1930s his antipathy to usury was becoming explicitly anti-Semitic.[37] Writing in response to Lino Caico, who had informed him of the German persecution of Jews, Pound declared: 'They are the GREAT destroyers of value/ the obliterators of all demarcations/ the shifters of boundary-stones.'[38] Anti-Semitism was inescapable: the Jews themselves were to blame for it, he argued to James Taylor Dunn: 'Even in Eng/ and Italy people are being forced

---

[35] Pound, *Jefferson and/or Mussolini*, 34, Pound's emphasis.

[36] Peter Nicholls argues that 'there are signs that Pound conceived these Cantos as an act of direct political intervention . . . perhaps even sanctions for Mussolini's seizure of power' (*Ezra Pound*, 112). In this same year, Pound also read the anti-Semitic conspiracy text, *Protocols of the Elders of Zion*—see Redman, *EPIF*, 202.

[37] See e.g., Pound's 'Race', *New English Weekly* 10: 1 (15 October 1936): 12–13.

[38] Quoted in Redman, *EPIF*, 177.

into anti-semitism by Jewish folly. I mean people who never thought of it before and who ON PRINCIPLE are opposed to race prejudice . . .'[39]

Given that the Italian Fascists were actively promoting anti-Semitism by 1938, to what degree is this shift attributable to Pound being immured in Fascist ideology?[40] How can we address this question historically when history and Semitism are so inextricably bound for Pound at this time?

At this point I propose to turn to the philosophy of Martin Heidegger, for whom the ontological nature of nationhood, political life, and knowledge are all bound to a determination of limits. Heidegger's involvement with National Socialism when he was rector of Freiburg University between 1933 and 1936 has been much discussed in recent years.[41] While it will be important to distinguish the different nuances between his thinking and that of Pound's, Heidegger's meditations on the ontology of politics will afford us a means of analysing Pound's anti-Semitism from a vantage point other than those that Pound offers us. Critics such as Jean-Michel Rabaté and Anthony Woodward have noted the affinity between the two figures. Rabaté, in particular, advocates a Heideggerian approach to Pound's poetry: 'my belief is that a detour through Heidegger can permit one to understand the "foundational" question of Pound as a poet and to understand its imbrication in a general historical perspective'.[42] However, neither Rabaté nor Woodward offers a protracted discussion of the correlations between the two, or of particular Heideggerian texts.

[39] Pound, letter to James Taylor Dunn, 18 March 1935, quoted in Redman, *EPIF*, 178. Such views had indeed become more prevalent in America, the main target of Pound's radio broadcasts. As Leonard Dinnerstein writes: 'Although Hitler may have been unpopular in the United States, his views of Jews were not . . . whereas before 1933 there were no official antisemitic organisations in this country, by 1939 over one hundred existed . . .' ('Antisemitism in Crisis Times in the United States: The 1920s and 1930s', in *Anti-Semitism in Times of Crisis*, ed. by Sander L. Gilman and Steven T. Katz [New York: New York University Press, 1991], 219).

[40] In 1938 the Italian Ministry for Popular Culture ('Minculpop') produced an anti-Semitic 'Race Manifesto' in accord with Nazi propaganda.

[41] See in particular, Victor Farias, *Heidegger and Nazism*, trans. by Paul Burrell and Gabriel Ricci (Philadelphia: Temple University Press, 1989); Jacques Derrida, *Of Spirit: Heidegger and the Question*, trans. by Geoffrey Bennington and Rachel Bowlby (1987; Chicago: University of Chicago Press, 1991); Pierre Bourdieu, *The Political Ontology of Martin Heidegger*, trans. by Peter Collier (1988; Cambridge: Polity, 1991); and Miguel de Beistegui, *Heidegger & the Political* (London: Routledge, 1998).

[42] Jean Michel Rabaté, *Language, Sexuality and Ideology in Ezra Pound's Cantos* (Albany: State University of New York Press, 1986), 2. See also Anthony Woodward, *Ezra Pound and The Pisan Cantos* (London: Routledge & Kegan Paul, 1980), 87–8.

Nor is the issue of their mutual anti-Semitism raised. In view of this, after offering a reading of some of Heidegger's rectoral addresses, I shall then turn to his *Parmenides* (1943), the only text in which he discusses politics at length, and which was first published when Pound was composing *The Pisan Cantos*.

Heidegger and the Institution of Terror

Heidegger took up the position of rector at Freiburg University in 1933 after his predecessor, von Möllendorf, was forced to resign because he had forbidden any posting of the anti-Jewish decrees set out in the Nazi's 'Law for the Constitution of the Civil Service' (issued on 1 April 1933).[43] While Heidegger also refused to endorse the decrees on acceding to his post—as he points out in a later interview—the decrees were enforced at the university anyway.[44] Moreover, in his inaugural rector's address, 'The Self-Assertion of the German University', and in several other speeches given in support of Hitler's decision to withdraw from the 'League of Nations', there is no equivocation concerning his allegiance to Nazism: 'the National Socialist revolution is not merely the assumption of power as it exists presently in the State by another party. . . . Rather, this revolution is bringing about *the total transformation of our German existence* [*Dasein*].'[45] Yet Heidegger also states that this transformation of 'existence', along with the university's 'self-assertion [*Selbstbehauptung*]', is a 'will to essence [*Wesen*]'.[46] Instructing students in 'self-examination', he argues, means revealing to them that this essence is rooted in an 'overpowering' national 'fate' (*Schicksal*). The institution thus institutes nothing: as with Pound's depiction of the Confucian 'luminous principle', it replicates a national essence that appears bearing the seal of its inborn nature.[47]

[43] See Richard Wolin's 'Introduction' to *The Heidegger Controversy: A Critical Reader*, ed. by Richard Wolin (1991; Cambridge, Mass.: MIT Press, 1993), hereafter cited as *HC*; also Hugo Ott's biography, *Martin Heidegger* trans. by Allen Blunden (London: HarperCollins, 1993), 229–40.

[44] Heidegger, ' "Only a God Can Save Us": *Der Spiegel's* Interview with Heidegger' (1966), in *HC*, 93.

[45] Heidegger, 'Declaration of Support for Adolf Hitler and the National Socialist State' (11 November 1933), in *HC*, 52, Heidegger's emphasis.

[46] Heidegger, 'The Self Assertion of the German University', in *HC*, 30, hereafter cited as 'Self Assertion'.

[47] Hwa Yol Jung draws connections between Heidegger and ancient Chinese philosophers—including Confucius—in 'Heidegger's Way with Sinitic Thinking', in *Heidegger*

For Heidegger, distinguishing between the institution and its Being is fundamental for inculcating knowledge. Grasping this distinction not only marks the beginning of authentic thinking, but also the thinking of an authentic ontological origin. Only when 'we stand firm in the face of German fate, extreme in its extreme distress [*Not*]' ('Self Assertion', 30), he declares, will the university be gathered into the necessity of its destiny. Its aim, consequently, must also be to 'create for our Volk a world of the innermost and most extreme danger, i.e., a truly *spiritual* world' ('Self Assertion', 33, Heidegger's emphasis). Self-assertion is thus synonymous with self-abnegation, through which the border of national culture is both drawn and withdrawn. For example, while outlining the importance of recognizing the danger specific to national spirit,[48] Heidegger obscures the specificity by equating the law of essence with a new Nazi Student Law:

Out of the resolve of the German students to stand firm in the face of the extreme distress of German fate comes the will to essence of the University. This will is a true will, provided that the German students, through the new Student Law, place themselves under the law of their essence and thereby delimit this essence for the very first time. ('Self Assertion', 34)

Issued on 1 May 1933, the legislation sought to integrate students into the National Socialist state by regulating them according to the *Führerprinzip*. Instead of national fate being safeguarded spiritually, then, its final determination resides with Hitler alone. Furthermore, this also requires securing political authority by policing against thinking differently:

Let not propositions and 'ideas' be the rules of your Being [*Sein*].
The Fuhrer alone *is* the present and future German reality and its law. Learn to know ever more deeply: from now on every single thing demands decision, and every action responsibility.
Heil Hitler![49]

The crisis of reason must be translated into a state of emergency. The Führer is the German destiny; the German destiny is the Führer—

---

and Asian Thought, ed. by Graham Parkes (Honolulu: University of Hawaii Press, 1987), 217–44. Pound also gets a mention, along with Ernest Fenollosa, for introducing 'etymosinology' to the West (223).

[48] See Derrida's analysis of Heidegger's use of 'spirit' in 'Self Assertion', in *Of Spirit*, 33–45.

[49] Heidegger, 'German Students' (12 November 1933), in *HC*, 47, Heidegger's emphasis.

thus Heidegger collapses the very difference upon which all his grounds of argumentation are based, while claiming that essence is finally embodying itself.[50] In 'Self Assertion', students are to be bound to the spiritual mission of the Volk through three bonds of service: 'labour service', 'military service', and 'knowledge service', each of which are *equally original* aspects of German essence' ('Self Assertion', 36, Heidegger's emphasis). There are no fundamental distinctions between each of the three because they are all working towards an obliteration of their differences: '*In its essence*, the knowledge of true Wissenschaft does *not* differ *at all* from the knowledge of the farmer, woodcutter, the miner, the artisan.'[51] So while such work is necessary 'to secure' the greatness of the state's 'existence' (*Dasein*), essentially it does nothing. The real labour is done by Being itself.

This work of *Wissenschaft* is nowhere better exemplified for Heidegger than in the case of Albert Leo Schlageter, a former Freiburg student who was executed for sabotage by occupying French forces in the Ruhr on 26 May 1923. Heidegger commemorates the death of this 'young German hero' in an address to the student body a decade later:

Schlageter died the *most difficult* of all deaths. Not in the front line as the leader of his field artillery battery, not in the tumult of an attack, and not in a grim defensive action—no, he stood *defenseless* before the French rifles . . . in his most difficult hour, he had also to achieve *the greatest thing of which man is capable*. Alone, drawing on his strength, he had to place before his soul an image of the future awakening of the Volk to honour and greatness so that he could die believing in his future.[52]

The founding of national ontology and political fundamentalism are 'executed' in both senses of the word. Schlageter's death is the 'most difficult' and the 'greatest' precisely because it could only 'have been borne . . . had a victory been won and the greatness of the awakening nation shone forth'.[53] The event of dying marks his difference from national essence. His death is *not* that of the Volk; thus the

---

[50] de Beistegui argues similarly: 'Having failed to take into account the specificity and the irreducibility of the ontic [existence], having envisaged the emergence of National Socialism solely in terms of a renewed dialogue with the most hidden powers of being, Heidegger became blind to some of the most central aspects of the regime he . . . supported' (*Heidegger and Politics*, 56–7).

[51] Heidegger, 'National Socialist Education' (22 January 1934), in *HC*, 58, Heidegger's emphasis.

[52] Heidegger, 'Schlageter' (26 May 1933), in *HC*, 40–1, Heidegger's emphases.

[53] Ibid., 40.

boundary between the political and the ontological is secured once more. It is not even an execution, but rather a sacrifice in the name of the homeland *by* the homeland: 'He was not permitted to escape his destiny so that he could die the most difficult and greatest of all deaths with a hard will and a clear heart.'[54] So while the greatest danger, the most 'extreme distress [*Not*]' has been faced with the utmost care and precautions, the nation's essence founds itself only by deferring its appearance in the world. The real death is still to come; in another place with another enemy. Schlageter thus learns the greatest lesson the German University has to teach. The execution is the final touch to his education, the point at which he has finally become qualified to teach. Yet it is Heidegger who must reconfigure the final moments of this 'hero's inner gaze' to discover a blind faith in the homeland. The death is not his, but it must become everyone's. That is the university's task: to create 'for our Volk a world of the innermost and most extreme danger' ('Self Assertion', 33); to organize its terror; to reveal its enemy so that each individual can hear the voice of destiny calling to defend it at all costs.[55]

The ground is thus laid for a comparison of Pound and Heidegger. For while they both outline a specific ontology of cultural violence and security, the experience of war elicits radically different responses in each. Heidegger from the early 1930s onwards was already advocating a philosophical 'turn' (*Kehre*), moving away from thinking ontology from the perspective of phenomenology to thinking it on its own grounds.[56] In contrast, Pound increasingly favoured the writings of Confucius as an alternative to Western metaphysics, seeing them as the means of formulating a kind of hyper-empiricism: 'Kung [Confucius] is superior to Aristotle by totalitarian instinct. His thought is never something scaled off the surface of facts . . .' (*GK*, 279). Yet Pound also struggles to conceal his need for a transcendence of power as much as Heidegger strives to deny the active part played by institutions in building Being. In both cases, the enforcement of an ontological division ends up demanding a specific use of force. By

[54] Ibid., 42.

[55] Martin Dillon, in *The Politics of Security: Towards a Political Philosophy of Continental Thought* (London: Routledge, 1996), argues that Heidegger's philosophy is undeniably a question of political security, for 'Security finds its expression as the principle, ground or *arche*—for which metaphysical thought is a search' (13).

[56] See Michel Haar, *Heidegger and the Essence of Man*, trans. by William McNeill (New York: State University of New York Press, 1993), xxviii–xxix, 60.

discussing Heidegger's *Parmenides* alongside Pound's *The Pisan Cantos*, I shall thus attempt to stake out a no-man's land from which we can begin to approach the following questions more effectively: to what extent does Pound attempt to develop his aesthetic practice into its own mode of incitement and cultural force? What is the relation of his aesthetic practice to the specific acts of terrorism that Pound later came to be associated with?

Heaven by Holocaust: The Pisan Cantos

> 'No wonder my head hurts, all of Europe fell on it; when I talk it is like an explosion in an art museum, you have to hunt around for the pieces.'[57]
>
> Pound

Pound had been coming under increasing pressure from the US government to cease broadcasting his propaganda. On 12 July 1941, the US State Department had informed him that his passport would be extended for only 6 months and could be used only to return to the US. Pound refused to heed the warning or to revoke his citizenship as William Joyce ('Lord Haw Haw'), an English radio propagandist for the Nazis, had done.[58] But with the bombing of Pearl Harbour and America's sudden involvement in the War, he realized the seriousness of his predicament. 'I'm cooked. This is my end', he is reported to have said, 'But I want you to bear witness that I am first of all an American citizen. I stand with my country, right or wrong. I will never speak over the air again.'[59] The resolution was short-lived. Pound recommenced broadcasting the day that the US Congress declared war. The need to reveal the forces that had drawn his country into conflict overrode all other concerns. Whereas other radio propagandists spoke anonymously, Pound, after consideration, rejected the idea outright: 'It seems to me that my speeches on the radio must

---

[57] Pound in an interview with James Jackson Kilpatrick (24 May 1958), quoted in Harry M. Meacham, *The Caged Panther: Ezra Pound and St. Elizabeth's* (New York: Twayne, 1967), 140.

[58] Joyce was hanged by the British government none the less. See J. A. Cole, *Lord Haw Haw: The Full Story of William Joyce* (1964; London: Faber & Faber, 1987). Pound had corresponded with Joyce, asking him for advice about broadcasting; he also signed some letters 'Heil Hitler'. See Humphrey Carpenter, *A Serious Character: The Life of Ezra Pound* (London: Faber & Faber, 1988), 594.

[59] Quoted in E. Fuller Torrey, *The Roots of Treason: Ezra Pound and the Secret of St Elizabeth's* (London: Sidgwick & Jackson, 1984), 160.

continue IN MY OWN NAME and with *my* voice and not anonymously. . . . Either one fights or one does not fight.'[60] He also insisted
on being introduced explicitly as an American citizen by the broad-
casters before each speech:

Italian radio acting in accordance with the Fascist policy of intellectual freedom and free expression of opinion by those who are qualified to hold it, following the tradition of Italian hospitality, has offered Dr. Ezra Pound the use
of the microphone twice a week. It is understood that he will not say anything whatsoever that goes against his conscience, or anything incompatible
with his duties as a citizen of the United States of America.[61]

As far as Pound was concerned, Italian radio was the last place he
could truly speak as an American. Speaking over the air-waves, he
stated, could not 'in and of itself be taken for treason', for it must depend on 'what is said and the motives for speaking'.[62] That the US
government might find his broadcasts objectionable would only
prove the extent to which it no longer believed in true freedom of
speech—which, argued Pound, 'becomes a mockery if it does not include the right of free speech over radio'.[63] Needless to say, the US
government did not take the same view. An FBI investigation of
Pound began in April 1942, and on 26 July 1943, the day that
Mussolini was forced out of government by General Badoglio and his
conservative faction, Pound and seven others were officially charged
with treason. The indictment stated that he

knowingly, intentionally, willfully, unlawfully, feloniously, traitorously and
treasonably did adhere to the enemies of the United States . . . giving to the
said enemies of the United States aid and comfort within the United States
and elsewhere.[64]

Pound later claimed that he remained unaware of the charges at
this time, but he was certainly aware that Italian Fascism had failed
in its aims. Mussolini's forced resignation and subsequent incarceration at the hand of the monarchists was made possible by the general
collapse that the regime had been moving towards since 1942. With
the economy in ruins from the war, and a general wave of strike

---

[60] Pound, letter to Cornelio di Marzio, 28 December 1941, published in Tim Redman,
'The Repatriation of Pound, 1939–42: A View from the Archives', *Paideuma* 8: 3 (Winter
1979): 456, Pound's emphasis.
[61] Quoted in Julian Cornell, *The Trial of Ezra Pound: A Documented Account of the Treason
Case by the Defendant's Lawyer* (London: Faber, 1966), 1.
[62] Quoted in Torrey, *The Roots of Treason*, 168.   [63] Ibid., 169.   [64] Ibid.

action in 1943, the Fascists had already lost the support of the popu-lace.[65] Mussolini was nevertheless rescued by the Germans and in-stalled in Salo, in the north of Italy, to head a new Republic. All its measures and legislations, however, were effectively placed under Nazi control. With the country divided, the new government in Rome was able to co-ordinate effective resistance; the final blow com-ing with the capture of Rome by the Allies on 4 June 1944. Shortly after this event, Pound was issued with a second, more general in-dictment which accused him of creating dissension between the US and its allies, inciting racial prejudice, and attempting to inculcate distrust in the American people for its government.[66] On 3 May 1945 he surrendered to American forces in Rapallo, and was subsequently placed in a specially reinforced cage in a detention centre in Pisa. His own country was holding him as an enemy to the very constitution he had been trying to save. Any hope of living in a new Jeffersonian state under Mussolini was finally dashed when the latter and his mistress, Claretta Petacci, were executed by resistance forces on 27 April 1945 and then publicly hanged in Milan the next day for display.

Yet Pound remained resolute: if the hope of the Italian Republic dwelt with its leader when he was living, it was dwelling with him still. The battle terrain had simply been shifted to higher grounds. After three weeks in his cage, forbidden from speaking to anyone, and with constant floodlight surveillance to ensure he did not attempt suicide, Pound began suffering from panic attacks. Diagnosed as having suf-fered a mental breakdown, he was finally allowed to move into a tent.[67] Provided, in addition, with a typewriter, he immediately com-menced *The Pisan Cantos*, which open with the image of Mussolini's corpse:

> The enormous tragedy of the dream in the peasant's bent
> shoulders
> Manes! Manes was tanned and stuffed,
> Thus Ben and la Clara *a Milano*
>   by the heels at Milano
> That Maggots shd/ eat the dead bullock
> DIGONOS, Δίγονος, but the twice crucified
>   where in history will you find it?

---

[65] See Morgan, *Italian Fascism*, 179–87.
[66] See Torrey, *The Roots of Treason*, 179–80.
[67] See Carpenter, *A Serious Character*, 652–7.

yet say this to the Possum: a bang, not a whimper,
  with a bang not with a whimper,
To build the city of Dioce, whose terraces are the colours of stars.
The suave eyes, quiet, not scornful,
          rain also is of the process.[68]

The state is with Mussolini, but Mussolini is not with the state. This is what the 'Maggots'—a derogatory term for the Partisans responsible for the execution—do not understand. That the leader had to be executed twice (actually and then ritually) is an acknowledgement of him being larger than life. This is why Mussolini's power is not so much that of Dionysus the twice born ('DIGONOS') as the 'twice crucified', for it builds itself through death, bringing its own end to an end. Accordingly, the city of Dioce, leader of the Medes, is to be secured sidereally with *il Duce*. Through destruction, the 'process', *contra* Eliot ('Possum'), reiterates its explosive force. As with Heidegger's Schlageter, then, Mussolini's death is not a termination for Pound but the sign of a *de*-termination that is yet to come.

Mussolini calls from beyond destruction. Mussolini calls for destruction. So we find Pound demonstrating his allegiance by declaring that, like Odysseus, he no longer has an identity:

               OὟ TIΣ
          OὟ TIΣ
'I am noman, my name is noman'
but Wanjina is, shall we say, Ouan Jin
or the man with an education
and whose mouth was removed by his father
      because he made too many *things*
          (*C*, 74: 440–1, Pound's emphasis)

Just as Odysseus escapes the cyclops by concealing his identity, Pound, denied the right to speak, names his own disappearance. Thus the Aboriginal figure of Wanjina, denied discourse by his father-god Ungur for speaking into existence too many things,[69] can be transformed into a 'Ouan Jin' (Chinese, *Wen Jen*, 'man of letters') who knows the difference between not creating, and creating from nothing. Upon this distinction the city of Dioce is founded and Pound's role as its guardian is secured. It all depends on arrogating one's own

[68] Ezra Pound, Canto 74, in *The Cantos of Ezra Pound* (1964; London: Faber, 1994), 439, hereafter cited with canto and page numbers and abbreviated as *C*.

[69] Concerning this myth, see I. M. Crawford, *The Art of the Wandjina: Aboriginal Cave Paintings in Kimberley, Western Australia* (Oxford: Oxford University Press, 1968).

destruction: 'a man on whom the sun has gone down / . . . first must destroy himself ere others destroy him' (C, 74: 444). Envisioning catastrophe, it dawns on Pound that self-destruction obliterates any relation to others. And by turning his nadir into *amor fati*, he finds his vocation in the rubble: 'As a lone ant from a broken ant-hill / from the wreckage of Europe, ego scriptor' (C, 76: 472).

The prestidigitation whereby Pound maintains a hold on what is essential for him even in losing it is evident throughout *The Pisan Cantos*. His predicament in Italy spells a cultural erasure; there is now 'no vestige save in the air / in stone is no imprint' (C, 74: 452). But the authentic foundations of culture are only revealed as such. Just as the present moment receives its clarity and completion through becoming a memory, so the foundations of the city of Dioce remain 'now in the mind indestructible' (C, 74: 456). Thus, the plans for the city must first be lost before Pound can declare: 'I surrender neither the empire nor the temples' (C, 74: 448), for these are built on the possibility of their impossibility: 'I believe in the resurrection of Italy quia impossibile est' (C, 74: 456). Negation brings completion; the city is secured by admitting danger into its grounds. Yet every time the event of disaster is overcome the significance of its end is annulled and the essential labour remains deferred. '4 times was the city remade' (C, 77: 479), we are told, before it was lodged safely in the mind. The reference here is to the North African legend of Wagadu, a spirit of dwelling who changed her name four times, and who 'endures no matter whether she be built of stone, wood [or] earth'.[70] Only when she has been found for the fourth time will she 'live so forcefully in the minds of men that she will never be lost again.'[71] The security of the dwelling thus resides between memory and its forgetting, between no place and every place. Pound knows it exists when he can no longer locate it. Caught between two extremes of having to uphold complete transcendence in order to bring about a new Republic into the world, he has to settle for a poetic middle-ground.[72] No stone bears the city, but neither is it 'here in hypostasis'; instead, 'this land

---

[70] Carroll F. Terrell, *A Companion to the Cantos of Ezra Pound* (Berkeley: University of California Press, 1993), 370. The Wagadu legend was recorded by Leo Frobenius in *African Genesis* (London: Faber & Faber, 1938), 109–10.

[71] Ibid.

[72] Nicholls argues similarly: 'The cleavage between material and ideal is seen by Pound as the result of the [war's] debacle, and "The Pisan Cantos" seeks a kind of intermediary zone where the contradiction can be dissolved in the images of air and water which admit us to the rhythm of the "process" ' (*Ezra Pound*, 178).

is of Dione' (*C*, 76: 472), the mother of Aphrodite. Only by turning suspension into his goddess can the diverging paths of the city be brought into view.

It is writing that is frequently offered as the means of bringing the suspension about:

> and that certain images be formed in the mind
> > to remain there
> > > *formato locho*
> > Arachne mi porta fortuna
> to remain there, resurgent *EIKONEΣ*
> and still in Trastevere
> for the deification of emporers
> and the medallions
> > to forge Achaia
> and as for playing checquers with black Jim
> > on a barrel top where now is the Ritz-Carlton
> and the voice of Monsieur Fouquet or the Napoleon 3rd
> barbiche of Mr Quackenbos, or Quackenbush
> > > (*C*, 74: 460–1)

The written images hold a power that challenges that of the gods themselves, as we see in the collocation of Arachne—the girl who challenged Athena to a spinning contest—with the '*formato locho*' ('formed trace'). Existing as 'resurgent *EIKONEΣ* [icons, images]' the 'deification of emporers' are thus weaved into Pound's memories of figures from his childhood—'black Jim', John Fouquet, and Abraham Quackenbush.[73] Everything has been minted anew, rescued from the destruction of history, to be hoarded in the present. As in Eliot's *The Waste Land*, Pound has shored up fragments against his ruin. Yet nothing speaks for itself. Each image can be resituated endlessly precisely because it is no longer tied to a particular mouth. Thus, anyone can enter into this spirit—which is why Pound sets about territorializing his city even from within the fragile bounds of his tent; saturating the quotidian with other memories and forcing, or rather forging, it into another time.[74]

---

[73] See Terrell, *A Companion to the Cantos of Ezra Pound*, 385–6.

[74] Daniel D. Pearlman also sees these cantos as being preoccupied with writing a vision of eternity: 'Canto 74 is an expression of faith that art corresponds to a permanent order in reality beyond Time or "accident" ' (*The Barb of Time: On the Unity of Ezra Pound's* Cantos [Oxford: Oxford University Press, 1969], 260). See also Woodward, *Ezra Pound and The Pisan Cantos*, 67–8.

How much must be forgotten, erased, before the new Republic can be founded in the present again? This is the question posed by Pound for the people to whom he is writing—'we who have passed over Lethe' (*C*, 74: 463).

For Heidegger, in the lectures he delivered on Parmenides between 1942 and 1943, politics is also inextricably bound to issues of memory and forgetting, and, in particular, to the myth of Lethe. Determining what politics *is*, he argues, means first addressing its ontological status. Returning to the Greek conception of the '*polis*', Heidegger writes that it was conceived as

the essence of the place [*Ort*], or, as we say, it is the settlement [*Ort–schaft*] of the historical dwelling of Greek humanity. Because the πόλις lets the totality of beings come in this way or that way into the unconcealedness of its condition, the πόλις is therefore essentially related to the Being of beings.[75]

The distinction between the *polis* and politics that Heidegger goes on to draw parallels the distinction he makes between Being and beings. 'No modern concept of "the political" will ever permit anyone to grasp the essence of the πόλις [*polis*]' (*P*, 91), because 'the essence of the πόλις is not determined politically' (*P*, 96). Heidegger elaborates this with an examination of Plato's *Politics*. For Plato, he writes, dwelling on the earth is a 'sojourn in the πόλις', a course that always has an end in sight: 'περίοδος θανατοφόρος [*periodos thanatophoros*]' (*P*, 93). While this course culminates in death, the story does not end there, for the 'Being of a man' then starts on a 'new course'. The essence of the *polis* begins with a death of politics, then. Only by facing one's death can a human being grasp the essence of humanity and comprehend the relation of the 'here' (existence) and the 'there' (essence).

For Heidegger, the 'final word' on the *polis* is given in the myth of Lethe and the warrior 'Er' in Book X of Plato's *Politics*. Er, having died in battle, is collected with the rest of the dead for cremation. When he has been brought home and placed on the funeral pyre, he awakes and reports what he had seen 'there' ('ἐκεῖ'). Accompanied by others, the journey has taken him to a demonic place ('δαιμόνιος τόπος'), which leads to the field of Lethe. Before this can be reached, however, an asphyxiating and all-consuming blaze must be crossed, which prepares for the absolute barrenness of the field itself. Its

---

[75] Martin Heidegger, *Parmenides*, trans. by André Schuwer (1982; Bloomington: Indiana University Press, 1992), 90, hereafter cited as *P*.

essential nature, writes Heidegger, is its absolute opposition to any form of presencing or 'self-disclosure'. But while it appears as a place of negation it is not denied its own place:

In the essential place of Λήθη [Lethe] everything disappears. Yet it is not only the completeness of the withdrawal or the presumed quantity of concealment that distinguishes this place. The point is rather that the 'away' of the withdrawn comes into presence itself in the essence of the withdrawal. The 'away' of what is withdrawn and concealed is surely not 'nothing', for the letting disappear that withdraws everything occurs in this place—in this place alone—and presents itself there. (P, 118–19)

In presenting itself as the place 'in' which disappearance and withdrawal occur, the spirit of Lethe forgets itself. For if it dwells only *after* it has left the vicinity, one should say, rather, that it dwells in its disappearance, and so negates its possibility of *taking place*.[76] Lethe has never reached itself before becoming errant. Like Pound's city of Dioce, it is always further 'away'.

On returning to earth, Er has the essence of the *polis* burned into his memory, but only to the extent that he has been momentarily able to leave his body and all earthly existence behind. The transcendent Being of the *polis* is also secured once he has departed from it. All that is required now is its final re-creation on earth, which the pyre presages for him. The myth is thus the saviour of authentic politics—so Heidegger translates Socrates' summation of the narrative:

And so, O Glaucon, a legend has been saved and did not get lost, and it could save us, too, if we would be obedient to it; and then we will fittingly traverse the river in the field of Λήθη and will not desecrate the 'soul,' i.e. the fundamental power to say beings. (P, 126)

In this sense, the myth is not merely a narration of a series of events, it is a demand for a specific relation of bodies, existence, and essence. It is not a story so much as a *mythology*, then, for to hear its message properly necessitates following a set of instructions.

Clearly, Heidegger's depiction of the relation of politics to myth corresponds to Pound's attempt to salvage the city of Dioce from the ruins of history.[77] Yet there is also a marked difference in emphasis. For despite insisting on myth as the primary manifestation of

---

[76] See de Beistegui's reading of the myth in *Heidegger & the Political*, 117–18.

[77] Both Rabaté (*Language, Sex, and Ideology* . . ., 3) and Woodward (*Ezra Pound and The Pisan Cantos*, 87) compare Pound's Pisan breakdown and cantos to Heidegger's 'turn' and writings on death.

political essence in the world, Heidegger also asserts that the myth in itself says nothing. While it may speak of origins, myth does not speak *originally*: 'The legendary word is a *response* to the word of an appeal in which Being itself dispenses itself to man and therewith indicates the paths a seeking might take within the sphere of what is disclosed in advance' (*P*, 128, emphasis mine). This is the same conceptual leger-demain manifest in Heidegger's treatment of the *polis*. Its essence ap-pears only once it has been brought to termination, although this very termination is then described as a deposition of essence. With Pound, in contrast, the safety of the new Republic lies in myth itself; *The Pisan Cantos* are supposedly laying its foundations. Whereas Heidegger's *polis* ultimately exiles politics and myth from its realm, then, Pound offers his poetry as actively instituting a new cultural spirit. The home of the future lies not in 'hypostasis', we are told, for 'Zeus lies in Ceres' bosom' (*C*, 81: 531), grounded in earth.

But Pound has his own discourse of concealment. The mountains of Pisa presage a new, terrene elysium because they are literally clouded over. Just as for Yeats a paradisal Sligo appeared through the mist, so 'clouds over the Pisan mountains' produce a miscegenated place for Pound: 'Mt Taishan @ Pisa' (*C*, 74: 441); 'Taishan-Chocorua' (*C*, 83: 544); 'a pseudo-Vesuvius / this side of Taishan' (*C*, 80: 509). Through this concealing 'breath' that both 'shines and di-vides' (*C*, 83: 545), Pound lifts Pisa into the numinous (Taishan is a sa-cred mountain in China) *and* makes this spirit appear on earth, turning it into a familiar memory (Chocorua is a mountain in his home state of New Hampshire). In terms of these images of veiling, Pound is not far from Heidegger's assertion that 'Language is . . . the language of being, like the clouds are the clouds of heaven.'[78] But whereas for Heidegger Being ultimately remains concealed behind its own screen, Pound ultimately remains committed to finding his gods in the mud:

> Moving ὑπὸ χθονὸς enters the hall of the records
>   the forms of men rose out of γέα
>   Le Paradis n'est pas artificiel
> [. . .]

---

[78] Whereas Pound associates the clouding of place with conjunctions of earth and spirit, Heidegger sees language and clouds as things behind which Being remains withdrawn: 'Language is . . . the language of being, like the clouds are the clouds of heaven' ('Letter on Humanism', in *Martin Heidegger: Basic Writings*, ed. and trans. by David Farrell Krell [London: Harper & Row, 1978], 242).

'Missing the bull's eye seeks the cause in himself'
'only the total sincerity, the precise definition'
[. . .]
the clouds over Pisa, over the two teats of Tellus, γέα.

(*C*, 77: 482)

The force of the place that arises from hiding its grounds—'no base seen under Taishan' (*C*, 83: 544)—is nevertheless rooted in soil. The 'forms of men' who rise out of earth ('γέα') refers to the men in the Cadmus myth who emerge from under the ground ('ὑπὸ χθονὸς') in full battle-gear and proceed to attack each other. The five remaining after the carnage assist Cadmus in building Thebes. Contrary to Baudelaire's *Les Paradis Artificiels*, Paradise is *not* artificial for Pound; it grows out of Nature itself. This is also connected in the passage to a Confucian ethics of personal responsibility: in order to harmonize heart and heaven one must first marry 'total sincerity' with 'precise [verbal] definitions'.[79] Looking into one's self thus brings recognition of the 'inborn nature' of things. But elsewhere, Pound's desire to 'study what is below . . . and penetrate upwards'[80] amounts to turning the earth into its own mysterious spirit:

<pre>
man, earth: two halves of the tally
but I will come out of this knowing no one
neither they me
            connubium terrae   ἔφατα πόσις ἐμός
                                      ΧΘΟΝΙΟΣ, mysterium
fluid ΧΘΟΝΟΣ o'erflowed me
    lay in the fluid ΧΘΟΝΟΣ;
            that lie
under the air's solidity
    drunk with ᾽ΙΧΩΡ of ΧΘΟΝΙΟΣ
        fluid, ΧΘΟΝΟΣ, strong as the undertow
    of the wave receding
but that a man should live in that further terror, and live
    the loneliness of death came upon me
        (at 3 P. M., for an instant)
</pre>

(*C*, 82: 540–1)

To enter into this chthonic spirit and become earth-born ('ΧΘΟΝΙΟΣ') means entering into the 'mysterium' and letting the earth dissolve one's borders. Like the waters from the river in Lethe,

79 See Pound, *Confucius*, 29, 95, 179.   80 Pound, *Confucian Analects*, 95.

the numinous fluid ('*ΙΧΩΡ*', the blood of gods) that is drunk brings oblivion. But experiencing such absolute dissolution is possible only if the experience itself is passed over—thus the gods can remain distanced as gods, and Pound can remain living. The transition to a new state, where Pound will know no one and no one will recognize him, can only exist as a myth. The realization *is* a flash of an instant, a moment of time—'3 P. M.'—in which death is seen as dwelling in the living present only to pass. Life and death in their pure states are thus both proximate and separated, like the 'two halves of the tally'. Yet for Pound 'in limbo [there are] no victories' (*C*, 77: 484). Time itself undoes the work of extremes through which the City of Dioce could be posed as alternately transcendent and materialized: 'Time is not, Time is the evil, beloved' (*C*, 74: 458). Pound's only recourse against such a beguiling and pertinacious enemy is to plot a coup through his poetry. Either he must pass out of temporal existence, like Er through the blaze that leads to Lethe—'had I the clouds of heaven / as the nautile borne ashore / in their holocaust' (*C*, 80: 514)—or else the deferral of transcendence must be taken as confirming its absolute difference and thus become a *promise* of both 'further terror' and a kingdom to come.

As we have seen from the works considered so far, terror and violence are invoked by both Pound and Heidegger for maintaining a vision of cultural spirit.[81] Moreover, in both cases this involves the negation of an Other's existence. In Heidegger's *Parmenides* a person's insight into existence primarily requires working out one's relation to Being rather than to another person (*P*, 103–6). Only by envisioning the 'uncanny' nature of Being, which both opposes earthly vision and appears opposed, can an individual understand his/her unique existential status. Similarly, for Pound, figuring his aesthetic spirit frequently means getting rid of other witnesses:

> Cassandra, your eyes are like tigers,
> with no word written in them
> You also have I carried to nowhere
> to an ill house and there is
> no end to the journey.
>
> (*C*, 78: 491)

---

[81] See also Heidegger's earlier *Being and Time*, trans. by John Macquarrie and Edward Robinson (1926; Oxford: Blackwell, 1990), in which 'authentic' individuality is based on 'Being-towards-death', 279–348.

Just as the marriage with the chthonic gods involves experiencing and passing over absolute negation, so the vision of death here must remain alien—namely, Cassandra's. Granted the gift of prophecy by Apollo, her terrifying vision of oblivion remains her own, indecipherable. The vision of Otherness draws a blank—'no word'; only in this way can it be borne. Similarly, the appearance of Aphrodite also introduces a terrifying beauty: 'δεινὰ ἔι, κύθηρα [you are terrible/terrifying, Kythera] / terrible in resistance' (C, 79: 506). Yet the terrifying aspect of the 'Lynxes' with gleaming eyes—'γλαυκῶπις' (C, 79: 504)—with which she is associated is also muted by the veil that keeps her Other-worldly: 'with the veil of faint cloud before her / κύθηρα δεινὰ as a leaf borne in the current / pale eyes as if without fire' (C, 80: 525).

Like Heidegger's vision of Being which carries specific political and ethical imperatives, Pound's images of Cassandra and Aphrodite are fundamentally about transmissions of authentic culture. The ethical machinations of this aesthetics are further explored in two connected passages. The first concerns an event of demonic vision that takes place in Pound's tent:

> Your eyen two wol sleye me sodenly
> I may the beauté of hem nat susteyne.
>
> [. . .]
> there came new subtlety of eyes into my tent,
> whether of spirit or hypostasis,
> but what the blindfold hides
> or at carneval
> nor any pair showed anger
> Saw but the eyes and stance between the eyes,
> colour, diastasis
> careless or unaware it had not the
> whole tent's room
> nor was the place for the full Εἰδὼς
> interpass, penetrate
> casting but shade beyond the other lights
> sky's clear
> night's sea
> green of the mountain pool
> shone from the unmasked eyes in half-mask's space
> What thou lovest well remains,
> the rest is dross
>
> (C, 81: 534–5)

The first two lines, a citation from Chaucer's *Merciles Beaute*, reiterate the theme of absolute beauty involving sublime terror. In order to gain insight into this spirit of purity, one must not exchange glances with it. It must remain 'careless or unaware it had not the whole tent's room' so that there will be no Otherness reflected in its gaze. Indeed, its eyes do not reflect on things—'night's sea / green of the mountain pool'—so much as *project* them as a vision. What we are offered is an image of seeing as its own spectacle, then, an immaculate perception that has no need of corporeal sensation (*carne vale* in Italian means 'farewell to flesh') because it envisions its own embodiment. Appearing as both sight and object, the 'diastasis' of this vision produces its own autonomy, or 'hypostasis'. By concealing himself, Pound thus aims to present a seeing that is no longer linked to a subject—as when he occludes his own 'I' in the line: 'Saw but the eyes and stance between the eyes'. There is no ambiguity of these eyes for him—only of the earthly 'half-mask space' which prevents them from *appearing* as a 'full' knowing ('Εἰδώς'). Rabaté argues that Εἰδὼς is grammatically a noun in this line, and that Pound turns it into a participle by giving it an omega (ω) instead of an omicron (o), thereby distinguishing the act of perception from the form of beauty.[82] But Εἰδὼς is also the past-perfect tense of Εἰδω ('to see' or 'to know'). Rather than signalling a distantiation of vision and form, then, I would argue that, for Pound, the word expresses a mode of perception that has envisioned its own perfection—just as Confucius taught: 'The law of the Great Learning . . . lies in developing and making visible that luminous principle of reason which we have received from the sky.'[83] In presenting the image this way, Pound denies any hand in its staging. Indeed, the spirit's imperative, we are told, is: 'Pull down thy vanity'; measure oneself and one's labour in relation to its nature: 'Learn of the green world what can be thy place / in scaled invention or true artistry' (*C*, 81: 535). And because the voice of others cannot be recognized in it, the spirit also illuminates the virtue of not bending to demotic dictates:

> But to have done instead of not doing
>   this is not vanity
> To have, with decency, knocked
> That a Blunt should open
>   To have gathered from the air a live tradition

---

[82] See Rabaté, *Language, Sex, and Ideology* . . ., 167–8.   [83] Pound, *Ta Hio*, 7.

or from a fine old eye the unconquered flame
This is not vanity.

$$(C, 81: 535-6)^{84}$$

The vision calls for action, and not even the decrees of parliament su-
pervene it. Thus we are offered Wilfred Scawen Blunt, the first Englishman imprisoned for defending Irish Home Rule, as a champion
of this 'live tradition'.

In another passage, the injunction to make visible the 'luminous
principle' leads Pound to view the world as emanating from his own
eyes:

> Summons withdrawn, sir).
> (bein' aliens in prohibited area)
> clouds lift their small mountains
>   before the elder hills
>
> A fat moon rises lop-sided over the mountain
> The eyes, this time my world,
>   But pass and look *from* mine
>   between my lids
>   sea, sky, and pool
>   alternate
>   pool, sky, sea,
> morning moon against sunrise
> like a bit of the best antient greek coinage
>   (*C*, 83: 548-9, Pound's emphasis)

The 'diastasis' of the previous vision has become the possibility of
holding two differing points of view simultaneously. The 'eyes' have
been seen in their full presence because only their space of appearance is ambiguous. Yet they have remained manifestly immaculate
precisely because of this 'half-masking'. Pound thus has 'full' know-
ledge of the $E\iota\delta\grave{\omega}\varsigma$ even without its full appearance—which is why he
must envision the world in the same way. Even before the world has
issued '*from*' his eyes to be set before them, he has perceived it to be
'my world'. The chiasmic exchange of 'sea, sky, and pool' is a distinctly secondary movement, for the journey has already been delimited, the origin and destination already foreseen. In this way, the
vision of the spirit has become minted as Pound's vision. There is no

---

[84] Regarding the drafting of these passages, see Ronald Bush, ' "Quiet, Not Scornful"?
The Composition of *The Pisan Cantos*', in *A Poem Containing History: Textual Studies in* The
Cantos, ed. by Lawrence Rainey (Ann Arbor: University of Michigan Press, 1997), 204-6.
Bush sees them as a confession of Pound's own 'failure and vanity' (205).

other way in which we can view this, for there is no longer an Other. He has reached the point where an alien 'summons' can no longer be heard.

Constructing an ontology of extremes that relates cultural practice and cultural essence, Pound undertakes a similar project to Heidegger. But he ends up adopting a position on the opposite side of the ontological divide. Whereas Heidegger portrays essence as determining all relations, Pound presents an appropriation of spirit to the extent that he becomes his own ontology. Not without a certain use of violence, though; essence has never destroyed itself enough before showing itself too much. As a consequence, its final determination is endlessly deferred, becoming either a recollection or a promise. The suspension makes the emergence of an alien force possible; indeed, for Pound the force of his enemy feeds on this limbo. Spreading the Confucian 'luminous principle' calls for a hero. Someone who will teach its rectitude to others and clear a space for it in the world by ridding it of its foes. Having been charged with treason by the US government in 1943, Pound was eventually deemed unfit for trial on the grounds of insanity.[85] It was not until after 1945, when he had been incarcerated in St Elizabeth's Federal Hospital for the Insane, in Washington, DC, that he met the right disciple: a young man named John Kasper.

Pound and John Kasper: A Guide to KKKulchur

Pound's relationship and correspondence with Kasper extend over fourteen years, from 1950 to 1963, the first nine of which Pound was in St Elizabeth's. Just 20 years old when he first met the poet, Kasper developed a passion for Pound on being exposed to his poetry and politics while still a science undergraduate at Columbia University.[86] Pound's letters to Kasper have not been located, but Kasper's unpublished letters (over 400 extant), held at the Beinecke Library at

[85] For detailed discussions of Pound's trial and subsequent incarceration, see Conrad L. Rushing, ' "Mere Words": The Trial of Ezra Pound', *Critical Inquiry* 14 (Autumn 1987): 111–33; Cornell, *The Trial of Ezra Pound*; and Torrey, *The Roots of Treason*. Regarding the veracity of the ruling, Torrey concludes: 'Pound's hospital record is replete with evidence that he was eminently capable of standing trial and in assisting his own defense' (205).

[86] See Carpenter, *A Serious Character*, 799–801; and C. D. Heymann, *Ezra Pound: The Last Rower, a Political Profile* (London: Faber & Faber, 1976), 227–9. Eustace Mullins discusses the relationship briefly, in *This Difficult Individual: Ezra Pound* (New York: Fleet, 1961), 22, 310, 312; as do Meacham, *A Caged Panther*, 56–69; and Torrey, *The Roots of Treason*, 229–31.

Yale and the Lilly Library at Indiana University, Bloomington, show that the relationship that developed was intense on both parts.[87] To date, however, there has been no extensive analysis of the letters or the friendship, despite the fact that Kasper's connection to Pound was cited by the US Federal government as a reason not to release Pound from St Elizabeth's. I can only surmise that the reason for the lack of critical attention is partly because Kasper's correspondence is often extremely disturbing, and partly because it is difficult to gauge exactly what Pound was writing to him. Difficult, but not impossible; as I shall show, many of Kasper's letters are responding to specific statements and instructions from Pound, and the poet's public reticence about the relationship was privately acknowledged by him as being a deliberate strategy.

Kasper addresses the poet as 'Grampaw' and 'Boss' (Pound's nickname for Mussolini) as early as 1951. He returned from their first meeting reportedly like 'a person inspired',[88] and immediately commenced a study of the *Cantos* and other texts prescribed by Pound, who also introduced him to other devotees such as Michael Lekakis and Louis Dudek. Willingness to follow the teachings of the poet translated immediately into an absolute devotion to Pound himself; in a lengthy letter praising the *Cantos*, Kasper writes 'I am willing to learn as many languages as you demand. To study history thoroughly . . . to learn how to make atom bombs.'[89] By October 1951, Kasper's admiration had developed into a veritable passion: 'You move all men to deed, deeds that are wise and virtuous. I praise you, I praise you, I praise you. I worship you, I love you.'[90] If, for Confucius, one man is enough to spread the word, the word, for Kasper, issued from Pound alone: 'you are the only teacher I have had';[91] 'when a man gets by the barriers and reads E.P. he loves E.P., and that wholly'.[92] So he set about spreading the knowledge, searching for other young disciples. In 1951, with Pound as their chief adviser, Kasper and another admirer of the poet, Thomas David Horton, founded the 'Square Dollar Press' which published under Pound's directions texts

[87] See Ezra Pound Papers, Lilly Library, Indiana University, Bloomington, MSS II, Letters of John Kasper, 1951–3; also Ezra Pound Papers, Beinecke Library, Yale University, YCAL MSS 43, Box 26, Folders 1124–34: John Kasper, Letters to Pound, 1951–61; and YCAL MSS 53, Box 9, Folder 210, John Kasper, Letters to Pound, 1952–63.

[88] Quoted in Carpenter, *A Serious Character*, 800.

[89] Kasper, letter to Pound, 15 May 1951, Lilly Library.

[90] Kasper, letter to Pound, 30 October 1951, Lilly Library.

[91] Ibid.   [92] Kasper, letter to Pound, 10 July 1951, Lilly Library.

such as Ernest Fenollosa's *The Chinese Written Character,* Alexander Del
Mar's *Barbara Villiers, or, A History of Monetary Crimes,* Thomas Hart
Benton's *Bank of the United States,* Pound's translation of *The Analects of
Confucius,* and a collection of extracts from the anti-Darwinian biolo-
gist Louis Agassiz selected by Kasper himself. In 1953, Kasper and
Horton also set up a company, 'United Distributors', dealing in
Pound's writings and those of the authors he admired. The venture
rapidly proved successful. By February, Kasper was writing to his
mentor that interest in their catalogue had been shown in Italy and
in Germany by 'some organization in Munich called "Freiheit fur
Reich" '.[93] Other advancements were made: 'Master, Banzai!' wrote
Kasper, after getting a positive response from the Juillard School with
regard to performing Pound's Villon songs and Cavalcanti opera.[94]

If 'the light of reason will produce sincerity as if cut clean by a
scalpel', as we are told in Pound's translation of Confucius's 'The Unwobbling Pivot', Kasper believed it sincerely by 1951, asking Pound if
he should not move to Washington, DC, and enter the 'one-man university' so that 'when I stepped out, I'd have two damaskan swords,
instead of a little kitchen knife to roll heads and slash dung'.[95] His
query was met with rebuke. The same thing happened when Kasper
and his friends, Paul and Lana Lett, set up the 'Make It New' bookshop for Pound in New York city, in October 1953. On 23 October,
Kasper wrote with pride of the 'grampian' window display he had
arranged, and sent some photographs of it. The display included an
assortment of Pound's letters to him, from 1951 to 1953:

> The letters are mainly concerned with education for a young man: study
> Sophocles, Dante, Agassiz[,] Blackstone etc. Or letters re the money prob-
> lem. . . . Nothing controversial or inflammatory except the bottom of one let-
> ter which reads: 'the filth of liberals and Marxists is their absolute refusal to
> think.'[96]

All other potentially 'compromising' references, Kasper wrote, had
been 'pasted over'. Pound's irate reply, as reported by Lana Lett, was
that he had 'no contact with the outside world'.[97] This, despite the
fact that according to Lett Pound was writing to Kasper up to 'eight

---

[93] Kasper, letter to Pound, 16 February 1953, Beinecke Library.
[94] Kasper, letter to Pound, 14 July 1951, Lilly Library.
[95] Kasper, letter to Pound, 30 August 1951, Lilly Library.
[96] Kasper, letter to Pound, 23 October 1953, Beinecke Library.
[97] Lana Lett quoted in 'Woman Tells of Financing Segregationist Shop', *New York Herald Tribune* (3 February 1957): 21.

times a day'.[98] Louis Dudek met with similar censure in 1953 when he wrote of the poet's 'voluminous, practical, benevolent correspondence' with editors and writers. 'God bloody DAMN it . . . SHUT up', replied Pound, 'You are not supposed to receive ANY letters from E.P. They are UNSIGNED and if one cannot trust one's friends to keep quiet . . .'.[99] Writing at a later point to a teacher, John Theobald, who began corresponding with the poet in 1957, Pound emphasizes the value of his secret invectives while clarifying the impact his own revisioning of school curricula could have: 'The UN-Printable part of my writing is what deals with/ ANYthing of importance./ I am NOT going to read sewing circle verse? [*sic*]/ I wd/ be interested in KILLING the dope in text books.'[100] Once again, he was effectively reserving the right to name his disappearance, like Odysseus in Canto 74. Thus Pound adopted the status of master only to the extent that he could also claim anonymity.

In Confucius's 'The Unwobbling Pivot' we are told that the 'realization' of 'inborn nature' is the 'process', and the 'clarification of this process is called education' (*Confucius*, 99). As Kasper's reference to Pound's pedagogic correspondence testifies, the poet was clearly invested in setting up a Confucian relation of master and disciple with Kasper, and the young man was all too willing to follow. But while the student followed him to the letter, developing the same prose style, *mise-en-page* and colloquial phrasing (including racist: 'kike', 'yitts', 'nigra', etc.), Pound pulled him up again when he learned that Kasper had placed some books in a play-pen in the bookshop with a sign reading 'Jewish Muck' over them. After being chastized earlier for lampooning Winston Churchill, Kasper explained such acts as a question of blind devotion: 'I wanted you to know I (emotionally) concurr [*sic*] w/ your politics in even their most superficial appearance. . . . I don't know a g.d. thing re politics.'[101] Yet this ambivalence is precisely what Pound's pedagogy was demanding from Kasper: a mind that mirrors the image, a mind that is 'not [the] image'— 'speculum non est imago' (*C*, 105: 762). In this way, Pound maintained a double-stance in relation to Kasper, distancing himself from

[98] Ibid. [99] Quoted in Carpenter, *A Serious Character*, 760.
[100] Pound, letter to John Theobald, dated '24 Sept befo-brek '57', in *Ezra Pound/ John Theobald Letters*, ed. by Donald Pierce and Herbert Schneidau (Reddin Ridge: Black Swan, 1984), 98.
[101] Kasper, letter to Pound, 11 November 1951, Lilly Library.

him while encouraging him to become a double.[102] So, on the one hand, Kasper's letters repeatedly request new instructions with respect to his own reading programme, the publishing of texts, and the running of the bookshop and distribution company in general: 'I am awaiting further word about my FUNCTION: whether I should forget entirely re the [publication of the Confucian] Odes and come to D.C. or stay here until further notice.'[103] On the other hand, the letters sometimes express disappointment at the poet's withdrawal of support. In response to a letter from Pound concerning Kasper's wish to publish a book on the Federal reserves, Kasper writes: 'Your letter received and I could wish a bit more elaboration/ you say you decline responsibility. Does that mean that K[asper] & H[orton] should not bring it out? I take it it does.'[104] Yet when Kasper wrote that he was no longer sure if he could keep running the bookstore, owing to financial problems and exhaustion, Pound was quick to berate him, as is evident from Kasper's reply:

Prince:

Please, I ain't a quitter. . . .

No sir, you never raised your heel yet, not once, and I am awful sorry to . . . cause any concern over this damn shop, it's only that for 4 years you have flowed through me so utterly, so alive, that I can't (even if I wanted to) think seriously of any thought but your thought, feel anything but it is your feeling. . . .

For that matter, this shop is not mine, it is yours.[105]

How can we make a clear judgement on Pound's responsibility when it involves dealing in such confusion? As far as Robert Casillo is concerned, Pound's relationships with his young St Elizabeth's habitués involved enforcing a highly controlled form of imitation, in contrast to the type that emerged in his radio speeches: 'at St Elizabeth's Pound himself was the unacknowledged mediator, and imitation was not only open but controlled by Pound. A clear difference separated him from his disciples, among whom Pound was the unap-

---

[102] The feeling of power that Pound experienced in ventriloquizing is evident in a letter he wrote to Adriano Ungaro about the radio speeches he had written to be read out by someone else: 'I like Morelli's reading of my stuff. The anonymous stuff is in some ways better than the personal / When anonymous I can be omniscient / when I speak in my own voice I have to be modest and stick to what I have seen at first hand' (quoted in Redman, *EPIF*, 211).

[103] Kasper, letter to Pound, 16 January 1953, Lilly Library.

[104] Kasper, letter to Pound, 11 August 1952, Lilly Library.

[105] Kasper, letter to Pound, 18 February [1955], Beinecke Library.

proachable model . . .'.[106] Certainly, instructing Kasper in aesthetic ambivalence helped Pound deny any responsibility for subsequent events. Throughout their correspondence, Pound reiterated the necessity for 'action' and the need to take on new recruits. With classes in Ancient Greek and some of Pound's favourite economists running at the bookstore, Kasper continually wrote of having found new disciples willing to fight for the Confucian 'process'—some of whom were subsequently introduced to the poet on Kasper's visits.[107] Indeed, recruitment had taken place even before the bookshop had been set up. December 1951: Kasper reports recruiting a 'militant Catholic', Thomas Ritt.[108] October 1952: 'I have gathered at least 2 "young" who know what's going on.'[109] November 1952: a '17 year old Nazi' has moved in with him.[110] 1955: he has found 'a new gunman, Eddie Moss (German not Jew) very goy, who is ready to liquidate any "big" hebrew'.[111] May 1955: he writes of a 'hillbilly', Tom Truelove: 'He was totally uneducated before Make It New. Now becoming vurry vurry, yais indeed, vurry useful.'[112] September 1955: 'Have acquired 2 additional gunmen in need of a pogrom. Details verbally.'[113] In addition, he has 'organised some Afro-American vitality to break the Jew-Grip'—security against the increasing number of Jewish attacks on the shop. All these people, Kasper writes, 'are as sincere as Confucius'. 1955: 'Tom T almost left for Miami last week to begin a pogrom'.[114] In this way, Kasper literally became the poet's middleman, for as well as introducing Pound to the new members, access to the poet was often initially possible only through Kasper. Regarding Ritt's induction, he wrote: 'He (Ritt) fully agrees it is best not to have any direct communication with Grampaw (correspondence) and is perfectly willing to

---

[106] Robert Casillo, *The Genealogy of Demons: Anti-Semitism, Fascism, and the Myths of Ezra Pound* (Evanston: Northwestern University Press, 1988), 309.

[107] Pound's daughter, Mary de Rachewiltz, maintains Pound's naïveté with respect to these gatherings: 'the young people who came to see him were a new species of human being in appearance: sloppy and ignorant. . . . It seemed to me no one had read or seen anything, certainly had not read much Pound. . . . if father threw a new name at them they ran off with it like crazy dogs with a bone. . . . The sad fact was that there was no one else willing or able to keep him company regularly and he needed an outside audience as an antidote to the inmates' (*Discretions* [London: Faber, 1971], 296–7).

[108] Kasper, letter to Pound, 11 December 1951, Lilly Library.

[109] Kasper, letter to Pound, 2 October 1952, Lilly Library.

[110] Kasper, letter to Pound, 7 November 1952, Lilly Library.

[111] Kasper, letter to Pound, [1955], Beinecke Library.

[112] Kasper, letter to Pound, 18 May 1955, Beinecke Library.

[113] Kasper, letter to Pound, 2 September 1955, Beinecke Library.

[114] Kasper, letter to Pound, [1955], Beinecke Library.

work through Kasp.'[115] While he frequently became jealous when a friendship developed between his master and these acolytes, the more Kasper's love increased, the more he sought to increase the ranks. By 1957, the drive for recruitment was intensified. Writing on Pound's seventy-third birthday, Kasper wrote:

Grampaw, Lord,

We earnestly pray you'll keep in good health . . . to see the day when you are soveraigne o'er all the wee birdies of the air and the beasties o' the fields and are Lord o'er all. Prince, seer of the inborn natures of men, reader of the semina motuum, Tiresias, just keep on keeping . . . sidgismundo, your army's gathering every day. Please, we need you for the offense and the charge.[116]

Letters like this might suggest that Kasper himself would not have been out of place in St Elizabeth's, but they also show the degree to which he had immersed himself in Pound's writings. The closing reference is to Sidgismundo Malatesta (1417–68), the main figure of Pound's earlier *Malatesta Cantos*, who refused to pay taxes to Popes Pius II and Paul II, and routed the papal army with his forces when only 13. Kasper had begun signing himself 'Little Sidge' in 1955.[117] The army was indeed gathering.

In 1955, Kasper's desire to spread the seeds of the movement had reached feverish heights, particularly as the time was so ripe. In 1954, the US Supreme Court ruled an end to segregated schools in the South. The process of integration began to be implemented in May 1955, which led to a widespread rekindling of white-supremacist organizations such as the Ku Klux Klan (KKK) and the more middle-class White Citizens' Councils.[118] Much of the anti-integrationist rhetoric was anti-semitic. Individuals like J. B. Stoner, who formed a 'Christian Anti-Jewish Party', declared the whole situation a Jewish plot, telling an Atlanta audience 'we ought to kill all Jews just to save

---

[115] Kasper, letter to Pound, 11 November 1951, Lilly Library.

[116] Kasper, letter to Pound, 30 October [1957], Beinecke Library.

[117] Kasper, letter to Pound, 4 September [1955], Beinecke Library.

[118] See Michael R. Belknap, *Federal Law and Southern Order: Racial and Constitutional Conflict in the Post-Brown South* (Athens: The University of Georgia Press, 1987); Benjamin Muse, *Ten Years of Prelude: The Story of Integration Since the Supreme Court's 1954 Decision* (Beaconsfield: Darwin & Finlayson, 1964); Allen D. Grimshaw (ed.), *Racial Violence in the United States* (Chicago: Aldine, 1969), 289–90, 320–6; Wyn Craig Wade, *The Fiery Cross: The Ku Klux Klan in America* (New York: Simon & Schuster, 1987), 276–305; and David Chalmers, *Hooded America: The History of the Ku Klux Klan* (Durham: Duke University Press, 1987), 344–56. For a study of the historical background to integration, see *The Age of Segregation: Race Relations in the South, 1890–1945*, ed. by Robert Haws (Jackson: University Press of Mississippi, 1978).

their unborn generations from having to go to hell'.[119] Asa 'Ace' Carter, leader of the Alabama 'Original KKK confederacy', followed suit, his Klansmen wearing pseudo storm-trooper outfits. Another campaigner for racial purity was Admiral John Crommelin, a World War II hero, who ran for Senate in Alabama in 1955 in order to save the state from Jewish subversion.[120] Kasper became his secretary and campaign manager. That Pound was implicated in the alliance; that Kasper was campaigning for Pound is clear from the letters.

New Year's Eve, 1955: Kasper sends a card, hoping that the New Year will bring 'The first American Pogrom' and '3 more generals to meet Gramp'.[121] The three 'generals' referred to are probably Admiral Crommelin, and two other figures who campaigned with Kasper: General Pedro del Valle, who had commanded the US marines in the battle of Okinawa; and George Lincoln Rockwell, who became the leader of the US neo-Nazi movement.[122] With the campaigning underway, Kasper requested material for speeches:

COPY. COPY. Can you write some short quotable slogans. Nothing highbrow. . . . /And 5 minute speeches. and 15 minute speeches.
on Segregation/States rights.
Mongrelization/Separation of Races.
NIGGERS.
and JEWS: the Admiral has taken up THE Question openly and it hasn't hurt him. The kike behind the nigger. . . .
Things look very good. The farmers are ON.[123]

Pound, still officially insane in St. Elizabeth's, obliged, as is evident from Kasper's expressions of gratitude: 'The Admiral sends his warmest regards and appreciation of all efforts from D.C. he has used at least 1/4 of Grampian summaries./ The pome [poem] will be used SOMEHOW.'[124] Two memos from Pound to Kasper also show the extent of the poet's advice on strategy:

don't get bogged in segregation. keept [sic] to BASIC principle, local control of local 'affairs'./ i.e. purchasing power./. . . . Get the ku kluxers to keep their

[119] Quoted in Wade, *The Fiery Cross*, 283.
[120] See Chalmers, *Hooded America*, 352–3; and Wade, *The Fiery Cross*, 303–4.
[121] Kasper, letter to Pound, 31 January [1955], Beinecke Library.
[122] Carpenter mentions Rockwell in *A Serious Character*, 827; as does Torrey in *The Roots of Treason*, 229.
[123] Kasper, letter to Pound, 10 April [1956], Beinecke Library.
[124] Kasper, letter to Pound, [1956], Beinecke Library.

their eye on the main issue, not the immediate irritant, granting it is the ac-
censio sanguinis/. . .[125]

Nothing is more damnably harmful to everyone, black and white than mis-
cegnation [sic], bastardization and mongrelization of EVERYthing. . . .
admit NO immigrants to registration who don't swear loyalty to state constitution. . . .
leave local option in principle, but make it unbearable in fact. Metaphor and
tradition: refusal of water and fire. ostracize 'em. surround 'em, cut 'em off,
but don't MIX principles for an immediate advantage . . .[126]

These extracts clearly show that Pound regarded the campaigning
largely to be about asserting local autonomy against Federal interference—all of which he relates to the Confucian process when signing
off in the first memo: 'Gramp/ job is SEED [semina motuum], to ripen
in 50 years'.[127] But his reference to organizing the KKK also suggests
that he was willing to accept the most extreme course of action in
order for the process to take root. This is more overt in the second
memo, which consists of eight dense pages of advice on political, economic, and aesthetic matters. Unsigned, it can nevertheless be identified as Pound's because Kasper raises 'the matter of "local option" '
at length in a letter from 1956 dated '30 June'.[128]

As the campaign rolled on through 1956, Kasper kept up a stream
of excited correspondence presaging success: 'You is com' like fast
freight through cow country, there's nothing they can do (try as they
may, the bastards) anymore to stop you.'[129] While he never officially
became a member of the KKK, Kasper maintained a very close affiliation. He and Crommelin teamed up with Asa Carter and were
continually appearing at Klan rallies and distributing their material:
'[Carter] has mobilised his 40,000 members behind us and on saturday we are having a 200 car cavalcade moving all over [Alabama]
distributing 100,000 of Rockwell's cartoons . . .'.[130] Pound himself received Klan material from Kasper, and although he did not join he
did try to persuade James Dickie to become a member.[131] By 1956,
having moved base to Washington, Kasper, however, was chief

[125] Pound, letter to Kasper, 17 May [1956], Beinecke Library.
[126] Pound, unsigned letter to Kasper, [1956], Beinecke Library.
[127] Pound, letter to Kasper, 17 May [1956], Beinecke Library.
[128] Kasper, letter to Pound, 30 June [1956], Beinecke Library.
[129] Kasper, letter to Pound, [1956], Beinecke Library.
[130] Kasper, letter to Pound, [1956], Beinecke Library. On Kasper's links with the Klan
see Chalmers, Hooded America, 306.
[131] See Torrey, The Roots of Treason, 231.

executive of Washington's 'Seaboard White Citizens' Council'. The organization bore the Confucian definition of metaphysics from 'The Unwobbling Pivot' on its stationery: 'Only the most absolute sincerity under heaven can effect any change' (*Confucius*, 95).

With the White Citizens' Councils inciting action throughout the South, things came to a head on 2 September 1956 in Clinton, Tennessee, when the first Southern school was officially integrated.[132] Kasper had been on the scene days before the official opening, living in his car, organizing rallies, and phoning residents, reportedly telling them: 'The niggers got to be pulled out of the high school. We're calling a meeting—you'd better come.'[133] Arrested before the opening date for vagrancy and 'circulating literature likely to cause an affray', his incitements had already worked. The school's re-opening resulted in two days of rioting and mob demonstration that led to 633 National Guardsmen, seven tanks, and two armoured personnel-carriers having to be brought in by the Federal government. Pound argued to Archibald MacLeish that Kasper was in no way responsible: 'Why pick on Kasp who was NOT on the scene of the riot, and was acquitted by jury in 44 minutes?'[134] However, as Benjamin Muse points out, Kasper's brief incarceration was itself a catalyst for the unrest. Asa Carter arrived the day after he was gaoled and began inciting a crowd to chant 'We want Kasper', which culminated in a march on the Mayor's house and threats to dynamite it.[135] It was the beginning of a series of riots, bombings, beatings, and murders that occurred throughout the South as desegregation became instituted.[136] Kasper was released on bail, as happened almost every time he was rearrested—the financial backing of the White Citizens' Councils proved a valuable asset for legal defence. Even after being sentenced to one year's imprisonment for contempt of court in July 1957,

[132] For a full account of these events and Kasper's involvement, see Muse, *Ten Years of Prelude*, 94–120.

[133] Quoted in 'Partisan of Prejudice: Frederick John Kasper', *New York Times* (24 July 1957): 12. Another of Kasper's methods, according to the article, involved circulating 'copies of photographs supposedly showing Negro soldiers mingling with white girls at a dance' (ibid.).

[134] Quoted in Carpenter, *A Serious Character*, 827.

[135] See Muse, *Ten Years of Prelude*, 95–6.

[136] In 1959 the Friends' Service Committee issued a report on racial violence that had occurred in the first four years after the Brown decision: it cited 530 cases, which included six African Americans killed, twenty-nine individuals shot (eleven white), forty-four people beaten, thirty homes bombed, and four synagogues bombed (Chalmers, *Hooded America*, 350).

Kasper and sixteen fellow segregationists were released on bail when their defence lawyers motioned for a new trial.[137] Throwing himself back into segregationist activism every time he was released, his sheer pertinacity eventually caught up with him, though, and led to a series of prison terms. By 1960, with Pound back in Italy after his release from St Elizabeth's in May 1958, Kasper, writing from behind bars, saw himself as taking up the poet's mantle: 'I am set up much like you were in your last years at St. E. Incoming mail is opened and read. Outgoing goes sealed and unread so long as I can find a way to mail it . . .'.[138]

Pound's relationship with Kasper certainly did not make the case for his release any easier. With segregationist activities becoming the newspapers' leading story in 1957, the relation of Kasper to Pound was widely publicized. As a result, several of Pound's friends who were campaigning for his release, including T. S. Eliot, Ernest Hemingway, e. e. cummings, and Allen Tate, pressed him to renounce any link.[139] Harry Meacham cites a letter he received from MacLeish expressing the extent of the problem they faced: 'The principle obstacle now is Kasper. . . . I have found P very reasonable and patient about the whole sad business . . . [but] I should never dream of suggesting to him that he do anything he doesn't want to do.'[140] On speaking to the Attorney General, William P. Rogers, on 13 April 1957, Meacham had been told that the Department of Justice 'felt that if he were released Pound might join Kasper in the South and people would be killed'.[141] Yet despite the damage the relation was doing to his case, each time the matter was raised Pound refused to condemn his friend,

---

[137] The Kasper trial was the South's first jury trial involving a Federal court against segregationists. A week before the verdict, John N. Popham in 'Civil Rights Jury Trial in Action', *New York Times* (14 July 1957) commented on the importance of the outcome: 'everyone here recognises that on the national scene the verdict will greatly color the argument on whether Southern white juries are loath to convict white defendants in racial conflicts' (iv, 7). Despite the intensity of attacks on Jews and African Americans after the Brown decision, the number of incarcerations was negligible because of the reluctance of Southern white juries to convict.

[138] Kasper, letter to Pound, 22 February, 1960, Beinecke Library.

[139] In a letter dated 10 September 1952, Lewis wrote to Pound questioning his motives for staying in St Elizabeth's: 'To take up a strategic position in a lunatic asylum is idiotic. If I dont [sic] see you make an effort to get out soon, I shall conclude, either that your present residence has a snobbish appeal for you, or that you are timid with regard to Fate' (Materer, *Pound/Lewis*, 273).

[140] MacLeish, letter to Meacham, 17 October 1957, quoted in Meacham, *A Caged Panther*, 60.

[141] Ibid., 121.

maintaining his essential philanthropy. 'I doubt if Kasper hates any-one', he told MacLeish, 'his action in keeping open shack for stray cats and humans seems to indicate a kind heart with no exclusion of nubians.'[142] Both kept up a constant correspondence throughout this time, with Kasper writing of new publishing possibilities, available homesteads for a Southern Pound university, and of the 'ATTACK programme' in general.

There is no question that Pound knew of Kasper's sincerity in en-forcing his master's values at all costs from fairly early in the cam-paign. Christmas, 1956:

hoping the New Year will find Providence (Schicksal sagt der Führer [des-tiny speaks for the leader]) turn the 'light of the Occident' loose from the mites and termites./ not disobeying orders, but here on urgent matters [drawings inserted of TNT, a bomb, a tree with a noose, and a dagger] all leading we hope to the dissemination of Ezratic civilization./ Praying the New Year will be healthy, vindictive, bloody, paradisal . . .[143]

Pound himself effectively sanctioned such campaigning, as his memos cited above testify. This is not to say that there were no disagreements about procedure. At times, Kasper appears unsure about the recti-tude of his actions, and about Pound's approbation: 'If I'm doin' wrong, going down the wrong road, getting corrupt in character, act-ing unconfucian, am in a rut or stupid, please say so. I would quit the Citizens [sic] Councils today if you asked me to.'[144] The fact that he continued with his activism suggests that Pound refrained from ask-ing him to stop—there is certainly no evidence of him doing so from Kasper's letters. Indeed, there are points at which Kasper seems to depend wholly on Pound's instruction, as when he writes in March 1957: 'General when can we come home?'[145]

Pound's 1942 radio call for authentic 'political violence' is precisely what Kasper was trying to instigate. Just as the violence against Afro-Americans was declared in Pound's speech to be extrinsic to the real Jewish issue *and* necessitated by it, so Kasper frequently saw his seg-regationism as essentially fighting Semitic influences. One of the

---

[142] Quoted in Torrey, *The Roots of Treason*, 230. Pound's—and thus Kasper's—insistence that integration was, at base, a Jewish issue led to a denial that being a segregationist meant being anti-African American rights. Pound told MacLeish that he was: 'vurry sceptik re/K's dislike of Afroamericans' (quoted in Carpenter, *A Serious Character*, 828).

[143] Kasper, letter to Pound, 25 December [1956], Beinecke Library.

[144] Kasper, letter to Pound, [1956], Beinecke Library.

[145] Kasper, letter to Pound, 28 March 1957, Beinecke Library.

corollaries of this is that he frequently dissolves his segregationist violence into issues of education. May 1957:

Still rabblerousin', still fightin'. . . .
we've slowed the entire race-mixing movement a helluvalot, and the bastards are getting scared. . . . Adm. Crommelin n' me spoke at Clinton Courthouse about 2 months ago. Crommelin opened up on the jews. The crowd went wild. Last Aug. when I first went to Clinton they didn't know what a kike was. I'm very proud of that educational feat. Also we've removed 3 jew's pimp's [*sic*] from the Anderson County school board, put in a new mayor, kicked out a jew school princilal [*sic*], [and] started a going paper (breaking news monopoly). . . .
Hillbillies talking of E[zra] P[ound] as readily as Dn'l Boone or Davey Crockett. . . . Kids digesting the digest [Confucius's 'The Great Digest'] and trying Kung [Confucius] in with Hard-Shell baptist outlook.[146]

It would, of course, be extremely rash to claim that all of this is the natural consequence of Pound's pedagogy and aesthetics. But neither should we dissociate these from the events with the facility that most critics have. Humphrey Carpenter, for example, is critical of the relationship, but comments that 'Ezra took little interest in the Kasper affair'[147] in terms of the trials and convictions. Yet in response to one of Kasper's court appearances in September 1956, Pound wrote to Brigit Patmore: 'Der Kasperl smiling in handcuffs and making the snooze [news] even in . . . Brit/ along with the LOOSEwypapers full page of fried nigger.'[148] Harry Meacham argues that 'When the definitive account of these events is written, I am sure that it will absolve Pound from any connection with Kasper beyond their literary collaboration.'[149] Aside from the clear evidence of Pound's advisory role in Kasper's campaigning, to reduce Pound's role in the relationship to the literary is to fail to recognize that Pound's poetics and pedagogy at this time were very much concerned with mediating relations between writing, politics, and action. Showing others the light of reason meant revealing what the process is not. For Pound, the necessity of instituting the process justified going to extremes. Just as Semitism could not be acknowledged as being part of this aesthetics, neither could the violence against it.

---

[146] Kasper, letter to Pound, 11 May 1957, Beinecke Library.

[147] Carpenter, *A Serious Character*, 829.

[148] Pound, letter to Brigit Patmore, 19 September 1956, Humanities Research Center, The University of Austin Texas.

[149] Meacham, *A Caged Panther*, 122.

'Maintain antisepsis, let the light pour': The Rock-Drill *and* Thrones
Cantos

The final two 'decads' of the *Cantos*, *Rock-Drill*, *LXXXV–XCV* (1956),
and *Thrones*, *XCVI–CIX* (1959), which Pound was composing throughout his relationship with Kasper, mark the point at which the epic as-
cends to Paradise in parallel with Dante's *Divine Comedy*. Yet these
cantos are also scattered with pedagogic passages of militancy and in-
vective. Relating such passages to Kasper's activities is justifiable
given that Pound himself makes explicit reference to Kasper's fellow
activists, as I shall demonstrate.

The first *Rock-Drill* canto opens with the ideogram 'Ling²':

> LING²
>
>
>
> Our destiny came in because of a great sensibility.
>
> (*C*, 85: 557)

It is a complex character; the upper radical [image] represents heaven,
clouds, and rain (the four small lines); the three boxes also represent
rain (though Pound also saw them as divine mouths), and means 'wiz-
ard', or 'sorcery'.[150] Usually rendered as 'the spirit of a being which
acts on others', Pound defines the character here as 'great sensibility',
and goes on to 'rhyme' it with his German neologism 'Sagetrieb'. A
coupling of *'sage'* ('legend', cognate of *'sagen'*, 'to say'), and *'trieb'*
('drive' or 'will'), Sagetrieb functions for Pound as both a force of language and an emplotment of spiritual force.[151] Like Heidegger's presentation of the myth of Lethe, it is offered as a *mythology*; a way of
reading 'the way'. It also voices the ontological vacillation that characterizes Pound's attempts to move from the earthly to the divine in
these last decads. Accordingly, a series of contradictory pedagogical
images arises—many of which Pound draws from Séraphin
Couvreur's Latin and French translation of the classic Confucian history, the *Chou King*.

[150] My breakdown of the character is taken from Paul Wellen, 'An Analytic Dictionary
of Ezra Pound's Chinese Characters', *Paideuma* 25: 3 (Winter 1996): 83.

[151] Rabaté relates Sagetrieb to Heidegger's musings on *Sage* in his post-fifties texts, *Language, Sex, and Ideology . . .*, 276–8.

The *Chou King* is itself a motley text, consisting of dialogues between emperors and ministers juxtaposed with exhortations from generals to their troops, and Pound invariably cites only fragments from it. The four basic Confucian principles ('TUAN') of 'jen' (humanity), 'i' (equity), 'li' (propriety), and 'chih' (wisdom), are 'from nature', we are told, and 'Not from descriptions of the school house' (*C*, 99: 725). Knowledge is thus received from heaven, like Pound's Pisan vision in the tent; it dwells in light, 'enrolled in the ball of fire' (*C*, 108: 778). But it also depends on the power of an institution to 'build light' (*C*, 94: 656); '1st / honest man's heart demands sane curricula' (*C*, 99: 725). Once again, empiricism and idealism are both mixed and segregated. Thus, the emanation of reason from light is also made to emanate from the body of a ruler: 'The Sage Emperor's heart is our heart' (*C*, 99: 709); 'the whole tribe is from one man's body' (*C*, 99: 722). In this way, Sagetrieb comes to mean understanding that the sage rules the tribe: 'that the king . . . shd / be king' and the state 'not a melting pot' (*C*, 94: 655). So although true love for the Confucian 'process' entails seeing that it dwells 'beyond civic order' (*C*, 94: 648), building the light also necessitates building ranks: 'train the fit men' (*C*, 85: 571); 'get men, it will grow . . . men strong as bears' (*C*, 86: 575). Policing racial separatism thus becomes a form of aesthetic practice: 'pity, yes, for the infected / but maintain antisepsis, / let the light pour' (*C*, 94: 649).

Pound is sedulous in linking these sagely apophthegms to particular historical periods and figures throughout *Rock-Drill* and *Thrones*. Referring to a range of different sources, instances of good governance and economic management are identified in Ancient Egypt, Medieval and Elizabethan England, the Rome of Antoninus, and several Chinese dynasties. Apollonius of Tyana and the Elizabethan judge Sir Edward Coke are also singled out as being particularly notable avatars of the 'great sensibility'. As Leon Surette has commented, in Apollonius Pound clearly saw parallels with himself.[152] As a sage and mystic in the first century AD, Apollonius travelled widely, counselled various kings (as Pound had attempted to counsel Mussolini), and was twice charged with treason, first by the emperor Nero and then by Domitian. Apollonius is thus praised for being 'unpolluted' (*C*, 91: 630) in his principled actions, just as Wilfred Scawen Blunt was praised in Canto 81 for 'gather[ing] a live tradition' in

[152] See Leon Surette, *A Light of Eleusis: A Study of Ezra Pound's* Cantos (Oxford: Clarendon, 1979), 240.

defending Irish Home Rule. A letter of 4 September 1955 from Kasper to Pound shows that the poet also saw Apollonius as being relevant to the young segregationist. Alluding to their correspondence about Kasper's earlier violence towards a married woman with whom he had had an affair, Kasper writes: 'numerous reasons have been set forth for the emotive excesses of that time, including observations of Apollonius of Tyana transmitted by Grampaw . . .'.[153]

Coke is another figure whom Pound sees as offering valuable lessons for contemporary culture. Yet as Peter Dale Scott has pointed out, there is also a more sinister side to Coke's role in history.[154] A prosecuting advocate in the trials of the Earl of Essex, and the Gunpowder plotters, he was ruthless in his denunciations, and in the trial of Sir Walter Ralegh, which he had arranged, he 'lost all control, speaking words which are held forever to his shame'.[155] Moreover, Coke's anti-Semitism led him to write favourably in his *Institutes* of Edward I's expulsion of Jews from England in 1275 as a way of countering usury. As Scott points out, this 'Statute on Jewry', which Coke quotes in *Institutes*, is incorporated by Pound into Canto 108 through a series of fragmentary quotations from it. Yet Pound never refers to the title of the Statute, nor does he refer to Jews at any point in the Canto, even when citing the number of subjects expelled—'15 000 three score' (*C*, 108: 779). The event is only summarized obliquely: 'Divers had banished / but the usuries no King before him' (*C*, 108: 779)—in other words, whereas other monarchs had banished Jews, none before Edward had forbidden usury. It is only by returning to Coke's text that the anti-Semitic context of the quotations becomes clear.

At other points in *Rock-Drill* and *Thrones*, Pound is more overt in his combativeness, to the point of turning Sagetrieb into diatribe:

> the light flowing, whelming the stars.
>   In the barge of Ra-Set
> On river of crystal
> So hath Sibile a boken isette.
> *Democracies electing their sewage*
> *till there is no clear thought about holiness*
> *a dung flow from 1913*

---

[153] Kasper, letter to Pound, 4 September [1955], Beinecke Library.

[154] See Peter Dale Scott, 'Anger in Paradise: The Poetic Voicing of Disorder in Pound's Later Cantos', *Paideuma* 19: 3 (Winter 1990): 47–63.

[155] Catherine Drinker Bowen, *The Lion and the Throne: The Life and Times of Sir Edward Coke* (Boston: Little Brown, 1956), 211.

> *and, in this, their kikery functioned, Marx, Freud,*
>   *and the american beaneries*
> *Filth under filth,*
>   (*C*, 91: 627–8, Pound's emphasis)

Pound originally marked the section in italics to be set in smaller type, as if the force of his enemy would diminish and be separated accordingly. But the difference in character is audibly lessened by the rapidity with which the lines on divine light are chanelled into the sewer; the full stop after 'So hath Sibile a boken isette' reads more like a colon leading into the next clause. In founding itself through opposition, authentic fate is thus illuminated only by simultaneously proscribing and prescribing a subversive historicity. And it needs two contradictory modes of writing to do this. One that apotropaically marks the enemy with a different voice, as with the use of italics. Another that resists *de*-scription, marking its separation from other voices, as with the ideogrammes that each retain a precise signification distinct to that of their phonemes.[156]

Pound makes it clear that he views ideogrammic writing as a cache of armaments in itself in an earlier essay, 'L'Ebreo, Patalogia Incarnata [The Jew, Pathology Incarnate]' (1941): '[the ideogramme] is a bulwark against those who destroy language . . . a sort of *rebus* . . . it has become a treasury of stable wisdom, an arsenal of live thought'.[157] In *Rock-Drill* and *Thrones* the character that best exemplifies this agonistic force is 'chen⁴':

> non coelum non in medio
>   but man is under Fortuna
> ?that is a forced translation?
>   La donna che volgo
> Man under Fortune,
>   CHÊN

>   (*C*, 86: 580)

---

[156] Jacques Derrida, in *Of Grammatology*, trans. by Gayatri Chakravorty Spivak (Baltimore: The Johns Hopkins University Press, 1978), notes Pound's historical achievement of foregrounding writing's break with speech: 'this irreducibly graphic poetics was, with that of Mallarmé, the first break in the most entrenched Western tradition. The fascination that the Chinese ideogram exercised on Pound's writing may thus be given all its historical significance' (92).

[157] Quoted in Nicholls, *Ezra Pound*, 153, Pound's emphasis. See also Rabaté, *Language, Sex, and Ideology* . . ., ch. 2; and Nicholls, *Ezra Pound*, 191–8.

The first line is a fragment of Couvreur's Latin version of a passage from the *Chou King*. As Nicholls, has noted, Pound's translation is indeed 'forced'; the specific passage translates as: 'It is not heaven which is not impartial; but man's lot is an unhappy one.'[158] That is to say, man might depart from the 'process', but the 'process' continues to work inexorably. Thus Pound translates the passage as 'man is under Fortuna', and then links this to a line from Cavalcanti's canzone to Fortune: '*Io sono la donna che volgo la ruota*' ('I am the lady who turneth the wheel').[159] Fortune in the canzone directs the turnings of the world, just as Dante's Fortune, in the *Inferno*, lends a divine hand to the distribution of wealth—Pound refers to this in Canto 96 (*C*, 670). Labouring beyond the civic order, Fortuna, for Pound, is thus the figure who brings earthly economics into line with the heavens. There is no abstraction intended here; this is why Pound links her to 'CHÊN' (chen⁴), which means 'to shake, to excite, to terrify', like 'a shock of thunder'.[160] As a fulminating force, Fortune is chief guardian of the 'great sensibility' (ling²). The connection is implicit, for ling² and chen⁴ share the same upper radical signifying a heavenly force raining down: 雨 .

But just as the ideogrammes' graphic significance needs to be voiced by a sage, so Fortune's divine power needs to be supplemented on the ground. Consequently, her terrifying aspect is at times overshadowed by instances of terroristic activism, particularly in *Thrones*. Oliver Cromwell ('Noll') is praised as a regicide (*C*, 107: 771), for example, and John Felton's assassination of the anti-parliamentarian Duke of Buckingham is also lauded as striking a blow for constitutionalism (*C*, 108: 781). In Canto 105 such resistance is brought closer to home when Pound invokes Kasper's fellow campaigners as defenders of faith:

> a Crommelyn at the breech-block
> or a del Valle,
> This is what the swine haven't got
> with their
> πανουργία [villainy]
> (*C*, 105: 765)

---

[158] Nicholls's translation, *Ezra Pound*, 186. For the relevant passage, see Séraphin Couvreur, *Chou King: les annales de la Chine* (Ho Kien fou, 1897), 388.

[159] The translation is Pound's, in *The Spirit of Romance* (London: Dent, 1910), 111.

[160] Wellen, 'An Analytic Dictionary of Ezra Pound's Chinese Characters', 65.

Referring to this passage, Scott writes that 'If Pound's poetry could be shown to have instigated anyone like Crommelin or Kasper in their terrorism, the case for teaching it as literature would be tenuous.'[161] A letter to Pound written by Kasper in July 1957 while awaiting trial for his activities shows that the above passage was indeed viewed by the segregationist as an imprimatur: 'New lines re Cromm/ and D.V. [del Valle] mighty fine and much appreciate seeing contemporary hist/ fitted between the permanent.'[162] This is not to say that Kasper would have refrained from his own 'πανουργία' without Pound's influence, but it does show the extent to which Pound's aesthetic pedagogy was mired in the terrorist events. My view is that this makes it all the more important that these later cantos continue to be taught and read critically.

Whatever the degree to which we see Pound's poetry as being linked to segregationist violence, his refusal publicly to chastise Kasper was a speech inaction of immense consequence. 'Well at least he's a man of action and don't sit around looking at his navel',[163] Pound told Meacham. By this stage Kasper had been arrested along with sixteen others for the dynamiting of the Hattie Cotton school in Nashville, on 10 September 1957. While he was released for lack of evidence, Kasper's letter in which he thanks Pound for the Crommelin and del Valle references shows that he was not averse to using terrorist action: 'This goddam trial has all busy [sic], trying to hang witnesses, assassinate judges, bomb courthouse etc.'[164] Louis Zukofsky declared that Pound was no more accountable for all of this 'than Aristotle for the Hollywood production of Alexander the Great'.[165] But it is Confucius who is closer to the mark, as Pound disingenuously summed it up for MacLeish: 'Kasper heard about Confucius and history.'[166] That Pound ultimately considered both Kasper's ventures

---

[161] Scott, 'Anger in Paradise', 58.

[162] Kasper, letter to Pound, 1 July 1957, Beinecke Library.

[163] Meacham, A Caged Panther, 62.

[164] Kasper, letter to Pound, 1 July 1957, Beinecke Library. Robert Alden in 'Seven Suspects held in School Blast', New York Times (11 September, 1957) reported that Kasper had been inciting violence in the days before the blast: 'In Nashville he has told them that it might be in order to use shotguns, dynamite or hanging ropes to keep their schools integrated' (25). Three days later Alden reported that Charles Reed, a KKK member, had told police that Kasper had arrived at his house with dynamite two days before the blast ('FBI Agents help Nashville Inquiry', New York Times [14 September 1957]: 1). The next day he wrote that Kasper had refused 'to confirm or deny' the charge ('Kasper questioned on Blast at School', New York Times [15 September 1957]: 1).

[165] Quoted in Meacham, A Caged Panther, 122.

[166] Quoted in Carpenter, A Serious Character, 829.

and his own evasion of accountability a boon is evident from a letter written to Wyndham Lewis in February 1957: 'Kasp/ has used expediency, and may have done some good, as the attempt to implicate grampaw in civic disorder don't seem to have got beyond the most stinking pinkerei.'[167]

As attempts at engendering new combative powers of culture, Pound's figures of Sagetrieb and Fortune can be seen as further examples of how relations between violence, terror, writing, and politics have been actively contested in the history of modern terrorism. And as with Conrad and Lewis, the engagement with terrorism, for Pound, is clearly a matter of relating the force of literature to an ontology of force more generally. Writing thus becomes a means of exploring 'potential' in all of the senses of the word: capacity, possibility (as opposed to actuality), energy, and subjunctivity. In the next chapter, I shall discuss how Walter Abish specifically correlates these types of potential in order to write on 1970s terrorism in West Germany.

---

[167] Pound, letter to Wyndham Lewis, 3 February 1957, in Materer, *Pound/Lewis*, 302.

4. Walter Abish: Plotting Everyday Terror

Sketches of Atrocity

In his introduction to the 1984 edition of Walter Abish's collection of short stories, *In the Future Perfect* (first published in 1975), Malcolm Bradbury declares the author to be 'quite the most important writer to have emerged in the United States over the past ten years, and the one whose serious inquiry is most surely still continuing.'[1] Winner of the 1981 PEN/Faulkner award for *How German Is It* (1980), his novel on terrorism and the lingering effects of Nazism in Germany, Abish has indeed been repeatedly cast by critics as one of the foremost exponents of contemporary, American, postmodernist fiction. For Bradbury, however, the affinity between Abish's prose and the postmodern is 'misleading', although he does assert that they 'share' one 'tendency': 'a refusal to name what we call reality as real, a sense that the language which authenticates this or that as history, geography or biography is a language of human invention' (*ITFP*, x). Given that Abish wrote *How German Is It* without ever having visited Germany, Bradbury's comment seems apposite. And certainly there is an ongoing fascination in Abish's fiction with what the writer has termed 'defamilarization'—which is no doubt partly attributable to his having lived in a number of countries from a young age.

Born in Vienna in 1931, Abish spent most of his childhood and adolescence in Shanghai, China, before moving to Tel Aviv, Israel, where he spent some time in military service. He then moved to New York city—gaining American citizenship in 1960—where he has worked as a writer and academic ever since. Defamiliarization has not just involved writing about foreign places for Abish, though; it has also entailed exploring different types of literary experimentation. In his *Alphabetical Africa* (1974), for example, travel in Africa becomes entangled in a journey through linguistic arbitrariness. Consisting of

---

[1] Walter Abish, *In The Future Perfect* (London: Faber, 1985), ix, hereafter cited as *ITFP*.

fifty-two chapters running from 'A' to 'Z' and then from 'Z' to 'A',
Chapter A contains only words beginning with 'a', Chapter B adds
words beginning with 'b', and so on. Thus, it is not until Chapter Z
that the narrative is able to draw on the full range of the English language, at which point the possibilities are gradually whittled back
down. What the text emphasizes in this way is not so much that things
depend for their 'authentication' on a language of 'human invention',
as Bradbury suggests; rather, language appears as an entity that introduces its own strictures. As Abish writes in 'Access', a short piece
in *In The Future Perfect* (1975), though: 'Language is not a barrier. Language enables people in all circumstances to cope with a changing
world. . . . I'm not really concerned with language. As a writer I'm
principally concerned with meaning' (*ITFP*, 72). In his subsequent fiction, Abish has thus tended more towards analysing the way in which
the 'familiar' is embedded more generally in the experience of everyday life. The fictional engagement with foreign places becomes a way
of making the familiar appear uncanny, as he has stated:

[In America] I *know* what is familiar, and I don't feel as free to break away
from it. On the other hand, I tend to establish or reestablish the familiar in
what is foreign, allowing the familiar to determine the subsequent defamiliarization. The result is a tension, a sense of . . . discomfort.[2]

An early example of such 'defamiliarization' is given in another
short story from *In The Future Perfect*, 'The English Garden'. The epigraph to the story, an extract from John Ashbery's 'Three Poems',
raises the problem of representational remainders immediately:
'Remnants of the old atrocity subsist, but they are converted into in-
genious shifts in scenery, a sort of "English Garden" effect, to give the
required air of naturalness, pathos and hope' (*ITFP*, 1). Brumholdstein, the town portrayed in the story, is built on the foundations of a
concentration camp, Durst: this is its atrocity. As the epigraph suggests, though, the past is not simply abolished by the transformations
of scenery; instead, it remains persistent, lurking. But if the aim of this
landscaping is to replace depths of trauma with an array of surfaces,
these surfaces are also portrayed as having two distinct sides. The first
paragraph of the story suggests as much through a displacing meta-
textuality:

---

[2] Walter Abish, 'Wie Deutsch Ist Es', interview with Sylvère Lotringer, in Sylvère
Lotringer (ed.), *Semiotext(e): The German Issue* 4: 2 (1982): 161, hereafter cited as *SGI*.

One page in the coloring book I bought showed details of the new airport, the octagonal glass terminal building to the left, and a Lufthansa plane coming in for a landing in the background. It is a German coloring book and the faces accordingly are coloring book faces, jolly faces, smiling and happy faces. By no means are they characteristically German faces. Nothing is intrinsically German, I suppose, until it receives its color.   (*ITFP*, 1)

The text comes up against its own limits: the colours and images of the colouring book are irreducible to the narrative rendering. That a sign or image cannot fully contain its own signification, or control its referent, is precisely why they can and need to be filled in. But this excess is not limited to representation, for things in general are also coloured by indeterminacy: 'Nothing is intrinsically German . . . until it receives its color'. Nor is anything just a signifier, for the colouring book, like the story itself, is recognized as involving a space of everyday life: 'thousands of children each day gravely apply a color . . . to everything that fills a space on the pages of the coloring book in much the same way it occupies, visually at least, a space in real life' (*ITFP*, 1). And because 'everything one encounters' in Germany requires a 'determining' of its 'lifelikeness', each determination must be seen as *making a reality possible*. That is to say, if the character of a thing is refigured with each performance, then what is made real is its own potentiality. Consequently, an event or thing remains to some degree a sign of itself—although this does not alter the fact that it *takes place* and *exists* as such.

Abish himself states that writing involves a form of surfacing: 'In a sense, the text is the writer's skin—the outermost delineation of his sensibility, his way of expressing, remembering furiously and rendering what he believes to be the exactitude of his feelings.'[3] Writing, as a process of turning inside-out, thus entails that the writer's subjective life is thrown into a wider field of existence:

Heidegger refers to being as something that does not take place within the skin. Existence itself means to stand outside oneself. Being is spread over a field, analogous to a field of matter, which represents its concerns. I think that everything, even the most contradictory could be on the surface of the same field.[4]

---

[3] Walter Abish, 'The Writer-To-Be: An Impression of Living', *SubStance* 9: 2 (1980): 104.
[4] Quoted in Jerome Klinkowitz, 'Walter Abish', interview, in *The Life of Fiction* (Urbana: University of Illinois Press, 1977), 69.

Abish's correlating of language and existence with Heideggerian notions of ontology makes Bradbury's assertion that the 'authentication'
of 'reality' lies in a language of 'human invention' problematic. Abish
himself opposes his idea of an expansive membrane of Being to the
sort of 'Humanism' which 'imposes a kind of center from which
everything radiates'.[5] And certainly, for Heidegger, it is language that
gathers man into Being, not man who determines existence through
language.[6] But to what degree can we see Abish's fiction as repro-
ducing Heidegger's thinking? In 'The English Garden' this question
can be examined by considering the presentation of 'Brumhold', the
'greatest living German philosopher' whom Abish bases on Heidegger. The details used to portray him correspond closely to Heidegger's writings and biography—his questioning of 'the intrinsic
meaning of a *thing*' (*ITFP*, 8, Abish's emphasis); his being 'drafted into
the militia in 1944' (*ITFP*, 8);[7] his reflections on the 'homeland' (*ITFP*,
4), and on 'Greek and German philosophy' (*ITFP*, 8). The town that
the narrator is visiting, Brumholdstein, is also named after him, although Brumhold, we are told by the narrator, 'is not the reason why
I am in Germany' (*ITFP*, 4). In fact, the philosopher appears only in
association with the colouring book when the narrator muses that a
picture of a professor lecturing 'could be Brumhold but he isn't.
Brumhold retired years ago' (*ITFP*, 4). But if the 'lifelikeness' of a person is also susceptible to the 'determinings' and colourings of others,
then a relation *can* be drawn between Brumhold and the picture, despite the ambiguity. This possibility, I would argue, is what differentiates Abish's writing from those of Heidegger on aesthetic practice.

The contrast is apparent if we analyse Heidegger's early essay,
'The Origin of the Work of Art' (1935), in which he discusses art's
installation of Being in the world. The work of art does not simply re-
produce 'some particular entity', he argues; rather, it is a 'reproduction of the thing's general essence'.[8] It installs 'the Being of beings'

---

[5] Ibid.

[6] In his 'Letter on Humanism' (1947) addressed to Jean-Paul Sartre, Heidegger states this
explicitly: 'Language is the house of Being. In its home man dwells' (in *Martin Heidegger: Basic
Writings*, ed. and trans. by David Farrell Krell [London: Harper & Row, 1978], 219).

[7] On Heidegger's conscription into the *Volksturm* in 1944, see Hugo Ott's biography,
Martin Heidegger, trans. by Allen Blunden (London: HarperCollins, 1993), 296–302.

[8] Martin Heidegger, 'The Origin of the Work of Art', in *Poetry, Language, Thought*, trans.
by Albert Hofstadter (New York: Harper & Row, 1971), 37, hereafter cited as 'Origin'.

within the world 'in its own way' ('Origin', 39). Offering the example of a Greek temple, Heidegger asserts that 'By means of the temple, the god is present in the temple' ('Origin', 41). But just when it appears that the building plays a primary part in Being's instauration, it turns out that the whole structure is a mere palimpsest: 'the presence of the god is itself the extension and *delimitation* of the precinct as holy' ('Origin', 42, my emphasis). The origin of the work of art never lies in the process of construction, for its foundations are always revealed as having been ontologically prefabricated. So, too, are the possibilities of existence in general, for it is the god's presence in the temple which 'first fits together and at the same time gathers around itself the unity of those paths and relations in which birth and death, disaster and blessing, victory and disgrace, endurance and decline acquire the shape of destiny for human being' ('Origin', 42). The temple is thus really a wall through which essence constructs its own distance in and from the world. Abish's portrayal of art and existence is much more open plan. Instead of being a simple 'reproduction of a thing's general essence', the act of fiction plays a part in composing the very nature of a thing. Rather than possibility being controlled by Being, things exist as real potentials. But this is not to say that nothing has inherent traits. 'Brumhold' is evoked because the colouring book depicts a lecturer; the figure arises from an interaction between the image and the narrator's interpretation. So whereas for Heidegger the 'basic design', the 'outline sketch' an art work draws of a thing's Being is always first traced and then coloured in by Being itself, in 'The English Garden', things, signs, and individuals refract and colour each other.

It all amounts to a different conception of the everyday. As far as Heidegger is concerned, the art work reveals that the ground of the 'ordinary' resides in 'extra-ordinary' essence. With Abish, everydayness in the world exudes its own capacity for becoming strange. This is partly because ordinary activities appear to have no higher guiding reason or meaning:

The coloring book simply activates the desire of most people to color something that is devoid of color. In this particular instant it is the normal activity of people in the process of going about their tasks: feeding the dog, the baby, the husband, the tropical fish, themselves, thereby acknowledging a need, not necessarily questioning the need, although they may ponder why . . . why must they feed the tropical fish and the baby and the husband. (*ITFP*, 5–6)

The lack of any transcendent, ordering principle means that habits are formed in relation to particular contexts or locations. Past and present answer not to destiny but to contingency, as is suggested in the passages on the concentration camp: 'Some of the people in Brumholdstein remember playing in that vast camp, by that time completely run down. . . . There were German signs all over the camp with arrows pointing in one or another direction. The signs are gone, the camp is gone' (*ITFP*, 6). The site of atrocity has thus been converted by shifts of scenery into a familiar urban scene. Nor is anything of the camp featured in the colouring book—which is an ominous omission, given that the book has been described as 'an indicator and recorder of all things that are possible' (*ITFP*, 5). It would appear that the camp has been relegated to oblivion, then, and that Brumholdstein is a tomb for the future to stand on. Yet this is immediately undermined when we are told that 'had a colouring book existed of Durst it too would have showed people diligently going about their everyday existence, standing upright, or sitting, or even reclining . . .' (*ITFP*, 7)—moreover, that 'many objects' featured in the current colouring book would also have been present in the camp. The transposition of atrocity and everydayness onto each other suddenly imbues the familiar pictures with a sense of uncanny ambivalence. Which is more disturbing: that the 'Benches, chairs, electric lightbulbs' and signs of the camp are 'now dispersed . . . missing' (*ITFP*, 7), or that the scenes currently portrayed in the book might be no different, in some ways, from those of the past? The story thus poses two further questions: is the Holocaust still lurking in everyday, German life? And is the tendency for signs and things, everydayness and atrocity, to blend a specifically German characteristic?

In so far as postmodernism has variously been defined by Lyotard, Jameson, and others as an 'incredulity' towards 'grand' or 'metanarratives';[9] a 'radical break' or '*coupure*' with history whereby everything is viewed as having come to an end;[10] and a 'dissolution' of a separate, 'autonomous sphere of culture' such that aesthetics is under the

---

[9] Jean-François Lyotard, *The Postmodern Condition*, trans. by Geoffrey Bennington and Brian Massumi (1979; Manchester: Manchester University Press, 1984), xxiv.

[10] Fredric Jameson, *Postmodernism; or, The Cultural Logic of Late Capitalism* (London: Verso, 1991), 1. Terry Eagleton, in *The Illusions of Postmodernism* (1996; Oxford: Blackwell, 1997), criticizes the notion that postmodernism marks a break with history: 'If we can *date* an end to History—if postmodernism took off in the 1960s, or the 1970s, or whenever it was that Fordism or autonomous culture or metanarratives supposedly ground to a halt—then we are still to some extent within the framework of that linear tale' (30, Eagleton's emphasis).

hegemony of 'commodity production generally',[11] the issues raised by 'The English Garden' are quintessentially issues of postmodernism. The colouring book and its images are a clear instance of commodified aesthetics. The problems of meta-narration, cultural history, and artistic agency are all sketched out in relation to it. But the impression Abish's text leaves us with is not one that sits easily with the characterizations of postmodernism just cited. On the one hand, it suggests that history is broken as easily as any object. When the writer William Aus tears up a photograph of some camp survivors, the narrator tells us: 'I did not lift a hand to stop him from effacing the past' (*ITFP*, 21). The signs are gone; the camp is gone. On the other hand, the facility with which a thing or an event can become coloured by different contexts and objects means that an environment is a vast memory bank: 'Anything in the world can trigger the recollection of an event' (*ITFP*, 14). As Abish writes elsewhere, this is an effect of the general surface of Being: 'a scuffed carpet, a crack in the wall becomes intentionally or unintentionally incorporated in that humanistic field, presenting to the reader a kind of pattern he can instantly recognise and evaluate'.[12] The intentions of the writer, the pattern of the text, and the interpretation of the reader are all part of a wider 'topography'. Yet this general immanence is volatile: a topography suffused by its elements is naturally open to being affected by them—though the force of these various elements is not necessarily equal. Indeed, it is precisely because what has been termed 'late-capitalism' has the capacity to increase its sphere of activity at an ever-increasing rate that we have to ask whether the ontological field described by Abish is mediated by commodification more than anything else. Conversely, though, a generalized immanence would suggest that processes of capitalism can themselves be affected by local cultural factors. C. Barry Chabot thus criticizes the sort of wholesale cultural homogenization that Jameson posits in *Postmodernism*, arguing that 'Since Jameson is attempting to develop a period concept that encompasses all of social life, he presumes that changes occur across a broad front and thus discounts the conditions specific to discrete cultural spheres.'[13] To what extent has the

---

[11] Jameson, *Postmodernism*, 4–5.   [12] Klinkowitz, 'Interview with Walter Abish', 69.
[13] C. Barry Chabot, 'The Problems of the Postmodern', in *Critical Essays on American Postmodernism*, ed. by Stanley Trachtenberg (New York: Hall, 1995), 107. John MacGowan also outlines problems of theoretical totalizing regarding late capitalism, in *Postmodernism and Its Critics* (Ithaca: Cornell University Press, 1991), ch. 1.

homogenizing tendency of postmodernism been contested culturally and historically? This question is considered at length in the novel that grows out of 'The English Garden', *How German Is It*, in which potentialities of signs, things, and events are explored in relation to terrorism and writing. By taking up the issue of quotidian mediation in this way, Abish also cites and rewrites an image of 'everydayness' that in the realm of theory, at least, has a distinct history—one that is inextricably linked to revolutionary violence, and which I shall now examine before turning to the novel.

Situationism and 'Happenings'

The most concerted and extreme engagement with the notion of 'everydayness' was that of the Situationist International. Emerging in Paris under the direction of Guy Debord, Raoul Vaneigem, Mustapha Khayati, and René Viénet, the group developed a radical interpretation of cultural production. Promulgating its ethos through twelve issues of their journal, *Internationale Situationiste*, published between 1957 and 1969, Situationism eventually developed other centres of activity, notably in Italy, Germany, Britain, and Holland. Essentially, the group sought to identify and resist what they viewed as the economic mediation of all facets of life. Debord states the case most explicitly in his major work, *Society of the Spectacle* (1967): 'Everything that was lived directly has moved away into a representation.'[14] As the rate of capitalist automation increases, so does its autonomy, he argues. Consequently, society has an ever-decreasing role in the modes of its production. Commodification becomes its own spectacle, and society is forced into the role of alienated spectator. Through the use of advertising images, the congruence of mass production and abstracted spectacles is manifested literally:

[The spectacle] is its own product and has made its own rules: it is a pseudo-sacred entity. It shows what it is: separate power developing in itself, in the growth of productivity by means of the incessant refinement of the division of labour into a parcelization of gestures which are then dominated by the independent movement of machines and working for an ever-expanding market. (*SOS*, §25)

---

[14] Guy Debord, *Society of the Spectacle* (Detroit: Black & Red, 1983), §1, hereafter cited as *SOS*.

The spectacle is the concomitant of capitalism become absolute. It marks the point at which 'the commodity has attained the *total occupation* of social life' (*SOS*, §42, Debord's emphasis). Henri Lefebvre's earlier definition of 'everydayness' as 'whatever remains after one has eliminated all specialized activities'[15] is thus no longer tenable, argues Debord. For as well as instituting a fracture between itself and the masses, the spectacle even mediates communication between individuals. 'Under what we have called the "colonization of everyday life" ', states Vaneigem, 'the only possible changes are changes of fragmentary roles.'[16]

Debord is similarly pessimistic about the potential for art to intervene. Living as we do in an epoch where the spectacle has gained control of time itself, he argues, the avant-garde can only replicate the dynamics of economic production: 'irreversible time is *unified on a world scale*' (*SOS*, §145, Debord's emphasis). As a result, art can only be 'simultaneously an art of change and the pure expression of impossible change. . . . Its avant-garde is its disappearance' (*SOS*, §191). At other points, though, this stance is contradicted. That the spectacle is the most extreme 'concrete-inversion of life' (*SOS*, §2) means that life gains its own autonomous difference through alienation. The spectacle's absolutism is an 'illusion', an 'unreal unity' that 'masks the class division on which the real unity of the capitalist mode of production rests' (*SOS*, §72). Capitalism's tendency to overturn its own limits and values is also identified as its weakness, all of which is viewed as facilitating the birth of a new form of aesthetic resistance: '*detournement*', usually translated into English as 'subversion' or 'diversion'. Deriving partly from Lautréamont's practice of plagiarism, the method was also indebted to the ideas developed in the 1950s by avant-garde movements such as Bauhaus Imagism and Lettrisme.[17] Debord defines *detournement* as 'the reuse of preexisting elements in a new ensemble',[18] whereby each element subsequently takes on a new meaning or importance. The 'possibility' of this occurring is attributed by Vaneigem, in *The Revolution of Everyday Life* (1967), to the proclivity for things to become 'devalorized'

[15] Cited in Guy Debord, 'Perspectives for Conscious Alterations in Everyday Life', in *Situationist International Anthology*, ed. and trans. by Ken Knabb (Berkeley: Bureau of Public Secrets, 1981), 69, hereafter cited as *SIA*.

[16] Raoul Vaneigem, 'Basic Banalities II', in Knabb, *SIA*, 122.

[17] Stewart Home traces these connections in *The Assault on Culture* (Stirling: AK, 1991), 22–40. On *detournement*'s relation to Lautréamont, see Mustapha Khayati, 'Captive Words: Preface to a Situationist Dictionary', in Knabb, *SIA*, 171–2.

[18] Guy Debord, '*Detournement* as Negation and Prelude', in Knabb, *SIA*, 55.

by the economic system.[19] For Khayati, *detournement* thus 'confirms the thesis, long documented by modern art, of the insubordination of words, of the impossibility for power to *totally recuperate* fixed meanings'.[20] Accordingly, bringing words and images into conflict was one of its main methods of assault; 'adroit perversions' of the classical novel form could be effected by incorporating illustrations that have no obvious connection to the text, they claimed.[21] Inserting politicized dialogue into comic strips—'the only truly popular literature'[22]—was another widely practised mode.

In general, *detournement* was presented as harnessing the degenerative forces of capitalism in order to open new forms of social collectivity. In this sense, it bolstered the group's other main form of active resistance; fostering 'unitary urbanism' by instigating the 'free creation of events', or 'situations'.[23] As capital's disintegrating effects become endemic, argues Debord, spaces of subversion appear spontaneously. The theatricality of situations work against the spectacle's separating effects, eliciting a free interaction of elements within an environment. This is how a new mode of political violence emerges; if the spectacle covers the social landscape, contends Vaneigem, it is countered by a burgeoning hinterland of everyday power that escapes its grasp: 'This revolution is nameless, like everything springing from lived experience. Its explosive coherence is being forged constantly in the everyday clandestinity of acts and dreams' (*Revolution*, 111). Forging new social ensembles therefore entails breaking down boundaries between the political and the aesthetic. Inducing a unification of space and time, states Vaneigem, is tantamount to building 'the first *foco* of the coming guerrilla war . . .' (*Revolution*, 228). And if any of the Situationists' exhortations seem contradictory or unclear, that is itself intentional:

The distortion and clumsiness in the way we express ourselves (which a man of taste called, not inaccurately 'a rather irritating kind of hermetic terrorism') comes from our central position . . . on the ill-defined and shifting

---

[19] Raoul Vaneigem, *The Revolution of Everyday Life*, trans. by Donald Nicholson-Smith (London: Rebel/Left Bank, 1993), 264, herafter cited as *Revolution*.

[20] Khayati, 'Captive Words', 171, Khayati's emphasis.

[21] Guy Debord and Gil J. Wolman, 'Methods of Detournement', in Knabb, *SIA*, 11.

[22] René Viénet, 'The Situationists and the New Forms of Action Against Politics and Art', in Knabb, *SIA*, 214.

[23] Guy Debord, 'Report on the Construction of Situations and on the International Situationist Tendency's Conditions of Organisation and Action', in Knabb, *SIA*, 23–4.

frontier where language captured by power (conditioning) and free language (poetry) fight out their infinitely complex war.[24]

The Situationists were not the only ones calling for a new theatrical politics. Avant-garde artists in several countries were attempting to alter the relation between politics and everydayness by staging 'happenings'. Allen Kaprow introduced the term in 1959, in New York, with his piece *18 Happenings in 6 Parts*, although as a genre of performance it emerged, like *detournement*, from the earlier dramatic innovations of Dada and Bauhaus. According to Michael Kirby, a happening can be defined as having two salient characteristics.[25] First, it jettisons the theatrical conventions of making time, space, or character external to the performance. As in the case of a bullfighter or public speaker, the action of the performer is not simply *representing* another event or figure—although different personae may occasionally be adopted. Second, the happening draws a collection of diverse elements or actions into the one space. Auditory, visual, and even olfactory qualities could all play an equal part, and as in Antonin Artaud's 'Theatre of Cruelty' the spectators were often incorporated into the performing space. While many happenings took place inside lofts or studios in the New York art scene, in Europe they tended to be staged outside in the cityscape. This was especially the case in Germany. Set up in 1957 in Düsseldorf, a group called 'ZERO' created urban happenings using kites and hot air balloons. Wolf Vostell, widely regarded as the 'father of the European Happening movement',[26] was also instrumental in moving performance into the city. In works such as *Citydrama* (1961), he gave the 'audience' a list of things to do at certain locations—for example, 'urinate into the debris and think of your best friend'.[27] Telephones, cars, trains and televisions were also used by him to create 'de/collage' environments. For Vostell, the happening was not a 'retreat from but *into* reality'.[28] For other artists this also meant a leap into politics.

As the left-wing and student movements in Europe galvanized over issues such as Vietnam and education, by 1968 the political orientation

---

[24] Vaneigem, 'Basic Banalities II', 123, my emphasis.

[25] See Michael Kirby's overview, 'Happenings: An Introduction', in *Happenings and Other Acts*, ed. by Mariellen R. Sandford (New York: Routledge, 1995), 1–28. *Happenings and Other Acts* hereafter cited as *Happenings*.

[26] Günter Berghaus, 'Happenings in Europe: Trends, Events, and Leading Figures', in Sandford, *Happenings*, 320.

[27] Quoted ibid., 320–1.   [28] Quoted ibid., 325, Vostell's emphasis.

of avant-garde groups was becoming more serious. Even *Tel Quel*, a Parisian collective of writers and theorists that had been more concerned with attacking structuralism, began to outline ideas on revolution—though mostly in terms of textuality. Organized principally by Philippe Sollers, the group and its journal—also called *Tel Quel*—provided a forum for a range of budding poststructuralists, including Roland Barthes, Louis Althusser, Michel Foucault, Jacques Lacan, Jacques Derrida, Luce Irigaray, and Julia Kristeva. Although the group had not initially been sympathetic to the rebellion by students that culminated in the general political demonstrations of May 1968, it went on to adopt Communist and then Maoist stances. As Patrick Ffrench has argued, though: '1968 appears as exorbitant and embarrassing with regard to the theory of the structuralist or poststructuralist theoretical orthodoxy, particularly that which had a political engagement. Only the Situationists, whose review dissolved a few years after the events escape this distance.'[29] May 1968 was indeed exemplary of what could be catalysed by 'unitary urbanism' for many Situationists, many of whom took an active role in the demonstrations. Happenings, too, were being offered by practitioners like Jean-Jacques Lebel as a form of revolutionary warfare. On 17 May 1968, Lebel's group, 'The Committee for Revolutionary Action' (CAR), along with student militants, stormed the Odéon Theatre in Paris and issued a manifesto calling for total cultural sabotage. 'The only theatre is guerrilla theatre', it declared, 'REVOLUTIONARY ART IS MADE ON THE STREETS.'[30]

Such conflation of politics and performance also frequently led to confusion over the status of the acts, though. In a letter to Vostell, Lebel wrote: 'I have ceased to be an artist'; the 'events' he was organizing could sometimes be described as 'happenings', he stated, but 'more often, they are simply life'.[31] The police, too, often reinforced the subversive nature of the acts by refusing to view them as anything but politically criminal. In the early 1960s, SPUR, the German Situationist branch, were repeatedly charged with immorality, blasphemy, and incitement to riot because of material published in their journal.

[29] Patrick Ffrench, *The Time of Theory: A History of Tel Quel (1960–83)* (Oxford: Clarendon, 1995), 106. See also Danielle Marx-Scouras, *The Cultural Politics of Tel Quel: Literature and the Left in the Wake of Engagement* (Pennsylvania: The Pennsylvania State University Press, 1996), ch. 4.

[30] Jean-Jacques Lebel, 'On the Necessity of Violation', in Sandford, *Happenings*, 275.

[31] Quoted in Berghaus, 'Happenings in Europe', 359.

When the 'Viennese Actionists and Austrian Socialist Students' Union' organized a happening involving vomiting, masturbating, defecating, and urinating while singing the national anthem, the organizers were immediately taken to court and charged with debasing Austrian state symbols. Members of 'Kommune 1', an alternative lifestyle community set up in March 1967 by Dieter Kunzelmann, met with a similar response when they started a 'Save the Police Committee'. Calling for a thirty-five hour week in order to give police 'spare time for reading, leisure activities with their wives and girlfriends . . . making love, and also time for chats with elderly passers-by to whom they can explain democracy',[32] several members were arrested when they showered some police officers with flowers. Yet even events that were not intended to be politically directed were overcoded as such. In a 1964 performance by Joseph Beuys of his piece *Kukei/ Akopee-No/ Brown Cross/ Fat Corners/ Model Fat Corners* at a festival in Aachen, he accidentally spilled some nitric acid on a spectator's trousers while attacking a piano with a drill. The man, a member of a right-wing students' group that had been protesting against the festival, stormed the stage with his friends and punched Beuys in the face. Bleeding from the nose, Beuys raised his hand in a Nazi salute before the police intervened. The response clearly gestures towards a troubling presence of political history—one that Abish avowedly found lacking in a later exhibition of Beuys's art at the Guggenheim museum: 'To me the entire work was made to represent an overwhelming German undertaking. . . . Mind you, nothing in the exhibition conveyed anything but this German drive. Of course, everything in the show reflected the past. But still, a Germany free of Nazi signs.'[33]

Certainly, violence generally played a much greater role in the happenings and avant-gardisme of Germany and Austria than elsewhere. In the late 1950s, Gustav Metzger, for example, was largely responsible for developing 'auto-destructive' art-works made out of corrosive materials.[34] Otto Mühl, Rudolf Schwarzkogler, Hermann Nitsch, and Günter Brus literally incorporated violence into their

---

[32] See Sadie Plant, *The Most Radical Gesture* (London: Routledge, 1992), 92. Similarly, Bazon Brock and Hermann Goepfert were arrested for their 'public actions' performed in front of the Frankfurt police station in 1962. They were protesting against the tyranny of death and the exclusion of human beings from being exhibited at the local zoo (Berghaus, 'Happenings in Europe', 333).

[33] Abish, 'Wie Deutsch Ist Es', 178.

[34] See Adrian Henri, *Environments and Happenings* (London: Thames & Hudson, 1974), 135–40; also Home, *Assault on Culture*, 60–4.

work by attacking their own bodies. Often using objects such as razors, nails, scissors, and saws, Brus damaged himself so severely in a performance of *Breaking Test* (1970) that he was never able to perform again.[35] According to Adrian Henri, the use of self-mutilation by these artists is symptomatic of their generation's relation to the war:

What is certainly disquieting is that Germany and Austria are the homes of this violently sadistic art, only a generation after the Nazis had embodied Sade's worst fantasies more thoroughly than he could have imagined. Is the work of Mühl, Brus and Nitsch an elaborate act of self-abasement for the sins of their fathers, or merely an echo of the hideous Nazi ethos?[36]

But are these the only possible interpretations? Can we not see such acts as expressing the general political upheaval and terrorism that were so prevalent throughout the 1960s and 1970s? Darko Suvin seems to suggest as much when he writes that these happenings beg a fundamental question: 'Do they shock for therapeutic or terroristic ends?'[37] Then again, what is the relation of the political violence that took place during this period to the horrors of World War II? And how German is it? In the following reading of Abish's *How German Is It*, I shall consider how the novel addresses these issues in its portrayal of 1970s West German terrorism and society.

How German Is It

Like 'The English Garden', *How German Is It* opens by raising a whole landscape of questions. Once again, the scene is Brumholdstein and the questions pertain to Brumhold:

How can anyone possibly fear the Germans, now that they have come to resemble all other stable, postindustrial, technologically advanced nations, now that their buildings are no longer intrinsically German but merely like everything else constructed in Germany, well built, solid, intended to last—and that their language, *die Deutsche Sprache*, as once before is again absorbing words from other languages. Still, notwithstanding the doubtful foreign elements in the language today, the German language remains the key to Brumhold's metaphysical quest. . . . How German is it? Brumhold might well ask of his metaphysical quest, which is rooted in the rich dark soil of *der*

---

[35] See Berghaus, 'Happenings in Europe', 360–7.

[36] Henri, *Environments and Happenings*, 165–9.

[37] Darko Suvin, 'Reflections on Happenings', in Sandford, *Happenings*, 301.

Schwarzwald, rooted in the somber, deliberately solitary existence that derives its passion, its energy, its striving for exactitude from the undulating hills, the pine forests, and the erect motionless figure of the gamekeeper in the green uniform.[38]

Despite the growth of urban uniformity, Brumhold's position is that there is an implacable and *natural* relation between metaphysics and the German nation. The essential questions of metaphysics are maintained as German, while the demarcation of this sphere protects Germanness. Yet the figure of the gamekeeper implies that the nation's metaphysics is as susceptible to trespassing as any field. If the nature of Brumhold's project is indeed rooted in the forest, what happens if the forest gives way to housing developments? In contrast to Razumov's image in *Under Western Eyes* of Russia smothered by a blank page of Spirit, this passage from Abish's text suggests that German nationality consists of a *contiguity* of language and landscape. The security of the two is entwined. Can the one be attacked through the other, then? As a writer and former terrorist, Ulrich Hargenau, the novel's main character, should know. When the story commences, he has just returned to Brumholdstein after having split up with his wife, Paula, and then lived for a few months in Paris where he had an affair. With the sojourn behind him, he faces the task of beginning a novel about it all. Paula, a member of the left-wing, terrorist 'Einzieh Group' when he had met her, had swiftly inducted him into the group's activism. When they were all eventually brought to trial, Ulrich's illustrious family background enabled Paula and himself to obtain a reprieve—the other eight members received lengthy sentences on the basis of his testimony: 'He merely told the truth to save their skin. It was not necessary to fabricate anything' (*HGII*, 22). For this action, he not only begins to receive increasingly threatening hate-mail, he and Paula are also castigated by the magazine *Der Spiegel*, which contrasts his actions to that of his father, Ulrich Von Hargenau, who was executed in 1944 by the Nazis for insubordination. His father's heroism—crying out (*à la* Heidegger's Schlageter) 'Long Live Germany' before being shot—becomes Ulrich's cowardice. The possibility of intervening in everyday life is thus raised from three different perspectives in the text: metaphysics, fiction, and terrorism, each of which I shall address separately.

---

[38] Walter Abish, *How German Is It* (1980; Manchester: Carcanet, 1982), 4–5, hereafter cited as *HGII*.

The skirmishes are outlined in a general form in the first two parts of the novel. For Ulrich, writing is his sole *modus vivendi*, the only way in which he can actively determine everyday life for himself. But while his truthful account in the Einzieh trial—all the more forceful because of his *name*—makes him the author of the terrorists' downfall, writing is also offered as resisting his intentions. It interposes its own distance. Because Ulrich's 'brain relie[s] on the words of his notebooks to designate its expectations' (*HGII*, 20), he gains an image of his future only *after* it has been written. Similarly, he can only begin to compose his experiences of a place once he has moved out of it both temporally and geographically: 'In general I prefer to write about a city only after I have put some distance between myself and the city in question' (*HGII*, 51). Before commemoration there must be an initial oblivion, as the title of Part One, 'The edge of forgetfulness', suggests. For Daphne Hasendruck, an American student working with Brumhold, what is striking about Ulrich's novels is precisely their inscrutability, even though she also finds them insufficiently discreet:

no matter how hard she tried the work remained somehow inaccessible to her. Although that was hardly surprising in someone who admitted that she found the exploration or probing of a relationship between people as something distasteful. She felt that the writer was trespassing, and Ulrich had to admit that writing in some respect was a form of trespassing. (*HGII*, 36)

The 'skin' of the text is both too foreign and too close to the bone for her. If, for Brumhold, language can be a 'gamekeeper' of national Being, here it functions for Daphne as a poacher of everyday intimacy. For Ulrich, such problems with communication are recurring and involve everyday experience generally: 'sometimes he felt as if his brain had become addicted to repetition, needing to hear everything repeated once, then twice in order to be certain that the statement was not false or misleading' (*HGII*, 15). Far from simply controlling language, Ulrich finds himself being split by it. The sporadic use of free indirect discourse throughout the novel further foregrounds the text's mechanics of doubling, allowing it to speak in the past and present, first person and third person, simultaneously. A primarily polyvocal novel is not readily acceptable to Ulrich, however; he would rather have all the different characters speak in the same neutral voice. This, he claims in an interview, is what he wants to achieve in his forthcoming book, *The Idea of Switzerland*—which is also the title of Part Two in which the interview takes place:

If someone withholds information, surely it is not merely for the sake of with-holding information. All the same, characters, like people, frequently mis-read each other's intentions. Anyhow, *The Idea of Switzerland* would neutralize these misreadings. I am, of course, thinking of the image Switzerland evokes in people. A kind of controlled neutrality, a somewhat antiseptic tranquility that even I find soothing. Obey the laws and there is nothing to fear. (*HGII*, 52).

Ulrich's space of literature thus speaks neutrally only if we have already heard it issuing dictates. But despite having cast literature as mediating critical consensus, Ulrich then declares that fiction's role is simply to ratify social conventions: 'A novel is not a process of rebellion. Just as it validates and makes acceptable forms of human conduct, it also validates and makes acceptable societal institutions' (*HGII*, 53).

Ulrich's statements on literary function might be inconsistent, but they nevertheless reflect some of the debates in West Germany surrounding literary responses to the nation's terrorist crisis at the time. The novelist Heinrich Böll, for example, was condemned in 1975 for defending the publication of Michael 'Bommi' Baumann's autobiographical *Terror or Love: The Personal Account of a West German Urban Guerrilla*. Winner of the Nobel Prize for literature in 1972, and President of PEN, Böll also came under attack for having published an article, 'Violence through Information', in which he criticized the West German print media for publishing assumptions about political violence as facts. The publicist Hans Habe wrote in response: 'Fascism would be [rampant] if PEN president Böll were to remain in his post'.[39] While Habe viewed the writer's stance as being irresponsibly provocative, Böll used his fiction to attack what he perceived to be the media's role in precipitating crisis. His novel *The Lost Honour of Katharina Blum: or, How Violence Develops and Where it Can Lead* (1974) tells a tale of a woman who assassinates a reporter on account of articles accusing her of terrorist associations: 'Here is a young women, cheerfully, almost gaily, going off to a harmless little private dance, and four days later, she becomes (since this is merely a report, not a judgement, we will confine ourselves to facts) a murderess, and this, if we examine the matter closely, because of newspaper reports.'[40] The

---

[39] Quoted in Kurt Groenewold, 'The German Federal Republic's Response and Civil Liberties', *Terrorism and Political Violence* 4: 4 (Autumn 1992): 148.

[40] Heinrich Böll, *The Lost Honour of Katharina Blum; or, How Violence Develops and Where it Can Lead*, trans. by Leila Vennewitz (London: Minerva, 1993), 134.

presentation of a volatile collusion of information and event is clearly meta-textual to some degree, applicable to the critical activism of the novel itself. But like Ulrich's notion of literary neutrality, such literary powers of critique remain open to interpretation. When Böll subsequently condemned the assassination by the terrorist '2nd of June Movement' of the President of West Germany's Superior Court of Justice in 1974, the terrorists criticized him for hypocrisy: 'What was Böll really saying in his *Katharina Blum* if not that the shooting of a representative of the ruling power machine is justified? But when "literary power" becomes material power, Böll goes over to the side of those whose word he used to scourge as lie . . .'.[41]

In *How German Is It* such issues about the relative forces of writing and activism lead to questions of metaphysics. By the end of Part Two, violence becomes a philosophical issue when Brumhold suddenly dies. Up to this point, his thinking has been interrogated on his own terms, especially regarding language's relation to things. If German remains the 'key' to his 'metaphysical quest', the narrator asks, to what extent does metaphysics change when the language is besieged by foreign terms?:

Brumhold might well ask of the language, How German is it still? Has it not once again, by brushing against so many foreign languages and experiences, acquired foreign impurities such as *okay* and *jetlag* and *topless* and *supermarkt* and *weekend* and *sexshop*, and consequently absorbed the signifiers of an overwhelmingly decadent concern with materialism? (*HGII*, 5)

Brumhold's thinking provides its own answer to this question: the essence of a thing—language included—is not defined by the thing itself: 'What is a thing? he asked rhetorically. Brumhold it must be pointed out, was not referring to a particular thing. He was not, for instance, referring to a modern apartment house, or a metal frame window, or an English lesson, but the *thingliness* that is intrinsic to all things . . .' (*HGII*, 19, Abish's emphasis). In contrast, Abish's text is making reference here to a specific theme in Heidegger's work: namely, the amalgamation of Being, framing, and security.

In his essay 'Building Dwelling Thinking' (1954), Heidegger argues that building, dwelling, and existing are all defined by the same power of Being. The Old English and High German word for building, '*buan*' means 'to dwell', he writes: 'ich bin, du bist' thus mean 'I

[41] Stefan Aust *The Baader-Meinhof Group: The Inside Story of a Phenomenon*, trans. by Anthea Bell (1985; London: Bodley Head, 1987), 267.

dwell, you dwell'.[42] None of this has anything to do with physical structures, though: 'This thinking about building does not presume to discover architectural ideas, let alone to give rules for building.'[43] Instead, Heidegger seeks to trace 'building back into that domain to which everything that *is* belongs.'[44] This domain he terms the 'fourfold'—a cohabitation of earth and sky, mortals and divinities. Its essence and presence take place only after a place in the world has been set for them: 'A boundary is not that at which something stops but, as the Greeks recognised, the boundary is that from which something *begins its presencing*.'[45] But this primary work of building is made strictly secondary by Heidegger when he portrays the fourfold as having been constructed even before the first stone has been laid. The demarcated zone merely 'admits the fourfold'[46] into itself rather than initially determining it, and so functions solely as a means of 'preservation'. In an earlier lecture, 'The Turning' (1949), Heidegger calls this structuration of essence '*Ge-stell*'—usually translated into English as 'enframing'. Its connection to security is made explicit:

Enframing comes to presence as the danger. But does the danger therewith announce itself *as* the danger? No. To be sure, men are at all times and in all places exceedingly oppressed by dangers and exigencies. But *the* danger, namely Being itself endangering itself in the truth of its coming to presence, remains veiled and disguised.[47]

Danger never takes place for Being because Being is never really exposed to the exigencies of places. Essence is therefore safeguarded from any external determination or violation—even though, as we saw in the last chapter, Heidegger has maintained it is nationally delimited. And as a consequence, all social structures are viewed by him as 'destined' and ontologically secured.[48]

For Heidegger, 'language is the house of Being', and the national security of Being hinges on enframing. Abish's text threatens this arrangement by offering a different view of its own framework. That *Ge-stell* must impose a definite temporal scission between ontology and the world is emphasized by Heidegger—the prefix that is

[42] Martin Heidegger, 'Building Dwelling Thinking', in *Poetry Language Thought*, 147.
[43] Ibid., 145.   [44] Ibid., Heidegger's emphasis.
[45] Ibid., 154, Heidegger's emphasis.   [46] Ibid., 151.
[47] Martin Heidegger, 'The Turning', in *The Question Concerning Technology, and Other Essays*, trans. by William Lovitt (New York: Harper, 1977), 36, Heidegger's emphasis.
[48] See Martin Heidegger, *Being and Time*, trans. by John Macquarrie and Edward Robinson (1926; Oxford: Blackwell, 1990), 434–7.

separated by the hyphen belongs to the past-perfect tense in German. In contrast, because Ulrich must interpose a spatial and temporal boundary between himself and an event or location *before* it can be presented or experienced, things are never identified before being actively configured. In addition, the novel's free indirect discourse does not express a separation of times or voices; instead, it opens them to conjunctions.[49] And as soon as this is a possibility, the foundations of Heidegger's thinking are undermined. Indeed, the novel itself intimates as much when shortly after Brumhold's death the pavement of Geigenheimer Street in Brumholdstein begins to cave in, exposing a mass grave from the concentration camp, Durst. Metaphysics collapses into history, as Abish himself states:

The reason I introduced Heidegger in the novel is because of his questionable political role in the thirties, as well as his extraordinary preoccupation with language. Here was a man who had to shape language in order to address the questions he found to be of overriding importance. His history, as I see it, was always a universal history that he somehow managed to locate in his own beloved forest. But was his history not shaped by specific historical events?[50]

Questioning the historicity of Heidegger's thinking necessitates an examination of his concept of '*Gewalt*' (violence/power). In his *Introduction to Metaphysics* (1935), violence is what defines humanity's power of existence more than anything else. It allows an individual to access and harness the overpowering nature of Being: 'Man is the violent one, not aside from and along with other attributes but solely in the sense that in his fundamental violence [*Gewalt-tätigkeit*] he uses power [*Gewalt*] against the overpowering [*Überwältigende*].'[51] But again, the violence of this act is always initially struck by Being rather than against it:

---

[49] Gilles Deleuze and Félix Guattari, in *A Thousand Plateaus: Capitalism and Schizophrenia*, trans. by Brian Massumi (Minneapolis: University of Minnesota Press, 1987), place great emphasis on indirect discourse when writing about language and collectivity: 'indirect discourse, *especially "free" indirect discourse*, is of exemplary value: there are no clear, distinctive contours; what comes first is not an insertion of variously individuated statements, or an interlocking of different subjects of enunciation, but a collective assemblage resulting in the determination of relative subjectification proceedings, or assignations of individuality and their shifting distributions within discourse' (80, authors' emphasis).

[50] Abish, 'Wie Deutsch Ist Es', 168–9.

[51] Martin Heidegger, *An Introduction to Metaphysics*, trans. by Ralph Mannheim (1935; New Haven: Yale, 1973), 150.

The violence of poetic speech, of thinking projection, of building configuration, of the action that creates states is not a function of the faculties that man has, but a taming and ordering of powers by virtue of which the essent is the power that man must master in order to become himself amid the essent, i.e. in order to be historical.[52]

Violence, if it is authentic, never has anything to do with 'mere arbitrary brutality',[53] Heidegger tells us. But if Being does not define its power before the act of violence, then violence cannot be seen as having its 'history' *essentially* destined. Rather, violence would be an event that brings the controlled security of Being to an end right from the start. For Jean Baudrillard, this is precisely why the primary importance of violence remains so repressed in Heidegger's thinking generally: 'the terrorism of authenticity through death remains a secondary process in that, by means of dialectical acrobatics, consciousness recuperates its "finitude" as destiny.'[54]

How German Is It's linguistic questioning of metaphysics has opened a space for violence to appear as a distinct issue—which it does, in the form of the 'Einzieh Group' and the 'Seventh of June Liberation Group'. The contest between the power of language and the force of violence is set up in the first two parts of the novel as a struggle between these terrorists and the media. Returning to Germany for Ulrich means coming to terms with having his family linked to the 'pathological and maniacal attempt' to overthrow the state. But if the media are responsible for thus defining terrorism and its aetiology, they also provide its main form of expression. Everytime Paula's friends go on hunger strike in prison, they 'receive some mention in the newspapers' (*HGII*, 22). The efficiency of terrorism is thus linked to its media impact, which presents problems of its own. For in spite of the constant bombings carried out by the Seventh of June Liberation Group, 'they have slipped from the front page, and accordingly from everyone's attention' (*HGII*, 56). For Ulrich, too, reputation is something the media gives and the media takes away: 'His somewhat inept performance in court, as reported widely in the press and on TV and radio, had fortunately been superseded by more recent events. An earthquake in Chile, a famine in Ethiopia, a coup d'état in Tanzania . . .' (*HGII*, 21). The serialization of disaster appears to

[52] Heidegger, *An Introduction to Metaphysics*, 157.   [53] Ibid., 151.
[54] Jean Baudrillard, *Symbolic Exchange and Death*, trans. by Iain Hamilton (1976; London: Sage, 1993), 190n.

have produced a general equivalence whereby the earthquake can be accorded the same status as the famine or act of terrorism. Yet, if one of the media's tendencies is to neutralize any catastrophe by allocating it causes and reasons, the novel also suggests that every anomaly can be viewed as equally threatening to state security. In this sense, the media destabilizes the very system of signification it attempts to construct. In part, this is because the identification of reasons and causes can only appear *after* the event and then be projected analeptically—as is also the case with Ulrich's writing. So, when the Einzieh Group blows up a post office, killing two employees, the papers rush to link the disaster to names and Ulrich is forced to realize that the significance of his own lies out of his hands: 'With one explosion the name Hargenau made all the papers again' (*HGII*, 40). That the victims of the explosion include two employees as well as two dozen sacks of first-class, unsorted mail becomes connected to the reports' confusion over the real status of the violence. The statement 'With one explosion the name Hargenau made all the papers again' suggests that the violence was exercised *by* the proper name, to the same degree that 'Hargenau' is the effect of the explosion. This slippage is reiterated in the next two sentences of the text: 'Great outrage at the senseless killings and the mutilation of thousands of letters. Those letters would never reach their destinations' (*HGII*, 40). Not only does the use of 'mutilation' regarding the letters further confound what is meant *literally* by violence, the conjunction between it and 'killings' makes it ambiguous as to whether there are even two separate instances being referred to. Indeed, there are a number of possible implications: if the explosion destroys all the letters, it also 'makes' all the papers; the violence done to the victims was essentially *graphic*; writing can explode; writing can be exploded. The *significance* of the event, like the 'destinations' of the letters themselves, admits its own accidence. At this stage, though, we need to ask how Abish's novel is itself mediating the elements of West German history it is depicting.

'The blood of Jews or the blood of cops'

> 'I suspect they're intellectuals who want to prove their theory is right.'[55]
>
> William Burroughs discussing West German terrorists.

---

[55] Interview with William Burroughs, 'Exterminating', in Lotringer, *SGI*, 84.

The Einzieh Group and the Seventh of June Liberation Group are based on the two main left-wing terrorist groups active in West Germany at the time; the 'Baader-Meinhof group', or 'Rote Armee Fraktion' (RAF), and the '2nd of June Movement', respectively.[56] Taking inspiration from the writings on guerrilla warfare by Che Guevara, Carlos Marighella, and Mao Tse-Tung, the groups preferred to describe themselves as 'urban guerrillas' rather than terrorists.[57] Offering themselves as the most radical expression of youth culture's opposition to 'capitalist imperialism' in general, they declared the USA's occupation of West Germany to be particularly offensive. That the West German government offered no resistance to the American presence was seen by many left-wing youths as being indicative of its support of America's power and the war in Vietnam. Moreover, the government's stringent attempts to reorder society, coupled with its intolerance of 'hippy' culture, only intensified the desire for rebellion.[58] Reacting to the vehement protests of students and radicals in May 1968, for example, the West German government passed a *Notstandsverfassung* ('emergency constitution') which allowed for the use of police and military force in the instance of 'internal emergencies'.[59]

[56] The best historical account of the RAF's development is Aust's *The Baader-Meinhof Group*. See also Joanne Wright, *Terrorist Propaganda: The Red Army Faction and the Provisional I.R.A., 1968–86* (London: Macmillan, 1991); Stefan T. Possony and L. Francis Bouchey, *International Terrorism—the Communist Connection—With a Case Study of West German Terrorist Ulrike Meinhof* (Washington: American Council for World Freedom, 1978); and Tom Vague, *Televisionaries: The Red Army Faction Story, 1963–93* (Edinburgh: AK, 1994). Michael 'Bommi' Baumann provides a history of the 'The Hash Blues Rebels', and '2nd of June Movement'—which took its name from the date of Ohnesorg's death—in *Terror or Love: The Personal Account of a West German Urban Guerrilla* (1975; London: John Calder, 1979).

[57] See Ernesto Che Guevara, *Guerrilla Warfare*, trans. by J. P. Morray (1960; Manchester: Manchester University Press, 1986); Mao Tse-Tung, *Basic Tactics*, trans. by Stuart R. Scram (London: Pall Mall Press, 1967), 77–136; and Carlos Marighella, *The Minimanual of the Urban Guerrilla* (1969; San Francisco: Arguello, 1978).

[58] See David Childs and Jeffre Johnson, *West Germany: Politics and Society* (London: Croom Helm, 1981), 38–9. For an overview of West German history at this time, see Michael Balfour, *West Germany: A Contemporary History* (London: Croom Helm, 1982), 133–231; also *Contemporary Germany: Politics and Culture*, ed. by Charles Burdick, Hans-Adolf Jacobsen, and Winifred Kudsus (Boulder: Westview, 1984).

[59] When the RAF increased the intensity of its militancy in the 1970s, the government brought in a series of anti-left-wing measures that were widely condemned for being draconian. Expressing public sympathy with the terrorists was enough to warrant arrest, although anyone suspected of having radical inclinations could be arrested. With the introduction of the 'Radicals Edict' (1972), or *Berufsverbot* (job ban) as it came to be known, suspected sympathizers could also be barred from employment. By 1976 the official list numbered over 500,000 people. In 1975, the Federal Court's rigid handling of the trial in which Ulrike Meinhof, Andreas Baader, Gudrun Ensslin, and Holger Meins were

Provoking widespread public opposition, such measures were declared by many radical political activists to be symptomatic of a new form of Fascism. The two events that proved this for them, and acted as a catalyst for militant action, were the police shooting of Benno Ohnesorg, a 26-year-old student, at a demonstration against the Shah of Iran on his visit to Berlin on 2 June 1967, and the shooting of the left-wing student leader, Rudi Dutschke, on 11 April 1968, by a man who had been incited by articles published in the conservative popular newspaper, *Bild-Zeitung*.[60] The leading figures of the Baader–Meinhof group—Ulrike Meinhof, Gudrun Ensslin, Astrid Proll, and Andreas Baader—joined forces during this period.

The frequency with which Auschwitz is coded into the actions of the state by the groups and then used to legitimate the most extreme response is striking. Ensslin makes the point most clearly after the death of Ohnesorg: 'this fascist state means to kill us all. We must organise resistance. Violence is the only way to answer violence. This is the Auschwitz generation and there's no arguing with them.'[61] Michael 'Bommi' Baumann, chief explosives expert of the 2nd of June Movement, argues similarly in *Terror or Love*. '[S]omething got started there', he says of Ohnesorg's shooting:

The general baiting had created a climate in which little pranks wouldn't work anymore. Not when they're going to liquidate you, regardless of what you do. Before I get transported to Auschwitz again, I'd rather shoot first. . . . These same people who gassed six million Jews, they harass you because of your hair, and that's been a part of it the whole time.[62]

The urban guerrilla is thus a Jew as much as the state is Nazi—indeed, Baumann pushes the historical analogy so far that Auschwitz is still in operation. Yet if this series of identifications heightens the extremity of the opposition between the militants and the government, it is also used to found an exchange between them, a common parlance: 'Violence is the only way to answer violence.'

As we have seen in relation to 'happenings', blurring the distinctions between politics and artistic performance was as much the work

convicted also did nothing to allay public accusations that the government was complicit in exacerbating the state of emergency to the point of acting like terrorists themselves. On these points, see Wright, *Terrorist Propaganda*, 177–89; and Aust, *The Baader-Meinhof Group*, 295–540, who covers the course of the trial in great detail.

[60] See Aust, *The Baader-Meinhof Group*, 41–7, 52–5; also Fritz Teufel, 'On Rudi Dutschke's Death', in Lotringer, *SGI*, 116–19.

[61] Quoted in Wright, *Terrorist Propaganda*, 110.   [62] Baumann, *Terror or Love*, 41.

of the West German government as it was of artists and radicals. Baumann's charge that 'little pranks wouldn't work anymore' refers to the inefficacy of the happenings that Kommune 1 had practised—members of both the RAF and the 2nd of June Movement had been involved in the group.[63] Under the direction of the former Situationist Dieter Kunzelmann, revolution and performance had become wholly combined, as in the 'Christmas happening' of 1966 when the group had attempted to set fire to papier mâché heads of Lyndon Johnson, Walter Ulbricht, and the East German chancellor under a Christmas tree—only Johnson's caught alight.[64] Baumann is none the less adamant that the group's main aim was to build an alternative culture rather than merely escalate militancy: 'we were building a group here that will start an action, but the idea was to develop a unity of collective life . . .'.[65] In this respect, the 2nd of June Movement and its earlier incarnation, 'The Hash Blues Rebels', differed from the Baader–Meinhof group, he argues, who placed militancy above all else.[66] According to Baumann, political violence was resorted to because alternative youth culture was already overcoded as politically violent by the state. But earlier leaflets of the The Hash Blues Rebels express a ready acceptance of militancy as a part of the unity of collective life they were trying to develop: 'IT IS TIME TO DESTROY . . . Build militant cadres in towns and cities. / Contact similar groups. / Shit on the society of middle age and taboos. Become wild and do beautiful things. Have a joint. Whatever you see that you don't like, destroy.'[67] In part, this confusion over their status reflects the indeterminate relations between politics and alternative culture at the time. But the point is that this instability was not simply determined by one side. Ambivalence was actively engendered by both the government and the radicals alike.

The confusion surrounding activism is evident from several events in 1968, the first being the response of Ulrike Meinhof to the 'superscale

---

[63] See also the interview with ex-2nd of June Movement member, Fritz Teufel, 'Terrorism with a Fun Face', in Lotringer, *SGI*, 134–46.

[64] See Jillian Becker, *Hitler's Children: The Story of the Baader–Meinhof Terrorist Gang* (London: Michael Joseph, 1977), 32–3.

[65] Baumann, *Terror or Love*, 54.

[66] For accounts by transitory members of the RAF of the slide into militancy, see the interview with Hans-Joachim Klein, 'Slaughter Politics', in Lotringer, *SGI*, 80–99; and the interview with Horst Mahler, 'Look Back on Terror', in Lotringer, *SGI*, 100–6.

[67] Baumann, *Terror or Love*, 56.

happening' arson attack by Belgian radicals on an American department store in Brussels:

> For the first time in any big European city, a burning store full of burning people gives that crackling Vietnam feeling (of being there and burning too), something previously unavailable in Berlin. . . . Sympathetic as we feel towards the pain of the bereaved in Brussels, yet receptive to new ideas, we cannot help admiring the bold and unconventional character of the Brussels department store fire, despite all the human tragedy involved. . . . three hundred complacent citizens end their exciting lives, and Brussels became Hanoi. None of us need shed any more tears for the poor Vietnamese over our morning paper at breakfast. Now you can just go to the clothing department of KaDeWe, Hertie, Woolworth, Bilka or Neckerman and light a discreet cigarette in the changing room.[68]

This second 'Vietnam' is offered as countering the first, as the price that had to be paid. But the exchange of violence is also made so complete here that despite the obvious numerical difference in casualties there is no longer any distinction made between the two events. Whether the arson attack is a subversion or reproduction of Vietnam on these terms becomes extremely unclear. The people caught in the fire are presented as both victims and culprits, Vietnamese citizens and consumers of American imperialism, just as Brussels is also Hanoi. At the same time, because the event is accorded a representational status, the real disaster is still figured as taking place elsewhere. The people burned in the fire have apparently played their parts well in showing that the real tragedy is in Vietnam, and that the US government is the perpetrator of real violence.

A subsequent arson attack on two stores in Frankfurt by Baader and Ensslin—aided by Thorwald Proll and Horst Söhnlein, a member of 'Action Theatre'—provoked similarly tangled interpretations, not least from Ensslin's father when interviewed:

> I—like the whole of Federal Germany—would object to any admonishments made in that way [the use of arson]. However, what she wanted to say is this: a generation that has seen the building of concentration camps, the encouragement of anti-Semitism and the committing of genocide among and in the name of its own people must not allow any revival of such things. . . . It has astonished me to find that Gudrun, who has always thought in a very rational, intelligent way, has experienced what is almost a condition of euphoric

---

[68] Quoted in Aust, *The Baader-Meinhof Group*, 34.

self-realization. . . . To me that is more of a beacon of light than the fire of the arson itself . . .[69]

Here the violence of the attack is interpreted as citing the atrocities of the Nazis only to the extent that it incites resistance to their return. The past is set alight by being actively rekindled. Moreover, the fire is also figured by Ensslin's father as a pyre upon which his daughter has attained a sublime political consciousness. A specific rationale of violence is thus projected analeptically so that the arson attack becomes a form of speech act—'what she wanted to say . . .'. The violence is not seen as exerting its own force, then, but as demonstrating that a 'beacon' of enlightenment is still burning.[70]

If the impact of such actions depends on the capacity for deeds to become pure propaganda, the arson attacks failed to make ideology speak louder than a bomb. Neither did the 2nd of June Movement's placement of a bomb in a Jewish Synagogue in Berlin on the thirtieth anniversary of Crystal Night. Baumann states the intention:

We sought out a point where everything met, the uncoped-with Nazi past, the Palestine problem with which we had recently been presented, and also we wanted a starting shot to announce the opening of Urban Guerrilla warfare. It was an operation that everyone was bound to take note of, from liberals to old Nazis . . .[71]

Although the bomb failed to explode, the group certainly achieved its aim of fuelling debate; the incident was reported by the media around the world.[72] But clearly the primary effect was to exacerbate the ambiguity of the difference between the group's overt anti-Fascist stance and the Fascism it accused its opposition of maintaining. A leaflet,

---

[69] Quoted in Aust, *The Baader–Meinhof Group*, 62. See also Becker, *Hitler's Children*, 53–6.

[70] Judith Butler, in *Excitable Speech: A Politics of the Performative*, ch. 1, discusses the problem of interpreting actions as speech acts, looking at recent US legal cases dealing with 'hate speech'.

[71] Baumann in Peter Neuhauser, 'The Mind of a Terrorist: Interview with Michael "Bommi" Baumann', *Encounter* 51: 3 (September 1978): 84. Hans Joachim Klein, another group member, expresses similar sentiments in J. Bougereau, *Memoirs of an International Terrorist: Conversations with Hans Joachim Klein* (Orkney: Cienfuegos, 1981), 13.

[72] Baumann acknowledges the part played by the media in reinforcing the group's social impact: 'Without the reporting there would be a void. We were built up by the press, after all' ('The Mind of a Terrorist', 83). Many RAF sympathizers thought that right-wing repression was also built by the press. The owner of *Bild-Zeitung*, Axel Springer, was held by some to be directly responsible for the shooting of Benno Ohnesorg. Shortly after the shooting, demonstrators led by Ulrike Meinhof chanted: 'Springer out of West Berlin! *Bild* fired the gun too!' (quoted in Aust, *The Baader–Meinhof Group*, 55).

'Shalom and Napalm', issued by the group shortly after the event, complicates matters further by aligning the Jews with neo-Fascism:

Israeli prisons in which, according to the testimony of escaped liberation fighters, Gestapo torture methods are used, are filled. . . . The Jews displaced by fascism have themselves become fascists who want to eradicate the Palestinian people in collaboration with Amerikan [*sic*] capital. . . . ALL POLITICAL POWER COMES FROM THE BARREL OF THE GUN![73]

But the presence and force of Fascism, which are offered as explaining and justifying the attempted bombing, have been reinstated *by* the placement of the bomb itself. What is posed as a simple reaction to a totalitarian system of power reveals instead an extreme instability of political performativity. The statement of opposition and self-legitimation in part derives its force from the initial gesture of violence, just as the subsequent leaflet and reports attempt to refigure the bomb's significance. And if this concatenation of actions and interpretations is not complicated enough, the difficulty in determining the political status of the bomb is compounded in so far as it was later revealed to have been supplied by a West German government informer, Peter Urbach.[74]

The grounds for such a general exchange between terrorism and German history, particularly regarding the Holocaust, had been prepared in advance by the Situationists and other Marxist critics. In *One Dimensional Man* (1964), Herbert Marcuse, a major influence on the Situationists, and declared by some to be an influence on the Baader–Meinhof group, describes the system of capitalist industrialization as producing a 'terroristic coordination of society'.[75] This metaphor is subsequently transposed indirectly onto the image of Auschwitz, which is also associated with rampant automation: 'Auschwitz continues to haunt, not the memory but the accomplishment of man—the space flights; the rockets and missiles . . . the pretty electronic plants, clean, hygienic and with flower beds . . .'.[76] In a series of lectures at Bremen after the war, Heidegger also conflated industrialization and Auschwitz to an incredible degree: 'Agriculture is now a motorized food industry, the same thing in its essence as the

---

[73] Quoted in Baumann, *Terror or Love*, 68.

[74] See Baumann, 'The Mind of a Terrorist', 84; also Wright, *Terrorist Propaganda*, 82–3.

[75] Herbert Marcuse, *One Dimensional Man* (London: Routledge, 1991), 3. On Marcuse as an inspiration for the RAF, see Wright, *Terrorist Propaganda*, 40–9; and Hans Josef Horchem, 'West Germany's Red Army Anarchists', *Conflict Studies* 74 (June 1974): 1–3.

[76] Marcuse, *One Dimensional Man*, 247.

production of corpses in the gas chambers and the extermination camps.'[77] For the Situationists, however, terrorism and Nazism are strictly opposed. According to Vaneigem, the propensity for everything to be made equivalent, owing to the dominance of exchange value over use value, amounts to living in a 'concentration camp world', where 'victims and torturers wear the same mask, and only the torture is real'.[78] Elsewhere, though, he imbues the Holocaust phenomenon with an almost romantic rebelliousness. Auschwitz and Hiroshima, he writes, were 'dreams of apocalypses, gigantic destructions' (*Revolution*, 47) that erupted out of relentless mechanization. The specific horrors of these events are further devalued by Vaneigem when he argues that: 'The clinical hecatomb of Auschwitz still has a lyrical quality when compared with the icy grasp of that generalized conditioning which the programmers of technocratic organisation are preparing for us . . .' (*Revolution*, 210). As with Lewis's and Pound's figurations of a solidary, enemy force, Nazism and the Holocaust are presented as calling for extreme counter measures. Terrorism, for Vaneigem, is the only possible response. An individual's decision to totally reject society is the 'Noon and eternity of the great refusal. Before it, the pogroms, and beyond it, the new innocence. The blood of Jews or the blood of cops' (*Revolution*, 179). Terrorism and totalitarianism might be opposed, then, but they are nevertheless bound into a system of exchange. The Holocaust and the present are interchangeable, indistinguishable, and terrorism must be made as systematically apocalyptic as Auschwitz itself. 'Guerrilla war is total war. This is the path on which the Situationist International is set' (*Revolution*, 263).

Given that the West German government and the militants were complicit in generating political ambivalence, we need to acknowledge that *historicity is itself contestation* in West Germany at the time. Thus, the various critical reactions that connected the political violence to the memory or denial of the Holocaust must themselves be seen as having influenced the very grounds of the historical debates and political struggles they seek to comment on. For Jane Kramer, all that is unclear in the critical responses is nevertheless rooted in the war: 'since Hitler, Germans have had an understandable problem in

---

[77] Quoted in Philipe Lacoue-Labarthe, *Heidegger, Art and Politics: The Fiction of the Political*, trans. by Chris Turner (Oxford: Blackwell, 1990), 34.

[78] Vaneigem, 'Basic Banalities II', 132.

distinguishing what is aberrant from what is symptomatic, and they are having that problem now as they try to come to terms with terrorism and their responses to it'.[79] For other commentators, it is not so much the war as the suppression of its memory that is the real problem in terms of terrorism. The 1960s in general contributed to an obliviousness in the youth, argues Michael Balfour: '[The radicals] were more the children of "Marx and Coca-Cola" than of Hitler'.[80] In contrast, other historians viewed this forgetting as symptomatic of a more generalized cultural repression.[81] According to Michael Schneider, this is what terrorism sought to expose: 'From the very beginning, the terrorism of the RAF was not that which it claimed to be—a representative act of liberation on behalf of the politically unaware masses of workers—but rather a murderous and suicidal act of unmasking.'[82] This consisted in revealing that Nazism was still politically and economically active, while imitating it through their actions: '[the militants] slipped, as it were, into the historical costume of the Nazi generation in order to "prosecute" in effigy the crimes which that generation had committed against their political and racial opponents.'[83] This is certainly an apt description of the confusion inherent to the 2nd of June Movement's attempted bombing of the Jewish synagogue; as Schneider argues, such imitative prosecution runs the risk of merely replicating what it is fighting against.[84]

The problems of historical politicizing during this period inevitably correspond to the problem of representing the Holocaust. After a relative silence on the subject of war crimes, the 1960s marked the beginning of an intense debate among historians, commonly known as the '*Historikerstreit*'. While Jürgen Habermas states that Auschwitz

---

[79] Jane Kramer, 'A Reporter in Hamburg', *The New Yorker* (20 March 1978): 46.

[80] Balfour, *West Germany*, 254.

[81] Tony Kushner discusses post-war American and British inattention to the Holocaust in *The Holocaust and the Liberal Imagination: A Social and Cultural History* (Oxford: Blackwell, 1994), ch. 7.

[82] Michael Schneider, 'Fathers and Sons Retrospectively: The Damaged Relationship Between Two Generations', *New German Critique* 31 (Winter 1984): 15.   [83] Ibid.

[84] For a further selection of the contrasting views concerning the militants' relation to the Nazi era, see Becker, *Hitler's Children*, 17–23; Saul Friedlander, *Memory, History, and the Extermination of the Jews in Europe* (Bloomington: Indiana University Press, 1993), 41–9; Jürgen Habermas, *The New Conservatism* [hereafter *NC*], trans. by Shierry Weber Nicholson (Cambridge: Polity Press, 1989), 186–9; Herbert Marcuse, 'Murder Is Not a Political Weapon', *New German Critique* 12 (Fall 1977): 7–8; Paul Oestreicher, 'The Roots of Terrorism. West Germany: A Special Case?' *The Round Table* 269 (January 1978): 76–8; and Melvin Lasky, 'Ulrike Meinhof and the Baader-Meinhof Gang', *Encounter* 44: 6 (June 1975): 11–17.

marks the point at which West Germany 'lost its power to generate myths'[85]—just as Theodor Adorno sees it as announcing the end of poetry—other historians sought to review its importance by placing it within a wider historical plot. For Ernst Nolte, this amounted to a radical revisioning of the Holocaust, which he outlines in a later essay: 'Could it be that the Nazis . . . carried out an "Asiatic deed" only because they regarded themselves and those like them as potential or actual victims of an "Asiatic deed"? Was not the Gulag Archipelago more original than Auschwitz?'[86] In this sense, the event becomes a matter of representation—'a distorted copy'—in further need of rewriting. It has become mythification *par excellence* (*muthos* in Greek is also 'emplotment').[87] To argue, then, that West German history and politics during this period were overdetermined by rampant commodification or the atrocities of the war is a point over which there has been no consensus, even at the time. Indeed, the issue is precisely what the West German government, the terrorists, and social commentators were fighting over in their various ways.

Terrorism, Potentiality, Real-ization

In combining issues of terrorism, Holocaust memory, and narrative, Abish's *How German Is It* certainly educes the salient antagonisms of the period. Yet I would argue that it also engages directly in the entwinings of discourse and violence, memory and performance, that I have been discussing to produce its own image of fiction's potential for intervention. Towards the end of the fourth and penultimate part of the novel, 'Sweet truth', the narrator raises the question: '*Can only*

[85] Habermas, *The New Conservatism*, 250.

[86] Ernst Nolte, 'Between Myth and Revisionism? The Third Reich in the Perspective of the 1980s', in *Aspects of the Third Reich*, ed. by H. W. Koch (London: Routledge, 1985), 36. For general discussions on the *Historikerstreit*, see in particular Dominick La Capra, 'Representing the Holocaust: Reflections on the Historians' Debate', in *Probing the Limits of Representation: Nazism and the 'Final Solution'*, ed. by Saul Friedlander (Cambridge, Mass.: Harvard University Press, 1992), 100–25; Eric L. Santner, *Stranded Objects: Mourning, Memory, and Film in Postwar Germany* (Ithaca: Cornell University Press, 1990), 1–35; and Jean-Paul Bier, 'The Holocaust and West Germany: Strategies of Oblivion, 1947–79', *New German Critique* 19 (Winter 1980): 11–29.

[87] For a historical overview of postwar responses by West German writers to warmemory and the Holocaust, see Walter Hinderer, 'The Challenge of the Past: Turning Points in the Intellectual and Literary Reflections of West-Germany, 1945–85', in *Legacies and Ambiguities: Postwar Fiction and Culture in West Germany and Japan*, ed. by Ernestine Schlant and J. Thomas Rimer (Baltimore: Johns Hopkins University Press, 1991), 81–98.

revolutions undermine the tyranny of the familiar day-to-day events?' (*HGII*, 157, Abish's emphasis). The problem is examined in detail with respect to three different images of everydayness. The first is that of a matchstick model of the Durst concentration camp built by Franz, a friend and former servant of Ulrich's father; the second is that of a photograph of two friends of Ulrich's architect brother, Helmuth, outside a house he has designed for them; the third is that of a colouring book sent to Ulrich by members of the Einzieh group. Each of these involves a distinct figuration of the familiar, which is itself posed as a general subject for debate earlier by Ulrich's schoolteacher friend, Anna Heller, in front of her class. After holding up a piece of chalk and deciding that it would be extremely difficult to ascertain whether it was the piece she had used in the morning, Anna concludes that 'the familiar' is more a matter of performativity than what Brumhold would have called the *'thingliness* that is intrinsic to all things . . . (*HGII*, 19, Abish's emphasis): 'What is familiar, then, is not this particular piece of chalk but the act of holding it, of using it' (*HGII*, 119). Stating that the quiddity of familiarity depends on everyday performance means that it is susceptible to contingency—not a position that Brumhold (or Heidegger) would readily accept.[88] For Anna, though, it also means that what appears strange or unpleasant can be made familiar:

if we think about the past, if we think about anything that happened in the past: yesterday, the day before, a week ago, aren't we to some extent thinking about something that we consider familiar? For if nothing else, the memory, pleasant or unpleasant as it may be, has become a familiar one. (*HGII*, 121)

This episode occurs shortly after the uncovery of Brumhold's mass grave. But the ease with which the uncanny or distasteful can become comfortably assimilated is challenged by Franz's model of the concentration camp.

A long time employee of the Hargenau household before being dismissed by Ulrich's mother, Franz has by no means reconciled himself to the past, as his frequent howling episodes testify. While he is known locally as 'the howler', only his wife, Doris, knows that his cries are 'not uniform'—for example, 'this particular look', we are told at one point, 'signified a momentous encounter with the past'

---

[88] See, for example, Heidegger on 'Being-familiar' and the 'uncanny', in *Being and Time*, 232–4.

(*HGII*, 73). Franz's incapacity to put his sentiments into words no doubt explains his recourse to model-making. Anna Heller, for one, finds the enterprise 'inexplicably gruesome and grotesque' on hearing of it from Helmuth. Vin, the wife of Brumholdstein's mayor, reacts similarly: 'Isn't it too awful for words', she remarks. Helmuth, however, disagrees: 'That's exactly what we need, isn't that so?' he asks the mayor, who replies by arguing that Franz's hobby is 'simply an expression of his detestation. I've got him down for a real antisocial type' (*HGII*, 96). In this way, the novel foregrounds the difficulty of verbally translating the model's meaning. Is it a memorial or is it simply reducing the commemoration of atrocity to kitsch? Whether it is the act of representing or what is being represented that is so repellent to the characters remains unclear. Do the aspersions they cast on it amount to good taste or bad repression? After being met with similar disdain when enquiring at the local library if they held the architectural plans for the camp, Franz is convinced that building such a sense of unease must be his primary goal:

He was not merely replicating a period of disaster. Or replicating what had ultimately been destroyed to make room for Brumholdstein. He was not merely replicating in every detail, and to scale, something that in its day had been as familiar to the people in Daemlin as the cows in the barn. What he was doing was to evoke a sense of uncertainty, a sense of doubt, a sense of dismay, a sense of disgust. That was to be the ultimate achievement. It was as if he recognised that all revolutions have in common an element of bad taste. In his case, to strive for bad taste was to strive for revolution. (*HGII*, 158)

But what form of revolution? For, like the 2nd of June Movement's synagogue bomb, Franz's model actively tries to reconstitute the space of extermination in order to attack complacency. Yet the effect of realism is still clearly a perversion of the referent; the model's precise scale is nevertheless a form of *detournement*. Even the memory of the Holocaust is thus open to resignification.[89] But this transformation cannot be reduced to a simple play of signifiers. What lends the model its dismaying impact is its ability to *re-place* the past—draw it into a different context *and* destabilize it to the point of usurpation. In contrast to the safe-guards of Heidegger's temple, a diversion of history is *real-ized* here; effectively made real.

[89] This point is debated in reference to numerous Holocaust memorials and museums in *The Art of Memory: Holocaust Memorials in History*, ed. by James E. Young (New York: Prestel-Verlag, 1994).

If the part played by representation in actively rebuilding the past is equivocal in Franz's enterprise, in Abish's second image of everydayness the fabrication of the present is overt. The pictures of Helmuth's friends Egon and Gisela posing in domestic style and comfort for *Treue* magazine are explicitly of 'the new democratic Germany', as well as being 'an invitation—what else?—to reinterpret Germany' (*HGII*, 129). Like the colouring book in 'The English Garden', the pictures both record and figure contemporary national traits. They are tributes to the way things can colour each other and create their own milieux of meaning: 'The red carnations authenticate the graceful shape of the fluted vase. The large mirror in its heavy gilded frame objectifies the view of the interior space and nicely frames what is clearly an attempt to achieve perfection' (*HGII*, 125). The whole scene is an advertisement for its own self-fashioning. Signification is determined within the environment because the environment appears to be suspended in its own self-reflected present, as if already a snapshot of itself. So, on the one hand, the pictures seem to suggest that contemporary German life has sealed itself hermetically from the past; that there has been a total historical change of scene. Everything is exposed and superficial: 'The meaning, the shades or layers of meaning, are to be found in their components: the ubiquitous gaberdine suit, the Paisley scarf . . .' (*HGII*, 126)—which is also why there is no reason to countenance the 'possibility' that the couple might be 'concealing in their attic or cellar, a member of the Einzieh . . .' (*HGII*, 129). On the other hand, this photographic arrangement of nationality is proffered as symbolizing a general epochal truth, an intrinsically German '*Standpunkt*', the reality of which is *revealed* rather than constructed:

All in all, it sums up the new German restlessness as well as the general anticipation of the greater German splendor yet to come. Are these not, also, the components of a German story? For, ultimately, what may come about is a matching of this finely developed sensibility, this heightened awareness of perfection and its actual realization. (*HGII*, 127)

What is at stake here is precisely a society of the spectacle. Just as Debord asserts that the spectacle manifests a prescriptive autonomy, so we are told that 'In a sense, everything in the eight-page article on Egon and Gisela in the magazine *Treue* is already conveyed and analyzed on the front cover—albeit in a more condensed manner' (*HGII*, 126). Yet just as Vaneigem argued that 'all transcendence depends on language and is developed through a system of signs and symbols (words, dance, ritual, music, sculpture, building . . .)' (*Revolution*, 101), so the photographs clearly advertise that they are staged, artificial. Ideality is not transcendent to the contingencies of social signs; it is produced in and by them as a thing. So while a proliferation of Egons and Giselas appears eminently possible, the pictures of the couple do not reflect the full reality of their situation: 'Something that is not shown is Gisela sulking. Gisela close to tears' (*HGII*, 130). At these times, she is to be found silently huddled in a corner of a room, usually on account of Egon's frequent affairs. His reaction to her distress on one of these occasions is to say that he will build her a 'tiny, tiny house' (*HGII*, 132) in the corner for her to inhabit—the image of domestic bliss begins to subdivide. But it is only through believing in 'the fundamental harmony that permeates our house' that Egon can comprehend a homeliness of contemporary German culture, against which the terrorist threat becomes clear:

It is a harmony that enables me to assess myself and my intentions in a fresh light. It is also, I might mention, the intrinsic harmony of our society that has enabled me to understand the full dimension of the terrorist threat to Germany. Clearly the Einzieh Group intends to overthrow our system of government by destroying Germany's newly acquired harmony. For harmony spell democracy, if you will, but democracy, alas, is a word that has been depleted of its meaning, its energy, its power. If anything can be said to represent the new Germany, it is the wish, the desire, no, the craving to attain a total harmony. (*HGII*, 131)

If total harmony is a fiction, this fiction still has real effects. Moreover, it is the illusion of harmony that makes total disruption such a real worry. The description of Egon and the photographer, Rita, driving in his Mercedes suggests as much: 'given the unpredictability of life, does it occur to them that at any moment, someone from behind one of those trees might be tempted to puncture their spotless windshield with a bullet, to puncture the perfection of their trip . . .' (*HGII*, 133).

Could everything be different, then? This question is the title of the fifth and final part of the novel, and also appears in the colouring book, *Unser Deutschland* (Our Germany), sent to Ulrich by Daphne Hasendruck, who now appears to be working with the terrorists. Whereas the photographs in *Treue* show how signs can effectively use realism to envisage a security of everydayness, in the colouring book the potential for an image to become actual is a cause for concern. The book is markedly different from the one depicted in 'The

English Garden', for many of the everyday scenes shown are explicitly disturbing. Alongside the familiar pictures of an airport, a group of workers mending a sewerage-pipe, a car on an autobahn, and an old freight train, there are also pictures of a car accident, a wall with 'DAS WORT IST EIN MOLOTOV COCKTAIL' (The Word is a Molotov Cocktail) (*HGII*, 178) inscribed on it, and a group of young women who carry automatic weapons and wear gas masks standing around the body of a man. Just as the colouring book in 'The English Garden' was understood to 'occupy visually, at least, a space in real life' (*ITFP*, 1) these images that Ulrich is confronted with embody their own threat; they are a death sentence. More than in the short story, then, the emphasis in this third image of everydayness is on an antagonistic force of signs. The colouring book is not a matter of representation so much as ultimatum.

Politics and fabulation overlap further towards the end of Part Five of *How German Is It* in a section entitled '*The purpose of an antiterrorist film*' (*HGII*, 243). According to Würtenberg's chief of police, the purpose of such a film amounts to constructing a complete terrorist profile that identifies 'their slang, their gestures, their preferences, their way of dressing . . . their weapons, their techniques, their political rhetoric . . .' in order to 'Depict as accurately as possible the threat they pose to the stability of this society' (*HGII*, 243). However, as the narrative voice points out, presenting an authentic picture of the threat is fundamentally a matter of deciding how to 'minimize' or 'exaggerate' the terrorists' 'strength' and 'callousness' (*HGII*, 243). Determining a special-effect of realism appears to be the only way the desired political effects can be realized: 'In order to clarify, to make evident a terrorist threat, the film has to distort, fabricate and often lie. But no matter how great these flaws are, the need for the film is self-evident' (*HGII*, 243). It is self-evident, though, because the film has already distorted this issue of its necessity:

If the film falls short of its aim—always a possibility—it may at least succeed in defining the rules, the bureaucratically, legalistically defined rules that govern the procedure by which the terrorists are to be eliminated. . . . Admittedly, the film is also an attempt to further escalate the continuous overreaction and overresponse of one side to the actions of the other. (*HGII*, 243)

That this whole procedure requires that the distinctions between events and representations, facts and fictions, 'terrorism' and counter-terrorism, become totally unclear in order to manipulate the public is no doubt why there is 'always a possibility' that it will not succeed. The fostering of an increasingly extreme opposition is undermined by the very ambiguities used to enforce it.

There is thus no general structure or code of everydayness in *How German Is It*. Nor is there a uniform relation between the force of events and the force of signification. Nor, as Debord claimed, is there a universalized, 'irreversible time' that controls all aesthetic production. Each of the three images of everydayness analysed above involves three distinct perspectives on the potential mediation, security, and disruption of social life. In part, this entails foregrounding different historical aspects: of the past with Franz's model; of the present with the photographs; of the future with the colouring book. Each of these emphases thus corresponds to specific aspects of performativity respectively: commemoration/repression (the model); figuration/description (the photos); prediction/pledge (the colouring book). Yet as we have seen, each image of everydayness also involves each of these modes to differing degrees. Performativity, or as I have been calling it, *real-ization*, is the element that gives the three images a commonality. Primarily, real-ization is the capacity for signs, things, or events to effect and affect a reality in the one blow. This might entail the production of a certain ideality or abstraction, as in the photographs, or it might involve the figuration of an event as Other— whether of the past (Durst) or the enemy (terrorism or Fascism). The point is that even abstraction and Otherness are to some degree constructed concretely in the act of real-ization, so that each instance admits a certain performative contingency. Moreover, the most abstract figuration can have an historical and experiential impact—whether it is Heidegger's Being calling for death, or Lewis's Vorticist separatism denying Suffragette militancy any import. That is not to say that language or 'reality', as Bradbury suggests, are primarily 'human inventions'. As each real-ization is a specific modulation of the everyday, it involves specific powers of existence. *What is engendered simultaneously manifests its own potential to affect a situation.* Indeed, what is clear from the real-izations discussed so far is that ideology and political agency, for example, can largely be an effect of a real-ization rather than its cause. For example, in the instance of the 2nd of June Movement's synagogue bomb, the spectre of Fascism in West Germany was cited and incited, made real, by placing the explosive there—which in turn bolstered the impact of the 2nd of June Movement's historical claims. The same holds for the effects of Abish's anti-terrorist film. In this

WALTER ABISH   229

respect, the *potentiality* of things presented in *How German Is It* must be seen in all senses of the term: it expresses how a state of affairs is precipitated, made possible; this possibility exists as an affective power (*potentia*) in itself; it also marks the antagonism of a force to other forces (like a 'potential' of energy in physics).[90] Without equating them, potentiality therefore denotes the capacity of events to impact on discursive production as well as the power of signs to designate and mediate an event. An image of how such potentials of action and discourse interact is given by Deleuze and Guattari in terms of hijacking:

In an airplane hijacking, the threat of a hijacker brandishing a revolver is obviously an action; so is the execution of the hostages, if it occurs. But the transformation of the passengers into hostages, and of the plane-body into a prison-body, is an instantaneous incorporeal transformation, a 'mass media act' in the sense in which the English speak of 'speech acts'.[91]

How German Is It ends by relating performativity back to the issue of history. Having narrowly escaped an attempted assassination by the terrorists, and then witnessed the bombing of a bridge that he was about to drive across, Ulrich decides to pay a visit to a psychoanalyst, Dr Ernst Magenbach. Ulrich's main concern, though, is that he was born too long after his father's execution to be his son: 'I practised a sort of self-deception. I still don't have the slightest clue as to who my father could be. . . . I am a bastard. Perhaps an appropriate role for a writer' (*HGII*, 250).[92] Both his identity and his vocation are viewed by him as having depended on fabricating memory. Even his Einzieh period seems a part of this plot to him: 'Is it possible that I agreed to work with the group because I wanted a role that would, in a respect, parallel the role my father played in '44?' (*HGII*, 251). Here, the issue

---

[90] A proper study of the philosophy and politics of potentiality is still to be written and would need to address writings of Aristotle, Leibniz, Spinoza, Schelling, Nietzsche, Heidegger, and Schmitt. Paul Ricoeur problematizes the Aristotelian opposition of potentiality (*dunamis*) and actuality (*energeia*) in relation to Heidegger, narration, and Being, in *Oneself as Another*, trans. by Kathleen Blamey (Chicago: University of Chicago Press, 1993), 299–317. See also Giorgio Agamben, *Potentialities: Collected Essays in Philosophy*, trans. by Daniel Heller-Roazen (Stanford: Stanford University Press, 1999).

[91] Deleuze and Guattari, *A Thousand Plateaus*, 81.

[92] By the end of the 1980s in West Germany, differences between the war and postwar generations were being explored increasingly through fictional and autobiographical narratives of son and father relations—*Väter Literatur* was the name given to the new genre. See Santner, *Stranded Objects*, 35–40; Schneider, 'Fathers and Sons, Retrospectively', 15–40; and Donna K. Reed, *The Novel and The Nazi Past* (New York: Peter Lang, 1985), 149–62.

of historical performativity is raised again. Ulrich's interpretation of
his actions as reconstructing the past differs from that of most historians, as we have seen, who largely view the West German militants as
attempting to break with Nazi memories. As far as Dr Magenbach is
concerned, Ulrich's prevarications can be overcome by 'instruct[ing]
the patient under hypnosis' to recall his childhood. After inducing
such a state, the psychiatrist tells Ulrich his arm is getting lighter and
beginning to rise; Ulrich then opens his eyes to find 'his right hand
raised in a stiff salute' (*HGII*, 252). This is taken as a sign that they are
'making progress', by Magenbach. Ulrich, on the other hand, is more
convinced that he was doing it 'for no better reason than not to im-
pede the hypnosis, or a wish to please the doctor' (*HGII*, 252). Is the
salute an unconscious reflex? Whether the action can be detached
from past events is the question the novel finishes with: 'Is it possible
for anyone in Germany, nowadays, to raise his right hand, for whatever the reason, and not be flooded by the memory of a dream to end
all dreams?' (*HGII*, 252).

In *The New Conservatism*, Habermas argues that 'the Nazi period will
be much less of an obstacle . . . the more calmly we are able to consider it as a filter through which the substance of [German] culture
must be passed . . .' (*NC*, 252–3). For Dominick La Capra, the closing
question of *How German Is It* problematizes Habermas's position:

Abish's final question, I would submit, lies at the heart of the current struggle
over memory in Germany today, and it profoundly complicates Habermas's
more sanguine metaphors of 'filter' and 'substance'—unless, that is, one can
imagine a filter that contaminates as it cleans.[93]

For La Capra, the Nazi past still carries contaminating effects—potentials that remain to be real-ized, and that affect the very instance
of commemoration. So far as Abish is concerned, though, the question of Ulrich's salute remains ambiguous: 'To me the salute contains
an ikonic position in a time frame. Hence, it is a gesture that cannot
be made innocently. The memory of a dream to end all dreams is a
vague statement. I had Hollywood in mind.'[94] This is not to say that
the issue of Germanness disappears. Once it is recognized that signs
carry their own specific force, their own potentials, they must be seen
as being capable of retaining their impact despite being subjected to

---

[93] La Capra, 'Representing the Holocaust', 157

[94] Quoted in Richard Martin, 'Walter Abish's Fictions: Perfect Unfamiliarity, Familiar
Imperfection', *Journal of American Studies* 17: 2 (August 1983): 241.

mass-production. Indeed, as Manfred Henningsen has argued, one of the first major public debates about the Holocaust in West Germany was in fact provoked by the screening of an American television series, 'Holocaust', in 1979.[95] In this respect, I would argue that Abish's novel explores questions of German history more generally by analysing *how* something becomes German, rather than simply asking whether it is German or not. As Adorno has argued, the question ' "What is German?" ' . . . presupposes an autonomous collective entity, "German", whose characteristics are then determined after the fact.'[96] Abish himself states that he was not interested in revealing a German essence in *How German Is It* so much as real-izing an assemblage of German signs: 'To me the [novel's] title is not primarily a question. Essentially it functions as a sign, the most effective sign I could find to describe the text. . . . I have introduced German signs. to create and to authenticate a "German" novel.'[97]

As I have been arguing, though, it is problematic to see the terrorism depicted in the novel as nationally overdetermined. It is also problematic to see such terrorism as being more prevalent at this time in West Germany than elsewhere; 'Action Directe' in France, the 'Brigate Rossi' in Italy, and the 'Angry Brigade' in England were all involved in similar left-wing terrorist activity. The West German groups were one part of a general political crisis which began in Europe and the US in the late 1960s. West Germany, in Abish's text, is the grounds upon which to build an image of how everydayness was entangled in specific clashes between representation and activism. *How German Is It* is effective not only because this confrontation was being pursued in West Germany at the time, but also because the Holocaust and terrorism were so frequently linked to cultural and political problems more generally. Germany in the novel is not simply a 'human invention', then, nor is it reducible to terrors of the past or present. Similarly, the terrorism depicted in *How German Is It* cannot simply be reduced to a media construction, or a state fabrication, or the detonation of a bomb by a group of radicals, for all these things are implicated in a more general topography. Inhabiting an ironic

[95] Manfred Henningsen, 'The Politics of Symbolic Evasion: Germany and the Aftermath of the Holocaust', in *Echoes From the Holocaust: Reflections on a Dark Time*, ed. by Alan Rosenberg and Gerald E. Myers (Philadelphia: Temple University Press, 1988), 403–5.

[96] Theodor Adorno, 'On the Question: "What is German" ', *New German Critique* 36 (Fall 1985): 121.

[97] Abish, 'Wie Deutsch Ist Es', 160, 161.

space in this topography of everyday life, Abish has stated that he endeavours to stake out a utopic field of resistance in his fiction:

I avoid the intentional and sometimes unintentional hierarchy of values that seems to creep in whenever lifelike incidents are depicted. Through the avoidance of a hierarchy that is related to values outside the actual work, language has a chance of becoming what Roland Barthes refers to as a field of action, and to quote him: 'the definition of and the hope for a possibility.'[98]

This resistance is not limited to abstract utopia; for Abish, the noplace (*ou topos*) of this 'field of action' can still take place. Contrasting his work to that of Claude Lévi-Strauss's analyses of social signification, Abish thus states: '[Lévi-Strauss] must, whether he likes the word or not, focus on the "real" as opposed to the "possible" or "probable". I sense that what I invent will become "real" . . .'.[99]

The notions of potentiality and real-ization that I have drawn from Abish's novel are clearly different from the security and violence of Being that Heidegger poses. Real-ization does not simply reverse his metaphysics of violence so that we can claim that ontology or signification is determined solely by physical force. Rather, in being linked to potentiality in all its senses, real-ization shows the degree to which political ontology can become entangled in everydayness in various ways. But in saying that real-ization can involve signs, things, individuals, and events, I am not suggesting that all of these become reduced to the same level of agency. The topography of potentiality through which real-izations take place points to new conjunctions and interactions among elements, not erosions of difference. For Heidegger, this kind of creation would involve a certain upheaval: 'the *violent one*, the creative man, who sets forth into the un-said, who breaks into the un-thought, compels the unhappened to happen and makes the unseen appear . . .'.[100] But for Heidegger, the un-said and un-thought is always the already-happened—in other words, Being. In *How German Is It*, violence and creativity are not limited to subjective agency, they are composed of and with a range of cultural elements. Which is not to say that the writing of fiction cannot entail a certain activism, as Abish's notion of novel as 'field of action' suggests. Indeed, in contrast to Ulrich's statement that 'A novel is not a process

---

[98] Quoted in Dieter Saalmann, 'Walter Abish's *How German Is It*: Language and the Crisis of Human Behaviour', *Critique* 26: 3 (Spring 1985): 107.

[99] Abish, 'Wie Deutsch Ist Es', 162.

[100] Heidegger, *Introduction to Metaphysics*, 161, Heidegger's emphasis.

of rebellion' (*HGII*, 53), Abish has stated that he viewed his initial decision to write as a turn to militancy: 'I chose to interpret my impulsive act as a poetic gesture. Arrabal defined a poet as someone who doesn't necessarily write poetry, but was a terrorist or provocateur.'[101]

How German Is It is certainly not a terrorist attack. What it does do is present an effective engagement with issues of postmodernism, history, and culture that are implicated in terrorism's impact. As Sadie Plant has argued, the postmodern writings of Baudrillard and Lyotard in particular are 'underwritten by situationist theory and the social and cultural agitations in which it is placed'.[102] Moreover, Baudrillard, Lyotard, and Jameson all invoke terrorism when characterizing dominant tendencies of contemporary culture. Baudrillard (whom I shall discuss further in the Conclusion) sets the trend in his early work, *For A Critique of the Political Economy of the Sign* (1968), asserting that capitalist commodification has reached such a saturation point that its codifications reverberate 'through the amplified system of signs up to the level of the social and political terrorism of the bracketting [*encadrement*] of meaning'.[103] Similarly, Lyotard argues that the power exercised by contemporary institutions in prescribing conditions for thinking and understanding is fundamentally 'terrorist'.[104] For Jameson, too, the hegemony of late-capitalism means that all hope for cultural change or subversion is relegated to fantasies of 'terrorism'.[105] But if terrorism has been made synonymous with cultural totalitarianism, thereby making the claim for a total theory of cultural production easier, Baudrillard at other points makes it clear that this state of overdetermination produces its own effects of paranoia. The system's desire for absolute control means that 'the slightest accident, the least catastrophe, an earth tremor . . .' takes on the proportions of an 'assassination attempt'.[106] Denoting both a complete determination and an utter disruption of culture, Baudrillard's

---

[101] Abish, 'The Writer-To-Be', 111.

[102] Plant, *The Most Radical Gesture*, 5. In a 1989 interview, Baudrillard stated: 'I was very, very attracted by Situationism. And even if today Situationism is past, there remains a kind of radicality to which I have always been faithful. There is still a kind of obsession, a kind of counter-culture, which is still there. Something that has really stayed with me' (Judith Wilson, 'An Interview with Jean Baudrillard', *Block* 15 [Spring 1989]: 18).

[103] Jean Baudrillard, *For a Critique of the Political Economy of the Sign*, trans. by Charles Levin (St Louis: Telos, 1981), 163.

[104] Lyotard, *The Postmodern Condition*, 63.   [105] Jameson, *Postmodernism*, 46.

[106] Baudrillard, *Symbolic Exchange and Death*, 161.

references to terrorism undo his attempt to found a *systematized* logic of oscillation between control and subversion.

It is all very well to contend that terrorism is neither a total system nor a total disruption of contemporary culture. Yet theorists of postmodernism contend that tendencies of economic power mean that historicity and local politics have indeed become increasingly bound to global networks—the events of 11 September 2001 being a case in point. To what extent, then, are theories of postmodernism useful in analysing more recent terrorist events? Have issues of postmodernism been implicated in the 'Troubles' of Northern over recent years, for example? These are the questions that I shall be discussing in the final chapter.

Conclusion
Re-Placing Terror:
Poetic Mappings of Northern
Ireland's 'Troubles'

A Postmodern State of Emergency?

According to Fredric Jameson, 'our daily life, our psychic experience, our cultural languages, are today dominated by space rather than categories of time'.[1] It is not just individual subjects who are faced with problems of 'locating' themselves; the decentreing effects of corporate multi-nationalism are evident right up to the level of the nation-state itself. As US President Bill Clinton announced to the UN General Assembly in 1997: 'Communications and commerce are global: investment is mobile; technology is almost magical. . . . There is no longer division between what is foreign and what is domestic— the world economy, the world environment, the world AIDS crisis, the world arms race—they affect us all.'[2] From this perspective, globalization is aligned with the recognition of a world community. For Jameson, however, multi-nationalism's proliferation is deleterious to local identity; global space devours place (*topos*) to the point that topography becomes subsumed within a larger map. Similarly, commentators on terrorism like Gearóid Ó Tuathail have argued that increasingly internationalized forms of insurgency have precipitated a new 'postmodern terrorism',

where threats now come from decentered bands of transnational terrorists more than from centered . . . states, and where threats are posed not to

---

[1] Fredric Jameson, *Postmodernism; or, The Cultural Logic of Late Capitalism* (London: Verso, 1991), 16.
[2] Quoted in Gearóid Ó Tuathail, 'The Postmodern Geopolitical Condition: States, Statecraft and Security at the Millennium', *Annals of the Association of American Geographers* 90: 1 (2000): 166.

territories and borders but to 'the space of flows'—to strategic transportation systems, vital economic centers, and critical infrastructures.[3]

In terms of the 11 September 2001 plane attacks in America, it is certainly true that the al-Qaida organization accused of being responsible for them operated 'transnationally'. Moreover, the attack on New York's World Trade Center, in addition to causing massive casualties, was clearly aimed at global economic power. But that is not to say that the effects of the attack were more economic than political. As the comments from Osama bin Laden and various US and UK government officials quoted in my Introduction evidence, America as nation-state was widely taken to be the primary target. To see the World Trade Center attacks as 'symbolic' strikes on the US is not enough; the building quite literally stood for the whole via concrete economic networks. Along with the scale of fatalities, the economic impact had clearly been envisioned by the terrorists as the most effective means of devastating the country. For this very reason, 11 September became a matter of 'war' rather than terrorism for the US government, thereby ensuring that the security of nation-states was very much at the heart of the ensuing conflict fought in Afghanistan.

The new 'postmodern terror' that Ó Tuathail writes of does not necessarily amount to a disappearance of state politics, then. But Jean Baudrillard, the theorist of postmodernism who has written most extensively on terrorism, would disagree. Politics and nationalism no longer hold real currency, he argues, for both have been hijacked by capitalist processes. Because the principles of exchange have permeated every sphere, including the referential power of signs, we are all at the mercy of a generalized 'code': 'Everything becomes undecidable, the characteristic effect of the domination of the code, which everywhere rests on the principle of neutralisation, of indifference.'[4] The system is thus seen to reduce all danger of anomaly to indeterminacy. Everything exists in a state of suspended animation: 'We are hospitalised by society. . . . Neither life nor death: this is security—this paradoxically, is also the status of the hostage.'[5] Baudrillard supports

---

[3] See, for example, Walter Laqueur, 'Postmodern Terrorism', *Foreign Affairs* 75: 5 (September–October 1996): 24–36; and Chris Hables Gray, *Postmodern War: The New Politics of Conflict* (New York: Guilford, 1997).

[4] Jean Baudrillard, *Symbolic Exchange and Death*, trans. by Iain Hamilton (1976; London: Sage, 1993), 9.

[5] Jean Baudrillard, *Fatal Strategies*, trans. by Philip Beitchman and W. G. J. Niesluchowski (1983; New York: Semiotext(e), 1990), 36.

this claim by arguing that a hostage who is held for ransom is someone whose existence no longer has any specific value: 'torn from
the circuit of exchange, the hostage becomes exchangeable against
anything at all'[6]—the lives of numerous political prisoners, a sum of
money, or a set of religious beliefs. Even the most extreme attempt at
disrupting social control thus ends up replicating it, he argues: 'In its
deadly and indiscriminate taking of hostages, terrorism strikes at precisely the most characteristic product of the whole system: the anonymous and perfectly undifferentiated individual . . .'.[7] Accordingly, any
political or nationalist position of terrorism is also absorbed in advance: 'Do the Palestinians strike at Israel by means of intermediary
hostages? No, it is through Israel as an intermediary that they strike at
a mythical, or not even mythical, anonymous . . . omnipresent social
order, whenever, whoever, down to the last of the innocents.'[8] Yet
Baudrillard also posits a contrary outcome for such hostage-taking;
the hostage can become an authentically terrifying figure, he argues,
for s/he is also 'secretly no longer negotiable, *precisely because of his
absolute convertibility*'.[9] As a nobody potentially standing for everybody
or anything, the hostage becomes priceless, thereby exceeding laws of
value and exchange. Consequently, argues Baudrillard, 'One must
conceive of terrorism as a utopian act, proclaiming inexchangeability
from the beginning, and violently so, experimentally staging an impossible exchange.'[10] From this perspective, terrorism restitutes an
epiphanous significance of values from the code's totalitarianism. By
instigating breakdowns in negotiation, terrorism 'pass[es] into the
symbolic order, which is ignorant of . . . calculation and exchange
. . .'.[11] The hostage is thereby made into 'a pure object, whose power
forbids either possessing or exchanging it'.[12]

The divergence of Baudrillard's two characterizations of terrorism
cannot be sustained. If unlimited substitution is characteristic of the

[6] Baudrillard, *Symbolic Exchange and Death*, 48.
[7] Jean Baudrillard, *In the Shadow of the Silent Majorities; or, The End of the Social, and Other Essays*, trans. by Paul Foss, John Johnston, and Paul Patton (New York: Semiotext(e), 1983), 56.
[8] Ibid., 55. Baudrillard makes similar statements in 'Baudrillard Shrugs: A Seminar on Terrorism and the Media with Sylvère Lotringer and Jean Baudrillard', in *Jean Baudrillard: The Disappearance of Art and Politics*, ed. by William Stearns and William Chaloupka (London: Macmillan, 1992).
[9] Baudrillard, *Fatal Strategies*, 48, my emphasis.
[10] Ibid., 49.   [11] Baudrillard, *Symbolic Exchange and Death*, 38.
[12] Baudrillard, *Fatal Strategies*, 47.

'code', then the code itself must be seen as fostering powers of the 'symbolic order'. Right from the start it would be unable to control the distinctions between serialized neutralization and unlimited differentiation. The claims that terrorism simply reproduces the tendencies of an autonomous capitalist system, or that it is wholly external to it, are thus sabotaged by Baudrillard himself. Elsewhere, however, he poses a third form of violent economy, where terrorism neither replicates nor abolishes a law of general exchange, but instead radically recodifies it:

> every death and all violence that escapes the state monopoly is subversive . . . [and] is closely akin to that associated with works of art: a piece of death and violence is snatched from the state monopoly in order to put back into the savage, direct and symbolic reciprocity of death, just as something in feasting and expenditure is retrieved from the economic order in order to be put back into useless and sacrificial exchange, and just as something in the poem or artwork is retrieved from the terrorist economy of signification in order to be put into the consumption of signs.[13]

Once the 'economy of signification' is viewed as having always been open to specific instances of violence and 'symbolic' savagery, it can no longer be viewed as an autonomous system. Instead, the 'monopoly' breaks apart and reveals its susceptibility to the impacts of locale, history, and minoritarianism. Moreover, as Baudrillard himself indicates here, such violence is still something that concerns the 'state'. Postmodernism, whether of terrorism or commerce, does not simply negate national governance, then; instead, it can be a factor that elicits a stronger assertion of state control. As far as Gearóid Ó Tuathail is concerned, the 'postmodern condition' thus remains resolutely 'geopolitical'. Globalization might traverse state boundaries, he argues, but it does not amount to a 'transcendence' of 'territoriality itself': 'The problematic defining the postmodern geopolitical condition is not the overstated "end of the nation state" but rather the globalization of the state'.[14] For Jameson, one of the consequences of multi-national space is an erosion of cultural and historical boundaries such that 'distance in general (including "critical distance" in particular) has very precisely been abolished . . .'.[15] But if we accept that the postmodern globalization is open to territorial mediation, then it must itself be seen as prone to crises.

---

[13] Baudrillard, *Symbolic Exchange and Death*, 175.
[14] Ó Tuathail, 'The Postmodern Geopolitical Condition', 169.
[15] Jameson, *Postmodernism*, 48.

In the last chapter, I argued that the 'topography' of terrorism figured by Abish opened postmodernism to historical negotiations because the 'real-izations' of signs and events embodied specific historical valencies. In this concluding chapter, I shall offer a geopolitical critique of postmodern space by examining the latter in relation to a specific crisis of place and statehood; namely, Northern Ireland and its political 'Troubles'. As will be evident, numerous commentators have seen postmodernism to be an issue for Northern Ireland, affecting everything from legislation to paramilitarism. Yet in many ways, considering the parts that nationalism, traditional religious beliefs, legislation, and historical revanchism have played in the region, one could be forgiven for thinking it the last place in which postmodernism might find a foothold. In light of this, I shall first offer a brief consideration of the politics surrounding Northern Ireland's territoriality, before looking at how a number of Northern Irish poets have addressed these issues in terms of postmodernism and the region's political violence.

Northern Ireland: The Grounds of Conflict

In the case of Northern Ireland territory has been a ground for conflict in many ways, just as it had been in Ireland as a whole ever since British colonization.[16] When the Anglo-Irish Treaty of 1921 separated six counties of Ulster from the newly-created Irish Free State and retained them as part of the UK, the stage was set for a drawn out battle over nationality and land. Northern Ireland became a region divided by religion and politics with Irish Republicans (almost exclusively Roman Catholic) and pro-UK Unionists (almost exclusively Protestant) pitted against each other. As far as the Republicans were concerned, the division of Ireland was particularly invidious because the new border secured an overall Unionist majority in the north with as much territory as possible. Having been implemented by the British government as a way of dealing with the conflicting pressures of

---

[16] For general historical backgrounds to Northern Ireland's governance see Thomas Hennessey, *A History of Northern Ireland* (Basingstoke: Macmillan, 1997); David Miller (ed.), *Rethinking Northern Ireland: Culture, Ideology and Colonisation* (London: Longman, 1998); and John Darby, 'Conflict in Northern Ireland: A Background Essay', in Seamus Dunn (ed.), *Facets of the Conflict in Northern Ireland* (Basingstoke: Macmillan, 1995). For an overview of the various interpretative approaches to Northern Ireland's political history, see John Whyte, *Interpreting Northern Ireland* (Oxford: Clarendon, 1998).

Republicanism and Unionism, the partitioning of Ireland immediately led to political upheaval in both the North and South. In the South a split in the recently established Irish Republican Army (IRA) developed between those staunchly opposed to the Anglo-Irish Treaty and those who had accepted it as a stepping stone towards independence for the island as a whole. With the pro-Treaty members gaining control of the new Free State parliament, civil war broke out after clashes between the Free State army and the IRA dissenters. The war came to an end with the anti-Treaty Republicans calling a ceasefire on 24 May 1923, more than 12,000 of its members having been incarcerated.[17] The cessation of the war did not mark an end to violence, though; after rebuilding its ranks the IRA continued to carry out attacks in the South until deciding in 1954 to focus its aggression against the British government.

The first years of Northern Ireland were similarly violent, seeing Unionists and Republicans clash all the more vehemently because of the civil war in the South. With the new devolved Northern government being controlled by the Unionist majority, many Republicans saw themselves as being still under colonial rule, and without proper recourse to political representation. For many Unionists, though, the Republicans were a community seeking to undermine legitimate governance—the IRA attacks on Crown forces and Protestants in the South only confiming their view. With power secured in their hands because of their majority, the Ulster Unionists thus maintained strict control of the Northern Ireland government right up until the 1960s. In 1963, however, Terence O'Neill, a liberal Unionist, was appointed the Northern Irish Prime Minister and began to encourage social modernization, including economic co-operation with the South of Ireland (a Republic since 1949), and a more lenient policy towards northern Catholics. This, along with the birth of a strong civil rights movement that supported anti-discrimination measures, was perceived by many Unionists to present a serious challenge to the status quo. Consequently, O'Neill was forced to resign in 1969 because of a lack of Unionist support, and the violence between Protestant and Catholic communities became so serious that the British government sent the Army into the region in 1969 to quell the disturbances, introduced internment without trial in 1971, and finally prorogued the Northern Ireland government in the following year. From this point

[17] Martin Dillon recounts the IRA's part in the civil war in *Twenty-Five Years of Terror: The IRA's War Against the British* (London: Bantam, 1999), 3–5.

onwards, the structure of political power in the region underwent a series of further upheavals. With the violence raging on the streets, a power-sharing government for Unionists and Republicans based on proportional representation was initiated by the British government with the Sunningdale Agreement in 1973. As a gesture towards Republicans, this included the creation of a 'Council of Ireland' consisting of representatives from both the North and South. For the majority of Unionists, though, the power-sharing in general, and the new Council in particular, amounted to an unacceptable compromise of the region's political identity. After protracted strikes by Unionist workers, the new administration was thus dissolved in May 1974 and replaced with direct rule by the British government.[18]

Devolution had failed; the power-base for the region was now firmly outside the territory. And to complicate matters further, Britain's and the Republic of Ireland's joining of the European Economic Community (EEC) in 1973 raised further questions about extra-territorial influence. This issue came to a head in November 1985 with the Anglo-Irish Agreement which was drawn up by the governments in London and Dublin to facilitate North–South cooperation. Widely seen as another concession to northern Republicans, it was thus met with further resistance from the majority of Unionists. The difference this time, however, was that the extra-territorial decision did not require Unionist support for it to be implemented. In order to allay Unionist disquiet, the Agreement thus stated that no change in the national status of Northern Ireland could take place without the 'consent' of a majority in the region. This was a major step; it meant that the region's governance was being conceived in terms of consensus rather than territoriality. Effectively, political power was acknowledged as being inherently provisional.

In December 1993, both the Anglo-Irish dimension and the issue of consensus were again reaffirmed in the 'Downing Street Declaration', which came out of a series of talks between politicians in London, Dublin, and Belfast. Including a statement that the British government acknowledged the right of people in Northern *and* Southern Ireland to bring about 'on the basis of consent . . . a united Ireland, if that is their wish',[19] the Declaration was enough to persuade

[18] Regarding the rise and fall of the devolved government, see, e.g., Tim Pat Coogan, *The Troubles: Ireland's Ordeal 1966–95 and the Search for Peace* (London: Hutchinson, 1995), 162–79; and Hennessey, *A History of Northern Ireland*, ch. 4.

[19] Quoted in Coogan, *The Troubles*, 370.

the IRA to call a ceasefire in August 1994, which was matched in December 1996 by the umbrella organization of pro-Unionist paramilitaries, the Combined Loyalist Military Command (CLMC). Both the Anglo-Irish Agreement and the Downing Street Declaration thus helped to clear the ground for the 1998 'Good Friday Agreement'.[20] Providing again for the creation of a devolved Northern Ireland government, the latter thus returned the executive power to the region. As a result, Unionists found the provision for a North–South council more palatable this time as it allowed them more determination of it than the Anglo-Irish Agreement had. Republicans also perceived advancements; for example, the Republic of Ireland's repeal of its constitutional claims to the North was mitigated by the Agreement's statement on citizenship: '[it is] the birthright of all the people of Northern Ireland to identify themselves and be accepted as Irish or British, or both, as they may choose . . .'.[21] Delivering peace to the region was thus partly bound to granting it a form of dual nationality.

These political developments from the late 1960s onwards have been deemed 'postmodern' and 'postnational' in a number of ways. For critics such as Richard Kearney, Conor McCarthy, and Cathall McCall, the accession of the UK and the Republic of Ireland to the EEC produced an initial shift towards postmodern power.[22] For McCall, it meant that the 'sovereignty of the modern nation state could no longer be guaranteed'.[23] Participation in the European Union (EU) since the early 1990s has done nothing to change the situation, he argues: 'regional actors are becoming increasingly integrated into a web of relationships that straddle regional, national, European and even international territorial boundaries'.[24] For McCarthy, this has contributed to precisely the sort of postmodern condition theorized by Lyotard:

[20] For an overview of the legislative developments, see Jonathan Tonge, 'From Sunningdale to the Good Friday Agreement: Creating Devolved Government in Northern Ireland', *Contemporary British History* 14: 3 (Autumn 2000): 39–60.
[21] The Home Office, London, and Northern Ireland Office (NIO Web-Site), 'The Belfast ("Good Friday") Agreement' (2000), 2.vi <http://www.nio.gov.uk/agreement.htm>.
[22] See, for example, Richard Kearney, *Postnationalist Ireland: Politics, Culture, Philosophy* (London: Routledge, 1997); Cathall McCall, *Identity in Northern Ireland: Communities, Politics and Change* (Basingstoke, Macmillan, 1999); Conor McCarthy, *Modernisation, Crisis and Culture in Ireland, 1969–92* (Dublin: Four Courts, 2000); and Eamonn Hughes, 'Introduction: Northern Ireland—Border Country', in *Culture and Politics in Northern Ireland, 1960–90*, ed. by Eamonn Hughes (Milton Keynes: Open University Press, 1991), 3–5.
[23] McCall, *Identity in Northern Ireland*, xi.   [24] Ibid., 66.

When . . . Lyotard describes the postmodern condition as 'incredulity towards metanarratives' his point can be given an Irish inflection by realising that the end of the 1960s saw the failure of the legitimating narrative of modernising bourgeois or statist nationalism in the Republic. At the same time, the 'modernisation' and liberalism of Terence O'Neill in Northern Ireland proved itself incapable of resolving the contraditions it had unleashed by encroaching on sectarian privilege . . .[25]

Associated with an incredulity towards both Republicans' and Unionists' statist narratives, it is hardly surprising that the tenets of postmodernism have been met with reservations in Northern Ireland and the Irish Republic alike. 'Such are the contradictions of Irish modernism that we have prematurely entered the post-modern era', comments Desmond Bell: 'We are experiencing, for example . . . "post-nationalism" with the national question materially unresolved.'[26] For Bill Rolston, postmodernism thus poses problems for Northern Ireland not as a descriptive term but as a prescriptive policy:

All the buzzwords of postmodernism are apparent in the utterances of those associated with the Community Relations Council and the Cultural Traditions Group—'tolerance', 'difference', 'diversity' and of course, the rejection of such essentialist notions as 'the nation'.[27]

From this perspective, postmodern policies have been used as a strategy to prevent Irish Nationalists, for example, from contesting that the region's 'multi-cultural diversity' remains firmly lodged within a UK framework. For Unionists, though, replacing this framework with that of the Irish Republic is hardly a solution to the problem.

As several critics have argued, the perceived prevalence of postmodern discourse has led many political and paramilitary groups to cling all the more intransigently to religious and political metanarratives. Anthony Buckley cites as an extreme example the Ulster Protestants who believe they are descended from the Pictish 'Cruthin'.[28] The contention was outlined by Ian Adamson in his books *The Cruthin*

[25] McCarthy, *Modernisation*, 197.

[26] Desmond Bell, *The End of Ideology* (Cambridge, Mass.: Harvard University Press, 1988), 229.

[27] Bill Rolston, 'What's Wrong with Multiculturalism?', in Miller, *Rethinking Northern Ireland*, 253.

[28] Anthony Buckley, 'Uses of History Among Ulster Protestants', in *The Poet's Place: Ulster Literature and Society; Essays in Honour of John Hewitt, 1907–87*, ed. by Gerald Dawe and John Wilson Foster (Belfast: Institute of Irish Studies, 1991), 259–71.

(1974) and *The Identity of Ulster* (1982), in which he argues that the Cruthin and not the Gaels were the earliest inhabitants of Ireland. Both Cu Chulainn, hero of the Gaelic epic *Tain Bo Cuailnge*, and St Patrick, the Irish national saint, are consequently garnered by him into the Cruthin heritage. Advocated by the Loyalist paramilitary group, the Ulster Defence Association (UDA), Adamson's work has gained some popular currency. In opposition to this, some Republicans have advocated a myth proposing that Irish inhabitants can trace their presence back to the geological division of the island from the European continent.[29] In both instances, the meta-narrative about territory is linked to claims about pre-history. For Richard Kirkland, such mythifying in the region has also been applied to history itself:

> the contesting narratives of Northern Ireland can be considered as strictly mythologised entities. . . . The litany of dates (for instance 1690 [William of Orange's defeat of Catholics at the Battle of the Boyne], 1798 [the defeat of Wolf Tone's Republican invasion from France], 1916 [Ulster Unionists killed in the Somme]) and the communal affinities which surround them in Northern Ireland are often taken as evidence of a mythologised community in the classic sense.[30]

The transformation of epochal events into mythical entities is thus seen as a way of bolting subsequent historical developments to a rigid narrative. As Clair Wills argues, such strategies are fundamentally 'antimodernist', manifesting a 'resistance to the impurities born with the fall into historical narrative'.[31] But when it comes to the political violence, other critics have argued that mythification does not simply arise *after* the event, for violence itself can play a part in myth-making. Rather than turning to myth as a supervention of history, paramilitaries are thus seen to be grounding separatist narratives materially *in* history. Offering the 1981 hunger strikes of Republican prisoners as an example, Paul Arthur claims that it contained 'all the ingredients of a successful myth in the making', just as the Easter Rising of 1916 can be seen as 'part of a *narrative*'.[32] Drawing on Lyotard, Allen Feldman argues similarly that events of political violence exist *as* 'narrative blocs':

---

[29] See Allen Feldman, *Formations of Violence: The Narrative of the Body and Political Terror in Northern Ireland* (Chicago: University of Chicago Press, 1991), 17–18.

[30] Richard Kirkland, *Literature and Culture in Northern Ireland Since 1965: Moments of Danger* (London: Longman, 1996), 5.

[31] Clair Wills, *Improprieties: Politics and Sexuality in Northern Irish Poetry* (Oxford: Oxford University Press, 1993), 106.

[32] Paul Arthur, ' "Reading" Violence: Ireland', in *The Legitimization of Violence*, ed. by David Apter (Basingstoke: Macmillan, 1997), 243, Arthur's emphasis.

Narrative blocs are plastic organisations involving language, material arti-
facts and relations. The narrative bloc of violence puts into play a constella-
tion of events and discourses about events, as Event. In turn, any oral history
of political violence privileges the event as a narrative symbol or function.[33]

Feldman is gesturing here towards a performativity of violence that
enforces a political or religious message. But such a view becomes
problematic if the metaphorizing attributed to the events leads
to them being seen as simply another form of textuality—as when
Feldman asserts that 'Political violence is a genre of emplotted
action. . . . *The event is not what happens. The event is that which can be
narrated.*'[34] The sheer physical force of violence is thus occluded.

For this reason, we should be careful in asking the sort of question
that Clair Wills poses in relation to Northern Ireland: 'can terrorism
in all its various forms be said to harbour a theory of narrative and
temporality?'[35] Alluding to theorists such as Baudrillard and Paul
Virilio, Wills goes on to qualify her question by offering postmodernism as problematizing terrorism's narrativity. If terrorist violence
is 'necessarily arbitrary', she argues, dependent on 'anonymity, rupture', then it becomes an anti-narrative, more like a 'postmodern
"*bricolage*" '.[36] This needs further questioning, though, states Wills, for
to view violence in this way comes close to denying it the possibility
of 'political representativeness'; she therefore concludes by calling for
the 'political structures of the nation-state' to be considered along
with the 'mythic or symbolic'[37] aspects of terrorism. But the physical
significance of terrorist violence itself remains unexamined in Wills's
study; an anti-narrative '*bricolage*' is still a form of aesthetic artefact.
Two questions remain, then: in what ways do the historical myths
and narratives surrounding terrorism in Northern Ireland interact
with the physical impact of its violence? And to what extent are postmodernist claims about territoriality, culture, and terrorism applicable to the region? In the remaining sections of this chapter I shall
examine how a number Northern Ireland poets can be seen as
addressing these questions. Focusing primarily on the Belfast poet
Ciaran Carson, I shall argue that Carson's poetic engagements with
terrorism and postmodernism offer a novel way of mapping the political violence in relation to its socio-political context.

---

[33] Feldman, *Formations of Violence*, 14.   [34] Ibid., Feldman's emphasis.
[35] Wills, *Improprieties*, 107.   [36] Ibid., 108.   [37] Ibid., 117.

Poetry and Place: Rewriting the Dinnseanchas

> There is something about the boundaries that seem to be drawn
> by the hand of the Almighty which is very different from the
> boundaries that are drawn by ink upon a map:—Frontiers
> traced by inks on other inks can be modified. It is quite another
> thing when the frontiers were traced by Providence.[38]

Eamonn de Valera, Prime Minister of the Irish Free State, quotes
Mussolini in 1939 with approval here, his basic point being that
Ireland's territorial integrity is nothing short of numinous, and if
Unionists cannot accept that then they should settle elsewhere. For
many Northern Ireland poets, negotiations with land, myth, and
spirituality have been an ongoing concern, precisely because these
hold such political import. John Hewitt, an Ulster Protestant by birth,
was one of the first poets to advocate a poetry of Ulster 'regionalism'
that would explore the concatenation of ancient Irish culture and
British 'colonialism'. The following extract from 'Once Alien Here'
(1948), an early poem, is a prime example:

> The sullen Irish limping to the hills
> bore with them the enchantments and the spells
> that in the clans' free days hung gay and rich
> on every twig of every thorny hedge,
> and gave the rain-pocked stone a meaning past
> the blurred engraving of the fibrous frost.
>
> So I, because of all the buried men
> in Ulster clay, because of rock and glen
> and mist and cloud and quality of air
> as native in my thought as any here,
> who now would seek a native mode to tell
> our stubborn wisdom individual,
> yet lacking skill in either scale or song,
> the graver English, lyric Irish tongue,
> must let this rich earth so enhance the blood
> with steady pulse where now is plunging mood
> till thought and image may, identified,
> find easy voice to utter each aright.[39]

---

[38] Eamonn de Valera quoted in Whyte, *Interpreting Northern Ireland*, 131.
[39] John Hewitt, *The Collected Poems of John Hewitt*, ed. by Frank Ormsby (Belfast: The
Blackstaff, 1991), 21. See also 'The Colony', 76–9.

In the first stanza, Hewitt portrays a magical relation of the Gaels to the land in which the clans' 'enchantments' and 'spells' transform nature into 'meaning' more powerfully than nature's own transformations. The Irish are thus seen to have transcribed a cultural significance onto their surroundings in a fashion that contrasts with Hewitt's own imagined relation to nature in the second stanza. Invoking past generations interred in 'Ulster clay', the landscape itself becomes the active agent for him, inhering in his 'mind' as much as in anyone else's. His hope is that the region thus performs a levelling function, providing the grounds for a more inclusive community. Rather than seeking to dominate it with 'the graver English, lyric Irish tongue', Hewitt imagines the landscape as promising a new organic cultural voice in which 'thought and image' might be married, and no doubt the poem's half-rhymes would be replaced with full, chiming couplets. In many of his critical writings, Hewitt puts forward similar views. On the one hand, he affirms an Ulster Planter ancestry that sets himself apart culturally from Gaelic roots: 'The ideas I cherish are British ideas . . . my intellectual ancestry goes back to the Levellers at the time of Cromwell.'[40] On the other hand, he proposes a 'regionalism' of Northern Ireland to accomodate cultural difference: 'Ulster, considered as a region and not as the symbol of any particular creed can, I believe, command the loyalty of every one of its inhabitants. For regional identity does not preclude, rather it requires, membership of a larger association.'[41]

While some poets and critics have criticized Hewitt's regionalism for not addressing the reality of political and religious separatism directly enough, others have viewed it as a progressive step.[42] Seamus Heaney, for example, writes that regionalism was 'original and epoch-making, a significant extension of the imagining faculty into the domain of politics'.[43] Nevertheless, he argues, 'it could not wholly

[40] Hewitt interviewed by Ketzel Levine in 1985, quoted in Gerald Dawe, 'Against Piety: A Reading of John Hewitt's Poetry', in Dawe and Foster, *The Poet's Place*, 216.

[41] John Hewitt, 'Regionalism: The Last Chance' (1947), in *Ancestral Voices: The Selected Prose of John Hewitt*, ed. by Tom Clyde (Belfast: Black Staff, 1987), 122.

[42] Richard Kirkland comments: 'Whatever regionalism might have been in Northern Ireland, it seems clear that for Hewitt at least it was a mode of evasion: a way of posing delusory ethical debates on the question of bourgeois identity in his work while avoiding any attempt to address political or *territorial* schism' (*Literature and Culture in Northern Ireland . . .*, 30, Kirkland's emphasis). See also Roy McFadden, 'No Dusty Pioneer: A Personal Recollection of John Hewitt', in Dawe and Foster, *The Poet's Place*, 176–7.

[43] Seamus Heaney, 'Frontiers of Writing' (1993), in Seamus Heaney, *The Redress of Poetry: Oxford Lectures* (London: Faber & Faber, 1995), 195.

reconcile the Unionist mystique of Britishness with the Irish National-ist sense of the priority of the Gaelic inheritance.'[44] Certainly Heaney and a number of other poets did set about exploring Union-ism and Irish Nationalism further, and while their 'reconciliation' of the two is also questionable, they did confront Northern Ireland's political Troubles that began in 1968 and raged throughout the next three decades. Brought together in the mid-1960s by Philip Hobsbaum, a lecturer in English literature at Queens' University, Belfast, Heaney along with Michael Longley, James Simmons, and John Montague wrote their poetry in dialogue with each other and subsequently became popularized as 'the Group'.[45] Although the co-terie dissipated by the early 1970s, the poets have explored issues of regionalism in similar ways, in part by engaging with the Irish genre of the '*dinnseanchas*' ('place-lore poem').

Dating back to early Christian Ireland, the *dinnseanchas* tradition-ally narrated the folk stories, legends, and history associated with a particular place, and usually provided an exegesis of its name. As Charles Bowen states, for the Celts 'Places would have been known to them as people were: by face, name and history. The last two would have been closely linked, for, as the *Dindshenchas* illustrates again and again, the name of every place was assumed to be an ex-pression of history.'[46] In John Montague's lengthy, ten-part poem, *The Rough Field*, written between 1961 and 1971, we find this traditional aspect of the *dinnseanchas* rewritten into the contemporary context of Northern Ireland. The poem's title is an English translation of 'Gar-vaghey' (*garbh achaidh* in Gaelic), Montague's home parish in County Tyrone. Musings on local onomastic lore are scattered throughout the poem's parts, but rather than figuring an easy correspondence of language, history, and place we are frequently presented with cultural fault-lines:

---

[44] Seamus Heaney, 'Frontiers of Writing'.

[45] Kirkland discusses the formation of 'the Group' in *Literature and Culture in Northern Ireland . . .*, 77–81. See also Seamus Heaney, 'The Group' (1978), in Seamus Heaney, *Preoc-cupations: Selected Prose, 1968–78* (London: Faber & Faber, 1980), 28–30.

[46] Charles Bowen, 'A Historical Inventory of the *Dindschenchas*', *Studia Celtica* 10: 11 (1975–6): 115. See also Caomhín Mac Giolla Léith, '*Dinnseanchas* and Modern Gaelic Poetry', in Dawe and Foster, *The Poet's Place*, 157–68; and Eleanor Knott and Gerard Murphy, *Early Irish Literature* (London: Routledge & Kegan Paul, 1966), 102–3.

Scattered over the hills, tribal
And placenames, uncultivated pearls.
No rock or ruin, dun or dolmen
But showed memory defying cruelty
Through an image-encrusted name.

[. . .]

The whole landscape a manuscript
We had lost the skill to read
A part of our past disinherited:
But fumbled, like a blind man,
Along the fingertips of instinct.[47]

If the landscape is seen to embody a 'manuscript' of cultural memory, the memory is in danger of being forgotten because of the loss of cultural skills in reading it. This potential fragmenting of cultural heritage is also foregrounded more generally by the poem's juxtapositions (mostly in its margins) of literary and historical texts from the sixteenth to the twentieth century that bear upon the region's settlement—ranging from John Derricke's *The Image of Ireland* (1581) to extracts from a 1960s pamphlet produced by an extremist Protestant organization. Rather than reconciling political and religious voices, then, the poem leaves them to stand alongside and in contrast to each other. Montague himself discusses the widening field of the poem's reference in the 'Preface' he added in 1989:

if I sometimes saw the poem as taking over where the last bard of the O'Neills left off, the New Road I describe runs through Normandy as well as Tyrone. And experience of agitations in Paris and Berkeley taught me that the violence of disputing factions is more than a local experience.[48]

The region's Troubles are thus experienced in relation to a wide array of historical events and forces.[49] And just as Conor McCarthy saw the 1960s modernizations of Terence O'Neill, coupled with nascent Europeanization, as eliciting an 'incredulity' towards statist meta-narratives, so we find cultural narration in Montague's poem being fractured into intertextual collage and pastiche.

---

[47] John Montague, *The Rough Field* (1972; Newcastle upon Tyne: Bloodaxe, 1990), 34–5.
[48] Ibid., vii.
[49] Richard Kearney writes of Montague that 'Myth is now seen as a way back into history rather than as a time that existed before it' (*Postnationalist Ireland*, 128).

A rather different rewriting of the *dinnseanchas* is evident in many of Heaney's poems from this period, particularly those featured in his collections *Wintering Out* (1972) and *North* (1975). Like Montague, Heaney had a Catholic upbringing, and his early poems in particular are very much rooted in exploring myth and place in relation to his cultural background. Having taught English literature for some time at Queen's University, Heaney left academe in 1972 and moved to the South where he concentrated on writing poetry. Already established as a poet of renown by his first collection, *Death of a Naturalist* (1966), Heaney's departure was noted by the pro-Unionist *Protestant Telegraph* which referred to him as 'the well-known Papist propagandist'.[50] Comments like these have no doubt contributed to his decision to defend poetry as having 'its existence in a realm separate from the discourse of politics', such that its 'political status' is essentially its detachment.[51] Yet Heaney has also insisted upon being recognized as an Irish rather than a British writer—most famously when he protested his inclusion in Blake Morrison's and Andrew Motion's *Penguin Book of Contemporary British Poetry* (1982). And when it comes to stating the influence of his cultural heritage he has at times been equally assertive:

Poetry is born out of the watermarks and colourings of the self. But that self in some ways takes its spiritual pulse from the inward spiritual structure of the community to which it belongs; and the community to which I belong is Catholic and nationalist. . . . I think that poetry and politics are in different ways, an articulation, an ordering, a giving of form to inchoate pieties, prejudices, world-views or whatever. And I think that my own poetry is a kind of slow obstinate papish burn emanating from the ground that I was brought up on.[52]

Such an organicism of language, culture, and place is certainly manifest in place-poems like 'Anahorish', 'Toome', Broagh', and 'Gifts of Rain' in *Wintering Out*. Indeed, place is often figured as its own lyric poem:

[50] Quoted in Bernard O'Donoghue, 'Involved Imaginings: Tom Paulin', in *The Chosen Ground: Essays on the Contemporary Poetry of Northern Ireland*, ed. by Neil Corcoran (Bridgend: Seren, 1992), 173.

[51] Seamus Heaney, 'Place and Displacement: Reflections on Some Recent Poetry from Northern Ireland', in *Contemporary Irish Poetry: A Collection of Critical Essays*, ed. by Elmer Andrews (Basingstoke: Macmillan, 1992), 130.

[52] Seamus Heaney, 'Unhappy and at Home', interview with Seamus Deane, *Crane Bag* I: I (1977): 62.

The tawny guttural water
spells itself: Moyola
is its own score and consort,

bedding the locale
in utterance,
reed music, an old chanter

breathing its mists
through vowels and history.[53]

Seeing the place as speaking for itself becomes a way of sealing it
hermetically from the 'lines of sectarian antagonism' that Heaney
writes of elsewhere as looping across the region like 'rabbit pads'.[54]
The river Moyola becomes a counter-historical stream that maintains
a terrene resistance to change, just as 'Broagh' is envisaged as a cultural stumbling-block and shibboleth—'that last / gh the strangers
found / difficult to manage'.[55] As in Hewitt's 'Once Alien Here',
Heaney offers his poetry here as a palimpsest of place, but whereas
for Hewitt the landscape offers new possibilities of voice, in Heaney's
early poems it often speaks a cultural atavism.[56]

The treatment of cultural locale in *Wintering Out* is linked more directly to violence in the much discussed 'The Tollund Man'. Inspired
by a reading of Peter Vilhelm Glob's book, *The Bog People* (1965), a
study of the preserved bodies of Iron Age sacrificial victims found in
Jutland bogs, the poem poses a direct analogy between this ancient
practice of sacrifice and the political killings in Northern Ireland.
Pondering a visit to see the eponymous Tollund victim, Heaney
writes in the last of three sections:

Something of his sad freedom
As he rode the tumbril
Should come to me, driving,
Saying the names

Tollund, Grabaulle, Nebelgard,
Watching the pointing hands
Of country people,
Not knowing their tongue.

[53] Seamus Heaney, 'Gifts of Rain', in *Wintering Out* (London: Faber & Faber, 1972), 25.
[54] Seamus Heaney, '*Omphalos*', in *Preoccupations*, 20.
[55] Seamus Heaney, 'Broagh', in *Wintering Out*, 27.
[56] On this point, see Eamonn Hughes, 'Could Anyone Write It? Place in Tom Paulin's
Poetry', in Richard Kirkland and Colin Graham (eds.), *Ireland and Cultural Theory: The
Mechanics of Authenticity* (Basingstoke: Macmillan, 1999), 165–8.

> Out there in Jutland
> In the old man-killing parishes
> I will feel lost,
> Unhappy and at home.[57]

The revenant spirit of the Tollund Man is imagined as a chthonic force. Faced by a people who no longer have the 'tongue' to respond to its culture, the spirit's uncanniness is mirrored in the poem's speaker feeling 'lost, / Unhappy and at home.' This analogy between Jutland and Northern Ireland is adumbrated by Heaney in his 1974 lecture, 'Feeling into Words'. Explaining that figures such as the 'Tollund Man' were sacrificed ritually to a 'Mother Goddess', he argues that

Taken in relation to the tradition of Irish political martyrdom for that cause whose icon is Kathleen ni Houlihan, this is more than an archaic barbarous rite: it is an archetypal pattern. And the unforgettable photographs of these victims blended in my mind with photographs of atrocities . . . in the long rites of Irish political and religious struggles.[58]

In this sense, Heaney's early poetics are resistant to admitting the sort of discordant, historical voices that Montague incorporates into *The Rough Field*. That is not to say that Heaney, like Hewitt, does not think of region and place as potentially germinating a wider community. Discussing the *dinnseanchas*, for example, he argues that 'Irrespective of our creed or politics . . . our imaginations assent to the stimulus of names . . . our sense of ourselves as inhabitants not just of a geographical country but of a country of the mind is cemented.'[59] But elsewhere in Heaney's writings from this period, it is not a liberalization of mind but a cultural separatism of myth that transcends geography:

There is an indigenous territorial numen, a tutelar of the whole island, call her Mother Ireland, Kathleen ni Houlihan . . . the Shan Van Vocht, whatever; and her sovereignty has been temporarily usurped or infringed by a new male cult whose founding fathers were Cromwell, William of Orange and Edward Carson, and whose godhead is incarnate in a rex or caesar resident in a palace in London.[60]

---

[57] Seamus Heaney, 'The Tollund Man', in *North* (London: Faber, 1975), 48.
[58] Seamus Heaney, 'Feeling into Words', in *Preoccupations*, 57–8.
[59] Seamus Heaney, 'The Sense of Place' (1977), in *Preoccupations*, 132.
[60] Heaney, 'Feeling into Words', 57.

The British colonization of Ireland is viewed here as an infringement of religion and myth as much as of territory; a usurpation of 'indigenous' spirit by secularism. Heaney's early poetic 'idiom' may thus be remote from 'the agnostic' world of 'economic interest' and 'political manoeuvres of power-sharing'[61] gripping Northern Ireland at the time, but because he sees the wider history of conflict as fundamentally religious and mythic, his poetics of place must be recognized as contesting political heritage itself.

Drawing on themes from *Wintering Out*, Heaney's next collection, *North*, presents a more pronounced 'mythopoeic' examination of power. Published in 1975, after some of Northern Ireland's worst years of political violence, the collection is divided into two parts and presents the conflict of Ireland and Britain as one of feminine myth versus masculine reason, these being embodied in the opposition of Antaeus and Hercules, respectively.[62] The main mythical structure is thus pointedly non-indigenous and so adduces a more generalized, archetypal conflict. With Ireland's colonization imagined as an act of rape in 'Act of Union', by the end of Part I the 'unassailed' Hercules has reduced Antaeus to 'a sleeping giant, / pap for the dispossessed'.[63] Such mythifying becomes more specific in 'Punishment', though, which further pursues the analogy of sacrifice in Jutland and Northern Ireland. By the third stanza of the poem it appears to be about another Jutland victim: 'I can see her drowned / body in the bog', but subsequent references to 'her shaved head', 'Little adulteress', and 'tar-black face'[64] suggest that the female is a victim of the 'tarring and feathering' that some Catholic extremists inflicted upon women of their own community whom they suspected of having sexual relations with British soldiers. The cultural analogies of *Wintering Out* have thus been replaced by conflation in 'Punishment', and for this reason *North* was criticized by a number of critics and poets. Reviewing the collection, Ciaran Carson wrote that Heaney had become 'the laureate of violence—a mythmaker, an anthropologist of ritual killing, an apologist for "the situation", in the last resort, a mythifier.'[65] Addressing 'Punishment' in particular, Carson continued:

[61] Ibid.
[62] Heaney outlines the opposition in 'Unhappy and at Home', 62.
[63] Heaney, 'Hercules and Antaeus', in *North*, 47.
[64] Heaney, 'Punishment', in *North*, 30.
[65] Ciaran Carson, 'Escaped from the Massacre?', *The Honest Ulsterman* 50 (Winter 1975): 183. See also Seamus Deane, *Celtic Revivals: Essays in Modern Irish Literature* (London: Faber, 1985), 180–1.

Being killed for adultery is one thing; being tarred and feathered is another. . . . [Heaney] seems to be offering his 'understanding' of the situation
almost as a consolation. . . . It is as if there never were and never will be any
political consequences of such actions . . .[66]

Carson is just one of a number of younger poets—from both Northern Ireland and the Republic—who began to address Northern
Ireland's Troubles by questioning the sort of archetypal underpin-
nings presented in Heaney's approach. For Carson, along with poets
such as Paul Muldoon, Tom Paulin, Medbh McGuckian, and Nuala
ni Dhomnaill (to name but a few), this has also involved a further
examination of the *dinnseanchas* in the context of postmodern claims
about linguistic arbitrariness, internationalism, and narrative fragmentation. As I do not have the space to do justice to all of these
poets, I shall first consider two examples of place-poems from Paulin
and Muldoon before turning to Carson's extended meditation on
Belfast and the Troubles in *The Irish for No* (1987) and *Belfast Confetti*
(1989).

Born in Leeds in 1949 Paulin spent his schooling years in Northern
Ireland before returning to England to attend university in Hull. With
a mother from Northern Ireland and a father from Tyneside in
England, Paulin initially considered himself an Ulster Unionist but
subsequently shifted in the early 1980s towards Presbyterian
Republicanism: 'there was something different in the air as the [1970s]
ended', he states: 'I started reading history again and found myself
drawn to John Hume's eloquence, his humane constitutional politics'.[67] As leader of the (predominantly Catholic) Social Democratic
Labour Party (SDLP), John Hume proposed the advancement of Irish
Nationalism and European 'regionalism' by parliamentary means.
For Paulin, the acceptance of Irish Republicanism is certainly not incompatible with Protestant beliefs; indeed, the two had already been
joined in figures such as the radical Presbyterian Wolf Tone. Viewing
this type of Republicanism as having 'more or less' gone 'underground'[68] since the capture and suicide of Tone in 1798, Paulin's 1983
collection *The Liberty Tree* sets about unearthing some of its possibilities
and offering a critique of contemporary Protestant-Unionist culture.

---

[66] Carson, 'Escaped from the Massacre?', 184–5.
[67] Tom Paulin, *Ireland and the English Crisis* (Newcastle upon Tyne: Bloodaxe, 1984), 16.
[68] Tom Paulin, interview with John Haffenden, in John Haffenden, *Viewpoints: Poets in
Conversation with John Haffenden* (London: Faber, 1981), 159.

In 'Desertmartin', for example, the poet presents changes in Protestant faith as symptomatic of an increasingly parochial extremism. The traditional Protestant emphasis on an individual's 'free' and direct relation to God is depicted as having given way to a 'servile' religious 'defiance' that binds (in Latin *religere* means 'to bind') its 'wee people' to the 'bondage of the letter' and its 'Big Man' leader[69]—a reference to the evangelist Protestant-Unionist Ian Paisley. Alluding to the belief held by a few Ulster Protestants that they are descendants of the ten tribes of Israel, Desertmartin's inhabitants have themselves become a lost tribe. In contrast to Heaney's archaeological emanations of cultural spirit, Paulin's 'bitter village' is figured as 'the dead centre of a faith', 'the territory of the law':

> Masculine Islam, the rule of the Just,
> Egyptian sand dunes and geometry,
> A theology of rifle-butts and executions:
> These are the places where the spirit dies.
> And now, in Desertmartin's sandy light,
> I see a culture of twigs and bird-shit
> Waving a gaudy flag it loves and curses.[70]

Postmodernization is not what has eroded culture here; rather, it is the staunch opposition of the community to any cultural diversity. The marriage of faith and sectarianism has engendered a separatism that depends on abstraction and violence. For Paulin, Desertmartin has literally become a cultural desert in which the Liberty Tree, symbol of the French Revolution's Republicanism, is prevented from taking root. Separatism has thus produced a separation from culture and turned the village into yet another haven of fundamentalism, one of the many 'places where the spirit dies'. Such overt polemicism has led the critic Edna Longley to criticize *Liberty Tree* for being political to the detriment of its poetry.[71] Yet in 'Desertmartin' Paulin can also be seen as rewriting the *dinnseanchas* to critique the belief that cultural

---

[69] Tom Paulin, 'Desertmartin', in *The Liberty Tree* (London: Faber, 1983), 16. Other notable place-poems by Paulin include: 'A Rum Cove, a Stout Cove', 'Manichean Geography I', and 'Manichean Geography II' in *The Liberty Tree*; 'Fivemiletown', 'Mount Stewart', and 'The Caravans on Luneberg Heath' in *Fivemiletown* (London: Faber, 1987); and 'History of the Tin Tent' and 'The Lonely Tower' in *Walking a Line* (London: Faber, 1994).

[70] Ibid., 17.

[71] See Longley's ' "When Did You Last See Your Father?: Perceptions of the Past in Northern Irish Writing, 1965–85' (1985), in *The Living Stream: Literature and Revisionism in Ireland* (Newcastle upon Tyne: Bloodaxe, 1994), 155.

myth, political violence, and poetry are joined organically at the '*omphalos*'.[72]

From another angle, Paul Muldoon's *dinnseanchas* rewritings introduce a paronomastic juggling of place-names that brings culture and arbitrariness into collision. Born in 1951 into a rural Catholic household in Country Armagh, Muldoon went on to study English literature at Queen's University where he was taught by Heaney and met other younger poets such as Carson, McGuckian, and Frank Ormsby. Aided by Heaney in publishing his first collection, *New Weather* (1973), at the age of 21, Muldoon went on to develop a distinct poetic style deploying linguistic play, intertextual pastiche, and a wide range of cultural registers. In 'Bechbretha', from his fifth collection, *Meeting the British* (1987), all of these elements are brought to bear upon a 'garden-party' at Government House in Hillsborough, County Down, 'ten or more summers ago'.[73] Along with the presence of Merlyn Rees in the poem, Northern Ireland Secretary of State from 1974 to 1976, this suggests that the event takes place shortly after the Sunningdale Agreement culminated in the collapse of the devolved Northern Ireland government. In 1975, Rees was responsible for holding a series of secret talks with the IRA, offering them the release of prisoners and an end to internment without trial in exchange for a ceasefire.[74] In Muldoon's poem, the whole atmosphere of political agency is similarly penumbral. Narrated, according to Muldoon, by 'someone like me',[75] the poem's speaker describes how the garden gathering is suddenly disrupted by a swarm of bees. At the speaker's suggestion, Rees calls for Enoch Powell to come from his home in Loughbrickland to their aid, at which point the speaker falls into a 'meditation' on the place-name:

> I described the 'brick' in Loughbrickland
> as a 'stumbling block'
> and referred to Bricriu Poison-Tongue
> of *Bricriu's Feast*.

---

[72] See Heaney's '*Omphalos*', in *Preoccupations*, 17–21.

[73] Paul Muldoon, 'Bechbretha', in *Meeting the British* (London: Faber, 1987), 18. For other place-poems by Muldoon, see in particular: 'Ontario' in *Meeting the British*; 'Seanchas' and 'The Lost Tribe' in *New Weather* (London: Faber, 1994); 'The Boundary Commission' in *Why Brownlee Left* (Winston-Salem: Wake Forest University Press, 1980); and 'The Right Arm' in *Quoof* (London: Faber, 1983).

[74] See Hennessey, *A History of Northern Ireland*, 250–9.

[75] Quoted in Wills, *Improprieties*, 102.

> Then I touched on Congal the One-Eyed,
> who was blinded by a bee-sting.
> This led me neatly to the *Bechbretha*,
> the Brehon judgements
> on every conceivable form
> of bee-dispute,
> bee-trespass and bee compensation.[76]

Like the story of a traditional Irish *seanachie* the speaker's disquisition proceeds via a series of etymological and folk-loric associations that touch upon issues of nationality and arbitration. Loughbrickland refers to the older name 'Loch Bricrenn' (Bricriu's Lake) and thus to the tale from the Ulster cycle, *Bricriu's Feast* (*Fled Bricrenn*), in which Bricriu, the mischief-making Ulster king, invites the three greatest Ulster heroes (among them Cu Chulainn) to a feast and plots to turn them against each other.[77] As Muldoon has indicated, the 'brick' is a stumbling block here partly because there is a debate over whether 'Bricriu' is a Viking or Irish name.[78] By association with the bees, we then jump to Congal, who is also associated with a tale of political feasting. In *The Banquet of Dun na n-Gedh and the Battle of Magh Rath*, Congal, the pagan Ulster king, is invited by Domnall, the Christian high king, to a feast, but finding himself placed on his host's left and served insulting food Congal subsequently declares war against Domnall. From here we move to the ancient 'Brehon judgements' which covered a range of disputes; as Clair Wills has argued, the issue of nationality thus arises because the judgements are linked to Ireland's Celtic roots but are nevertheless foreign—from Brehon.[79]

Given the context of the garden party hosted by Merlyn Rees, the speaker's seemingly arbitrary ramble becomes a honeycomb (*brice meala* in Gaelic) of pointed allusions that are subsequently prevented from reaching any point when Enoch Powell arrives and gains everyone's attention by 'brush[ing] the swarm into a box / and cover[ing] it with the Union Jack'.[80] With obvious reference to Bernard Mandeville's *The Fable of the Bees* (1714), the poem could thus be read as an allegory of Northern Irish political problems being contained within the fabric of the British state. By the end of the poem, Merlyn

---

[76] Muldoon, 'Bechbretha', 19.
[77] See M. A. O'Brien, 'Fledd Bricrenn', in *Irish Sagas*, ed. by Myles Dillon (Dublin: Radio Eireann, 1959), 66–78.
[78] Muldoon quoted in Wills, *Improprieties*, 103.   [79] Ibid.
[80] Muldoon, 'Bechbretha', 19.

Rees, for one, is certainly in good spirits; appearing 'through a secret door / [. . .] (which raised a nervous laugh / among the Castle Catholics)',[81] he produces a handkerchief and declares it to be that of 'Melmoth the Wanderer'.[82] This closing reference is to Charles Robert Maturin's *Melmoth the Wanderer* (1820), in which the eponymous protagonist, in a Faustian deal, bargains his soul in return for 150 years of power and knowledge on earth. Government rule at a price, then, although the fact that 'Melmoth' was adopted as an alias by the exiled Oscar Wilde perhaps also suggests that Merlyn's (Merlin's) political sleights-of-hand involve fashioning disguises. Read in the light of Rees's discussion with the IRA which secured an IRA ceasefire in February 1975, the bewildering swarm of references in the poem certainly captures the confusion of the political negotiations.[83] Moreover, it all shows the extent to which Muldoon uses the *dinnsean-chas* to depict a marriage of myth and politics in order to deflate it. As Muldoon has stated, the poem is a parody of the type of everyday proselytizing in the region: 'At the end [the speaker is] scrabbling around for bits of data to substantiate what his argument might be— it's an old style ridiculous Northern Ireland speech of which a couple are made every day. Yes, it's a speech about racial purity . . .'.[84] As with Paulin's 'Desertmartin', then, 'Bechbretha' manifests an 'incredulity' towards statist meta-narratives by portraying such a concatenation of narrative strands that the speaker loses the plot. Arbitration is forced to negotiate the arbitrary.[85]

With Ciaran Carson's interpretations of the *dinnseanchas*, the relation between a place and its onomastic lore is similarly broken apart. Etymology interposes a 'verbal swamp', as Carson suggests in his own reading of the word 'brick': 'Its root is in *break*, related to the flaw in cloth known as a *brack*; worse, it is a cousin of *brock* . . . rubbish, refuse, broken down stuff'.[86] Musing on Belfast's bricks as contributing not only to its buildings but also its rioting (as 'ammunition'), Carson considers the implications for the city more generally:

[81] Muldoon, 'Bechbretha', 19.   [82] Ibid., 20.

[83] As one of the IRA negotiators later commented: 'We were engaged in so many rounds of talks with British officials that our heads were filled full of nonsense and useless information' (quoted in Martin Dillon, *Twenty Five Years of Terror*, 196).

[84] Quoted in Wills, *Improprieties*, 104.

[85] This is also the case in Muldoon's poem 'The More a Man Has the More a Man Wants' in *Quoof*, 40–64, a long sonnet sequence which follows the fortunes of Gallogly, a terrorist, while exploring a range of intertextual and linguistic possibilities.

[86] Ciaran Carson, 'Brick', in *Belfast Confetti* (Newcastle upon Tyne: Bloodaxe, 1989), 72, hereafter cited as *BC*.

the land we inhabited [as children] has long since been built over. . . . Belfast
has again swallowed up the miniature versions of itself in its intestine war.
The inevitable declension: *Brick.*
                                    Brack.
                                    Brock.

                                                    (*BC*, 75, Carson's italics)

Etymology weaves its own connections here, but these are also contrasted against the background of the city's transformations. Linguistic arbitrariness is thus confronted by material contingency. In
Carson's other Belfast poems, this confrontation is used to map the
impact of terrorist violence more specifically.

Ciaran Carson's Belfast Poems

Born in Belfast in 1948 Carson has spent most of his life working in
the city and was for many years Traditional Arts Officer for the Arts
Council of Northern Ireland. Publishing his first poetry collection,
The New Estate, in 1976, he then had a ten-year period of poetic silence
which Neil Corcoran has claimed was part of a 'personal search' for
new modes of poetic expression adequate to the Troubles' devasta-
tions.[87] The collections which brought the long hiatus to a close were
The Irish for No and *Belfast Confetti*, both of which draw on a range of
experiences of living through Belfast's volatile times. In the short
prose-piece 'Question Time', one of several that appear in *Belfast Confetti*, Carson recounts a bicycle ride down memory lane that takes him
from one side of Belfast's 'Peace Line' to the other. Having wandered
into the Protestant 'Shankill Road' area, he makes his way back to the
familiar Catholic territory of the 'Falls Road', only to find himself
being hauled off his bike by three men who then drag him into a
building, frisk him, and interrogate him:

> *You were seen coming from the Shankill.*
> *Why did you make a U-turn?*
> *Who are you?*
> [. . .]
> *You were seen. You were seen.*
> *Coming from the Shankill.*
> *Where are you from?*
> *Where is he from?*

---

[87] See Neil Corcoran, *Poets of Modern Ireland: Text, Context, Intertext* (Cardiff: University of
Wales Press, 1999), 179–80.

The Falls? When? What Street?
What was the number of the house?
How far down the street was that?
When was that?
What streets could you see from the house?
Cape Street? Yeah.
Frere Street? Yeah. Where was Cape Street?
[. . .]
How old were you then?
(*BC*, 62, Carson's emphasis)

Continuing along these lines for some time, his assailants eventually persuade themselves that Carson's knowledge of the Falls Road area and its history sufficiently vouchsafes his identity. For Carson, the trauma of the encounter is indissociable from the men's threatening insistence that a cartographic slip on his part is a matter of life and death. As the elision in the passage of all Carson's responses emphasizes, there is no question of him stopping them in their tracks; he is being plotted by them:

The map is pieced together bit by bit. I am this map which they examine, checking it for error, hesitation, accuracy; a map which no longer refers to the present world, but to a history, these vanished streets; a map which is this moment, this interrogation, my replies. Eventually I pass the test. I am frisked again, this time in a regretful habitual gesture. *A dreadful mistake,* I hear one of them saying, *has been made,* and I get the feeling he is speaking in quotation marks, as if this is a bad police B-movie and he is mocking it, and me, and him.   (*BC*, 63, Carson's emphases)

Notably, the borders of 'the map', 'this map', that Carson is forced to embody become increasingly indefinite as the interrogation proceeds. Charting his present 'hesitations' and 'accuracy' along with his capacity to remember 'vanished streets' and people, the map becomes a singular diagram of the whole encounter: 'this moment, this interrogation, my replies'. If the interrogators are satisfied that they have extracted a watertight script, for Carson there remains the conviction that the script is contingent upon slips of memory, hesitations, and the sheer ability to reply and not break down; in short, it involves a dangerous performativity. Dangerous because it admits an unstable series of possibilities. We see this in the second part of the passage: frisking him again with a 'habitual gesture', the interrogator's subsequent statement of regret sounds to Carson like a quotation, 'as if this is a bad police B-movie, and he is mocking it, and me and him.'

That the interrogators are certainly *not* the police only heightens the ironic distance that the speaker seems to adopt in relation to his own script. Whether the irony is intended or not, this possibility of speaking or performing as another is precisely what undermines the preceding surety of the interrogators' sectarian mapping.

As this scene of interrogation implies, possibility is not an abstract matter in Belfast at this time; rather, it is part of a whole cityscape of terror. The fact of not knowing what lies around the corner means that even entering a bar is cause for concern, as Carson writes in the poem 'Last Orders': 'you never know for sure who's who, or / what / You're walking into. I for instance, could be anybody [. . .] how simple it would / be for someone / Like ourselves to walk in and blow the whole place, and / ourselves, to Kingdom come' (*BC*, 46). If the writings of Northern Ireland poets such as Carson and Muldoon are saturated with the conditional and the subjunctive, it is precisely because potentiality in Northern Ireland is a very real concern.[88] All the more reason for paramilitaries and security forces alike to try and map situations. But, as Carson points out, in 'Turn Again', the possibility of mapping is frequently undermined by the city's own shifting contours: 'Todays plan is already yesterday's—the streets that were there / are gone. / And the shape of the jails cannot be shown for security reasons' (*BC*, 11). So while the image of the map arises throughout Carson's work, mapping itself is invariably made provisional because when it comes to the city, 'Everything will be revised': 'No don't trust maps, for they avoid the moment: ramps, barricades, diversions, Peace Lines' ('Question Time', *BC*, 58).

How to chart the dangerous potentiality of Belfast, then? This is the problem that Carson surveys in a number of poems that continue in the line of the *dinnseanchas*.[89] It is not just an issue of urban cartography, but of delineating variables of political terror itself. In this section, then, I shall chart some of the directions that Carson's survey takes by looking at images of mapping that are scattered throughout *Belfast Confetti*, *The Irish for No*, and his autobiographical memoir of Belfast, *The Star Factory* (1997). In addition, I want to consider the

---

[88] On the uses of the subjunctive and conditional see Jonathan Allison, ' "Everything Provisional": Fictive Possibility and the Poetry of Paul Muldoon and Ciaran Carson', *Études Irlandaises* 20: 2 (Autumn 1995): 89–93.

[89] Fran Brearton also examines some of Carson's mapping poems in 'Mapping the Trenches: Gyres, Switchbacks and Zig-zag Circles in W. B. Yeats and Ciaran Carson', *Irish Studies Review* 9: 3 (Winter 2001): 373–86.

following question: if poetry is linked by Carson to charting such potentials, then what are the potentials of the poem as a type of map?

I am, perhaps, being hasty in saying that Belfast's volatility undermines its cartography, for in Carson's poems we frequently find the city exploding into a map of its own. Pondering the burnt-out Smithfield Market, for example, he glimpses in the 'charred beams' a 'map' of 'obliterated streets, the faint impression of a key. Something many-toothed, elaborate, stirred briefly in the / labyrinth.'[90] The flickering remains thus seem to hold a synecdochic code for the city's conflicts—like the mythic labyrinth holds its minotaur, or the 'Maze' prison its paramilitaries. But the 'key' remains shadowed, abstracted, here, like a general truth to be excavated. In contrast to this there are the images of explosions, such as the following from *The Star Factory*:

> Minutes or hours would pass before the device went off, and the delivery van became instant shrapnel, a rapidly-increasingly exploded diagram of itself, visible in antiquated slo-mo newsreel footage or the eye of memory . . .

> Sometimes the city is an exploded diagram of itself, along the lines of a vastly complicated interactive model aircraft kit whose components are connected by sprued latitudes and longitudes.

> At the same time it mutates like a virus, its programme undergoing daily shifts of emphasis and detail.[91]

In these passages, the city maps itself only to the extent that it explodes the map or diagram. As the second passage suggests, this explosivity is thus a matter of charting possibilities: instead of a code to the city's transience we are presented with the mutability of a model that is itself seen to be 'interactive'. And if the city's cartography manifests its own immanent and dangerous temporality, then its present tense becomes modified by 'ifs' and 'maybes' and its subjunctivity, its possibility, becomes real.[92] Contemplating a photograph that is described as being that of a 1970s Belfast street riot, for example, Carson's reaction to its facticity is to qualify it with a barrage of modal auxiliaries:

---

[90] Ciaran Carson, 'Smithfield Market', in *The Irish For No* (Newcastle upon Tyne: Bloodaxe, 1987), 37.

[91] Ciaran Carson, *The Star Factory* (London: Granta, 1997), 274, 15.

[92] Like Carson, I am using 'subjunctivity' in the more general sense of denoting 'contingency', 'potential', as well as 'the degree of realism or probability of a literary work' (*OED*).

the camera has caught only one rioter in the act. . . . The others, these other *would-be* or *has-been* or *may-be* rioters have momentarily become spectators . . . some *might* be talking of the weather . . . some others are looking down Bosnia street at what is happening or what *might* happen next. ('Question Time', *BC*, 58, my emphases)

The final use of zeugma here says it all, for the photograph is itself a montage, for Carson, of 'what is happening' *and* 'what might happen next'. Certainly the image manifests its own contingency, having been taken at a particular place and point in time. But Carson emphasizes elsewhere that such contingency is wholly yoked to the historical terrain: 'everything is contingent and provisional; and the subjunctive mood of these images is tensed to the ifs and buts, the yeas and nays of Belfast's history' ('Revised Version', *BC*, 67).

Carson's exploration of the city's volatility presents materiality exploding into different potentials so that mapping itself must become provisional. Against this cartography, Carson contrasts the plots and mappings of paramilitaries and the security forces. We have already seen an example of paramilitaries forcing Carson to embody the right map. What is emphasized in images of security surveillance is technological mediation:

if there is an ideal map, which shows the city as it is, it may exist in the eye of that helicopter ratcheting overhead, its searchlight fingering and scanning the micro-chip deviations: the surge of funerals and parades, swelling and accelerating, time-lapsed, sucked back into nothingness by the rewind button; the wired up alleyways and entries; someone walking his dog when the façade of Gass's Bicycle Shop erupts in an avalanche of glass and metal forks and tubing, rubber, rat-trap pedals, toe-clips and repair kits. ('Question Time', *BC*, 58)

The ideality of this map is again qualified by the subjunctive—'if there is . . . it may exist'. But more importantly, if the helicopter does offer the only 'ideal' survey, this survey is in no way a pure representation for it entails its own 'fingering' and 'scanning' mediation whereby what is seen is 'time-lapsed' and 'sucked back into nothingness by the rewind button'. This map secures what it surveys only by editing it. Belfast is itself a tale of at least two cities, then. On the one hand streets and situations frequently explode into diagrams of their own potential; on the other hand, security forces use virtual mapping to contain the possibility of violence. Two levels of the city, two types of map—although the helicopter's scanning is also notably embedded in the 'micro-chip' of 'wired up alleyways and entries' themselves. The point is that counter-terrorism here means securing a dominance of the virtual over the material. An image of this is given in the poem 'Queen's Gambit' which describes the planning and execution of a security operation:

> [. . .] Operation 'Mad Dog', as it's known
> now,
> Is the sketch that's taking shape on the Army HQ blackboard,
> chalky ghosts
> Behind the present, showing what was contemplated and
> rubbed out
> [. . .]
> Unbeknownst to [the perpetrators] they'll be picked up in the
> amplified light
> Of a Telescope Starlight II Night Observation Device
> (NOD)—*Noddy*, for short,
> But not before the stoolie-pigeon spool is reeled back;
> amplified,
> Its querulous troughs and peaks map out a different curve of
> probability.
>
> (*BC*, 37–8)

Here the spectral 'sketch' on the Army HQ blackboard is a plotting of future events, just as the 'Night Observation Device' functions to mediate analeptically what will have taken place. Both the sketch and observation technology are thus deployed to control the shape of events. It is the exploding diagrams of the city versus the containing map of the security forces. What they have in common, for Carson, is provisionality: both admit contingency and 'revision'. Nevertheless, they remain ontologically distinct: physical force and powers of virtual surveillance might confront each other but they retain their own potentials and are never reduced to the same level. This is important to note, because Carson also brings a similar distinction to bear upon the relation of terrorist events to his own poetic responses, as I shall be demonstrating shortly. First, though, I want to consider how his insights relate to a wider context of provisionality in terms of terrorism and anti-terrorist legislation in Northern Ireland.

Terrorism and Legislation in Northern Ireland

The history and politics of the Northern Ireland Troubles is a book-length subject; indeed, with more than 10,000 studies written since

1968, John Whyte has argued that 'in proportion to size' Northern Ireland is probably 'the most heavily researched area on earth'.[93] Rather than attempting a historical overview of the region's terrorism, then, in this section I want to highlight some salient structural issues that have contributed to the more general state of provisionality and are germane to Carson's Belfast poems.

Between 1968 and 1999 there were 3,289 deaths caused by the Troubles, with more than 35,000 shootings, 15,000 bombings, and over 40,000 people wounded.[94] As a consequence, it has been estimated from surveys that more than half of the region's population have known someone who has been killed or injured.[95] On the Republican side, the IRA has been the largest and most active paramilitary organization to play a part in the conflict. Regrouping in 1969 in the face of Catholic and Protestant clashes over civil rights, the IRA presented themselves initially as a community defence force, confronting both Loyalist paramilitaries and the British troops who had been sent to control the situation.[96] From the early 1970s, though, the IRA adopted more overtly terroristic methods, attacking commercial and government buildings and initiating bombing campaigns in England. Along with the Irish National Liberation Army (INLA) founded in 1974, the IRA also maintained a constant campaign against Loyalist paramilitary organizations such as the UDA and the Ulster Volunteer Force (UVF). With an estimated 12,000 members at its peak, the UDA has been the largest paramilitary group in Northern Ireland, and like the IRA began in 1971 as a community defence group.

[93] Whyte, *Interpreting Northern Ireland*, xviii. For accounts of the Troubles in general, see, for example, Tim Pat Coogan, *The Troubles*; Martin Dillon, *Twenty-Five Years of Troubles*; Yonah Alexander and Alan O'Day (eds.), *Terrorism in Ireland* (London: Croom Helm, 1984); Yonah Alexander and Alan O'Day (eds.), *Ireland's Terrorist Trauma: Interdisciplinary Perspectives* (Hemel Hempstead: Harvester Wheatsheaf, 1989); and Seamus Dunn (ed.), *Facets of the Conflict in Northern Ireland* (Basingstoke: Macmillan, 1995). The best general resource about Northern Ireland's political violence is the *Conflict Archive on the Internet* (CAIN) (The University of Ulster at Magee),<http://cain.ulst.ac.uk>, which includes chronologies of events, conflict background, bibliographies, statistics, articles, and links to UK government and political party web-pages.

[94] Bernadette C. Hayes and Ian McAllister, 'Sowing Dragon's Teeth: Public Support for Political Violence and Paramilitarism in Northern Ireland' (2000), *CAIN Web Service* <http://cain.ulst.ac.uk/issues/violence/docs/hayes/hayes00.htm>, 1.

[95] Mari Fitzduff and Liam O'Hagan, 'The Northern Ireland Troubles: Background Paper' <http:cain.ulst.ac.uk/othelem/incorepaper.htm>, 4.

[96] For a history of the IRA see Peter Taylor, *Provos: The IRA and Sinn Fein* (London: Bloomsbury, 1997); and Kevin J. Kelley, *The Longest War: Northern Ireland and the IRA* (London: Zed, 1982).

Playing a major part in orchestrating the Unionist workers' strike in opposition to the Sunningdale Agreement, it was largely responsible for forcing Catholics out of mixed areas in the early 1970s. Along with the UVF, it has also been deemed responsible for the majority of sectarian attacks against Catholics.

With paramilitary groups like these carrying out violence on a daily basis, much of the Troubles was more about revenge-killings, defending territory, and eradicating the opposition than simply turning events into a narrative symbol or function. This is not to say that political and religious ideals have played no part in paramilitary actions, and certainly there have been numerous events that have stood out symbolically against the background of everyday violence: to name but a few—the UVF's killing of fourteen Catholics in a Belfast bomb attack on 4 December 1971; the 'Bloody Sunday' shooting of fourteen Catholics by the British Army at a Derry civil rights march on 30 January 1972; the IRA's 'Bloody Friday' killing of five protestants, two British soldiers, and two Catholics in a Belfast bomb attack on 21 July 1972; the killing of thirty-three civilians by Loyalist car bombs in Monaghan and Dublin on 17 May 1974; the killing of twenty civilians by two IRA bomb attacks on public houses in Birmingham on 21 November 1974; the killing of five members of the Conservative Party (and nearly Margaret Thatcher, the Prime Minister) in a bomb attack on the Grand Hotel in Brighton on 16 October 1984; the killing of ten Protestants and a policeman in an IRA bomb attack on a Remembrance Day Ceremony in Enniskillen on 8 November 1987; the unsuccessful IRA mortar bomb attack on Prime Minister John Major at 10 Downing Street on 7 February 1991; the IRA bombing of the Baltic Exchange in London on 10 April 1992 which killed three people and caused £800 million worth of damage; the IRA bombing of Canary Wharf in London on 9 February 1996 which killed two people and caused £85 million worth of damage; and the killing of twenty-nine civilians in the bomb attack in Omagh by the splinter group the Real IRA on 15 August 1998. If we return to the assertions made by Wills, Feldman, and Arthur on narrative and mythic aspects of terrorist violence, it is certainly the case that a number of the attacks cited here were initiated, in part, as symbolic events. Moreover, instances such as 'Bloody Sunday', 'Bloody Friday', and the Enniskillen and Omagh bombings have certainly attained mythic proportions in the minds of paramilitary and civilian communities alike. It is also notable, though, that in cases such as the major IRA bombings aimed against the British government, the ends of violence were envisaged not simply as the enforcing of a separatist narratives, or as the defence of ideology, but as a means of physically forcing political dialogue.[97] Regardless of whether this tactic was successful or not, the point is that we need to address the effects of violence on discursive power in addition to questioning discursive overdeterminations of terrorist events.

One way of doing this is by considering the anti-terrorism legislation introduced by the British government in the face of Northern Ireland's conflict. With the region's violence looking as if it would spiral out of control in the early 1970s, the British government introduced the Northern Ireland (Emergency Provisions) Act (EPA) in 1973. The Act introduced a number of new measures: increased powers for the Royal Ulster Constabulary (RUC) and Army allowing them to arrest anyone suspected of terrorist activity; the proscription of terrorist organizations; and the creation of special non-jury courts to try those accused of terrorism. These powers were subsequently augmented by the Prevention of Terrorism (Temporary Provisions) Act (PTA) of 1974 which was rushed through the British Parliament in a number of days after the IRA's Birmingham pub bombings.[98] As well as extending the EPA's measures to the whole of the UK, the PTA also introduced further powers of detention and interrogation. Because of the extreme nature of their provisions, both the EPA and the PTA were designed to be 'temporary', yet they were continually renewed owing to the incessant nature of the Northern Ireland conflict—until their replacement by the permanent provisions of the UK Terrorism Act (2000). The British government was thus forced to alter its own legislative performativity in relation to Northern Ireland's political violence—not only by adopting extreme measures, but also by initially making the emergency provisions temporary. The volatility of the region was thus implicated in the provisionality of the

---

[97] Martin Dillon writes that a month after the Baltic Exchange bombing '[an] intermediary told the Provisionals that the British government hoped they would make greater use of the line of communication. From an IRA viewpoint, that message was interpreted as a clear signal that bombing London was the catalyst for generating dialogue' (*Twenty-Five Years of Terror*, 310).

[98] For general discussions of Northern Ireland and anti-terrorism legislation, see Clive Walker, *The Prevention of Terrorism in British Law* (Manchester: Manchester University Press, 1992); Paddy Hillyard, *Suspect Community: People's Experience of the Prevention of Terrorism Acts in Britain* (London: Pluto, 1993); and Conor Gearty and John A. Kimbell, *Terrorism and the Rule of Law: A Report on the Laws Relating to Political Violence in Great Britain and Northern Ireland* (London: Civil Liberties Research Unit, King's College, London, 1995).

legislation designed to deal with it. Simultaneously, though, the anti-terrorist laws have mediated the performative capacities of paramilit-aries. For example, it is illegal to display 'sectarian' clothes, flags, or symbols in Northern Ireland, or to wear a hood or balaclava. Lead-ers of groups such as Sinn Fein and the UDA were also banned for some time from speaking directly in the media by a 'Broadcast Ban' introduced in 1988.[99] The extent of performative mediation is most evident, though, in the 2000 Terrorism Act's definition of terrorism as the 'use *or* threat of action'.[100] As I argued in the Introduction, this effectively renders the difference between violence and discourse am-biguous.

To make general claims about the narrational or symbolic nature of terrorism thus becomes problematic if we consider that violence, symbol, and performativity have been mediated in Northern Ireland in very specific ways. Moreover, it is not simply a matter of a more general agonism of narratives, for physical force has played its own part in disrupting the production of discourses—whether political, legal, or cultural. Coupled with the provisions for territory and nationality evident in the 1998 Good Friday Agreement and earlier legislation, the anti-terrorist laws can be seen as contributing to a complex and general state of provisionality in Northern Ireland. Commenting on this complexity of the Troubles, John Whyte's re-sponse is to call for a new 'cartography' of power: any attempt may fail at capturing the situation in its entirety, he argues, but 'Whichever projection the cartographer uses will create a distinc-tion.'[101] The distinction of Carson's poetic mappings lies first in ex-amining the general state of provisionality relating to territory, events, and security, and second in linking these to performative potentials of both violence and language. In the next section I shall address this second aspect of his poetry and consider the cartographic potentials of the poems themselves.

[99] See Adrian Guelke, 'Paramilitaries, Republicans and Loyalists', in Dunn, *Facets of the Conflict*, 126.

[100] The Home Office, London, 'Terrorism Act 2000' (Her Majesty's Stationery Office Web-Site, 2000), 1.1 <http://www.hmso.gov.uk/acts/acts2000/00011>, my emphasis. See also Clive Walker, 'Briefing on the Terrorism Act 2000', *Terrorism and Political Violence* 12: 2 (Summer 2000): 1–36.

[101] Whyte, *Interpreting Northern Ireland*, 249.

The Poem's Map: Making the World Possible

We have seen that, for Carson, Belfast explodes intermittently into a map of its own dangerous potentials. This type of map or diagram is still envisaged *as an event in itself,* though, not as an abstract figure or a pre-fabricated plot. If we return to his image of the city in *The Star Factory* as 'an interactive model aircraft kit' we find that there is 'no instruction leaflet' to this model; 'I must write it',[102] he claims. Composing a poem or writing a narrative is thus seen to be a distinct process that engenders its own powers of interpretation. Recounting his father telling a story, for example, Carson comments that 'he makes curvy waves of possibility which punctuate or illustrate the story's rhythm and its tendency to gather into ornate runs and turns'.[103] The story tells a tale of its own affective capacities that are correlated elsewhere with the power of names. Examining the Belfast Street Directory, Carson writes:

I am reminded how the arbitrary power of the alphabet juxtaposes impossibly remote locations. . . . streets named after places form exotic junctures not to be found on the map of the Empire: Balkan and Ballarat, Cambrai and Cambridge, Carlisle and Carlow. . . . I am trying to think of myself as a bookworm, ruminating through the . . . Directory in teredo mode, following my non-linear dictates, as I make chambered spirals in my universe, performing parabolas by browsing letters and the blanks between them.[104]

In parallel to the material events that 'revise' the city's contours, Carson presents such linguistic exploration as producing a cartography of other possible-worlds. This is not a move towards abstraction, though, for the naming and coding of the city are also linked to powers of surveillance in his writing:

In the small hours, at the height of the Troubles, when incidents of arson or assassination occurred routinely, I used to listen to the short-wave police radio, from which I learned the alphabet of *Alpha, Bravo, Charlie, Delta* . . . So convincing was the aural landscape that I sometimes believed the police could overhear me . . .[105]

It is this notion of an 'aural landscape' that Carson collocates with a form of poetic mapping, a mapping that remains ontologically distinct from the city's own exploding diagram, even though the two are

---

[102] Carson, *The Star Factory,* 15. [103] Ibid., 2. [104] Ibid., 8.
[105] Ibid., 172.

placed in relation. So, in his collection of poems, *Opera Et Cetera*
(1996), we are presented with a sequence of twenty-six ten-line poems
whose titles run from 'Alpha', 'Bravo', Charlie' through to 'Zulu',
each of which forms a series of linguisitic connections around each
letter or word.[106] Carson thus engages directly with the aural landscape associated with virtual surveillance, and uses the alphabet to
form 'exotic junctures', thereby re-scripting other possible networks
as poems. If we consider this in relation to the rewritings of the
dinnseanchas already examined, we can see that Carson explodes the
genre much like Montague's *Rough Field* in so far as locale similarly
becomes internationalized. And because this is facilitated partly
by the sort of arbitrary connections of names displayed in much of
Muldoon's poetry, several critics have ascribed a definite postmodernism to Carson's refigurings of the *dinnseanchas*.[107] Carson does not
present an unquestioning incorporation of the postmodern, though;
indeed, in 'Queen's Gambit' he appears to criticize glib cultural con-
flations: 'It's all the go, here, changing something into something else,
/ like rhyming Kampuchea with Cambodia. It's why Mickey Mouse
wears / those little white gloves' (*BC*, 36). The linguistic commutation
of places thus becomes problematic when linked to a more general
Disneyfication of culture. For this reason, Carson (*contra* early
Heaney) is careful to recognize his poetic plays on place for what they
are—linguistic explorations—and to set them *against* material contingencies of local topography.[108] As for Gearóid Ó Tuathail, then,
Carson's gestures towards a 'postmodern condition' are qualified by
the 'geopolitical'. The provisionality he explores is not a generalized
disintegration of cultural borders and identities, it is a specific state of
socio-political power 'tensed' to the 'history' of Belfast and Northern
Ireland no less than the poems themselves.

Carson's poetry presents a potential for engagement precisely
because the landscape of power and terror in Belfast does not just
include 'physical force' but also the discursivity of legislation, the
media, and local stories along with virtual powers of surveillance
technology. The presence of the IRA, for example, is acknowledged

[106] Ciaran Carson, *Opera Et Cetera* (Newcastle upon Tyne: Bloodaxe, 1996).

[107] See Sean O'Brien, *The Deregulated Muse* (Newcastle upon Tyne: Bloodaxe, 1998),
191–2, Neil Corcoran, *Poets of Modern Ireland*, 180–1; Richard Kirkland, *Literature and Culture
in Northern Ireland . . .*, 42; and Wills, *Improprieties*, 105n.

[108] John Kerrigan compares Carson's and Heaney's approach to place with reference
to Heidegger in 'Earth Writing: Seamus Heaney and Ciaran Carson', *Essays in Criticism* 48:
2 (April 1998): 144–68.

at one point as having been augmented largely by rumour-mongering: 'IRA men were practically invisible . . . seeming to exist by rumour or osmosis in a narrative dimension largely inaccessible to the over-whelmingly non-combatant Catholic population.'[109] While Carson accepts that narratives or information about terrorism can have their own power, then, this does not compromise his resistance to conflat-ing violent events with language. The only people who do conflate the two in his poetry are terrorists:

> There was this head had this mouth he kept shooting off.
> Unfortunately.
> It could have been worse for us than it was for him.
> Provisionally.
> But since nothing in this world is certain and you don't know
>   who hears what
> We thought it was time he bit off more than he could chew.
> Literally.
> By the time he is found there'll be nothing much left to tell
>   who he was.
>
> ('The Mouth', *BC*, 70)

Broken into metonymical parts, the victim is figuratively dismem-bered in the terrorist's account even before he has been killed. And because 'loose-talk costs lives', as a 1974 IRA poster proclaimed,[110] the victim's verbosity is translated into an act of violence ('shooting off') and then countered with a violence that is recounted as a met-alepsis—'We thought it was time he bit off more than he could chew. / Literally'. The punishment is thus doubly violent; not only does it involve the victim's death, this death has 'Literally' become figura-tive. By the end of the stanza, tropes and killing have become con-joined to produce a silenced figure—the victim. Clearly, such terrorist rhetoric is what the commentators who posit a 'troping' or 'narrativizing' of terrorism are drawing on. But Carson's response is to identify this transformation *as a form of violence in itself*, and all the more reason to distinguish the act of poetry from the material force of bombings and shootings.

Despite offering his mapping poems as ontologically distinct from the city's exploding cartography, we nevertheless find the language in Carson's poems breaking open in response. As is evident from the

---

[109] Carson, *The Star Factory*, 117.
[110] The poster is reprinted on the *CAIN Web Service*, <http://cain.ulst.ac.uk/images/posters/ira/poster61r.jpg>.

passages quoted, Carson often uses enjambement to separate adjectives, genitives, articles, and conjunctions from dependent nouns and clauses, thus foregrounding the sense of not knowing what lies around the corner.[111] The frequent use of zeugma also emphasizes multiple effects of actions by splitting verbs into two directions or possibilities. In this way the poems' performativity is interposed somewhere between the city's exploding map and the security forces' surveillance technology: they attempt to give expression to the impact of violence at the same time as mediating it by making it expressible and figuring other connections. This still amounts to seeing material states of affairs and modes of poetic expression as two distinct but mutually affecting variables. Deleuze and Guattari outline a similar form of interaction in terms of 'content' (materiality) and 'expression' (language): 'the way an expression relates to a content is not by uncovering or representing it. Rather, forms of expression and content communicate through a conjunction of their quanta of relative deterritorialization, each intervening, operating in the other.'[112] This is simply to say that materiality and language each has its performative variables which are open to being affected by those of the other.

By charting this type of dynamic, Carson offers new ways of thinking about the Troubles in terms of the relation of violence to textuality. Once we are forced to think of linguistic variables as being placed in variation by states of affairs, we need to think of a new type of trope to account for the linguistic turnings. This is suggested by the images of confetti strewn throughout the poems in *Belfast Confetti*. Appearing intermittently like a musical refrain, confetti comes to be associated with a number of different people, things, and places—for example: drops of blood and a wedding photograph of a man killed in the Troubles ('All the Better to See You With', *BC*, 24, 25; and 'Jump Leads', *BC*, 56); snow being watched while contemplating a lost love ('Snow', *BC*, 21); aeroplanes in the distance ('Loaf', *BC*, 18); and a street spattered with bits of corrugated iron ('Queen's Gambit', *BC*, 33). The troping of the confetti is thus serialized, as scattered as its pieces, each image being torn into a separate poem and yet simultaneously

---

[111] Regarding lineation, Carson cites a number of inspirations: 'Storytelling is there: the line breaks are points of suspense, where you need to see what happens next. The length of the line is a story-teller's deliberate fast-paced gabble. It's also based around the *haiku*'s seventeen syllables, and the intention is to have a kind of *haiku* clarity within the line. . . . And it's not unlike Irish (sean-nos) singing' (quoted in Corcoran, *Poets of Modern Ireland*, 181).

[112] Gilles Deleuze and Félix Guattari, *A Thousand Plateaus: Capitalism and Schizophrenia*, trans. by Brian Massumi (Minneapolis: University of Minnesota Press, 1987), 88.

permeated with the other images. Moreover, this is further complicated in so far as 'Belfast Confetti' is a slang expression for the assortment of objects—broken bricks, bottles, etc.—used by 'generations of
rioters' in Northern Ireland against the armed forces ('Brick', *BC*, 72).
The charting of the confetti throughout the various poems thus draws
together associative possibilities of language in relation to the dangerous contingencies of the political situation. As with his refiguring of the
dinnseanchas, Carson thus presents the confetti as a form of exploded
trope: what I have termed elsewhere the 'diaphor'.[113] In the concluding section, I shall outline the difference of the diaphor in more detail,
and then use it to provide a brief overview of the other literary figures
of terror and violence that I have described in the previous chapters.

The Diaphor: Surveying the Tropes of Terror and Violence

In Greek *diaphora* means 'difference', although it has several other
meanings: to tear asunder; to carry over; to bear; to permeate both
space and time. As far as Heraclitus was concerned, it is fundamental to the concept of Being: 'the all is divisible and indivisible' he
claimed, 'agreeing with itself through differing in itself' (*diapheromenon
heauto sumpheretai*). When Heidegger, in his lecture 'Language' (1950),
relates *diaphora* to the difference between essence and existence, he
clearly has Heraclitus in mind. Recasting the relation of essence to
existence as one of 'world' and 'things' respectively, Heidegger outlines a middle-term, an inter-being, which he associates with language and terms '*Unter-schied*' ('dif-ference'):

> The intimacy of world and thing is present in the separation of the between;
> it is present in the dif-ference. . . . The intimacy of the dif-ference is the
> unifying element of the *diaphora*, the carrying out that carries through. The
> dif-ference carries out world in its worlding, carries out things in their thing-
> ing.[114]

In this sense, the *diaphora* is posed by Heidegger as a middle ground
that 'carries out' essence into existence *and* differentiates the two,
much like the temple-precinct he traces in 'The Origin of the Work of
Art'. Yet as Derrida argues in 'Différance', the power of Heidegger's

---

[113] See Alex Houen, ' "Various Infinitudes": Narrative, Embodiment, Ontology in
Beckett's *How It Is* and Spinoza's *Ethics*', in *Post-Theory* (Edinburgh: Edinburgh University
Press, 1998): 176–87.
[114] Heidegger, 'Language', in *Poetry, Language, Thought*, 202.

diaphora is subordinated because it is predetermined by essence's primordial structuring.[115] Dif-ference as middle being is not a mediation of ontology for Heidegger but a medium, for 'The intimacy of world and thing is not a fusion.'[116] Against this hierarchical structuring of ontology, I argued in the last chapter that Abish posits a topography of immanent potentiality that fuses particular things and discourses to a wider socio-political field. The possibility of existence is not prefigured by a transcendent Being; rather, things exist as real potentials. Consequently, difference is opened to interactions and is no longer seen as simply subordinate to a presumed identity or essence. Writing of Aristotle's treatment of *diaphora*, Deleuze thus calls for a differentiating of difference *in itself*:

the manner in which Aristotle distinguishes between difference and diversity or otherness points the way: only in relation to the supposed identity of a concept is specific difference called the greatest. . . . [His] *diaphora* of the *diaphora* is only a false transport: it never shows difference changing in nature . . .[117]

This notion of 'difference changing in nature' is what I propose the diaphor, as literary figure, manifests. It is no longer the question of a 'transference' (*metapherein*) from one discrete term to another, as in the case of metaphor. Nor is it reducible to the dynamic of a synechdochic part-for-whole. Rather, the diaphor figures a thing *as a variable in itself* and opens it to a multitude of associations. As with Carson's presentation of the confetti, the diaphor is not simply a series of metaphors, either; it is a figure that is torn in a number of directions at once such that it is affected by the contingencies of a wider cultural topography. In this way it presents a mutable mapping of language and tropes.

Throughout this study I have attempted to show how relations between violence, terror, and textuality have been approached differently by literary writers in their engagements with terrorism. In each case writing on these relations have necessitated recourse to a novel form of literary figure: for the Stevensons, the 'report'; for Conrad, 'entropolitics' and the 'aesthetic Idea' of the 'spectre'; for Lewis, the

[115] Jacques Derrida, 'Différance', in *Margins of Philosophy*, trans. by Alan Bass (1972; Chicago: University of Chicago Press, 1986), 22.

[116] Heidegger, 'Language', 202.

[117] Gilles Deleuze, *Difference and Repetition*, trans. by Paul Patton (1968; New York: Columbia University Press, 1994), 31–2.

'literary strike' and 'allegorical assault'; for Pound, 'Sagetrieb'; for
Abish, 'real-ization'; and for Carson, the 'diaphor'. My aim in edu-
cing these figures has been to show some of the diverse ways in which
terrorism and literature have interacted since the 1880s, and so to
question the kinds of structural aetiology of terrorism and its mediation that have been predominant in terrorism studies. In part, then,
this has meant using a literary approach in order to pose new
approaches to the complicated impact that terrorism has had on
cultural life. Such an approach is called for, I have argued, precisely
because fiction, narrative, myth, mediation, representation, performativity, and literary/critical theory have been increasingly invoked in
terrorism studies, stretching as it does across several academic fields.
In many instances, however, the use of these terms and theories has
not taken into account the particular debates on them from within literary studies; instead, narrative and myth, for example, have been
used to present general theories of terrorism's discursive production
or mediation. In each of the preceding chapters, though, I have
argued that literary writers have viewed the relation of terrorism
and textuality as being mediated by a range of other factors—from
thermodynamics and evolution theory for Conrad, to urban cartography and postmodernism for Carson. In this sense, each of the literary figures that I have proposed is 'tensed', to use Carson's term, to a
particular historical terrain. They are figures of historicity. However,
I am not presenting this figural approach as simply a method of drawing analogies between literary and socio-political fields, or of
attributing the literary valencies to a more primary cultural base. The
point of tropes like Conrad's 'entropolitics', Lewis's 'literary strike', or
Pound's 'Sagetrieb' is that the very relations between literature and
social context, text and violence, *are figured differently in each case*. It is not
a question of simply drawing correspondences between discrete cultural elements, then; instead, the figures present their own inter-
pretive and affective dynamics that are nevertheless entangled in
specific cultural contaminations. In short, each of the figures manifests its own diaphorical quality.

Consider Conrad's 'entropolitics', for example. Drawing on the
complicated exchanges taking place between thermodynamics, law,
theories of evolution, and Anarchism at the time, entropolitics is a
troping of cultural dynamics that also posits its own performativity.
And as with Carson's confetti diaphor, it is not just a mapping of
the relation between texts and violence, it is also a figuring of single

'micropolitical' events in relation to a 'macropolitical' field. By showing how the exchanges within this field involve texts and tropes, entropolitics figures its own agency and opens itself to various interactions. This is also the case with Conrad's 'aesthetic Idea' of the 'spectre', in which imagination and experience take on an *other* existence as distinct bodies of sensation. The spectre is literally an image of writing's potentiality. And by linking the force of terror to its transference, Conrad shows how volatile terrorism *and* its mediation can be.

In contrast to Conrad's notion of immanence, Lewis's 'literary strike' presents interruptive abstraction. However, it is no less immured in a wider cultural field. Inspired by Sorelian Syndicalism, British strikes, Futurism, and other avant-garde movements, the force of abstraction is drawn from a number of areas. And while it is intended to counter endemic transference between cultural and economic spheres, it is also figured as aiding the disruption of society as a systematized whole. Proposing a host of disjunctions—time from space, actions from texts, the individual from the masses—Lewis thus rejects metaphor as facilitating conjunctions and rejects synecdoche because there is no 'whole' to be a part of. Favouring in 'Enemy of the Stars' a syntax of collage instead, his writing nevertheless posits congeries of discrete elements together. As with entropolitics, then, the literary strike poses its own agency in relation to a social field, and like Lewis's 'allegorical assault' also involves relations between violence and textuality. Such literary militancy may not have produced any significant political effects, as Lewis himself acknowledges, but seen in relation to debates at the time on the Suffragettes' and avant-gardists' relative activisms, a figure like the allegorical assault does bear testament to the way in which relations between political violence and representation have been historically contested. As a refiguring of literary force, the allegorical assault is thus as much about transforming the performativity of allegory itself.

Pound's 'Sagetrieb' is also an attempt at building a unique literary power, and similarly draws on a complicated network of ideas, including Italian Fascism, American anti-integrationism, and a range of economic theories. Like Carson's poetic mappings, though, the connections that Sagetrieb charts are not limited to the cultural contexts that Pound lives in—as his Confucianism and *The Cantos'* various literary and historical allusions evidence. So, while he presents the trope in part as responding to issues of local politics, Sagetrieb is also torn into a number of different directions: epistemology, aesthetics, and politics more generally. The reason it is so difficult to define its relation to Kasper's terrorist activities is because it figures a specific ontology of ambivalence in relation to pedagogy, violence, and textuality. Transcendent to political power and yet calling for a hero to defend it, Sagetrieb, like Lewis's allegorical assault, manifests its own internal variations to the point of contradicting itself. Pound's figuration of the 'Jew usurer' is no different, vacillating as it does between denoting a particular body and a general process. For this reason, posing Pound's anti-Semitism or anti-integrationism as manifestations of a modernist aesthetic is problematic, precisely because his aesthetics is proposing an alternative ontology of violence and cultural contamination at the time.

Literary periodicity has its own role to play in these figures, then. In the cases of Conrad, Lewis, and Pound the tropes of terror and violence they present harness different modernist practices in addition to elements of historical context. But this does not mean that the tropes are structurally overdetermined by correlating modernism on the one hand and historical context on the other. Lewis's literary strike, for example, is a contestation of avant-garde practice *and* historical context, just as Conrad's spectres mark an original revisioning of Russian Nihilism *and* modernism in relation to the Sublime. While the tropes have a definite historical import, then, the authors' rewritings of literary practice figures a more general potentiality for the tropes themselves. In this respect, each of them can also be applied to different contexts—as I've argued, Lewis's allegorical assault, for example, is pertinent to contemporary discussions about conspiracy theory—but only in so far as this entails fresh interpretations of the trope. It is simply a matter of seeing the consistency of the figures as residing with their capacity for variation. This is their diaphoricity.

For Abish and Carson, variation and potentiality are foregrounded issues because they both see contemporary terrorism and culture as manifesting contingency and provisionality. Tracing the impact of terrorism in 1970s West Germany, Abish is fascinated with militancy because he sees the subversion of everydayness as no less an issue for literary practice. As in Conrad's *The Secret Agent*, he critiques terrorism in terms of the potential for violence and signs to interact. The 'real-ization' I ascribed to Abish's portrayal of signs and violence as events is thus similar to Conrad's entropolitics, for Abish also relates micropolitical performativity to a macropolitical 'topography'. As I have argued, though, this performative capacity does not render these events as merely arbitrary 'human constructs' devoid of particular value. For Abish the potentials of individual signs and events mean that they have their own affective forces. Such forces are never simply overdetermined by human invention or economic processes; for this reason, they always need to be interpreted in relation to the specificities of historical context. In this sense, Abish uses 1970s West Germany to problematize certain postmodernist claims about culture and terrorism, just as Carson does with Belfast more recently. In many of Carson's poems, postmodernism is also implicitly addressed by explorating performativity—from bombings to speech acts—and thereby interrogating contexts of power more generally. In the context of terrorism studies such exploration is essential because the attempt to contain terrorism's complexity with theories of rigid social dynamics has been so prevalent. As I have attempted to show, accounting for terrorist violence by linking it to generalized grounds—whether of ideology, myth, narrative, modernism, or postmodernism—has sometimes amounted to a form of violence in itself. By analysing terrorism's impact in relation to a variety of cultural factors, I have thus tried to resist solidifying it into a structure greater than it is. For whether it is West German terrorists linking their violence to Fascism, or Baudrillard rooting hostage-taking in global-capitalism, the effect of such magnification is frequently to magnify the terrorism itself. One way to separate terror from its 'ism' is to try and map the multiplicity of factors involved in it. Only by thus drawing critique into the crises can we help to prevent violence and discourse from forming further explosive compounds.

Bibliography

Abish, Walter, *Alphabetical Africa* (New York: New Directions, 1974).
—— *How German Is It* (Manchester: Carcanet, 1982).
—— *In The Future Perfect* (London: Faber, 1985).
—— 'Wie Deutsch Ist Es', Interview with Sylvère Lotringer, in Lotringer (ed.), *Semiotext(e): The German Issue*, 158–70.
—— 'The Writer-To-Be: An Impression of Living', *SubStance* 9: 2 (1980): 104–14.
Adamson, Ian, *The Cruthin: The Ancient Kindred* (Newtownards: Nosmada, 1974).
—— *The Identity of Ulster: The Land, the Language, and the People*, (Bangor: Pretani, 1987).
Adorno, Theodor, 'On the Question: "What is German" ', *New German Critique* 36 (Fall 1985): 121–31.
Agamben, Giorgio, *Potentialities: Collected Essays in Philosophy*, trans. by Daniel Heller-Roazen (Stanford: Stanford University Press, 1999).
Alden, Robert, 'Kasper questioned on Blast at School', *New York Times* (15 September 1957): 1.
—— 'FBI Agents help Nashville Inquiry', *New York Times* (14 September 1957): 1.
—— 'Seven Suspects held in School Blast', *New York Times* (11 September, 1957): 25.
Alexander, Yonah, and Alan O'Day (eds.), *Ireland's Terrorist Trauma: Interdisciplinary Perspectives* (Hemel Hempstead: Harvester Wheatsheaf, 1989).
—— (eds.), *Terrorism in Ireland* (London: Croom Helm, 1984).
——, and Seymour Maxwell Finger (eds.), *Terrorism: Interdisciplinary Perspectives* (New York: John Jay, 1977).
Allen, Grant, *Force and Energy: A Theory of Dynamics* (London: Longman, 1888).
—— *For Maimie's Sake: A Tale of Love and Dynamite* (London: Chatto & Windus, 1886).
Allison, Jonathan, ' "Everything Provisional": Fictive Possibility and the Poetry of Paul Muldoon and Ciaran Carson', *Études Irlandaises* 20: 2 (Autumn 1995): 87–93.
Alter, Peter, 'Traditions of Violence in the Irish National Movement', in Mommsen and Hirschfield (eds.), *Social Protest*, 137–54.
Altieri, Charles, 'The Concept of Force as Modernist Response to the Authority of Science', *Modernism/Modernity* 5: 2 (April 1998): 77–93.

American Civil Liberties Union, 'Civil Liberties Implications of the Anti-Terrorism Act of 1995' (American Civil Liberties Union: Freedom Network Web-Site, 1996), <http://www.aclu.org/congress/terract.html>.

Amis, Martin, 'Fear and Loathing', *The Guardian*, G2 (18 September 2001): 4.

Anderson, Margaret, 'Judicial Opinion (Our Suppressed October Issue)', *The Little Review* 4: 8 (December 1917): 46–9.

Ansell-Pearson, Keith, *An Introduction to Nietzsche as Political Thinker* (Cambridge: Cambridge University Press, 1994).

—— 'Women and Political Theory', in *Nietzsche, Feminism and Political Theory*, ed. by Paul Patton (London: Routledge, 1993), 27–48.

Antliff, Mark, *Inventing Bergson: Cultural Politics and the Parisian Avant-Garde* (Princeton: Princeton University Press, 1993).

Annual Register, 1884: A Review of Public Events at Home and Abroad (London: Ridingtons, 1885).

Annual Register, 1913: A Review of Public Events at Home and Abroad (London: Longman's, 1914).

Annual Register, 1914: A *Review of Public Events at Home and Abroad* (London: Longman's, 1915).

Apter, David (ed.), *The Legitimization of Violence* (London: Macmillan, 1997).

—— 'Political Violence in Analytical Perspective', in Apter (ed.), *The Legitimization of Violence*, 1–32.

—— *Rethinking Development: Modernization, Dependency and Postmodern Politics* (Newbury Park: Sage, 1987).

Arthur, Paul, ' "Reading" Violence: Ireland', in Apter (ed.), *The Legitimization of Violence*, 234–91.

Aubry, G. Jean, *Joseph Conrad: Life and Letters*, 2 vols. (London: Heinemann, 1927).

Aust, Stefan, *The Baader-Meinhof Group: The Inside Story of a Phenomenon*, trans. by Anthea Bell (London: Bodley Head, 1987).

Ayers, David, *Wyndham Lewis and Western Man* (London: Macmillan, 1992).

Bakunin, Mikhail, *Statism and Anarchy*, trans. by Marshall S. Shatz (Cambridge: Cambridge University Press, 1990).

Balfour, Michael, *West Germany: A Contemporary History* (London: Croom Helm, 1982).

Barker, J. Ellis, 'The Labour Revolt and its Meaning', *Nineteenth Century* 70: 415 (September 1911): 441–60.

Barkun, Michael, 'Religion, Militias and Oklahoma City: The Mind of Conspiratorialists', *Terrorism and Political Violence* 8: 1 (Spring 1996): 50–79.

Batchelor, John, *The Life of Joseph Conrad: A Critical Biography* (Oxford: Blackwell, 1994).

Baudrillard, Jean, 'Baudrillard Shrugs: A Seminar on Terrorism and the Media with Sylvère Lotringer and Jean Baudrillard', in *Jean Baudrillard: The Disappearance of Art and Politics*, ed. by William Stearns and William Chaloupka (London: Macmillan, 1992), 283–302.

—— *Fatal Strategies*, trans. by Philip Beitchman and W. G. J. Niesluchowski (New York: Semiotext(e), 1990).

—— *For a Critique of the Political Economy of the Sign*, trans. by Charles Levin (St Louis: Telos, 1981).

—— *In the Shadow of the Silent Majorities; or, The End of the Social, and Other Essays*, trans. by Paul Foss, John Johnston, and Paul Patton (New York: Semiotext(e), 1983).

—— *Symbolic Exchange and Death*, trans. by Iain Hamilton (London: Sage, 1993).

Baumann, Michael, *Terror or Love: The Personal Account of a West German Urban Guerrilla* (London: John Calder, 1979).

Becker, Jillian, *Hitler's Children: The Story of the Baader–Meinhof Terrorist Gang* (London: Michael Joseph, 1977).

Beer, Gillian, *Open Fields: Science in Cultural Encounter* (Oxford: Clarendon, 1996).

Belknap, Michael R., *Federal Law and Southern Order: Racial and Constitutional Conflict in the Post-Brown South* (Athens: The University of Georgia Press, 1987).

Bell, Desmond, *The End of Ideology* (Cambridge, Mass.: Harvard University Press, 1988).

Benjamin, Walter, *The Origin of German Tragic Drama*, trans. by John Osborne (London: Verso, 1990).

Benson, Donald, 'Facts and Constructs: Victorian Humanists and Scientific Theorists on Scientific Knowledge', in *Victorian Science and Victorian Values: Literary Perspectives*, ed. by James Paradis and Thomas Postlewait (New York: The New York Academy of Sciences, 1981).

Berghaus, Günter, 'Happenings in Europe: Trends, Events, and Leading Figures', in Sandford (ed.), *Happenings*, 310–88.

Bergson, Henri, *Creative Evolution*, trans. by Arthur Mitchell (London: Macmillan, 1920).

—— *Duration and Simultaneity*, trans. by Leon Jacobson (Indianapolis: Bobbs-Merrill, 1965).

—— *Matter and Memory*, trans. by Nancy Margaret Paul and W. Scott Palmer (New York: Zone, 1991).

—— *Mind Energy*, ed. and trans. by H. Wildon Carr (London: Macmillan, 1920).

Bier, Jean-Paul, 'The Holocaust and West Germany: Strategies of Oblivion, 1947–79', *New German Critique* 19 (Winter 1980): 11–29.

Blackwood's Edinburgh Magazine, 'Fenianism—its Force and its Feebleness: By an Ex-Member of the Fenian Directory', unsigned, 131: 798 (April 1882): 454–67.

Blanchot, Maurice, 'The Limits of Experience: Nihilism', in *The New Nietzsche*, ed. by David B. Allison (Cambridge, Mass.: MIT Press, 1990).

—— *The Writing of the Disaster*, trans. by Ann Smock (Lincoln: University of Nebraska Press, 1992).

Böll, Heinrich, *The Lost Honour of Katharina Blum; or, How Violence Develops and Where it Can Lead*, trans. by Leila Vennewitz (London: Minerva, 1993).

Borch-Jacobsen, Mikkel, *The Freudian Subject* (Basingstoke: Macmillan, 1989).

Bougereau, J., *Memoirs of an International Terrorist: Conversations with Hans Joachim Klein* (Orkney: Cienfuegos, 1981).

Bourdieu, Pierre, *The Political Ontology of Martin Heidegger*, trans. by Peter Collier (Cambridge: Polity, 1991).

Bowen, Catherine Drinker, *The Lion and the Throne: The Life and Times of Sir Edward Coke* (Boston: Little Brown, 1956).

Bowen, Charles, 'A Historical Inventory of the *Dindschenchas*', *Studia Celtica* 10: 11 (1975–6): 113–37.

Bowyer Bell, J., 'Terrorist Scripts and Live-Action Spectaculars', *Columbia Journalism Review* 17: 1 (1978): 43–60.

Brearton, Fran, 'Mapping the Trenches: Gyres, Switchbacks and Zig-zag Circles in W. B. Yeats and Ciaran Carson', *Irish Studies Review* 9: 3 (Winter 2001): 373–86.

Bridge, Cyprian, 'Sub-Aqueous Warfare', *Fraser's Magazine* 98 (October 1878): 458–70.

Brush, Stephen G., *The Kind of Motion we Call Heat: A History of the Kinetic Theory of Gases in the Nineteenth Century*, 2 vols. (Amsterdam: North Holland, 1986).

—— *The Temperature of History: Phases of Science and Culture in the Nineteenth Century* (New York: Franklin, 1978).

Buckley, Anthony, 'Uses of History Among Ulster Protestants', in Dawe and Foster (eds.), *The Poet's Place*, 259–71.

Burdick, Charles, Hans-Adolf Jacobsen, and Winifred Kudsus (eds.), *Contemporary Germany: Politics and Culture*, (Boulder: Westview, 1984).

Bürger, Peter, *Theory of the Avant-Garde*, trans. by Michael Shaw (Minneapolis: University of Minnesota Press, 1984).

Burke, Edmund, *A Philosophical Enquiry into the Origin of our Ideas of the Sublime and Beautiful*, ed. by J. T. Boulton (London: Routledge, 1958).

—— *Letters on a Regicide Peace* in *The Works of the Right Honourable Edmund Burke*, 5 vols. (London: Rivington, 1877–84), v.

Bush, Ronald, ' "Quiet, Not Scornful"? The Composition of *The Pisan Cantos*', in *A Poem Containing History: Textual Studies in* The Cantos, ed. by Lawrence Rainey (Ann Arbor: University of Michigan Press, 1997), 169–211.

Butler, Judith, *Excitable Speech: A Politics of the Performative* (Routledge: London, 1997).

Cahm, Caroline, *Kropotkin and the Rise of Revolutionary Anarchism, 1872–1886* (Cambridge: Cambridge University Press, 1989).

Conflict Archive on the Internet (CAIN) (University of Ulster at Magee), <http://cain.ulst.ac.uk>.

'Calchas', 'The Anglo-Russian Agreement', *Fortnightly Review* 87: 490 (October 1907): 535–50.

Carpenter, Humphrey, *A Serious Character: The Life of Ezra Pound* (London: Faber & Faber, 1988).

Carson, Ciaran, *Belfast Confetti* (Newcastle upon Tyne: Bloodaxe, 1989).

—— 'Escaped from the Massacre?' *The Honest Ulsterman* 50 (Winter 1975): 183–6.

—— *The New Estate* (Belfast: Blackstaff Press, 1976).

—— *The Irish For No* (Newcastle upon Tyne: Bloodaxe, 1987).

—— *Opera Et Cetera* (Newcastle upon Tyne: Bloodaxe, 1996).

—— *The Star Factory* (London: Granta, 1997).

Carus, Paul, 'Max Stirner, the Predecessor of Nietzsche', *The Monist* 21: 3 (July 1911): 376–97.

Casillo, Robert, *The Genealogy of Demons: Anti-Semitism, Fascism, and the Myths of Ezra Pound* (Evanston: Northwestern University Press, 1988).

Chabot, C. Barry, 'The Problems of the Postmodern', in *Critical Essays on American Postmodernism*, ed. by Stanley Trachtenberg (New York: Hall, 1995).

Chace, William M., *The Political Identities of Ezra Pound and T. S. Eliot* (Stanford, Calif.: Stanford University Press, 1973).

Chalmers, David, *Hooded America: The History of the Ku Klux Klan* (Durham: Duke University Press, 1987).

Che Guevara, Ernesto, *Guerrilla Warfare*, trans by J. P. Morray (Manchester: Manchester University Press, 1986).

Childs, David, and Jeffre Johnson, *West Germany: Politics and Society* (London: Croom Helm, 1981).

Clarke, I. F. (ed.), *The Great War with Germany, 1890–1914: Fictions and Fantasies of the War-to-come* (Liverpool: Liverpool University Press, 1997).

—— (ed.), *The Tale of the Next Great War: Fictions of Future Warfare and Battles Still-to-come* (Liverpool: Liverpool University Press, 1995).

Cohn, Norman, *Warrant for Genocide: The Myth of the Jewish World-Conspiracy and the Protocols of the Elders of Zion* (Chico, Calif.: Scholars, 1981).

Cole, J. A., *Lord Haw Haw: The Full Story of William Joyce* (1964; London: Faber & Faber, 1987).

Commonweal, 'Anarchy at the Bar', unsigned (12 May 1894): 67.

Confucius, *Confucian Analects*, trans. by Ezra Pound (London: Peter Owen, 1956).

—— *Ta Hio: The Great Learning*, trans. by Ezra Pound (Seattle: Folcroft, 1970).

Conrad, Joseph, 'Autocracy and War', in *Notes on Life and Letters* (London: Dent, 1924), 83–114.

—— *The Mirror of the Sea, and A Personal Record* (Oxford: Oxford University Press, 1988).

—— *The Secret Agent* (Harmondsworth: Penguin, 1990).

—— *Under Western Eyes* (Harmondsworth: Penguin, 1989).

Coogan, Tim Pat, *The Troubles: Ireland's Ordeal 1966–95 and the Search for Peace* (London: Hutchinson, 1995).

Cookson, William (ed.), *Ezra Pound: Selected Prose 1909–65* (London: Faber, 1973).

Cooper, H. H. A., 'Terrorism and the Media', in Alexander and Finger (eds.), *Terrorism: Interdisciplinary Perspectives* (New York: John Jay, 1977), 141–56.

Corcoran, Neil, *Poets of Modern Ireland: Text, Context, Intertext* (Cardiff: University of Wales Press, 1999).

'Cornelia', 'Epidemic Hysteria', *The English Review* 17 (July 1914): 498–508.

Cornell, Julian, *The Trial of Ezra Pound: A Documented Account of the Treason Case by the Defendant's Lawyer* (London: Faber, 1966).

Cornerford, R. V., *The Fenians in Context: Irish Politics and Society, 1848–82* (Dublin: Mercier, 1978).

Cornhill Magazine, 'Dynamite', unsigned, 3: 15 (September 1884): 273–91.

Coroneos, Con, 'Conrad, Kropotkin and Anarchist Geography', *The Conradian* 18 (Autumn 1994): 17–30.

Couvreur, Séraphin, *Chou King: les annales de la Chine* (Ho Kien fou, 1897).

Cox, Harold, 'Holding a Nation to Ransom', *Nineteenth Century* 71 (March 1912): 401–10.

Crawford, I. M., *The Art of the Wandjina: Aboriginal Cave Paintings in Kimberley, Western Australia* (Oxford: Oxford University Press, 1968).

Crowder, George, *Classical Anarchism: The Political Thought of Godwin, Proudhon, Bakunin, and Kropotkin* (Oxford: Clarendon, 1991).

Crowe Ransom, John, 'Poetry: A Note in Ontology', in *Critical Theory Since Plato*, ed. by Hazard Adams (New York: Harcourt, 1971).

Daily News, 'Rebel Art in Modern Life', unsigned (7 April 1914): 14.

Dangerfield, George, *The Strange Death of Liberal England* (London: MacGibbon & Kee, 1966).

Darby, John, 'Conflict in Northern Ireland: A Background Essay', in Seamus Dunn (ed.), *Facets of the Conflict in Northern Ireland* (Basingstoke: Macmillan, 1995), 15–23.

Dasenbrock, Reed Way, *The Literary Vorticism of Ezra Pound and Wyndham Lewis: Towards the Condition of Painting* (Baltimore: The Johns Hopkins University Press, 1985.

Dawe, Gerald, 'Against Piety: A Reading of John Hewitt's Poetry', in Dawe and Foster (eds.), *The Poet's Place*, 209–24.

Dawe, Gerald, and John Wilson Foster (eds.), *The Poet's Place: Ulster Literature and Society; Essays in Honour of John Hewitt, 1907–87* (Belfast: Institute of Irish Studies, 1991).

de Beistegui, Miguel, *Heidegger & the Political* (London: Routledge, 1998).

de Bolla, Peter, *The Discourse of the Sublime: Readings in History, Aesthetics and the Subject* (Oxford: Blackwell, 1989).

de Rachewiltz, Mary, *Discretions* (London: Faber, 1971).

Deane, Seamus, *Celtic Revivals: Essays in Modern Irish Literature* (London: Faber, 1985).

Debord, Guy, '*Detournement* as Negation and Prelude', in Knabb (ed.), *Situationist International Anthology*, 55–6.

—— 'Report on the Construction of Situations and on the International Situationist Tendency's Conditions of Organisation and Action', in Knabb (ed.), *Situationist International Anthology*, 17–25.

—— 'Perspectives for Conscious Alterations in Everyday Life', in Knabb (ed.), *Situationist International Anthology*, 68–75.

—— *Society of the Spectacle* (Detroit: Black & Red, 1983).

—— and Gil J. Wolman, 'Methods of Detournement', in Knabb (ed.), *Situationist International Anthology*, 10–13.

Del Grand, Alexander, *Italian Fascism: Its Origins and Developments* (Lincoln: University of Nebraska Press, 1982).

Deleuze, Gilles, *Difference and Repetition*, trans. by Paul Patton (New York: Columbia University Press, 1994).

—— *Kant's Critical Philosophy: The Doctrine of the Faculties*, trans. by Hugh Tomlinson and Barbara Habberjam (Minneapolis: University of Minnesota Press, 1984).

—— and Félix Guattari, *A Thousand Plateaus: Capitalism and Schizophrenia*, trans. by Brian Massumi (Minneapolis: University of Minnesota Press, 1987).

deMause, Lloyd, 'The Apocalypse in Our Heads', *The Journal of Psychohistory* 23: 1 (Summer 1995): 18–25.

Dennis, Ian, 'The Terrorism Act 2000', *The Criminal Law Review* (December 2000): 931–2.

Der Derian, James, *Antidiplomacy: Spies, Terror, Speed and War* (Oxford: Blackwell, 1992).

Derrida, Jacques, *Acts of Literature*, trans. by Nicholas Royle, ed. by Derek Attridge (London: Routledge, 1992).

—— *Of Grammatology*, trans. by Gayatri Chakravorty Spivak (Baltimore: The Johns Hopkins University Press, 1978).

—— *Margins of Philosophy*, trans. by Alan Bass (Chicago: University of Chicago Press, 1986).

—— *Specters of Marx: The State of Debt, the Work of Mourning, and the New International*, trans. by Peggy Kamuf (London: Routledge, 1994).

—— *Of Spirit: Heidegger and the Question*, trans. by Geoffrey Bennington and Rachel Bowlby (Chicago: University of Chicago Press, 1991).

—— *Writing and Difference*, trans. by Alan Bass (Chicago: University of Chicago Press, 1978).

Didion, Joan, 'Varieties of Madness', *The New York Review of Books* 45: 7 (23 April 1998): 17–21.

Dillon, Martin, *The Politics of Security: Towards a Political Philosophy of Continental Thought* (London: Routledge, 1996).

Dillon, Martin, *Twenty-Five Years of Terror: The IRA's War Against the British* (London: Bantam, 1999).

Dinnerstein, Leonard, 'Antisemitism in Crisis Times in the United States: The 1920s and 1930s', in *Anti-Semitism in Times of Crisis*, ed. by Sander L. Gilman and Steven T. Katz (New York: New York University Press, 1991), 212–26.

Dodson, Sandra, 'Conrad and the Politics of the Sublime', in *Conrad and Theory*, ed. by Andrew Gibson and Robert Hampson (Amsterdam: Rodopi, 1998), 6–38.

Doob, Leonard (ed.), *'Ezra Pound Speaking': Radio Speeches of World War II* (Westport: Greenwood, 1978).

Dunn, Seamus (ed.), *Facets of the Conflict in Northern Ireland* (Basingstoke: Macmillan, 1995).

Eagleton, Terry, *The Ideology of the Aesthetic* (Oxford: Blackwell, 1990).

—— *The Illusions of Postmodernism* (Oxford: Blackwell, 1997).

Eco, Umberto, 'The Roots of Conflict', *The Guardian*, Saturday Review (13 October 2001): 2.

Eisenberg, Anne, 'The Unabomber and the Bland Decade', *Scientific American* 278: 4 (30 April 1998): 27.

Ellison, Julie, 'Aggressive Allegory', *Raritan* 3: 3 (Winter 1984): 98–115.

Ellmann, Maud, *The Poetics of Impersonality: T. S. Eliot and Ezra Pound* (Sussex: Harvester, 1987).

English, James F., 'Anarchy in the Flesh: Conrad's "Counterrevolutionary" Modernism and the *Witz* of the Political Unconscious', *Modern Fiction Studies* 38 (Autumn 1992): 616–30.

English, James T., 'Scientist, Moralist, Humanist: A Bergsonian Reading of *The Secret Agent*', *Conradiana* 19 (1987): 139–56.

Farias, Victor, *Heidegger and Nazism*, trans. by Paul Burrell and Gabriel Ricci (Philadelphia: Temple University Press, 1989).

Farnen, Russell F., 'Terrorism and the Mass Media: A Systemic Analysis of a Symbiotic Process', *Terrorism* 13: 2 (1990): 99–143.

Fawcett, E. Douglas, *Hartmann the Anarchist; or, The Doom of the Great City* (London: Arnold, 1893).

Fawcett, Waldon, 'The Submarine Boat and its Future', *Scientific American* 81: 24 (9 December 1899): 376–7.

Feldman, Allen, *Formations of Violence: The Narrative of the Body and Political Terror in Northern Ireland* (Chicago: University of Chicago Press, 1991).

Ffrench, Patrick, *The Time of Theory: A History of Tel Quel (1960–83)* (Oxford: Clarendon, 1995).

Fitzduff, Mari, and Liam O'Hagan, 'The Northern Ireland Troubles: Background Paper', *CAIN Web Service*, <http:cain.ulst.ac.uk/othelem/incorepaper.htm>.

Fleishman, Avrom, *Conrad's Politics: Community and Anarchy in the Fiction of Joseph Conrad* (Baltimore: The Johns Hopkins University Press, 1967).

Flett, Kathryn, 'Images that Mocked all Powers of Description', *The Observer* (16 September 2001): 19.

Ford, Franklin L., 'Reflections on Political Murder: Europe in the Nineteenth and Twentieth Centuries', in Mommsen and Hirschfield (eds.), *Social Protest*, 1–12.

Foshay, Toby Avard, 'Wyndham Lewis's Vorticist Metaphysic', *Ariel* 24: 2 (April 1993): 45–63.

Freeman, Barbara Claire, *The Feminine Sublime: Gender and Excess in Women's Fiction* (Berkeley: University of California Press, 1995).

Freud, Sigmund, 'A Note upon the "Mystic Writing Pad" ', in Strachey (ed. and trans.), *The Standard Edition of the Complete Psychological Works of Sigmund Freud*, xix: 225–32.

—— 'The Uncanny', in Strachey (ed. and trans.), *The Standard Edition of the Complete Psychological Works of Sigmund Freud*, xvii: 219–52.

Freud, Sigmund, and Josef Breuer, *Studies on Hysteria*, in Strachey (ed. and trans.), *The Standard Edition of the Complete Psychological Works of Sigmund Freud*, ii.

Friedlander, Robert A., 'The Origins of International Terrorism', in Alexander and Finger (eds.), *Terrorism: Interdisciplinary Perspectives*, 30–45.

Friedlander, Saul, *Memory, History, and the Extermination of the Jews in Europe* (Bloomington: Indiana University Press, 1993).

Frobenius, Leo, *African Genesis* (London: Faber & Faber, 1938).

Furniss, Tom, *Edmund Burke's Aesthetic Ideology: Language, Gender, and Political Economy in Revolution* (Cambridge: Cambridge University Press, 1993).

'G.', 'Strikes', *Fortnightly Review* 96 (February 1912): 235–47.

Gearty, Conor, *The Future of Terrorism* (London: Phoenix, 1997).

—— (ed.), *Terrorism* (Aldershot: Dartmouth, 1996).

—— and John A. Kimbell, *Terrorism and the Rule of Law: A Report on the Laws Relating to Political Violence in Great Britain and Northern Ireland* (London: Civil Liberties Research Unit, King's College, London, 1995).

Geifman, Anna, *Thou Shalt Kill: Revolutionary Terrorism in Russia, 1894–1917* (Princeton: Princeton University Press, 1993).

Gesell, Silvio, *The Natural Economic Order*, trans. by Philip Pye (London: Owen, 1958).

Gilbert, Geoff, 'A Career in Modernism: Wyndham Lewis, 1909–31', Ph.D. thesis (University of Cambridge, 1995).

Gillan, Audrey, 'Bin Laden Appears on Video to Threaten US', *The Guardian* (8 October 2001): 1.

Gillies, M. A., 'Conrad's *The Secret Agent* and *Under Western Eyes* as Bergsonian Comedies', *Conradiana* 20 (1988): 195–213.

Glob, Peter Vilhelm, *The Bog People: Iron-Age Man Preserved*, trans. by Rupert Bruce-Mitford (London: Faber, 1969).

Glover, David, 'Aliens, Anarchists and Detectives: Legislating the Immigrant Body', *New Formations* 32 (Autumn/Winter 1997): 22–33.

GoGwilt, Christopher, *The Invention of the West: Joseph Conrad and the Double-Mapping of Europe and Empire* (Stanford: Stanford University Press, 1995).

Graver, David, 'Vorticist Performance and Aesthetic Turbulence in *Enemy of the Stars*', *PMLA* 107: 3 (May 1992): 482–96.

Gray, Chris Hables, *Postmodern War: The New Politics of Conflict* (New York: Guilford Press, 1997).

Green, Alice Stopford, 'Women's Place in the World of Letters', *Nineteenth Century* 41 (June 1897): 964–74.

Greer, Tom, *A Modern Daedalus* (London: Griffith, Farran, Okeden & Welsh, 1885).

Grimshaw, Allen D. (ed.), *Racial Violence in the United States* (Chicago: Aldine, 1969).

Groenewold, Kurt, 'The German Federal Republic's Response and Civil Liberties', *Terrorism and Political Violence* 4: 4 (Autumn 1992): 136–50.

Guelke, Adrian, *The Age of Terrorism and the International Political System* (London: Tauris Academic Publishers, 1995).

—— 'Paramilitaries, Republicans and Loyalists', in Dunn, *Facets of the Conflict*, 114–30.

Guy, Josephine, *The British Avant-Garde: The Theory and Politics of Tradition* (London: Harvester Wheatsheaf, 1991)

Haar, Michel, *Heidegger and the Essence of Man*, trans. by William McNeill (New York: State University of New York Press, 1993).

Habermas, Jürgen, *The New Conservatism*, trans. by Shierry Weber Nicholson (Cambridge: Polity Press, 1989).

Hachey, Thomas E., *Britain and Irish Separatism: From the Fenians to the Free State, 1867–1922* (Washington, DC: Catholic University of America Press, 1984).

Hansen, Miriam, 'T. E. Hulme, Mercenary Modernism, or, Fragments of Avantgarde Sensibility in Pre-World War 1 Britain', *ELH* 47: 2 (Summer 1980): 355–85.

Harley, John Hunter, 'Syndicalism and Labour Unrest', *Contemporary Review* 101 (March 1912): 348–57.

Harrison, Brian, *Peaceable Kingdom: Stability and Change in Modern Britain* (Oxford: Clarendon, 1982).

—— *Separate Spheres: The Opposition to Women's Suffrage in Britain* (London: Croom Helm, 1978).

Hatton, Joseph, *By Order of the Czar: The Tragic Story of Anna Klosstock, Queen of the Ghetto*, 3 vols. (London: Hutchinson, 1890).

Haws, Robert (ed.), *The Age of Segregation: Race Relations in the South, 1890–1945* (Jackson: University Press of Mississipi, 1978).

Hay, Eloise Knapp, *The Political Novels of Joseph Conrad* (Chicago: University of Chicago Press, 1963).

Hayes, Bernadette C., and Ian McAllister, 'Sowing Dragon's Teeth: Public Support for Political Violence and Paramilitarism in Northern Ireland' (2000), *CAIN Web Service* (University of Ulster at Magee), <http://cain. ulst.ac.uk/issues/violence/docs/hayes/hayeso0.htm>.

Heaney, Seamus, *Death of a Naturalist* (London: Faber, 1966).

—— *North* (London: Faber, 1975), 48.

—— 'Place and Displacement: Reflections on Some Recent Poetry from Northern Ireland', in *Contemporary Irish Poetry: A Collection of Critical Essays*, ed. by Elmer Andrews (Basingstoke: Macmillan, 1992), 124–44.

—— *Preoccupations: Selected Prose, 1968–78* (London: Faber & Faber, 1980).

—— *The Redress of Poetry: Oxford Lectures* (London: Faber & Faber, 1995).

—— 'Unhappy and at Home', Interview with Seamus Deane, *Crane Bag* 1: 1 (Spring 1977): 61–7.

—— *Wintering Out* (London: Faber & Faber, 1972).

Heidegger, *Being and Time*, trans. by John Macquarrie and Edward Robinson (Oxford: Blackwell, 1990).

—— 'Declaration of Support for Adolf Hitler and the National Socialist State', in Wolin (ed.), *The Heidegger Controversy*, 49–52.

—— 'German Students', in Wolin (ed.), *The Heidegger Controversy*, 46–7.

—— *An Introduction to Metaphysics*, trans. by Ralph Mannheim (New Haven: Yale, 1973).

—— 'Letter on Humanism', in *Martin Heidegger: Basic Writings*, ed. and trans. by David Farrell Krell (London: Harper & Row, 1978), 189–242.

—— 'National Socialist Education', in Wolin (ed.), *The Heidegger Controversy*, 55–60.

—— ' "Only a God Can Save Us": *Der Spiegel's* Interview with Heidegger', in Wolin (ed.), *The Heidegger Controversy*, 91–116.

—— *Parmenides*, trans. by André Schuwer (Bloomington: Indiana University Press, 1992).

—— *Poetry Language Thought*, trans. by Albert Hofstadter (New York: Harper & Row, 1971).

—— *The Question Concerning Technology, and Other Essays*, trans. by William Lovitt (New York: Harper, 1977).

—— 'Schlageter', in Wolin (ed.), *The Heidegger Controversy*, 40–2.

—— 'The Self Assertion of the German University', in Wolin (ed.), *The Heidegger Controversy*, 29–39.

Hennessey, Thomas, *A History of Northern Ireland* (Basingstoke: Macmillan, 1997).

Henningsen, Manfred, 'The Politics of Symbolic Evasion: Germany and the Aftermath of the Holocaust', in *Echoes From the Holocaust: Reflections on a Dark Time*, ed. by Alan Rosenberg and Gerald E. Myers (Philadelphia: Temple University Press, 1988), 396–411.

Henri, Adrian, *Environments and Happenings* (London: Thames & Hudson, 1974).

Herman, Edward, and Gerry O'Sullivan, *The 'Terror' Industry: The Experts and Institutions that Shape Our View of Terror* (New York: Pantheon, 1989).

Hewitt, Andrew, *Fascist Modernism: Aesthetics, Politics, and the Avant-Garde* (Stanford: Stanford University Press, 1993).

Hewitt, John, *The Collected Poems of John Hewitt*, ed. by Frank Ormsby (Belfast: The Blackstaff, 1991).

—— 'Regionalism: The Last Chance' (1947), in *Ancestral Voices: The Selected Prose of John Hewitt*, ed. by Tom Clyde (Belfast: Black Staff, 1987).

Heymann, C. D., *Ezra Pound: The Last Rower, a Political Profile* (London: Faber & Faber, 1976).

Higgins, Rosalyn, and Maurice Flory (eds.), *Terrorism and International Law* (London: Routledge and London School of Economics, 1997).

Hillis Miller, J., *Poets of Reality* (Cambridge: Harvard University Press, 1966).

Hillyard, Paddy, *Suspect Community: People's Experience of the Prevention of Terrorism Acts in Britain* (London: Pluto, 1993).

Hinderer, Walter, 'The Challenge of the Past: Turning Points in the Intellectual and Literary Reflections of West-Germany, 1945–85', in *Legacies and Ambiguities: Postwar Fiction and Culture in West Germany and Japan*, ed. by Ernestine Schlant and J. Thomas Rimer (Baltimore: The Johns Hopkins University Press, 1991).

Hoffman, Bruce, *Inside Terrorism* (London: Victor Gollancz, 1998).

Holton, Bob, *British Syndicalism 1910–1914: Myths and Realities* (London: Pluto, 1980).

Holton, Sandra Stanley, *Feminism and Democracy: Women's Suffrage and Reform Politics in Britain, 1900–18* (Cambridge: Cambridge University Press, 1986).

The Home Office, London, 'Terrorism Act 2000' (Her Majesty's Stationery Office Web-Site, 2000), <http://www.hmso.gov.uk/acts/acts2000/00011>.

The Home Office, London, and Northern Ireland Office, 'The Belfast ["Good Friday"] Agreement' (NIO Web-Site, 2000), <http://www.nio.gov.uk/agreement.htm>.

Home, Stewart, *The Assault on Culture* (Stirling: AK, 1991).

Horchem, Hans Josef, 'West Germany's Red Army Anarchists', *Conflict Studies* 74 (June 1974): 1–13.

Houen, Alex, ' "Various Infinitudes": Narrative, Embodiment, and Ontology in Beckett's *How It Is* and Spinoza's *Ethics*', in *Post-Theory* (Edinburgh: Edinburgh University Press, 1998), 176–87.

Hughes, Eamonn, 'Could Anyone Write It? Place in Tom Paulin's Poetry', in Richard Kirkland and Colin Graham (eds.), *Ireland and Cultural Theory: The Mechanics of Authenticity* (Basingstoke: Macmillan, 1999), 159–80.

—— 'Introduction: Northern Ireland—Border Country', in *Culture and Politics in Northern Ireland, 1960–90*, ed. by Eamonn Hughes (Milton Keynes: Open University Press, 1991), 1–12.

Hulme, T. E., 'Modern Art and its Philosophy', in *Speculations: Essays on Humanism and the Philosophy of Art*, ed. by Herbert Read (London: Routledge & Kegan Paul, 1987).

Hunt, Bruce J. 'Doing Science in a Global Empire: Cable Telegraphy and Electrical Physics in Victorian Britain', in *Victorian Science in Context*, ed. by Bernard Lightman (Chicago: University of Chicago Press, 1997).

Hunter, Allan, *Joseph Conrad and the Ethics of Darwinism: The Challenges of Science* (London: Croom Helm, 1983).

Huxley, Thomas H., 'Capital—The Mother of Labour', *Nineteenth Century* 27 (March 1890): 513–32

—— *Science and Culture, and Other Essays* (London: Macmillan, 1881).

—— *Selections from the Essays of T. H. Huxley*, ed. by Alburey Castell (New York: Appleton-Century-Crofts, 1948).

Ingraham, Barton L., *Political Crime in Europe: A Comparative Study of France, Germany, and England* (Berkeley: University of California University Press, 1979).

Isaak, Jo Anna, *The Ruin of Representation in Modernist Art and Texts* (Ann Arbor: UMI Research Press, 1986).

James, Henry, *The Princess Casamassima* (Harmondsworth: Penguin, 1987).

Jameson, Fredric, *Fables of Aggression: Wyndham Lewis, the Modernist as Fascist* (Berkeley: University of California Press, 1979).

—— *The Political Unconscious: Narrative as a Socially Symbolic Act* (London: Methuen, 1981).

—— *Postmodernism; or, The Cultural Logic of Late Capitalism* (London: Verso, 1991).

Jenkins, Edward, *A Week of Passion; or, The Dilemma of Mr. George Barton the Younger* (London: Bliss Sands, 1897).

Jennings, Jeremy, *Syndicalism in France: A Study of Ideas* (London: Macmillan, 1990).

Johnson, George, *Architects of Fear: Conspiracy Theories and Paranoia in American Politics* (Los Angeles: Torcher, 1983).

Judge, Edward H., *Plehve: Repression and Reform in Imperial Russia* (Syracuse: Syracuse University Press, 1983).

Jung, Hwa Yol, 'Heidegger's Way with Sinitic Thinking', in *Heidegger and Asian Thought*, ed. by Graham Parkes (Honolulu: University of Hawaii Press, 1987).

Kadlec, David, 'Pound, *Blast*, and Syndicalism', *ELH* 60: 4 (Winter 1993): 1015–31.

Kahn, Douglas, and Gregory Whitehead (eds.), *Wireless Imagination: Sound Radio, and the Avant-Garde* (Cambridge, Mass.: MIT Press, 1992).

Kant, Immanuel, *Critique of Judgement*, trans. by J. H. Bernard (London: Macmillan, 1914).

—— *Observations on the Sublime and the Beautiful*, trans. by John T. Goldthwait (Berkeley: University of California Press, 1960).

Kant, Immanuel, 'On a Newly Raised Superior Tone in Philosophy', trans. by Peter Fenves, in *On the Rise of Tone in Philosophy: Kant and Derrida*, ed. by Peter Fenves (Baltimore: The Johns Hopkins University Press, 1992).

Karl, Frederick R., and Laurence Davies (eds.), *The Collected Letters of Joseph Conrad, 1898–1902*, 5 vols. (Cambridge: Cambridge University Press, 1986).

Kasper, John, Letters to Ezra Pound, Ezra Pound Papers, Lilly Library, Indiana University, Bloomington, MSS II, Letters of John Kasper, 1951–3.

—— Letters to Ezra Pound, Ezra Pound Papers, Beinecke Library, Yale University, YCAL MSS 43, Box 26, Folders 1124–34: 'John Kasper, Letters to Pound, 1951–61'.

—— Letters to Ezra Pound, Ezra Pound Papers, Beinecke Library, Yale University, YCAL MSS 53, Box 9, Folder 210: 'John Kasper, Letters to Pound, 1952–63'.

Kearney, Richard, *Postnationalist Ireland: Politics, Culture, Philosophy* (London: Routledge, 1997).

Kelley, Kevin J., *The Longest War: Northern Ireland and the IRA* (London: Zed, 1982).

Kent, Susan Kingly, *Sex and Suffrage in Britain, 1860–1914* (Princeton: Princeton University Press, 1987).

Kerrigan, John, 'Earth Writing: Seamus Heaney and Ciaran Carson', *Essays in Criticism* 48: 2 (April 1998): 144–68.

Khayati, Mustapha, 'Captive Words: Preface to a Situationist Dictionary', in Knabb (ed.), *Situationist International Anthology*, 170–5.

Kifner, John, 'Oklahoma Blast: A Tale in Two Books', *New York Times* (21 August 1995): A12.

Kirby, Michael, 'Happenings: An Introduction', in Sandford (ed.), *Happenings*, 1–28.

Kirkland, Richard, *Literature and Culture in Northern Ireland since 1965: Moments of Danger* (London: Longman, 1996).

Kirschner, Paul, 'Topodialogical Narrative in *Under Western Eyes* and the Rasoumoffs of "La Petite Russie" ', in *Conrad's Cities: Essays for Hans Van Marle*, ed. by Gene M. Moore (Amsterdam: Rodopi, 1985), 224–54.

Klein, Hans-Joachim, 'Slaughter Politics', in Lotringer (ed.), *Semiotext(e): The German Issue*, 80–99.

Klein, Scott, 'The Experiment of Vorticist Drama: Wyndham Lewis and "Enemy of the Stars" ', *Twentieth Century Literature* 37: 2 (1991): 225–39.

Klinkowitz, Jerome, 'Walter Abish', Interview, in *The Life of Fiction* (Urbana: University of Illinois Press, 1977), 60–71.

Knabb, Ken (ed. and trans.), *Situationist International Anthology* (Berkeley: Bureau of Public Secrets, 1981).

Knott, C. G., *The Life and Scientific Work of Peter Guthrie Tait* (Cambridge: Cambridge University Press, 1911).

Knott, Eleanor, and Gerard Murphy, *Early Irish Literature* (London: Routledge & Kegan Paul, 1966).

Kramer, Jane, 'A Reporter in Hamburg', *The New Yorker* (20 March 1978): 44–88.

Kropotkin, Peter, 'Anarchism', in *Anarchism and Anarchist Communism* (London: Freedom, 1987), 7–21.

—— 'The Revolution in Russia', *Nineteenth Century and After* 83: 316 (December 1905): 865–83.

—— 'The Scientific Bases of Anarchy', *Nineteenth Century* 21 (February 1887): 238–52.

Kruchenykh, Aleksei, and Kazimir Malevich, 'Victory Over the Sun', reprinted in *The Drama Review* 15 (Fall 1971): 107–24.

Kubiak, Anthony, *Stages of Terror: Terrorism, Ideology, and Coercion as Theatre History* (Bloomington: Indiana University Press, 1991).

Kushner, Tony, *The Holocaust and the Liberal Imagination: A Social and Cultural History* (Oxford: Blackwell, 1994).

La Capra, Dominick, 'Representing the Holocaust: Reflections on the Historians' Debate', in *Probing the Limits of Representation: Nazism and the 'Final Solution'*, ed. by Saul Friedlander (Cambridge, Mass.: Harvard University Press, 1992), 100–25.

Lacoue-Labarthe, Philipe, *Heidegger, Art and Politics: The Fiction of the Political*, trans. by Chris Turner (Oxford: Blackwell, 1990).

Laqueur, Walter, *The Age of Terrorism* (London: Weidenfeld & Nicolson, 1987).

—— 'Postmodern Terrorism', *Foreign Affairs* 75: 5 (September–October 1996): 24–36.

Lasky, Melvin, 'Ulrike Meinhof and the Baader-Meinhof Gang', *Encounter* 44: 6 (June 1975): 9–23.

Lawson, Mark, 'The Power of a Picture', *The Guardian* G2 (13 September 2001): 10.

Le Bon, Gustave, *The Crowd: A Study of the Popular Mind*, trans. by Robert K. Merton (New York: Penguin, 1977).

Lebel, Jean-Jacques, 'On the Necessity of Violation', in Sandford (ed.), *Happenings*, 268–84.

Lebzeltzer, Gisela C., *Political Anti-Semitism in England, 1918–1939* (London: Macmillan, 1979).

Lee, Vernon, 'M. Sorel and the "Syndicalist Myth"', *Fortnightly Review* 98: 538 (October 1911): 664–80.

Léith, Caomhín Mac Giolla, '*Dinnseanchas* and Modern Gaelic Poetry', in Dawe and Foster (eds.), *The Poet's Place*, 157–68.

Lesesne, Mary Richardson, *Torpedoes; or, Dynamite in Society* (Galveston, Texas: Shaw & Baylock, 1883).

Lévinas, Emanuel, *Otherwise than Being, or Beyond Essence*, trans. by Alphonso Lingis (Dordrecht: Kluwer, 1991).

Levine, George, 'The Novel as Scientific Discourse', in *Why the Novel Matters: A Postmodern Perplex*, ed. by Mark Spilka and Caroline McCracken-Fleischer (Bloomington: Indiana University Press, 1990), 238–45.

Lewis, Wyndham, *The Art of Being Ruled* (London: Chatto & Windus, 1926).

—— *Blasting and Bombardiering* (London: Calder & Boyars, 1967).

—— *Count Your Dead: They Are Alive!* (London: Lovat Dickson, 1937).

—— *Creatures of Habit and Creatures of Change: Essays on Art, Literature and Society, 1914–1956*, ed. by Paul Edwards (Santa Rosa: Black Sparrow, 1989).

—— *The Diabolical Principle and the Dithyrambic Spectator* (London: Chatto & Windus, 1931).

—— 'Enemy of the Stars' (1932 version), in *Wyndham Lewis: Collected Poems and Plays*, ed. by Alan Munton (Manchester: Carcanet, 1979), 141–91.

—— 'Imaginary Letters, IX', *The Little Review* 4: 6 (April 1918): 50–4.

—— *Rude Assignment: An Intellectual Biography* (Santa Barbara: Black Sparrow, 1984).

—— *Time and Western Man* (Santa Rosa: Black Sparrow, 1993).

—— (ed.), *Blast 2: War Number* (Santa Rosa: Black Sparrow, 1993).

—— (ed.), *Blast: Review of the Great English Vortex* 1 (Santa Rosa: Black Sparrow, 1997).

Lilly, W. S., 'The Philosophy of Strikes', *Nineteenth Century* 70 (October 1911): 627–42.

Linden, Marcel, and Wayne Thorpe, 'The Rise and Fall of Revolutionary Syndicalism', in van der Linden and Thorpe (eds.), *Revolutionary Syndicalism*, 1–24.

Livingston, Steven, *The Terrorism Spectacle* (Boulder and Oxford: Westview Press, 1984).

Lombroso, Cesare, 'Illustrative Studies in Criminal Anthropology: The Physiognomy of the Anarchists', *The Monist* 1: 3 (April 1891): 321–43.

Longley, Edna, *The Living Stream: Literature and Revisionism in Ireland* (Newcastle upon Tyne: Bloodaxe, 1994).

Lotringer, Sylvère (ed.), *Semiotext(e): The German Issue* 4: 2 (1982).

Lovejoy, Arthur Oncken, 'The Practical Tendencies of Bergsonism', *International Journal of Ethics* 23 (July 1913): 429–43.

Lovell, John, 'British Trade Unions 1875–1933', in *British Trade Union and Labour History: A Compendium*, ed. by L. A. Clarkson (London: Macmillan, 1990).

Lyon, Janet, *Manifestoes: Provocations of the Modern* (Ithaca: Cornell University Press, 1999).

Lyotard, Jean-François, *Lessons on the Analytic of the Sublime*, trans. by Elizabeth Rottenberg (Stanford: Stanford University Press, 1994).

—— *The Postmodern Condition*, trans. by Geoffrey Bennington and Brian Massumi (Manchester: Manchester University Press, 1984).

McCall, Cathall, *Identity in Northern Ireland: Communities, Politics and Change* (Basingstoke, Macmillan, 1999).

McCarthy, Conor, *Modernisation, Crisis and Culture in Ireland, 1969–92* (Dublin: Four Courts, 2000).

McEwan, Iain, 'Only Love and Then Oblivion. Love Was All They Had to Set Against Their Murderers', *The Guardian* (15 September 2001): 1.

McFadden, Roy, 'No Dusty Pioneer: A Personal Recollection of John Hewitt', in Dawe and Foster (eds.), *The Poet's Place*, 169–80.

MacGowan, John, *Postmodernism and Its Critics* (Ithaca: Cornell University Press, 1991).

McInerney, Jay, 'Brightness falls', *The Guardian*, Saturday Review (15 September 2001): 1.

Mackay, Donald, *The Dynamite Ship* (New York: Manhattan, 1888), 5, 155.

Mahler, Horst, 'Look Back on Terror', in Lotringer (ed.), *Semiotext(e): The German Issue*, 100–6.

Mallock, W. H., 'Physics and Sociology', *Contemporary Review* 68 (December 1895): 883–908.

Marcuse, Herbert, 'Murder Is Not a Political Weapon', *New German Critique* 12 (Fall 1977): 7–8.

—— *One Dimensional Man* (London: Routledge, 1991).

Marighella, Carlos, *The Minimanual of the Urban Guerrilla* (San Francisco: Arguello, 1978).

Marinetti, Filippo Tommaso, *Let's Murder the Moonshine: Selected Writings*, trans. by R. W. Flint and Arthur A. Coppatelli (Los Angeles: Sun and Moon, 1991).

Marshall, Peter, *Demanding the Impossible: A History of Anarchism* (London: HarperCollins, 1992).

Martin, Richard, 'Walter Abish's Fictions: Perfect Unfamiliarity, Familiar Imperfection', *Journal of American Studies* 17: 2 (August 1983): 229–41.

Marx, Karl, *The German Ideology*, trans. by C. P. Magill (London: Lawrence and Wishart, 1940).

—— *Grundrisse: Foundations of the Critique of Political Economy*, trans. by Martin Nicholaus (Harmondsworth: Penguin, 1987).

Marx-Scouras, Danielle, *The Cultural Politics of Tel Quel: Literature and the Left in the Wake of Engagement* (Pennsylvania: The Pennsylvania State University Press, 1996).

Masters, Ardyce, and James Masters, 'Reflections on the Oklahoma City Bombing', *The Journal of Psychohistory* 23: 1 (Summer 1995): 26–9.

Materer, Timothy (ed.), *Pound/Lewis: The Letters of Ezra Pound and Wyndham Lewis* (London: Faber & Faber, 1985).

Matyushin, Mikhail, 'Futurism in St Petersburg', reprinted in *The Drama Review* 15: 4 (Fall, 1971): 101–6.

Maurras, Charles, *L'Avenir de l'intelligence* (Paris: Flammarion, 1927).

May, Todd, *The Political Philosophy of Poststructuralist Anarchism* (Philadelphia: University of Pennsylvania Press, 1994).

Meacham, Harry M., *The Caged Panther: Ezra Pound and St. Elizabeth's* (New York: Twayne, 1967).

Meade, L. T., *The Siren* (London: F. V. White, 1898).

Melchiori, Barbara Arnett, *Terrorism in the Late-Victorian Novel* (London: Croom Helm, 1985).

Melley, Timothy, *Empire of Conspiracy: The Culture of Paranoia in Postwar America* (Ithaca: Cornell University Press, 2000).

Mengham, Rod, 'From Georges Sorel to *Blast*', in *The Violent Muse: Violence and the Artistic Imagination in Europe, 1910–39*, ed. by Rod Mengham and Jana Howlett (Manchester: Manchester University Press, 1994), 33–44.

Metchnikoff, Leon, 'Revolution and Evolution', *Contemporary Review* 50 (September 1886): 412–37.

Meyers, Jeffrey, *The Enemy: A Biography of Wyndham Lewis* (London: Routledge & Kegan Paul, 1980).

Miller, David, *Anarchism* (London: Dent, 1984).

—— (ed.), *Rethinking Northern Ireland: Culture, Ideology and Colonisation* (London: Longman, 1998).

—— 'The Use and Abuse of Political Violence', *Political Studies* 32: 3 (1984): 401–19.

Miller, Reuben, 'The Literature of Terrorism', *Terrorism* 11: 1 (1988): 63–87.

Mir, Hamid, 'Muslims Have the Right to Attack America', *The Observer* (11 November 2001): 2.

Mitchell, Barbara, 'French Syndicalism: An Experiment in Practical Anarchism', in van der Linden and Thorpe (eds.), *Revolutionary Syndicalism*, 25–42.

Mommsen, Wolfgang J., and Gerhard Hirschfield (eds.), *Social Protest, Violence and Terror in Nineteenth- and Twentieth-Century Europe* (London: Macmillan, 1982).

Montague, John, *The Rough Field* (Newcastle upon Tyne: Bloodaxe, 1990).

Morgan, Philip, *Italian Fascism, 1919–45* (London: Macmillan, 1995).

Morrison, Blake, and Andrew Motion (eds.), *The Penguin Book of Contemporary British Poetry* (Harmondsworth: Penguin, 1982).

Moser, Thomas C., 'An English Context for Conrad's Russian Characters: Sergey Stepniak and the Diary of Olive Garnett', *Journal of Modern Literature* 11: 1 (March, 1984): 3–44.

Muldoon, Paul, *Meeting the British* (London: Faber, 1987).

—— *New Weather* (London: Faber, 1994).

—— *Quoof* (London: Faber, 1983).

—— *Why Brownlee Left* (Winston-Salem: Wake Forest University Press, 1980).

Mullins, Eustace, *This Difficult Individual: Ezra Pound* (New York: Fleet, 1961).

Murphy, Richard, *Theorizing the Avant-Garde: Modernism, Expressionism, and the Problem of Postmodernity* (Cambridge: Cambridge University Press, 1998).

Muse, Benjamin, *Ten Years of Prelude: The Story of Integration Since the Supreme Court's 1954 Decision* (Beaconsfield: Darwin & Finlayson, 1964).

Myers, Greg, 'Nineteenth-Century Popularizations of Thermodynamics and the Rhetoric of Social Prophecy', in *Energy and Entropy: Science and Culture in Victorian Britain*, ed. by Patrick Brantliger (Bloomington: Indiana University Press, 1990).

Najder, Zdzisław, *Conrad in Perspective: Essays on Art and Fidelity* (Cambridge: Cambridge University Press, 1997).

—— *Joseph Conrad: A Chronicle* (Cambridge: Cambridge University Press, 1983).

Neuhauser, Peter, 'The Mind of a Terrorist: Interview with Michael "Bommi" Baumann', *Encounter* 51: 3 (September 1978): 81–8.

The New Freewoman: An Individualist Review, 'Views and Comments', unsigned, 6: 1 (1 September 1913): 104–5.

—— 'Views and Comments', unsigned, 8: 1 (15 October 1913): 163–4.

Newton, R. Heber, 'Anarchism', *Arena* 27: 1 (January 1902): 1–12.

New York Herald Tribune, 'Woman Tells of Financing Segregationist Shop', unsigned (3 February 1957): 21.

New York Times, 'Partisan of Prejudice: Frederick John Kasper', unsigned (24 July 1957): 12.

—— 'Vorticism, the Latest Cult of Rebel Artists', unsigned (9 August 1914): 10.

Nicholls, Peter, *Ezra Pound: Politics, Economics and Writing: A Study of* The Cantos (London: Macmillan, 1984).

—— 'Futurism, Gender, and Theories of Postmodernity', *Textual Practice* 3: 2 (Summer 1989): 202–21.

Nietzsche, Friedrich, *Beyond Good and Evil*, trans. by Walter Kaufmann (New York: Random House, 1966).

—— *Ecce Homo*, trans. by R. J. Hollingdale and Walter Kaufmann (New York: Random House, 1967).

—— *The Gay Science*, trans. by Walter Kaufmann (New York: Random House, 1974).

—— *The Will to Power*, trans. by Walter Kaufmann and R. J. Hollingdale (London: Vintage, 1968).

—— *Thus Spake Zarathustra*, trans. by R. J. Hollingdale (Harmondsworth: Penguin, 1969), 179.

Nolte, Ernst, 'Between Myth and Revisionism? The Third Reich in the Perspective of the 1980s', in *Aspects of the Third Reich*, ed. by H. W. Koch (London: Routledge, 1985).

Norman, Sherry (ed.), *Conrad: The Critical Heritage* (London: Routledge, 1973), 198.

Ó Broin, León, *Revolutionary Underground: The Story of the Irish Republican Brotherhood, 1858–1924* (Dublin: Gill and Macmillan, 1976).

Ó Tuathail, Gearóid, 'The Postmodern Geopolitical Condition: States, Statecraft and Security at the Millennium', *Annals of the Association of American Geographers* 90: 1 (2000): 166–78.

O'Brien, M. A., 'Fledd Bricrenn', in *Irish Sagas*, ed. by Myles Dillon (Dublin: Radio Eireann, 1959).

O'Brien, Sean, *The Deregulated Muse* (Newcastle upon Tyne: Bloodaxe, 1998).

O'Donoghue, Bernard, 'Involved Imaginings: Tom Paulin', in *The Chosen Ground: Essays on the Contemporary Poetry of Northern Ireland*, ed. by Neil Corcoran (Bridgend: Seren, 1992), 171–88.

Oestreicher, Paul, 'The Roots of Terrorism. West Germany: A Special Case?' *The Round Table* 269 (January 1978): 75–80.

O'Hanlon, Redmond, *Joseph Conrad and Charles Darwin: The Influence of Scientific Thought on Conrad's Fiction* (Edinburgh: Salamander, 1984).

Orr, John, and Dragan Klaic (eds.), *Terrorism and Modern Drama* (Edinburgh: Edinburgh University Press, 1990).

Ott, Hugo, *Martin Heidegger*, trans. by Allen Blunden (London: Harper-Collins, 1993).

Pankhurst, Christabel, 'Militancy: A Virtue', *The Suffragette*, 1: 13 (10 January 1913): 186.

—— 'Militant Methods', in *Suffrage and the Pankhursts*, ed. by Jane Marcus (London: Routledge & Kegan Paul, 1987), 117–23.

—— 'Standards of Morality', *The Suffragette* 1: 25 (4 April 1913): 404.

Pankhurst, Sylvia, *The Suffragette Movement: An Intimate Account of Persons and Ideals* (London: Virago, 1977).

Pater, Walter, 'Prosper Mérimée', in *Miscellaneous Studies* (London: Macmillan, 1910), 11–37.

Paulin, Tom, *Fivemiletown* (London: Faber, 1987).

—— Interview with John Haffenden, in John Haffenden, *Viewpoints: Poets in Conversation with John Haffenden* (London: Faber, 1981), 157–73.

—— *Ireland and the English Crisis* (Newcastle upon Tyne: Bloodaxe, 1984).

—— *The Liberty Tree* (London: Faber, 1983).

—— *Walking a Line* (London: Faber, 1994).

Pearlman, Daniel D., *The Barb of Time: On the Unity of Ezra Pound's Cantos* (Oxford: Oxford University Press, 1969).

Peppis, Paul, *Literature, Politics, and the English Avant-Garde: Nation and Empire, 1901–18* (Cambridge: Cambridge University Press).

Perloff, Marjorie, *The Futurist Moment: Avant-Garde, Avant-Guerre, and the Language of Rupture* (Chicago: Chicago University Press, 1986).

'Perseus', 'Europe and the Russian Revolution', *Fortnightly Review* 84: 468 (1 December 1905): 959–75.

Pierce, Donald, and Herbert Schneidau (eds.), *Ezra Pound/John Theobald Letters* (Reddin Ridge: Black Swan, 1984).

Plant, Sadie, *The Most Radical Gesture* (London: Routledge, 1992).

Poggioli, Renato, *The Theory of the Avant-Garde*, trans. by Gerald Fitzgerald (Cambridge, Mass.: Harvard University Press, 1968).

Poincaré, Henri, 'Sur le probleme des trois corps et les équations de dynamique', *Acta Mathematica* (February 1890): 1–270.

Popham, John N., 'Civil Rights Trial Jury in Action', *New York Times* (14 July 1957): iv, 7.

Possony, Stefan T., and L. Francis Bouchey, *International Terrorism—the Communist Connection—with a Case Study of West German Terrorist Ulrike Meinhof* (Washington: American Council for World Freedom, 1978).

Pound, Ezra, *The Cantos of Ezra Pound* (London: Faber, 1994).

—— *Confucius: The Great Digest and Unwobbling Pivot*, trans. and commentary by Ezra Pound (London: Owen, 1952).

—— 'The Classics "Escape" ', *The Little Review* 4: 11 (March 1918): 32–4.

—— 'Convenit esse Deos', in *Machine Art & Other Writings: The Lost Thought of the Italian Years: Ezra Pound*, ed. by Maria Luisa Ardizzone (Durham: Duke University Press, 1996), 135–40.

—— 'Editorial', *The Little Review* 4: 1 (May 1917): 3–6.

—— *Guide to Kulchur* (London: Owen, 1966).

—— 'The Individual in his Milieu', in Cookson (ed.), *Ezra Pound*, 242–53.

—— 'The Italian Score', *New English Weekly* 7: 6 (23 May 1935): 107.

—— *Jefferson and/or Mussolini* (London: Nott, 1935).

—— 'Mang Tsze (The Ethics of Mencius)', in Cookson (ed.), *Ezra Pound*, 95–111.

—— 'Race', *New English Weekly* 10: 1 (15 October 1936): 12–13.

—— *The Spirit of Romance* (London: Dent, 1910).

—— Towards Orthology', *New English Weekly* 6: 26 (11 April 1935): 534.

Powell, Colin, 'Interview on ABC News' (US State Department Web-Site, 12 September 2001), <http:www.state.gov/secretary/rm/2001/index.cfm?docid=4188>.

—— 'Interview on BBC News' (US State Department Web-Site, 21 September 2001), <http:www.state.gov/secretary/rm/2001/index.cfm?docid=5004>.

—— 'Remarks to the Overseas Security Advisory Committee' (US State Department Web-Site, 7 November 2001), <http: //www.state.gov/secretary/rm/2001/index.cfm?docid=5974>.

Pugh, Martin, *Electoral Reform in War and Peace, 1906–18* (London: Routledge & Kegan Paul, 1978).

Perdue, William, *Terrorism and the State: A Critique of Domination through Fear* (Westport: Praeger, 1989).

Quarterly Review, 'The Recent Strikes', unsigned, 215 (November 1912): 573–98.

'R. L.', 'Peace and Internal Politics: A Letter from Russia', *Fortnightly Review* 84: 463 (1 July 1905): 136–50.

Rabaté, Jean Michel, *Language, Sexuality and Ideology in Ezra Pound's* Cantos (Albany: State University of New York Press, 1986).

Radzinowicz, Leon, and Roger Hood, *A History of English Criminal Law, Volume 5: The Emergence of Penal Policy in Victorian and Edwardian England* (Oxford: Clarendon, 1990).

Rainey, Lawrence, 'Taking Dictation: Collage Poetics, Pathology, and Politics', *Modernism/Modernity* 5: 2 (April 1998): 142–8.

Reclus, Elisée, 'The Evolution of Cities', *Contemporary Review* 67 (February 1895): 246–64.

Redman, Tim, *Ezra Pound and Italian Fascism* (Cambridge: Cambridge University Press, 1991).

—— 'The Repatriation of Pound, 1939–42: A View from the Archives', *Paideuma* 8: 3 (Winter 1979): 447–57.

Reed, Donna K., *The Novel and The Nazi Past* (New York: Peter Lang, 1985).

Reynolds, Paige, ' "Chaos Invading Concept": *Blast* as a Native Theory of Promotional Culture', *Twentieth Century Literature* 46: 2 (Summer 2000): 238–67.

Ricoeur, Paul, *Oneself as Another*, trans. by Kathleen Blamey (Chicago: University of Chicago Press, 1993).

Ridley, F. F., *Revolutionary Syndicalism in France: The Direct Action of its Time* (Cambridge: Cambridge University Press, 1970).

Roberts, David, *The Syndicalist Tradition and Italian Fascism* (Manchester: Manchester University Press, 1979).

Rolston, Bill, 'What's Wrong with Multiculturalism?', in Miller (ed.), *Rethinking Northern Ireland*, 253–74.

Rose, W. K. (ed.), *The Letters of Wyndham Lewis* (London: Methuen, 1963).

Roy, Arundhati, 'The Algebra of Infinite Justice', *The Guardian*, Saturday Review (29 September 2001): 1–2.

Rushdie, Salman, 'Let's Get Back to Life', *The Guardian*, Saturday Review (6 October 2001): 1.

—— 'A War that Presents Us All with a Crisis of Faith', *The Guardian*, Saturday Review (12 November 2001): 12.

Rushing, Conrad L., ' "Mere Words": The Trial of Ezra Pound', *Critical Inquiry* 14 (Autumn 1987): 111–33.

Saalmann, Dieter, 'Walter Abish's *How German Is It*: Language and the Crisis of Human Behaviour', *Critique* 26: 3 (Spring 1985): 105–21.

Said, Edward, 'Identity, Negation, Violence', *New Left Review* 171 (September/October 1988): 49–60.

—— 'Islam and the West are Inadequate Banners', *The Observer* (16 September 2001): 27.

Sandford, Mariellen R. (ed.), *Happenings and Other Acts* (New York: Routledge, 1995).

Santner, Eric L., *Stranded Objects: Mourning, Memory, and Film in Postwar Germany* (Ithaca: Cornell University Press, 1990).

Saturday Review, 'Anarchists as Pests', unsigned, 101 (9 June 1906): 712.

—— 'Anarchism, Socialism and Rubino', unsigned, 94 (22 November 1902): 634.

—— 'Anarchy and Assassination', unsigned, 92 (14 September 1901): 324.

—— The Dynamite Plot', unsigned, 55: 1433 (14 April 1883): 516.

Savinkov, Boris, *Memoirs of a Terrorist*, trans. by Joseph Shaplen (New York: Boni, 1931).

Schlesinger, Philip, Graham Murdock, and Philip Elliott (eds.), *Televising Terrorism: Political Violence in Popular Culture* (New York: Commedia, 1983).

Schmid, Alex, and Albert Jongman, *Political Terrorism: A New Guide to Actors, Authors, Concepts, Data Bases, Theories and Literature* (New Brunswick, NJ: Transaction, 1988).

Schneider, Michael, 'Fathers and Sons Retrospectively: The Damaged Relationship Between Two Generations', *New German Critique* 31 (Winter 1984): 3–51.

Scott, Peter Dale, 'Anger in Paradise: The Poetic Voicing of Disorder in Pound's Later Cantos', *Paideuma* 19: 3 (Winter 1990): 47–63.

Scott, Thomas L. (ed.), *Pound/The Little Review: The Letters of Ezra Pound to Margaret Anderson* (London: Faber, 1988).

Scott-James, R. A., 'Blast', *New Weekly* 2 (4 July 1914): 88.

Seltzer, Mark, *Serial Killers: Death and Life in America's Wound Culture* (New York: Routledge, 1998).

Serres, Michel, *Hermes: Literature, Science, Philosophy*, ed. by Josué V. Harari and David F. Bell (Baltimore: The Johns Hopkins University Press, 1992).

Sherry, Norman, *Conrad's Western World* (Cambridge: Cambridge University Press, 1971).

Sherry, Vincent, *Ezra Pound, Wyndham Lewis and Radical Modernism* (Oxford: Oxford University Press, 1993).

Short, K. R. M., *The Dynamite War: Irish-American Bombers in Victorian Britain* (Dublin: Gill and Macmillan, 1979).

Simon, Jeffrey D., *The Terrorist Trap: America's Experience with Terrorism* (Bloomington: Indiana University Press, 1994).

Smith, Crosbie, and M. Norton Wise, *Energy and Empire: A Biographical Study of Lord Kelvin* (Cambridge: Cambridge University Press, 1989).

Smith, Zadie, 'How it Feels to Me', *The Guardian*, Saturday Review (13 October 2001): 8.

Sorel, Georges, *L'Avenir Socialiste des Syndicats* (Paris: Librairie de l'art Sociale, 1898).

—— *Reflections on Violence*, trans. by T. E. Hulme (New York: Collier, 1961).

The Spectator, 'Anarchy and Industry', unsigned, 4464 (17 January 1914): 174.

—— 'The Dynamite Danger', unsigned, 2856 (24 March 1883): 383.

—— 'The Fear of Dynamite', unsigned, 2859 (14 April 1883): 478.

—— 'Paradox in Politics', unsigned, 4121 (15 June 1907): 929–30.

—— 'Russia and Great Britain', unsigned, 4259 (12 Feb 1910): 247.

'Specto', 'Russia's Line of Least Resistance', *Fortnightly Review* 84: 466 (October 1905): 573–92.

Spencer, Herbert, *On Social Evolution: Selected Writings of Herbert Spencer*, ed. by J. D. Y. Peel (Chicago: University of Chicago Press, 1972).

Stephens, James Fitzjames, *A History of the Criminal Law in England* (London: Macmillan, 1883).

'Stepniak' (Sergei Kravchinsky), *The Career of a Nihilist* (London: Scott, 1889).

—— 'The Dynamite Scare and Anarchy', *The New Review* 6 (May 1892): 529–41.

—— *Underground Russia* (London: Smith & Elder, 1883).

Sterling, Claire, *The Terror Network: The Secret War of International Terrorism* (London: Weidenfeld & Nicolson, 1981).

Stevenson, Robert Louis, and Fanny Van de Grift Stevenson, *The Dynamiter* (Stroud: Sutton, 1991).

Stewart, Balfour, *The Conservation of Energy: An Elementary Treatise on Energy and its Laws* (London: Henry S. King, 1873).

Stewart, Balfour, and J. Norman Lockyer, 'The Sun as a Type of the Material Universe', *Macmillan's Magazine* 18 (July 1868): 246–52.

Stewart, Balfour, and Peter Guthrie Tait, *The Unseen Universe; or, Physical Speculations on a Future State* (London: Macmillan, 1875).

Stirner, Max, *The Ego and Its Own*, trans. by David Leopold (Cambridge: Cambridge University Press, 1995).

Stites, Richard, 'Women and the Russian Intelligentsia', in *Women in Russia*, ed. by Dorothy Atkinson, Alexander Dallin, and Gail Warshofsky Lapidus (Hassocks: Harvester, 1978), 39–62.

—— *The Women's Liberation Movement in Russia: Feminism, Nihilism, and Bolshevism 1860–1930* (Princeton: Princeton University Press, 1978).

Strachey, James (ed. and trans.), *The Standard Edition of the Complete Psychological Works of Sigmund Freud*, 24 vols. (London: Hogarth Press and the Institute of Psycho-analysis, 1953–74).

The Suffragette, ed. by Christabel Pankhurst, 'Foreword', unsigned, 1: 1 (18 October 1912): 1.

—— 'The Inner Policy of the W.S.P.U.', unsigned, 2: 68 (30 January 1914): 353.

—— 'Letters a Conglomerated Mass', unsigned, 1: 12 (3 January 1913): 177.

—— 'The Majesty of the Law', unsigned 1: 22 (14 March 1913): 341.

—— 'Pillar Box Trial at the Old Bailey', unsigned, 1: 13 (10 January 1913): 184

—— 'Retribution', unsigned, 2: 74 (13 March 1914): 491.

Surette, Leon, *A Light of Eleusis: A Study of Ezra Pound's* Cantos (Oxford: Clarendon, 1979).

Suvin, Darko, 'Reflections on Happenings', in Sandford (ed.), *Happenings*, 285–309.

Taylor, Peter, *Provos: The IRA and Sinn Fein* (London: Bloomsbury, 1997).

Terrell, Carroll F., *A Companion to the Cantos of Ezra Pound* (Berkeley: University of California Press, 1993).

Teskey, Gordon, *Allegory and Violence* (Ithaca: Cornell University Press, 1996).

Teufel, Fritz, 'On Rudi Dutschke's Death', in Lotringer (ed.), *Semiotext(e): The German Issue*, 116–19.

—— 'Terrorism with a Fun Face', in Lotringer (ed.), *Semiotext(e): The German Issue*, 134–46.

Thomson, William, 'On the Age of the Sun's Heat', *Macmillan's Magazine* 5 (March 1862): 388–93.

Tickner, Lisa, *The Spectacle of Women: Imagery of the Suffrage Campaign, 1907–14* (London: Chatto & Windus, 1987).

Tiffany, Daniel, *Radio Corpse: Imagism and the Cryptaesthetic of Ezra Pound* (Cambridge, Mass.: Harvard University Press, 1995).

The Times (London), 'Academy Outrage', unsigned (5 May 1914): 8.

—— 'National Gallery Outrage', unsigned (11 March 1914): 9.

—— 'Political Crime', unsigned (12 March 1896): 11.

—— 'The Outrage at Victoria Station', unsigned (27 February 1884): 10.

Tonge, Jonathan, 'From Sunningdale to the Good Friday Agreement: Creating Devolved Government in Northern Ireland', *Contemporary British History* 14: 3 (Autumn 2000): 39–60.

Torrey, E. Fuller, *The Roots of Treason: Ezra Pound and the Secret of St Elizabeth's* (London: Sidgwick & Jackson, 1984).

Tratner, Michael, *Modernism and Mass Politics: Joyce, Woolf, Eliot, Yeats* (Stanford: Stanford University Press, 1995).

Trotter, David, *The Novel in English History* (London: Routledge, 1993).

Tse-Tung, Mao, *Basic Tactics*, trans. by Stuart R. Scram (London: Pall Mall Press, 1967).

Tyrell, Lynne, 'Sexual Dualism and Women's Self-Creation: On the Advantages and Disadvantages of Reading Nietzsche for Feminists', in *Nietzsche and the Feminine*, ed. by Peter J. Burgard (Charlottesville: University Press of Virginia, 1994).

US Bureau of Public Affairs, 'United Against Terrorism' (US State Department Web-Site, 7 November 2001), <http://www.state.gov/r/pa/rls/index.cfm?docid=5968>.

—— 'The United States and the Global Coalition against Terrorism, September–November 2001' (US State Department Web-Site, November 2001), <http://www.state.gov/r/pa/pubs/fs/index.cfm?docid =5889>.

Vague, Tom, *Televisionaries: The Red Army Faction Story, 1963–93* (Edinburgh: AK, 1994).

van der Linden, Marcel, and Wayne Thorpe (eds.), *Revolutionary Syndicalism: An International Perspective* (Aldershot: Scolar, 1990).

van der Vat, Dan, *Stealth at Sea: The History of the Submarine* (London: Weidenfeld & Nicolson, 1994).

Vaneigem, Raoul, 'Basic Banalities II', in Knabb (ed.), *Situationist International Anthology*, 121–3.

—— *The Revolution of Everyday Life*, trans. by Donald Nicholson-Smith (London: Rebel/Left Bank, 1993).

Viénet, René, 'The Situationists and the New Forms of Action Against Politics and Art', in Knabb (ed.), *Situationist International Anthology*, 213–16.

Wade, Wyn Craig, *The Fiery Cross: The Ku Klux Klan in America* (New York: Simon & Schuster, 1987).

Walker, Clive, 'Briefing on the Terrorism Act 2000', *Terrorism and Political Violence* 12: 2 (Summer 2000): 1–36.

—— *The Prevention of Terrorism in British Law* (Manchester: Manchester University Press, 1992).

Wardlaw, Grant, *Political Terrorism: Theory, Tactics, and Counter-measures* (Cambridge: Cambridge University Press, 1989).

Watts, Cedric, *Joseph Conrad's Letters to R. B. Cunninghame Graham* (Cambridge: Cambridge University Press, 1969).

Wees, William C., *Vorticism and the English Avant-Garde* (Manchester: Manchester University Press, 1972).

Weinberger, Barbara, *Keeping the Peace?: Policing Strikes in Britain, 1906–26* (New York: Berg, 1991).

Wellen, Paul, 'An Analytic Dictionary of Ezra Pound's Chinese Characters', *Paideuma* 25: 3 (Winter 1996): 59–100.

Wells, H. G., *The War of the Worlds* (Bloomington: Indiana University Press, 1993).

Whibley, Charles (William Blackwood), 'Musing without Method', *Blackwood's Magazine* 170: 1032 (October 1901): 559–69.

Whitworth, Michael, 'Inspector Heat Inspected: *The Secret Agent* and the Meanings of Entropy', *The Review of English Studies* 49: 193 (1998): 40–59.

Whyte, John, *Interpreting Northern Ireland* (Oxford: Clarendon, 1998).

Wieviorka, Michel, *The Making of Terrorism*, trans. by David Gordon White (Chicago: University of Chicago Press, 1993).

Wills, Clair, *Improprieties: Politics and Sexuality in Northern Irish Poetry* (Oxford: Oxford University Press, 1993).

Wilson, Judith, 'An Interview with Jean Baudrillard', *Block* 15 (Spring 1989): 16–19.

Wolin, Richard (ed.), *The Heidegger Controversy: A Critical Reader* (Cambridge, Mass.: MIT Press, 1993).

Woodward, Anthony, *Ezra Pound and The Pisan Cantos* (London: Routledge & Kegan Paul, 1980).

Wright, Joanne, *Terrorist Propaganda: The Red Army Faction and the Provisional I.R.A., 1968–86* (London: Macmillan, 1991).

Wynne, Brian, 'Physics and Psychics: Science, Symbolic Action, and Social Control in Late Victorian England', in *Natural Order: Historical Studies of Scientific Order*, ed. by Barry Barnes and Steven Shapin (Beverley Hills: Sage, 1979).

Yack, Bernard, *The Longing for Total Revolution: Philosophic Sources of Social Discontent from Rousseau to Marx and Nietzsche* (Princeton: Princeton University Press, 1986).

Yeats, W. B., *Collected Poems* (London: Macmillan, 1990).

—— and Lady Gregory, 'Where There is Nothing', in *'Where There is Nothing' and 'The Unicorn from the Stars'*, ed. by Katherine Worth (Washington, DC: Catholic University of America Press, 1987), 54–118.

Young, James E. (ed.), *The Art of Memory: Holocaust Memorials in History* (New York: Prestel-Verlag, 1994).

Young, Robert, 'The Historiographical and Ideological Contexts of the Nineteenth-Century Debate on Man's Place in Nature', in *Changing Perspectives in the History of Science*, ed. by Mikulas Teich and Robert Young (London: Heinemann, 1973), 344–438.

Žižek, Slavoj, *The Sublime Object of Ideology* (London: Verso, 1989).

Zulaika, Joseba, and William Douglass, *Terror and Taboo: The Follies, Fables, and Faces of Terrorism* (London: Routledge, 1996).

Index